MODERN

JAPANESE LITERATURE

Modern
JAPANESE
LITERATURE

an anthology

compiled and edited by

Donald Keene

GROVE PRESS, INC.   NEW YORK

First Evergreen Edition 1960

Library of Congress Catalog Card Number: 56-8439

Fourteenth Printing

This volume is published in accordance with
an arrangement between Unesco and
the Japanese Government

MANUFACTURED IN THE UNITED STATES OF AMERICA

DISTRIBUTED BY RANDOM HOUSE, INC., NEW YORK

GROVE PRESS, INC., 196 WEST HOUSTON STREET,

NEW YORK, N.Y. 10014

Frontispiece by Nenjirō Inagaki. Reproduced by courtesy of Mikumo Wood-block
Print Company, Kyoto, Japan.

Material from WHEAT AND SOLDIERS reprinted by permission of Rinehart &
Company, Inc.

TO TED AND FANNY DE BARY

Japanese names are given in this book in the Japanese order: that is, the surname precedes the personal name. Thus, in the name Natsume Sōseki, Natsume is the family name, Sōseki the personal name.

The pronunciation of Japanese in transcription is very simple. The consonants are pronounced as in English (with g always hard), the vowels as in Italian. There are no silent letters. Thus, the name Mine is pronounced "mee-nay." In general, long vowels have been indicated by macrons, but in some stories they have been omitted, as likely to seem pedanticisms.

TRANSLATORS

Sam Houston Brock
Robert H. Brower
Harold G. Henderson
Howard Hibbett
Glenn Hughes
Baroness Shidzué Ishimoto
Yozan T. Iwasaki
Donald Keene
Ivan Morris
W. H. H. Norman
Shio Sakanishi
G. W. Sargent
Edward Seidensticker
Burton Watson
Meredith Weatherby

It may come as a surprise to some readers that this volume, devoted to the Japanese literature of the last eighty or so years, should be as long as my *Anthology of Japanese Literature,* which covers more than a thousand years. The disproportion is largely to be explained in terms of the amount of literature which has poured from the printing presses in recent times. All the literature which survives from, say, the thirteenth century can hardly compare in bulk with what any single year now produces. But it is not only by mere numbers that modern Japanese literature earns the right to be heard; its quality is remarkably high, and compares with that written anywhere in the world.

The choice of material for inclusion has been difficult to make. It is a commonplace of literary history that many works highly esteemed in their own day are subsequently doomed to oblivion. It also happens, though less frequently, that a book which passed almost unnoticed in its own time is later seen to be a treasure of the literature. These are the dangers which beset the compiler of anthologies of modern works, and I cannot hope to have escaped them altogether. I shall be very glad if no glaring injustices have been made. I have included very little solely for "historical" reasons. The novels of the 1890's have suffered in particular as a result of this policy. Although they are still highly regarded by some Japanese critics, they seem unbearably mawkish today, as I think most people will agree who have read the existing translations of such works as Ozaki's *Golden Demon.*[1]

It is the custom of Japanese critics to divide the modern period into the reigns of the three Emperors: Meiji (1868-1912), Taishō

[1] For an admirably detailed account of the literature written between 1868 and 1912, the reader should consult *Japanese Literature in the Meiji Era* by Y. Okazaki, translated by V. H. Viglielmo. (Tokyo, 1955.)

(1912-1926), and Shōwa (since 1926). These distinctions have some meaning, as our use of "the twenties" or "the thirties" conjures up an era, but it has not been felt necessary to observe the lines of these demarcations in a book intended for Western readers.

Few of the translations given here have ever before appeared in print. Most were made especially for this volume, and I wish to express my thanks to all the translators. I am particularly indebted to Edward Seidensticker for his willingness on repeated occasions to drop whatever else he was doing and turn out for this book a remarkably fine translation. Carolyn Kizer has kindly looked over my translations of modern poetry and offered many valuable pointers. Other help, at a time when I needed it badly, I have acknowledged, however inadequately, in the dedication.

I am grateful to Kawabata Yasunari, President of the Japanese P.E.N. Club, for his kind intercession in obtaining permission to use works by living authors. Acknowledgments are also due to: International Publishers Co. for *The Cannery Boat;* the *Japan Quarterly* for *The Mole;* Alfred A. Knopf, Inc., publishers of *Some Prefer Nettles,* for permission to use other works by Tanizaki; W. H. H. Norman and the Hokuseido Press for *Hell Screen;* Glenn Hughes for *The Madman on the Roof* (from *Three Modern Japanese Plays*); New Directions for "Villon's Wife"; and Rinehart & Co., Inc., for *Earth and Soldiers* (from *Wheat and Soldiers*).
Kyoto–New York

CONTENTS

Short Bibliography

The transformation of Japan within the space of about forty years from an obscure oriental monarchy to one of the great powers is accounted a miracle of the modern age. With the most rapid efforts Japan shook off the encumbering weight of a past of isolation and ignorance, and astonished the world by victory in a war with Russia and the winning of an equal alliance with England. Military successes and the development of industrial enterprises—and also the growth of scientific learning—made Japan the leader of eastern Asia.

Many striking parallels may be drawn between the history and the literature of Japan during this period. In 1868, when the youthful Emperor Meiji assumed control of the government after six centuries of rule by military men, Japanese literature had dropped to one of its lowest levels. The popular authors of the time specialized in books of formless, almost meaningless gossip. The country, which had been turned in on itself during almost 250 years of isolation, seemed to have exhausted its own resources. The gaiety had left the gay quarters, the center of much of the literature of the seventeenth and eighteenth centuries; and the rouged animation of anecdotes about the courtesans of the day was ugly and meretricious. And yet, within the same forty years that elapsed between the Meiji Restoration and the Russo-Japanese War, Japanese literature moved from idle quips directed at the oddities of the West to Symbolist poetry, from the thousandth-told tale of the gay young blade and the harlots to the complexities of the psychological novel.

The military and commercial successes of Japan have been attributed by Western critics to the Japanese genius for imitation, and this very skill has been often considered a discredit, as if it were somehow more admirable to imitate badly. The literature and art of modern Japan have been open to similar attack by those who deplore any deviations from what they consider to be the "pure Japanese." Such critics would condemn the writers and artists of today to expressing their anxieties about a world in disorder through the medium of exquisite poems on the cherry blossoms or monochrome sketches of pines and waterfalls. But, as the Japanese have discovered, the cleavage is impossible: the industrial plant, democracy, economics, Symbolist poetry, and abstract painting all go together, and are today an inseparable part of the lives of cultivated people in Japan as everywhere in the world.

The acceptance of what we think of as Western traditions did not take place in Japan without a struggle. For a time (as in China) an attempt was made to maintain the principle of "Western techniques and Eastern spirit." This meant that Japan should welcome Western machinery and other material benefits while retaining unaltered the customs and philosophy of the East. It might seem that it was a feasible dichotomy, that there was no reason why, say, a machine operator could not lead his life in accordance with Confucian principles. The fact was, however, that the industrialization of Japan tended to make the ideals of the family system impossible to fulfill. Even had the West offered nothing but technical knowledge, Japan would probably have had to abandon or modify seriously her traditional ways.

During the twenty or so years that followed the Meiji Restoration of 1868, the Japanese were frantically occupied in learning about—imitating, if one will—the West. They built for themselves railway and telegraph systems, printed newspapers and photographs. Ordinary citizens became interested in political problems for the first time, and there was a movement to enable them to take a more active part in the government. A modern political and industrial state was taking shape, characteristically Japanese in many features of its composition, but modeled on similar institutions in the West. In literature the changes came more slowly. This is not surprising: it took a much greater knowledge of the West to write a good psychological novel than it did to run a railway. We find traces of the West scattered everywhere, of course. Even the conservative writers mentioned in their works the rickshaws, banks, newspapers, and other novelties of the time. The celebrated dramatist Kawatake

Mokuami wrote a play about an English balloonist who dazzled the Japanese by descending from the sky over Tokyo, and a leading Kabuki actor was required to pronounce a speech written in English for the play. In a puppet drama of 1891 there is a love scene between a geisha and a foreigner, which is filled with scraps of English: "*Wasureyō mono ka* last year *no* spring, I *no* fine day *Sumida no hana yori* Paris London. . . ." In the domain of translation from Western works, the Japanese moved from *Self-Help* by Samuel Smiles (a book which sold hundreds of thousands of copies) to the political novels of Bulwer-Lytton and Disraeli, and eventually to Zola.

It is easy to see why the Japanese eagerly devoted themselves to study of the working of the steam engine or the pump, or even to the practical information contained in *Self-Help,* but it is interesting that they turned so quickly to Western literature. The first complete translation of a Western novel was that of Bulwer-Lytton's *Ernest Maltravers* in 1878. This innocuous story belies the vaguely pornographic overtones of its Japanese title, "A Spring Tale of Flowers and Willows." The title may have been initially necessary to sell the book, but what made it so great a success with the Japanese was the revelation that the men of the West had a tender side to their sternly practical lives. The emphasis on the material superiority of the West had been so insistent that the more spiritual aspects of Western life, even when revealed in so etiolated a fashion as we might expect from the pen of Bulwer-Lytton, came as a great surprise to most Japanese. The political background of the novel also offered Japanese writers fresh ideas as to what they might put into their own works.

One should not overlook the role of Christian missionaries in arousing among Japanese an interest in the literature of the West. The Christian religion had been prohibited in Japan during the early seventeenth century, and rigorous measures had been adopted to prevent its recrudescence. In 1873, under foreign pressure, the ban was lifted, and the influence of Christianity rapidly spread to all parts of the country. Some men were led, as Christian concern with their fellows began to occupy them, to a kind of socialism. Others felt a new sense of individuality and the desire to express it. The hymns which the Christian converts sang were of importance both in the introduction of Western music and in the beginnings of the new poetry. The Bible was the first Western book known to many Japanese, and its words convinced them that there was more to the West than mere "techniques."

It goes without saying, however, that unless the Japanese had felt a need to create a new literature no amount of foreign influence would have mattered. There was no reason why the books of chatter about the denizens of the licensed quarters could not have continued to dominate the literary scene. What the foreign examples did was to afford the Japanese the means of expressing their new ideas and their consciousness of being men of the enlightened Meiji era. This was not by any means the first time that Japanese had felt dissatisfied with the prevailingly low level of the literature of the first half of the nineteenth century. The poet Ōkuma Kotomichi (1798-1868) had declared himself proud to be a man of his times, and scorned to write, as most poets did, in the old-fashioned diction of a thousand years before. But despite his protests, Ōkuma's poems are written in the traditional *waka* form, and delightful though they are, do not strike us as being in any sense revolutionary. A poem in thirty-one syllables can be exquisite, it can be moving, but it obviously can never be a full exposition of a poet's thoughts or attempt to deal with subjects in which the intellect as well as the heart is involved. Some Japanese had tried to escape from the limitations of the *waka* by writing Chinese poems and prose—the only foreign literature known in Japan before the opening of the country —but, with some brilliant exceptions, their compositions were less explorations of the possibilities of the medium than cold and sterile repetitions of alien imagery.

When the poets of the 1880's felt a need to express their emotions in terms more suitable to their age than the traditional forms permitted, they had access to a new idiom. The first collection of English and American poems in translation was published in 1882. The choice of poems was not inspired, but with Tennyson's "Charge of the Light Brigade," Gray's "Elegy," some Longfellow, and even a few morsels of Shakespeare to build on, the Japanese were soon expressing in very varied terms their reactions to life in the brave new world of the Meiji era. That their early attempts were not masterpieces need surprise no one. Everything had to be learned afresh, for the old traditions were more of a hindrance than a help. Interestingly enough, it was not until much later that Japanese poets discovered that the complexities of modern life—or, at any rate, some of them—could be treated in the *waka* and *haiku* as well.

The Essence of the Novel (1885) by Tsubouchi Shōyō is one of the first important critical works of the time. Tsubouchi was a student of English literature, and what he read of the aesthetic principles on which it is founded convinced him that great changes must take place in the writing of Japanese fiction. The preface to the book threw a challenge in the faces of Japanese authors and readers alike: the sorry state of Japanese literature was no less the fault of readers who buy the sensational, pornographic fiction than of the men who wrote the books. Tsubouchi's challenge was, as a matter of fact, more impressive than either the full statement of his views or the original works he later wrote. His critical opinions were for the most part those of foreign writers, and applied by him to Japanese works. For example, Tsubouchi rejected the didactic novel, represented in Japan by such writers as Bakin, in favor of the artistic novel, the beauty of which is its own excuse for being. Quotations from Sir Walter Scott, Thackeray, and a variety of other nineteenth-century giants buttressed his arguments. Sometimes he was caught in a dilemma, as when he had to deal with artistic novels of amorous content. Tsubouchi wrote, "The Frenchman Dumas wrote some extremely cruel works, and some romantic tales of illicit unions, but he never stooped to lascivious description of the mysteries of the bedchamber, such as are common in Japanese vulgar works. There is no objection to his novels being read aloud before the entire family."

Shortly after his *Essence of the Novel,* Tsubouchi published the *Character of Modern Students,* a work intended to embody his artistic theories. It is not much of a book, and hardly distinguishes itself from the popular fiction which Tsubouchi so roundly condemned. Perhaps the most interesting thing about this novel is that the heroes are students (modeled on Tsubouchi's friends) who speak a jargon heavily larded with English, and thus identify themselves as being "enlightened."

The first important novel of the new Japanese literature was *The Drifting Cloud* (1887-1889) by Futabatei Shimei. It is written almost entirely in the colloquial, which in itself was a great achievement. Undoubtedly Futabatei was influenced by Turgenev, some of whose stories he translated, but *The Drifting Cloud* is an original work and no mere imitation. The conversations capture with a marvelous exactness the speech of the day, and the character portrayals are brilliant. It is astonishing that within twenty years after the Meiji Restoration the imprint of the West had become so strong on Japanese society, and that any novelist caught up in the frantically rapid evolution of that society could have observed it with such detachment and humor. A new kind of hero made his appearance in Japanese fiction. Unlike the all-conquering soldiers and lovers we find in earlier writings, the leading character of *The Drifting Cloud* is timid before the woman he loves, loses his job, becomes the object of the laughter and contempt of everyone, and finally exasperates even the reader with his ineptitude. In one typical scene Bunzō (the hero), having been rebuffed by his sweetheart, lies on his bed, grief-stricken. But he is incapable even of keeping his thoughts on his sorrow—they wander to a consideration of the grain of the wood in the ceiling, from that subject to the remembrance of his physics teacher, a bearded foreigner, and then to a book which had once impressed him. Suddenly he recalls with a cry his lost love. We see in Bunzō a Japanese overwhelmed by the pushings of a world composed of people who have read *Self-Help*.

Futabatei's extraordinary novel did not sweep all before it. Another, more powerful group of authors continued older traditions while paying lip service to the new. Such works as Ozaki Kōyō's *Golden Demon* (1897) combined a lushly poetic style with sentimental plots filled with the wildest improbabilities. Enormously popular in their own day, they have dated as *The Drifting Cloud* has not. One work in a more traditional vein which retains its vitality is *Growing Up* (1895) by the woman novelist Higuchi

Ichiyō. This tale of children in the Yoshiwara, the licensed quarter of Tokyo, is closer in style to the seventeenth-century novel than to works of its own day, but the sharpness of its details and its descriptions still excites our admiration today.

While the novel and the short story were making striking advances, the Japanese drama and poetry continued in much the same vein as before. In the case of the drama, the exigencies of the theatre were such that no great changes were immediately possible. The most that one could expect was an occasional Western touch, whether the striking of a clock or the appearance of a character in Western dress. Within the framework of the existing dramatic arts certain steps were taken to achieve greater historical accuracy in the presentations, sometimes with ludicrous results. In the 1890's the Shimpa (or "New School") drama gained public favor with plays based on such contemporary events as the Sino-Japanese War of 1894. Shimpa, however, relied more on dramatizations of novels than on original plays, and its greatest successes were with the *Golden Demon* and similarly melodramatic works. Some Western plays (including Shakespeare) were performed by Shimpa, but it was not until the foundation of new theatre movements after the Russo-Japanese War that Western dramas received serious productions.

In poetry we find in the 1880's and 1890's numerous translations of European works, and in their wake Japanese poems on similar themes. The most successful of these poems, one step removed from the originals, was undoubtedly "The Song of the Autumn Wind" (1896) by Shimazaki Tōson. Although clearly derived from Shelley's ode, it was graceful enough to survive in its own right as a Japanese poem, and indeed marked the beginning of modern poetry in the country. It begins:

> Softly the autumn wind has come,
> Rising from the western sea . . .

and has some rather striking verses:

> Scattering East and scattering West,
> Like priests of Brahma who taught the way,

Tossed about by autumn winds,
The leaves go fluttering down.

A poem by another poet of the day startles us with its opening lines:
"Oh, to be in Yamato, now that October's there." Such close imitations of European models amuse us, but it should be remembered
that the only examples of new poetry which could inspire the Japanese were familiar European ones. If they had based their poetry
movement on, say, Chinese verse, the results would seem less comic.
Japanese translations were, in fact, the way that much European
literature came to be known in China and elsewhere in eastern Asia.

The speed of the development of the forms and themes of poetry
during the 1890's and 1900's was astonishing. In 1896 Shimazaki
delighted his contemporaries with his lines after Shelley; in 1909
Kitahara Hakushū began his "Secret Song of the Heretics" with:

I believe in the heretical teachings of a degenerate age, the
witchcraft of the Christian God . . .

and a few years later he wrote lines like this:

My sorrow wears the thin flannel garb of one-sided love.

Within the space of fifteen years the Japanese poets had leaped from
Shelley to the French Symbolists, and it was not long before
Dadaism, Surrealism, and all the other movements in French poetry
had their Japanese admirers. There was a difference between these
borrowings and the earlier imitations of the poetry, painting, and
other arts of China. The Chinese poetry written by Japanese was
generally a tissue of allusions to Chinese scenes and events, and
only rarely betrayed its Japanese origins; the Dadaist or Surrealist
poetry was almost always about Japan, or at least as much about
Japan as anywhere. Imitation of Chinese models had bound the
Japanese to rigid conventions which kept most poets from describing
their own experiences. The imitation of French models, on the other
hand, freed poets to explore parts of their experience and imagina-

tion which could never before have found expression in poetry. The poets did not always wear this freedom easily. Some of them spilled over into unbridled and perhaps meaningless fantasy; others became so cryptic that a poem of a single line requires pages of exegesis. What, for example, are we to make of this verse written in English, a stanza of a longer poem in the same vein?

> (well, go on!)
> qwiim qwick qwiim qwick
> qririm qririm qririm. . . .
> qwiim qwick qwiim qwick
> qririm qririm qririm. . . .
> (ah rain bow!)

Granted that this stanza has a logic of its own and a compelling directness of expression, one might wish for a trifle more content.

The poets who wrote in the more conservative *waka* and *haiku* forms also began to discover the new possibilities in expression. The *waka* reached modernity about thirty years ahead of the *haiku*, which proved the least flexible medium, but even the *haiku* caught up, as the following creations witness:

Hitohachi no kigiku   A bowl of yellow chrysanthemums.

or:

Hi e yamu   I am sick with the sun.

People have attempted to divine the meanings intended by the poets, but it remains a real question whether *any* such short poetic utterances can be called *haiku*. Liberation may sometimes be too complete.

On the whole, modern Japanese drama and poetry have not been the equal of the novels, short stories, and other works of prose. There are some remarkable exceptions, but one cannot escape the feeling that the drama and poetry have yet to reach their full maturity. In the drama we find survivals of the old-fashioned plots beloved of the Kabuki audiences, and the modern theatre has been slow to catch on. Among the few modern plays which have won lasting popularity have been those by Kikuchi Kan, including *The Madman on the Roof* (1916), given in this volume. More recently, the play *Twilight Crane*[1] (1949) by Kinoshita Junji won acclaim for its skillful use of Japanese folklore. As yet, however, the number of playwrights is small and most audiences seem to prefer period pieces to works on contemporary subjects.

The modern movement in poetry has been a greater success, in spite of the eccentricities detailed above. There is a personal and very moving quality in some of the more straightforward poetry, and the Japanese Surrealists at times rival their French masters. One must admit, however, that much of the modern poetry seems curiously lacking in substance. There is in particular an extraordinary dearth of intellectual interest. One finds the pangs of love, the praise of nature, and the battle cry of the workers, but of the poet's concern with intellectual matters we find little trace. The gloom of *The Wasteland* pervades a considerable portion of modern Japanese poetry, but we search in vain for T. S. Eliot's preoccupation with such subjects as ritual and religion, the poetry of the past, and the ways in which time alters all things. This poverty in Japanese poetry is not difficult to understand. The modern poets are by their own choice cut off from the heritage of Japanese (and Chinese) literature. No falling cherry blossoms or reddening maple leaves are permitted to grace their verses except ironically, and the rest of the repertory of images worn smooth by centuries of poets is considered too remote and dead to be of relevance. On the other hand, knowledge of Western poetry is not very profound either among poets or readers. A Japanese poet is unlikely to think of quoting Dante; if he did, the quotation as such would have little meaning to most readers. Japanese modern poetry tends thus to be bounded by the translatable parts of foreign poetry: the decadence of Rimbaud without his overtones, the gloom of T. S. Eliot without his sense of tradition, the fantasy of Max Jacob without his religion. There is little joy or hope in this poetry except in the "affirmative" writings from

[1] Translated by A. C. Scott in *Playbook* (New York: New Directions, 1956).

the left. The sorrow over the falling of the cherry blossoms is now sorrow over the crumbling walls of a bombed-out site; instead of soaking his sleeve with tears, the poet shouts his grief to the wind.

That the poetry is prevailingly dark, traditionless, and nonintellectual does not mean that it lacks value. Within the limits the modern poets have set for themselves there is much beautifully conceived and sometimes hauntingly moving poetry. The poems of Hagiwara Sakutarō are perhaps the best of recent years. They seem the deepest felt, and, although clearly influenced by European examples, retain a feeling for the music and potentialities of the Japanese language. Hagiwara is also known as the first poet to have successfully composed in the colloquial.

The changes in the drama and poetry which have only slowly been accomplished, or which must await the future for fruition, were realized in prose at the beginning of this century, thanks to the emergence of an extraordinary cluster of gifted writers. One specific event of importance in the achievement of maturity in the novel was the four years' residence in Germany, from 1884 to 1888, of Mori Ōgai, the first major Japanese writer to have lived in Europe. Mori produced a volume of translations of German poetry in 1889, and in the following year published *The Dancing Girl,* the account of an unhappy attachment between a German dancer and a young Japanese. With this touching story the "romantic" movement in Japanese literature is considered to have begun; it is important in any case as the earliest work of the new literature to have been written by a man who had actually lived in Europe and knew at first-hand something of its emotional and spiritual life. *The Dancing Girl* was, in Mori's words, an *"Ich roman"*—a story so closely based on personal experiences as to be a kind of dramatized diary. This type of autobiographical fiction was to occupy a disproportionately large place in modern Japanese literature.

The other titan of Meiji literature, whose name is usually linked with Mori's, was Natsume Sōseki. Natsume began his career as a scholar of English literature, and from 1900 to 1903 studied in England. In 1905 he published his first work of fiction, *I Am a Cat.* In the following years he produced a series of novels which were enthusiastically acclaimed in his day and even now retain their popularity. His early works, such as *Botchan* (1906), are filled with light, satirical touches; but Natsume's tone darkened as he turned to subjects of increasingly philosophical content. His novels deserve a larger place in this anthology, but unfortunately their reflective tone and rather deliberate pace do not permit extracts to be made successfully from the later works.[2] Suffice it to say that in the years since his death Natsume's popularity has never wavered, and his books are still finding new readers today.

The appearance of Natsume on the scene would in itself have represented a major event in Japanese literature, but by an unusual set of circumstances the whole of the literary world burst into an almost unprecedented period of creativity during the years 1905-1915. This was the decade when some writers, like Mori Ōgai and Shimazaki Tōson, who had previously enjoyed a measure of fame, produced their best works; when others, like Natsume Sōseki and the poet Ishikawa Takuboku, wrote all of their literary production; and when still others, like Nagai Kafū and Tanizaki Junichirō, began their long, distinguished careers. The Russo-Japanese War of 1904-1905 undoubtedly was at least indirectly responsible; the victory may well have given the Japanese the confidence to produce great literature. Be that as it may, there is an almost bewildering profusion of talent in this decade. The next three decades were not to produce more than a fraction of the number of new writers of importance as appeared between the years 1905 and 1915.

The termination of the Russo-Japanese War may be said, in political terms, to have heralded the coming of age of Japan after its period of apprenticeship to the West. Japan had arrived among the powers, and her literature now began to win itself a place in the attention of the world. That the war had in some sense crystallized the new literary movement in Japan does not mean that the writers of the time were jingoists exulting over the victory. On the contrary, even those men whose hearts had leaped at initial reports of Japanese successes were disillusioned by the time the war was over.

[2] Some complete translations of novels by Natsume have been made, notably that of *Kokoro*, by I. Kondo.

Tayama Katai's *One Soldier* (1908) suggests the mingled feelings the war aroused in the minds of sensitive writers.

Japanese chroniclers of the literary history of the modern period divide the various authors into a large number of schools—neo-Realist, Naturalist, Sensualist, etc.—and these schools in turn are splintered into subsections, denoting influences and associations. Such categories are of little concern to Western readers and need hardly bother us here. We should, however, note the immense ferment of activity in many directions. The passion for European literature continued, but to it was added a growing interest in the old Japan. Nagai Kafū published in 1909, the year after his return from five years' stay in the United States and France, *The River Sumida,* an exquisitely fashioned elegy for the vanishing Tokyo of the past. Nagai was influenced by French examples, but in subtle ways that might easily escape notice. Japanese literature was passing from a period when European works were slavishly imitated to one when an awareness and receptivity to them was not permitted to blot out the native heritage.

The conflict between the claims of East and West is particularly apparent in the works of Tanizaki Junichirō. His early productions dealt mainly with themes which might have been suggested by the writings of Edgar Allan Poe, and are marked by strong overtones of sadism and masochism. This period reached its height with *A Fool's Love* (1924), the story of a man who is so fascinated by a coarse, European-looking waitress that he tolerates her repeated cruelties. Even in this work, however, there is implied a condemnation of the excessive worship paid to Western things. In the next major novel, *Some Prefer Nettles* (1928),[3] the hero is drawn both to an Eurasian prostitute and to a Kyoto beauty. Each stands for a world, and we sense that it is Japan which will win. The later novels of Tanizaki expand this conservative aspect of his work. Many of them deal with events of Japanese history of the recent or distant past. *The Thin Snow* (1944-1947), perhaps Tanizaki's masterpiece, tells of the Japan of the years immediately before the

[3] Translated by Edward G. Seidensticker (New York: Knopf, 1955).

Pacific War, but contains many suggestions of *The Tale of Genji,* a work which Tanizaki has translated into modern Japanese.

Another writer who first gained celebrity in the ten years after the Russo-Japanese War was Shiga Naoya. His works, probably more than those of any other modern author, have exercised a commanding influence over the Japanese literature of today. He did not invent the "I novel," as we have seen, but his success with this genre led many other writers to seek to salvage bits worthy of preservation from the incidents of their lives. This absorption with the petty details of their own lives may represent an attempt on the part of Japanese writers to create individuality for themselves. I am tempted to link this literary tendency with the extraordinary craze for the camera in Japan. The desire to preserve the memory of a meeting or celebration with a commemorative photograph is, after all, not so different from the intent of many "I novels." In both cases it is assumed that the faithful portrayal of an individual makes for individuality, but, as some of the lesser imitators of Shiga Naoya have demonstrated, this is not necessarily the case.

Akutagawa Ryūnosuke, who also published his first works during the decade after the Russo-Japanese War, was able to create true individuality in his novels without intruding himself. In 1915 *Rashōmon* appeared, a work whose brilliant, rather unhealthy style has magnetized readers ever since. *Rashōmon,* like many others of Akutagawa's works, germinated from a story in one of the old collections. To the framework of events of an ancient tale Akutagawa added modern psychological insights and the glitter of his style. Towards the latter part of his career Akutagawa also wrote some autobiographical fiction, and it too is touched with the morbid glow of his more objective writings.

The novels of the twenties, thirties, and forties were dominated largely by men who had made a name for themselves during the previous decade. A few important new writers did emerge, notably Yokomitsu Riichi and Kawabata Yasunari. Both men were associated with a school called the "neo-Sensationalist." This ambiguous term meant in practice that its adherents were opposed alike to the rising "proletarian" school and to the unrelieved use of realism prac-ticed by certain writers. Yokomitsu and Kawabata proved themselves to be superlative craftsmen and masters of the art of psychological fiction.

The proletarian literature movement of the twenties occupied the attention of many young authors, and has since been rediscovered and extravagantly admired. Viewed by any normal standards of literature, however, its productions were remarkably poor. The great virtue of proletarian writings was that they dealt with aspects of Japan largely ignored by more famous writers. Apart from the novel *Earth* (1910) by Nagatsuka Takashi, a ponderous if accurate portrayal of the lives of hard-pressed farmers, there had been a marked reluctance on the part of most Japanese writers to treat the farmers, fishermen, and laboring classes, who make up the bulk of the Japanese population. The proletarian writers filled this gap but, we may feel, in an excessively crude manner. Occasionally, as in Kobayashi Takiji's *Cannery Boat* (1929), there is so vivid a description of the conditions under which the proletariat lives that the work still commands our attention. But painfully detailed accounts of the misery of the oppressed classes, interspersed with scenes of joyous workers marching hand in hand to overthrow the capitalists, do not rate very high literarily. We can only marvel today that so many earnest writers produced so little of lasting value.

The military disasters of the thirties and forties into which the Japanese people was plunged by the ruling cliques produced almost no literature of consequence. Most writers did what they could to prevent becoming embroiled in the propaganda efforts of the militarists. A few showed open sympathy with Japan's "mission," but apart from the diaries of Hino Ashihei, the China Incidents and the Pacific War did not engender much literature which can be read with pleasure today.

It has only been since the end of the war in 1945 that important new writers have begun to appear again in numbers. It is still too soon to be able to predict with confidence which of their works will last, but the writings of Dazai Osamu capture so perfectly the postwar scene that it is hard to imagine that they will be forgotten. The present volume concludes with an extract from a novel by Mishima

Yukio, a remarkably gifted young writer whose varied production augurs well for the future of Japanese literature. As European traditions are finally absorbed, not only by the novels but by the drama and poetry as well, we can expect that the amazing renaissance of literature in Japan during the past half-century or so will continue to be one of the wonders of the modern literary world.

MODERN

JAPANESE LITERATURE

THE BEEFEATER

[from Aguranabe, 1871] by Kanagaki Robun (1829-1894)

It would be hard to defend on purely literary grounds the writings of the years immediately following the Meiji Restoration of 1868, but in the books of anecdotes and curiosities which were the bestsellers of the day, we find many fascinating glimpses into the life of the Japan which was just emerging. The beefeater described in this selection was a typical man of his age. For many centuries the Japanese had been forbidden by Buddhist law to eat beef. With the coming of the foreigners, however, a demand for beef was created, and by the early years of the Meiji period restaurants which sold beef had sprung up in the cities. Details of the costume and the manners of the beefeater reveal to us the comic aspects of the "enlightenment" which was taking place. The intent of this piece would seem largely to have been to parody the advocacy of the superiority of Western civilization by such men as the great educator Fukuzawa Yukichi (1834-1901).

•

A man about thirty-five, rather swarthy it is true, but of clear complexion, thanks apparently to the daily use of soap, which purges all impurities. His hair, not having been cut for some hundred days, is long and flowing, and looks as if it is in the process of being let out altogether, in the foreign style. Naturally enough, he uses that scent called Eau de Cologne to give a sheen to his hair. He wears a padded silken kimono beneath which a calico undergarment is visible. By his side is his Western-style umbrella, covered in gingham. From time to time he removes from his sleeve with a painfully contrived gesture a cheap watch, and consults the time. As a matter of fact this is merely so much display to impress others, and the chain is only gold-plate. He turns to his neighbor, who is also eating beef, and speaks:

Excuse me, but beef is certainly a most delicious thing, isn't it? Once you get accustomed to its taste, you can never go back to deer or wild boar again. I wonder why we in Japan haven't eaten such a clean thing before? For over 1620—or is it 1630—years people in the West have been eating huge quantities of beef. Before then, I understand, beef and mutton were considered the king's exclusive property, and none ever entered the mouth of a commoner, unless he happened to be something on the order of a daimyo's chief retainer. We really should be grateful that even people like ourselves can now eat beef, thanks to the fact that Japan is steadily becoming a truly civilized country. Of course, there are some unenlightened boors who cling to their barbaric superstitions and say that eating meat defiles you so much that you can't pray any more before Buddha and the gods. Such nonsense shows they simply don't understand natural philosophy. Savages like that should be made to read Fukuzawa's article on eating beef. In the West they're free of superstitions. There it's the custom to do everything scientifically, and that's why they've invented amazing things like the steamship and the steam engine. Did you know that they engrave the plates for printing newspapers with telegraphic needles? And that they bring down wind from the sky with balloons? Aren't they wonderful inventions! Of course, there are good reasons behind these inventions. If you look at a map of the world you'll see some countries marked "tropical," which means that's where the sun shines closest. The people in those countries are all burnt black by the sun. The king of that part of the world tried all kinds of schemes before he hit on what is called a balloon. That's a big round bag they fill with air high up in the sky. They bring the bag down and open it, causing the cooling air inside the bag to spread out all over the country. That's a great invention. On the other hand, in Russia, which is a cold country where the snow falls even in summer and the ice is so thick that people can't move, they invented the steam engine. You've got to admire them for it. I understand that they modeled the steam

engine after the flaming chariot of hell, but anyway, what they do is
to load a crowd of people on a wagon and light a fire in a pipe
underneath. They keep feeding the fire inside the pipe with coal, so
that the people riding on top can travel a great distance completely
oblivious to the cold. Those people in the West can think up inventions like that, one after the other. . . . You say you must be going?
Well, good-bye. Waitress! Another small bottle of sake. And some
pickled onions to go with it!

TRANSLATED BY DONALD KEENE

THE WESTERN PEEP SHOW

[from Tōkyō Shin-hanjō-ki, 1874] by Hattori Bushō (1842-1908)

This selection describes one way in which the early curiosity of the Japanese about the West was satisfied. The style is a mock version of the heavy antithesis of Chinese balanced-prose, and there are even allusions to the ancient philosophers.

•

No less than the soaring eagle, the dung fly beats its wings; the naked savage parades himself with the airs of the elegantly clad. Hence it comes about that the peep show has won such popularity and, together with the photograph, proudly flaunts its banners to-day. It all began when someone opened a place in Asakusa. Within a few months there were peep-show establishments in a number of localities, particularly in the section formerly dominated by mansions of the daimyo. The peep show must have been an invention of those who eat without tilling the fields and who wear clothes which are not of their own weaving. As yet no respected businessmen seem to be promoting this entertainment.

The viewing parlors are for the most part small painted shacks, the fronts of which have been given a hasty coat of whitewash. The rear, however, is neglected, suggesting nothing so much as a slattern who powders her face but leaves her back dirty. Some of these parlors are several stories tall, and the wooden boards with which they are built are painted to resemble stone, exactly like the entrance to some quack doctor's residence. Inside the building, at intervals several feet apart, are arranged a number of machines, and one goes from one machine to another peeping at its display. The front of the machine has eyes like a giant snake, each of which neatly fits the two human eyes. The viewer peeps at the world as through the eye of a needle, and the cost is a mere one sen. Some machines contain

pictures of the scenery of countries all over the world; others are of
completely imaginary subjects:

The steel bridge of London is longer than a rainbow; the palace
of Paris is taller than the clouds. An enraged Russian general pulls
out a soldier's whiskers; a recumbent Italian lady kisses her dog.
They have bought an American conflagration to sell us; they have
wrapped up a German war to open here. Warships push through the
waves in droves; merchant ships enter port in a forest of masts. A
steam engine climbs a mountain; a balloon flies in the sky. Seated
one may contemplate the Cape of Good Hope; lying down one may
gaze at the Mediterranean. The lion which devours the human being
invariably kills from the trunk; the black men who paddle boats
remain stuck for all eternity to the bottom.[1] You look at a picture
of a museum and despise the pawnshop next door; you peep at a
great hospital and lament the headaches of others. As the spectator
approaches the last peep show he becomes increasingly aware how
cheap the admission price has been. In the last show, the Goddess of
Beauty lies naked in bed. Her skin is pure white, except for a small
black mole under her navel. It is unfortunate that she has one leg
lifted, and we cannot admire what lies within. In another scene we
regret that only half the body is exposed and we cannot see the behind; in still another we lament that though face to face we cannot
kiss the lips. This marvel among marvels, novelty among novelties,
is quite capable of startling the eyes of rustics and untutored individuals.

The above are only a few examples of what one can see. Although
the peep show is popular entertainment, when compared to other
familiar types it is not without its educational benefits. Unlike the
"tigers" of Asakusa, which are actually dyed cats, or the "dragons"
of Yorozuyo Bridge, which are snakes with painted scales—displays
whose falseness becomes apparent in a couple of days, when the
paint wears off—the peep shows offer the latest curiosities of the
world and the customs of every nation. It is like touring the world at
a glance, and should broaden men's knowledge while delighting
their eyes. It may be true, as some say, that we cannot be sure

[1] Meaning, probably, that the pictures, unlike life, are always the same.

whether these pictures are true or false without going to the countries they represent, but they are by no means in the same category with a cat painted like a tiger. But, of course, they are no more than second-hand articles from some old ragpicker's shop.

TRANSLATED BY DONALD KEENE

THE THIEVES

[Shima Chidori Tsuki no Shiranami, 1881]
by Kawatake Mokuami (1816-1893)

Mokuami was one of Japan's greatest dramatic geniuses. His works number over three hundred, many of which are still performed in Kabuki theatres. He is known particularly for portrayals of thieves and other characters of the underworld. Mokuami was fortunate in that his plays were performed by Kabuki actors of extraordinary brilliance. In The Thieves, *for example, the ninth Danjūrō created the part of Mochizuki, the fifth Kikugorō that of Shimazō, and the first Sadanji that of Senta. However, the very fact that Mokuami was so consummately skilled in meeting the requirements of the Kabuki theatre and its actors sometimes lessened the purely literary value of his works.*

The Thieves *is considered by many to be Mokuami's masterpiece. It was written when he was sixty-five years old as his farewell to the theatre, although he actually continued writing for some years afterward. This was the first of his works composed without any collaborators, as was the common practice. The reform of the thieves at the end and the prevalence of the sentiment of "encouraging virtue and chastising vice" has been attributed to Mokuami's desire to end on a virtuous note his career as a chronicler of the underworld. Mentions of the telegraph, the legal reforms after the Meiji Restoration, etc., lend a contemporary tone to this play.*

Only the last act of The Thieves *is given here, but it is complete in itself.*

Characters

SHIMAZO
SENTA
MOCHIZUKI AKIRA
A NOODLE SELLER
PILGRIMS

SCENE: *Before the Yasukuni Shrine in Tokyo. At left* [1] *is a large stone torii, with low stone fences on either side. Above are towering pines. At rear are a pair of copper lanterns and numerous stone lanterns. The shrine is dimly visible to the far rear. It is night.*

As the curtain is drawn aside the noodle seller is setting down his wares. Two men in pilgrim's costume are eating near him. A clock is striking somewhere.

FIRST PILGRIM: Another bowl of noodles!

NOODLE SELLER: Yes, sir.

SECOND PILGRIM: While you're at it, I'll have another too.

NOODLE SELLER: Yes, sir. (*He prepares the noodles.*)

FIRST PILGRIM: There seem to be fewer people out selling noodles at night nowadays.

NOODLE SELLER: That's right. They're all in the suburbs, and nobody's left downtown.

SECOND PILGRIM: But every year you see more and more people selling fried dumplings.

NOODLE SELLER: Yes, there has been a change. (*He serves the two customers, who continue talking and eating.*)

FIRST PILGRIM: Unusually good, isn't it?

SECOND PILGRIM: Yes, it is. It's extremely well seasoned.

NOODLE SELLER: There aren't many noodle shops in this neighborhood. It's a little out of the way. I'm very careful with the ingredients and the preparation, and most people are kind enough to wait for me to come. I usually am about sold out by the time I make my first round.

---

[1] That is, stage left; to the right as far as the audience is concerned.

FIRST PILGRIM: That doesn't surprise me. The noodles are prepared just as well as in a regular shop.

SECOND PILGRIM: I don't wonder that people wait for something as good as this.

NOODLE SELLER: It's kind of you to say so. Where are you gentlemen going dressed that way?

FIRST PILGRIM: We set out this afternoon to worship at the big temple in Horinouchi. We hadn't much time to lose, what with the shortening of the days, but we stopped anyway at a restaurant.

SECOND PILGRIM: We spent a little time drinking there to refresh ourselves, but it was already dark before we left, and now it's become very late.

NOODLE SELLER: You must be very tired.

FIRST PILGRIM: Who is honored at this shrine?

NOODLE SELLER: The men who died in the wars.[2] It was for the Emperor's sake that they died, even the soldiers of humble birth, and that's why it has been made so impressive.

SECOND PILGRIM: I've always gone by without ever looking inside, but it really looks pretty when you see it this way.

NOODLE SELLER: You should have a look at it by day. There are fountains in the ponds, and the trees in the garden are something to see. Flowers bloom all year round. It's well worth a special trip to see it, even if you come a long way.

FIRST PILGRIM: Here's your money.

NOODLE SELLER: Thank you. (*He takes the money.*)

SECOND PILGRIM: We've got to hurry now.

FIRST PILGRIM: What time is it?

NOODLE SELLER: It has just struck ten.

SECOND PILGRIM: That's like a line out of a Kabuki play, isn't it— asking the noodle seller the time.

NOODLE SELLER: It *is* a familiar phrase.

FIRST PILGRIM: Now that we know the time, we really must be hurrying.

[2] The Yasukuni Shrine was founded in 1869 to honor those who had died fighting for the Meiji Restoration. It has become the shrine for soldiers who have died in all subsequent wars.

NOODLE SELLER: I must also be starting on my round.

SECOND PILGRIM: Well then, good-bye.

NOODLE SELLER: Good-bye, sir.

VOICE: Noodles, over here!

(*At a cry from the left the noodle seller goes off in that direction. The two pilgrims move off the stage onto the* hanamichi.[3] *The music begins.*)

NARRATOR: As is the wont of autumn nights,

> A wind is in the sky.
>
> The clouds move quickly, to disclose
>
> Patches of stars here and there.
>
> And now a man comes quickly by:
>
> Senta pauses beneath a tree.

(*Senta enters from left to the tolling of a bell and the howl of the wind. The lower part of his face is concealed. He strikes an attitude.*)

SENTA: Ten o'clock has struck, but Shimazo hasn't appeared yet. He must have decided to shut his shop for the night before he left. I can't believe that he won't come, since he promised me. Brrrr—the wind up here is strong! It's not just cool, it's downright cold. The effects of the sake I drank this evening seem to have worn off. I hope he comes before eleven.

NARRATOR: He looks around—a pile of stones

> Is close at hand and there he sits.
>
> Before he has waited long, he sees
>
> In the starlight Shimazo, who rushes up.

SHIMAZO: (*He steps onto the* hanamichi *where he stops and looks at the stage.*) I'm sure that man next to the torii is Senta. It's already struck ten and he must be waiting for me. I'll hurry now.

NARRATOR: Accustomed as he is to night's dark roads,

> He quickly strides up to the torii.

SHIMAZO (*reaching the stage*): Is that you over there, Senta?

SENTA: Oh, it's you, brother. I'm glad you came.

---

[3] The *hanamichi* is the raised passageway that goes from the back of the theatre through the audience to the stage.

SHIMAZO: I was still at home when I heard ten o'clock strike. I must be half an hour late. Have you been waiting long?

SENTA: I've only just arrived. I stopped at a restaurant for a couple of drinks on the way. Come sit over here.

SHIMAZO: You've found a convenient place to sit, haven't you? (*He dusts the stones with his towel, and the two men sit.*) You asked me to go somewhere with you tonight. Whose house are we going to?

SENTA: To a house below Kagurasaka. The man who lives there used to be one of the direct retainers of the Shogunate. He now calls himself a teacher of calligraphy. He's a low dog who can't be trusted. Even before the collapse of the Shogunate he was dismissed for his outrageous intimidation of the people, but he got pardoned in the general amnesty after the Restoration. Since then he has been lending money—stolen money, for all I know. He's a very prosperous gentleman now, and he goes by the name of Mochizuki Akira. I intend to break in there tonight, kill him and his wife, and clean out all his money. Then I'll head for Osaka.

SHIMAZO: I happen to know something about this Mochizuki. He certainly has money, but you could get it by just threatening him. Why must you kill him and his wife?

SENTA: I have my reasons.

SHIMAZO: What reasons could you have for killing them?

SENTA: The woman Mochizuki now publicly recognizes as his wife was until April of this year a famous geisha in Shirakawa. I was so madly in love with her that sometimes I would stay with her ten days running. I spent a fortune trying to get her to give in to me, but she had her sights trained on higher targets, and wouldn't listen to me. I had about decided to take her by force if necessary, when I was surrounded by the police and barely managed to make a getaway. I wandered from one place to another, finally ending up here. Then I learned by chance where she is living now. Yesterday I went to her house, intending to extort some money from her. But Mochizuki, what with his experience at intimidating people, was too clever for me, and was unimpressed by my threats. He offered to return the hundred yen I gave the girl when she was at Shirakawa, and ordered me to take the money and leave at once. After having been talked to in such a way I felt that it would be too humiliating to take the money. I left empty-handed and thoroughly disgusted. But tonight will be the second round of my revenge, and this time I want you to go with me. We'll wipe out my old score with them by killing Mochizuki and his wife, and divide whatever money we find. Once this is over I plan to spend six months or so in Osaka. Well, that's the favor I have to ask you. I know you may not like it, but I ask you as my brother to help me in this job.

SHIMAZO (*reflects for a while*): I'm sorry, but I can't possibly do what you ask.

SENTA: Why can't you?

SHIMAZO: I've had a complete change of heart and I've given up crime.

SENTA: I don't want to bore you by saying the same things over and over, but it's all very well for you to give up crime—if I am arrested tomorrow you will be implicated all the same. They may let you off lightly and give you ten years, but if it's a heavy sentence, you may spend the rest of your life at hard labor.

SHIMAZO: I'm perfectly well aware of that, even without your saying it. I have every expectation that the police will catch up with me. But I have a little hope, and I have had good reasons for changing my ways. Listen.

NARRATOR: In the deepening night around him
There are not even shadows of passers-by,
And in the grasses only the insects' cries.

SHIMAZO (*looks around him intently*): After I left you, I went back to the town where I was born. My father and sister were the same as ever, but my son, whom I had entrusted to my father's care, walked with a limp. I was flabbergasted to hear how the boy became a cripple. My father had left a sharpened cleaver on a shelf, and late one night the family cat knocked it off, in the process of catching a mouse. It fell on the leg of my son, who was sleeping below, and hurt him so badly that he was crippled. He now has trouble walking. The strange thing is that the night he got hurt was the twentieth of April, and it was just before midnight. That was the same night that you and I broke into Fukushimaya's house, and the time was also exactly the same. And the place where I slashed Fukushimaya was the left leg too.

NARRATOR: The sin of the father is visited upon the child,

The proverb goes, but seldom so swiftly!

SHIMAZO: This forced me to realize that I must renounce my criminal ways. At the time that I made this decision I had exactly four hundred yen left of the loot from our robbery. I went back to Tokyo from the country, intending to bring the amount up to five hundred yen, which was my share, and return it to Fukushimaya. I decided I would give myself up to the police, accept whatever punishment was coming to me, and become an honest man. I started a wineshop in order to raise the money. Now you know how I came to be honest and why I can't do what you ask.

NARRATOR: Thus he told of the punishment for evil,

But Senta would not hear him.

SENTA: You mean that just because your son was hurt on the same night that you stabbed Fukushimaya, you're now in such a panic that you've lost your courage?

SHIMAZO: Yes, as you say, I've lost my courage. I realize what the punishment for that crime was. Not only for me—as a result of our stealing the thousand yen, Fukushimaya finally had to sell his land and his shop went into bankruptcy. He disappeared without a trace. I searched fruitlessly for him everywhere. Today, quite by chance, a well-mannered little girl came to my shop and ordered two quarts of soy sauce. I asked where I should deliver them, and she told me they were for Fukushimaya. I took the soy sauce myself, wondering if it would prove to be the same family. As I suspected, it was. The two of them, father and daughter, are leading a life of such misery in their alley tenement that it pained me almost too much to look at them. It was fortunate I arrived when I did—they were in desperate need of a hundred yen, which I gave them without saying why. I want now to return the balance and give myself up. But at the moment, it so happens that my father has come to Tokyo from the country, to tell me how happy he is that I've reformed, and I'll have to postpone surrendering myself for a while.

I was so surprised this evening when you appeared, saying something about an urgent request. We couldn't very well talk at home, with my father and sister there. Besides, my house is separated from the neighbors only by a thin wall. I thought it would be safer for both of us to talk here, where no one can hear us.

Now you have my whole explanation of why I can't go with you. I know you're disappointed in me. I'm sorry.

SENTA: You've always been a very cool sort up to now. I wonder what's come over you. If you've been punished because, as people say, the gods have put a curse on you for an evil deed, I should also have been punished. And if everybody gets what he deserves, that means that Fukushimaya must have been robbed as a punishment for having sold bad merchandise. It's the will of Heaven that his business has folded and that he's been forced into a life of poverty. What could be more foolish than to return the money to him? I've been living very comfortably during the past six months since the robbery, obviously because my sins were not bad enough for Heaven to punish me. Come on with me tonight and give up your chicken-hearted moralizing.

SHIMAZO: This is one favor I can't do for you, no matter how much you ask me. I have given up crime for once and for all. If you can't do the job alone, so much the better. You can change your ways tonight too.

SENTA (*with an angry gesture*): There's no use talking to you any more, I can see. But do you mean to say you've forgotten how when we were in prison we made ourselves blood brothers? How we cut each other's arm with a broken shell and drank the blood? We swore that from then on we would stick together, through life and death. You can't have forgotten. If you won't do what I ask, it means you no longer feel any loyalty.

SHIMAZO: No, it's because I *am* your friend that I want to stop you.

SENTA: Explain yourself.

SHIMAZO: I don't know all the details of the grudge you bear towards Mochizuki, but let's suppose that you succeed in running off with all his money tonight after you have killed the two of them. The police will suspect you at once, since you went there only yesterday to blackmail them. An alarm will be telegraphed all over the country. You'll never escape. You'll be caught in three days. Then, when they sentence you, it won't be as a thief but as a murderer, and you're certain to be beheaded. You may be able to lay your hands on a thousand yen tonight, but if you're caught within three days, you won't have spent more than fifty yen of it. What could be more stupid than to throw away your life for such a trifling amount? If you take my advice and go straight, I will be a real brother to you in every way and do whatever I can for you. What I am saying is for your own good. If you can't manage to give back the whole five hundred yen you got as your share, return whatever you can to Fukushimaya, and then go with me to the police and confess everything.

SENTA: You're not forty yet, but already you seem to have lost your nerve. I still have enough fight left in me so that even if I'm surrounded on all sides, I'll keep on until I drop. If I gave myself up now they might, I suppose, commute the sentence by one degree, and I would be condemned to ten years at hard labor! You call me stupid, but you're not very bright yourself.

SHIMAZO: Ten years of hard labor? That shows how little you understand such things. The government will show special clemency if you return the money you stole and surrender. They'll reduce a ten year sentence to seven or even five years. And when once you serve out the sentence all the crimes you have committed are washed into the sea and are completely forgotten. If you can really pass this test and work day and night with all your strength

NARRATOR: It is certain that you will receive

Blessings from Heaven which once punished you.

SHIMAZO: If these were still the old days of the Shogunate, when any theft over ten yen was punishable by death, I could see why you might prefer to take a parting fling at crime, since you were doomed to die in any case. But now the penal code has been changed, and even a burglar who steals a thousand yen escapes with life imprisonment. If, instead of being grateful that you live

in such times as these, you throw away your life by killing somebody, it shows you're not very enlightened. Don't show such
neglect for the precious body you have received from your parents. Change your heart and join me.

NARRATOR: Senta with crooked heart falsely took
  Shimazo's straight words of understanding.

SENTA: The reason why you're going straight is that you have a son
you love, besides your father and your sister. I can see why you'd
like to become an honest man. But I have neither parents nor family, and even if I reformed, it wouldn't make anybody happy. I'll
go on stealing all the rest of my life. If I make a mistake and get
killed for it, well, that will be an end to it.

SHIMAZO: You really are completely stupid. Even admitting that your
parents are no longer in this world, don't you think they're worrying about you in their graves? If people simply vanished without
a trace when they died, nobody, not even the Emperor, would pay
respects to the dead. Something must surely remain. You've got to
change your ways, renounce your crimes, and bring happiness to
your parents in the other world.

SENTA: Why should I bother with making them happy? They're my
parents, yes, but all that means is that out of their own pleasure
they created me. I feel no gratitude or obligation to them. Let
them suffer now at their own pleasure.

NARRATOR: In his fit of wrath he uses vile words;
  Shimazo hearing them is completely dismayed.

SHIMAZO: I hadn't thought you were such a thick-headed fool. From
tonight on I'll not talk to you any more, and you can go to hell
for all I care.

SENTA: And what do you mean by that? When we swore to be
brothers, we promised to stick together whatever happened, in
life or in death. If you won't do what I ask you, we're no longer
brothers. I am breaking our relationship. We're strangers from
tonight on. If I get caught tonight I'll send the police after you, so
you had better be ready and waiting.

SHIMAZO: Haven't you listened to anything I've been saying?

SENTA: If we are still brothers, I'll obey whatever you say, since you are the older. But once we become strangers, we're equal, and then why should I listen to what you or anyone else says?

SHIMAZO: If you won't listen, don't. And now that I no longer have any obligations to you, I'm going to turn myself in. They will be coming to arrest you. Don't be a coward and run away.

SENTA: I won't turn and run. Come and get me any time you like. I'll be risking my life when I break into Mochizuki's house to-night, but whether I kill two people or three, I have only one head they can cut off. If you try to stop me with any underhanded trick, you are a dead man, Shimazo.

(*He removes his kimono from one shoulder to permit freer move-ment of his arm, then draws from his cloak a dagger hidden in its folds. He brandishes it before Shimazo, who glances at it con-temptuously, and with a scornful laugh assumes a posture of de-fiance.*)

SHIMAZO: If that's the best you can threaten, it's not very impressive. I don't suppose you've forgotten how I swore to be your brother because of the help you gave me when I was sick in prison, but when we served our term and got out, I was the one who taught you how to stage a robbery. What do you think you're doing now, waving a dagger at me? Are you planning to stab me? I don't doubt you can cut off the corner of a tombstone, but you can't cut off my head! If you think you can, go ahead and try!

NARRATOR: He thrusts himself forward with no sign of fear;
          Senta hesitates, uncertain whether to strike.

SENTA: What else can I do but stab him?

(*He slashes at Shimazo, who dodges and with a stick engages Senta in a wild scuffle. Shimazo cracks the stick against Senta's wrist and the dagger drops to the ground. Senta tries to retrieve it, but is prevented by Shimazo. The two men strike poses. They then grapple again. Shimazo finally strikes Senta to the ground. He picks up the dagger and presses it against Senta's chest.*)

SHIMAZO: Well, Senta, all it would take for me to kill you now is just one thrust, and there is nothing you can do about it. You won't reconsider even if it costs you your life?

(*He releases the pressure of the dagger.*)

SENTA: Who is going to change his ways? If you want to kill me, go ahead. That will make a murderer out of you, but I won't be the only one to die. Go ahead and kill me.

SHIMAZO: Yes, even though you're a scoundrel, you're still a human being, and I realize that if I kill you I'll die for it.

SENTA: If you realize that, kill me. Come on, kill me. Kill me quickly.

(*He pushes himself against Shimazo, who takes Senta by the front of his kimono and forces him to the ground.*)

SHIMAZO: You've asked for it—I will kill you.

NARRATOR: Holding the dagger downwards, Shimazo
      Lifts his arm to stab him, but hesitates:
      Villain though Senta is, until today
      They had called each other brother.
      Stirred by his emotion Shimazo relents.

SHIMAZO: You tell me to kill you, and I know I should. But I can't bring myself to do it. I once thought of you as my brother. If you will only realize that what you have done is wrong, and give up being a thief, I'll help you all the rest of my life. And as for the five hundred yen—your share of the loot—I'll make it up somehow, if only you turn over a new leaf. As I said, I intend to surrender to the police as soon as I have returned the money to Fukushi-maya. I've made up my mind to throw myself on the mercy of the government, and am confident that they will shorten my sentence. To give yourself up after returning the money is not a very spectacular thing to do, but even thieves will recognize you as a hero for it. Would you rather be praised and enabled to live out your full life, and even be of some service to your country, or abused and forced to die? You've reached the boundary between life and death now. Be sure you are doing the right thing.

NARRATOR: Shimazo, full of forgiveness, a true brother,
      Speaks words of advice that sink with the breeze
      Of the autumn night into the flesh
      Of Senta the villain who, as one waking
      From nightmares, returns to virtue's ways.

SENTA: (*He gradually looks up, and in an attitude of repentance lifts his head.[4] When he has raised it fully, he wipes away his tears and joins his hands in supplication.*) Forgive me, brother. You have convinced me. I'll change my ways.

SHIMAZO: You're really serious?

SENTA: What else is there to do? You've always advised me more patiently, more kindly than any blood relation, even though I've been such a monster. That was because we were sworn brothers, but today at last your words have sunk in. They have completely changed me. To prove to you that I'm not lying—

(*He picks up the dagger and attempts to kill himself, but Shimazo stops him.*)

SHIMAZO: Senta, what are you doing? I was giving you such harsh advice because I wanted to save your life. Do you think I would talk that way if I dreamt it would drive you to kill yourself? Now that you've repented, what makes you do such a thing?

(*He twists away the dagger.*)

SENTA: I'm not like you—even though I reform, I'm no use to anybody. I thought that if I died it would be for the good of the world, and I felt like killing myself.

SHIMAZO: Don't be stupid. Value your life and live like a good man. Try to make an honest living, even if you have to open a little shop somewhere. That is sure to bring happiness to your dead parents. Don't revert to your evil ways!

SENTA: I renounce robbery. I will make offerings on the anniversaries of the deaths of my poor parents, to whom I have brought so much suffering all these years, even if I can only afford to give water.

SHIMAZO: That will bring them greater joy than you can imagine. And do you completely give up the idea of breaking into Mochizuki's house tonight?

SENTA: Yes, I do.

SHIMAZO: I am very relieved to hear your words.

SENTA: I could have spared you much suffering if only I had seen the light earlier. Brother, forgive me.

(*He bows his head to the ground in apology.*)

---

[4] This is the acting climax of the play, and a familiar feature of the Kabuki drama. The actors would register various changes of expression in a series of poses.

SHIMAZO: Your apology shows you have become an honest man. I forgive you.

SENTA: I wish I could go with you now to return what I took from Fukushimaya, but I haven't five yen, much less five hundred. My only way of raising money is to accept the hundred yen Mochizuki offered me yesterday.

SHIMAZO: Since it is Mochizuki's wish, you should. Then, if you can sell this dagger for two hundred yen, it will make three hundred yen all told. That's still two hundred yen short, of course.

SENTA: Now that I've given up stealing, I haven't the means of earning even one yen.

MOCHIZUKI (*appearing from behind the torii to the left*): I will present you with the two hundred yen you need.

SHIMAZO: Who are you?

SENTA: Mochizuki!

MOCHIZUKI: This is the first time I meet you, Shimazo. Let me present myself. I am Mochizuki. Yesterday I had the unexpected pleasure of speaking with Senta. This evening I happened to be passing through the grounds of the shrine on my way back home from business downtown. I heard whispering and wondered what was afoot. I've heard everything, and that's why I'm offering you the two hundred yen.

SHIMAZO: I don't know about Senta, but I've never had the honor of meeting you and . . .

SENTA: For you to offer to give me so much money . . .

MOCHIZUKI: It is a slight token of gratitude to Shimazo.

SHIMAZO: But why?

MOCHIZUKI: If Senta had broken into my house tonight because of his old grudge, I might easily have been killed, or if lucky enough to escape with my life, suffered a severe wound. I escaped this danger because of Shimazo. I offer the money in gratitude.

SHIMAZO: Then you really intend to give the two hundred yen?

SENTA: I didn't think you could be so merciful. If I had broken into your house tonight, I would certainly have ended up by having my head cut off.

SHIMAZO: You see, bad actions never lead to useful results. When you do good, your need is answered. Now you have the money.

MOCHIZUKI: I suppose you've heard all kinds of rumors about me, but the fact is that I also used to be a member of a desperate band of criminals. I know what you feel, and I am delighted that you both have abandoned the evil ways of that life.

SENTA: May I presume on your most merciful nature to make another request? Would you please give me the hundred yen you offered me yesterday as quittance money?

SHIMAZO: Please also buy this dagger. It is a very valuable one and well worth two hundred yen.

MOCHIZUKI: I shall certainly give you the money I offered, Senta. And, Shimazo, since it is your wish, I'll offer two hundred yen for the dagger.

SHIMAZO: Your generosity will enable Senta to pay back in full the five hundred yen which he received as his share of the Fukushimaya robbery. I will go home to get the balance I owe Fukushimaya. We will return all of the thousand yen.

SENTA: How amazing that we have been able to find so much money in one night!

MOCHIZUKI: It is Heaven's reward for your having given up crime.

SHIMAZO: When we have returned the thousand yen to the long-suffering Fukushimaya . . .

SENTA: We will at once confess the robbery at the police station.

MOCHIZUKI: I am sure that your sentence will be light.

SENTA: If word of this appeared in the newspapers it would set a good example for thieves.

SHIMAZO: We owe everything, without any doubt, to Mochizuki.

MOCHIZUKI: I helped you because I too was once a thief.

[*The remaining lines of the play are in verse and declaimed.*]

SENTA: We who are now gathered here

SHIMAZO: Are thieves, like rough waves that recoil

SENTA: From the sands of the beach of crimes towards the open sea.

MOCHIZUKI: Only to return with the tide to virtue itself.

NARRATOR: They rejoice over their return to grace.

Now is the immaculate hour before sunrise.

(Music of flutes and drums to which is added the tinkle of a bell. All strike poses.)

That music, at the Yasukuni Shrine,

SHIMAZO: Means the cleansing rite of every day.

SENTA: The cries of the cock chase away impurity

SHIMAZO: Boldly in the hour before the dawn.

MOCHIZUKI: The sky is clearing now.

The dawn has come!

(Fast beating of wooden clappers to signal the closing of the Kabuki curtain, and ringing of bell.)

TRANSLATED BY DONALD KEENE

Many writers of the early Meiji period continued the scholarly tradition of writing poetry and prose in Chinese. The growth of interest in the West tended increasingly to lessen the popularity of classical Chinese studies, but it was Natsume Sōseki, a scholar of English literature, who wrote the most distinguished poetry in Chinese of any Japanese of recent times.

●

Niagara Falls

The startled traveler wakes to the thunder by his pillow,
Rises and climbs among old trees to the roaring brink.
In the deep night, white all heaven and earth;
The moon comes, parting the curtain of a million misty pearls.
Narushima Ryūhoku (1837-1884)

In the Army

To fret at the time, to bewail the age—how pointless!
More sense in howling at the moon or fashioning rhymes on
  flowers.
Should anyone come to camp and ask for me today,
Say that the General went to bed drunk and has not yet
  wakened.
Fujita Koshirō (1842-1865)

Song of Victory: The Battle of Port Arthur

With the King's million I struck the proud foe;
From the plains drove upon the fort until the dead were piled
  in hills.

With this shame must I now face their fathers:
To our song of victory today, how many men return?

General Nogi Maresuke (1849-1912)

Self-derision

With hateful eyes I wait withdrawal from the world,
Lazy, with this doltish ignorance, to try its fame.
Turning my back upon the days, I slander my contemporaries;
I read old books to curse the ancients.
With the talent of a donkey, a lagging roan,
Head vacuous as the autumn locust's shell,
Abounding only in passion for the mists,
I shall rate rivers, from my rude hut classify the hills.

Natsume Sōseki (1867-1916)

TRANSLATED BY BURTON WATSON

THE ESSENCE OF THE NOVEL

[Preface to Shōsetsu Shinzui, 1885] by Tsubouchi Shōyō (1859-1935)

The Essence of the Novel was a work which exercised great influence during the early Meiji period. Tsubouchi defined in it the methods and purposes of the novel (as opposed to the tale or the romance) largely in terms of European, particularly English, examples. The preface, given here, is probably the most interesting part of the work for Western readers; the rest of the book tends to be a reiteration of ideas familiar to us from Victorian works of literary criticism.

•

What a glorious tradition the novel can boast in Japan! We have from ancient times such works as *The Tale of Genji,* and in more recent centuries Saikaku and other novelists have won considerable fame with their writings. The novel has enjoyed an ever increasing popularity, and writers have eagerly turned out historical romances, humorous tales, or love stories, as their particular talents dictated. However, as the result of the upheavals which accompanied the Meiji Restoration, for a time the popular writers ceased their activity, and the novel itself consequently lost ground. It has only been recently that a revival has occurred. The time indeed seems propitious for the production of novels. Everywhere historical romances and tales are being published, one more unusual than the next. It has reached such a point that even newspapers and magazines are printing reworkings of the hackneyed old novels, and thanks to this trend, the number of novels being produced is now beyond all reckoning. There is a simply staggering production of books, all of them extremely bad.

This holy reign of Meiji may well be said to have witnessed an absolutely unprecedented popularity of the novel in Japan. At the end of the Tokugawa period, it is true, such writers as Bakin and Tanehiko [1] wrote a great many books which enjoyed immense popularity. Old and young, men and women, town dwellers and villagers alike, all eagerly pored over the historical romances. But this was still a far cry from approaching the present wild popularity of the novel. It should not be forgotten that during the early years of this century the reader, however extravagant he might be, purchased and read only the outstanding books. The inferior novels were, in the nature of things, overwhelmed by the good ones and, unable to enjoy public circulation, were doomed to perish in manuscript. Or, even supposing they managed somehow to get printed, most of them became food for bookworms and very rarely emerged from their obscurity. As a result, the variety and number of such works was understandably rather smaller than at present. Things are quite different today. Every novel or romance, however improbable a tale it may be, however vulgar a love story, whether a reworking, a retranslation, a republication, or a new work, regardless of its merits or quality, is certain to win the same popularity. Is this not extraordinary? Ours must indeed be called an era of unprecedented prosperity for the novel.

There is certainly no dearth of those who fall under the heading of "writers of popular fiction," but most of them are merely rehashers, and not a single one has distinguished himself as an author. The novels which have lately appeared have one and all been either reworkings of Bakin and Tanehiko or else fakes in the manner of Ikku and Shunzui. The writers of popular fiction seem to have taken as their guiding principle the dictum that the essence of the novel lies in the expression of the approved moral sentiments. They accordingly erect a framework of morality into which they attempt to force their plots. The scope of their works is basically so narrow that even when they are not deliberately trying to ape the old writers, they end up by unconsciously falling into the old ruts and the old ideas of their predecessors. How can we but deplore this?

However, that things have come to such a pass is not to be blamed

[1] Takizawa Bakin (1767-1848) and Ryūtei Tanehiko (1783-1842).

exclusively on the inferiority of the writers. Far from it—the indiscriminate readers throughout the country also must shoulder their share of the blame. It has long been the custom in Japan to consider the novel as an instrument of education, and it has frequently been proclaimed that the novel's chief function is the castigation of vice and the encouragement of virtue. In actual practice, however, only stories of bloodthirsty cruelty or else of pornography are welcomed, and very few readers indeed even cast so much as a glance on works of a more serious nature. Moreover, since popular writers have no choice but to be devoid of self-respect and in all things slaves to public fancy and the lackeys of fashion, each one attempts to go to greater lengths than the last in pandering to the tastes of the time. They weave their brutal historical tales, string together their obscene romances, and yield to every passing vogue. Nevertheless they find it so difficult to abandon the pretext of "encouraging virtue" that they stop at nothing to squeeze in a moral, thereby distorting the emotion portrayed, falsifying the situations, and making the whole plot nonsensical. One awkwardness is piled on another until it becomes quite beyond any mature person to read the book with a straight face. The writers quite irresponsibly dash off their fiction without any conception of what the object of such literature should be. They continue to cling obstinately to their old, misguided practices. Is this not the height of the ridiculous? Or rather—is this not the height of the lamentable?

I myself from childhood days have had a taste for fiction, and I used to read such works whenever I had the leisure. More than ten years of irreplaceable time went by in such pursuits, but they enabled me to acquire a considerable amount of knowledge about fiction old and new. Believing moreover that I have obtained a fair understanding of what the true object of fiction should be, I now make so bold as to display my theories to the world, aware as I am of their inadequacies. I hope that this book will help clear up the problems of readers and, at the same time, that it will be of service to authors, so that by dint of steady planning from now on for the improvement of our novels we may finally be able to surpass in quality the European novels, and permit our novels to take a glorious place along with painting, music, and poetry on the altar of the arts. I hope that the learned and gifted men who will read these pages will not be too severe on my inadequacies, but will instead grant their favor to what I have to say and to the spirit which infuses my words. Their careful and thoughtful consideration will be a source of joy not only to myself but to the whole literary world.

TRANSLATED BY DONALD KEENE

THE DRIFTING CLOUD

[Ukigumo, II, 7. 1888] by Futabatei Shimei (1864-1909)

The Drifting Cloud, *written 1887-1889, is the first modern Japanese novel both in subject matter and style: it deals mainly with young Japanese educated under the new "enlightenment," and it is written in a colloquial style very close to the actual conversation of the time. The chief character—he can hardly be called the hero—is Utsumi Bunzō, a hapless young man who loses his job in the Civil Service because he does not toady to his superiors. His aunt Omasa, in whose house he lives, at first wishes to marry her daughter Osei to him, but when he loses his job she shows him only contempt. Osei, a superficially "enlightened" girl, proud of her education and Western ideas, turns from Bunzō to the aggressive sycophant Honda Noboru, the up-and-coming Meiji bureaucrat par excellence. The novel is full of vivid and amusing scenes which depict life in the eighties in Japan with a sharpness that borders at times perhaps on caricature. We can only regret that this unprecedented novel was never completed. The following excerpt occurs at a point where Osei is beginning to be won by the blandishments of Noboru.*

•

Sunday was a brilliantly clear day, the likes of which they had not seen in a long while. The wind was gentle and not a particle of dust stirred. It was the second of November, the beginning of the "month of chrysanthemums" according to the old calendar, and ideal weather for pleasure seekers.

The members of the household had been busy since morning with preparations for the excursion to view the chrysanthemums. Osei fretted so over the fit of her finery that she quite got on Omasa's

nerves. The hairdresser's tardiness in arriving, which precipitated
another crisis, was naturally enough blamed on the maid. Finally,
in rapid succession, a teapot passed down from remote antiquity
acquired a harelip with which it had not been born, an earthenware
mortar firmly placed on a shelf ran away all by itself, and, just
when everything was in a state of the extremest confusion, an
unfortunate visitor, one notorious as a long stayer, appeared. They
attempted to lay as much emphasis as they could on the words
"We're leaving in just a few minutes for Dangosaka," but these
had no more effect than the remedies of the most arrant quack. The
visitor settled down with utter self-possession to a lengthy chat, with
an air of being permanently installed. What a dreadful nuisance!
Nevertheless they did as duty required, and the danger passed more
easily than expected. Hardly had the visitor left—which eventually
did occur—than the hairdresser arrived. The preparations for the
excursion were duly completed and by eleven the household had at
length calmed down. Occasionally one even heard loud peals of
laughter.

Bunzō, the man of misfortune and woe, had nothing about *him* of
chrysanthemum-viewing. If we could compare Noboru to the
cherry blossoms in the pride of their springtime flowering, Bunzō
resembled, rather, a withered cattail in the shade. He had decided
that if there was nothing he could do to oppose the excursion, he
would at least not let himself be humiliated by it. He chose to let
circumstances take their course and give himself the airs of a martyr.
The day before yesterday when Noboru invited him along, he had
resolved to refuse outright. Since then, he had maintained a detached calm which suggested that whether people were excited or
not was a matter of as little concern to him as the neighbor's colic.
But he was inwardly not quite equal to this feigned tranquillity.
Everything he saw or heard, always with the same expression of
serene pleasure on his face, of the others' excitement served to
remind him again of his happiness of yesterday, and he sighed, his
spirits damp as the sky in May. Which was not very enjoyable.

No, it was not enjoyable. When yesterday Osei asked Bunzō if he
were going, he had replied that he was not. To which she had said

in the coolest possible tone, "Oh, really?"—which was not enjoy-able. Bunzō felt that if she wanted him to go she should have coaxed him. And if he remained obstinate and still would not go, she should have said something like, "Unless I can go with you, I won't go at all."

"But I am not jealous," he suddenly recalled, and tried to rational-ize his mood to himself. But he still felt a tickling sensation of uneasiness.

He didn't want to go, he didn't want to stay at home either, and this dilemma put him in a bad humor. He was angry, although at no one in particular. He could not sit still, but kept jumping up as though he had remembered some urgent business, only to decide that he hadn't. He could not seem to quiet down, no matter what he did.

Bunzō thought he might be able to distract himself with a little reading, and took the first book from his shelf that came to hand. He tried reading, but it brought no distraction whatsoever. He glowered at the volume with a peevish expression as if he were trying to outstare the page. The book was not a bad one, but no matter how many times he read and reread the opening lines of the first chapter he could not make any sense out of it. With mad-dening clarity, on the other hand, he could hear Osei's laughter in the downstairs parlor, and once this sound had taken possession of his ears, it would not go away for quite some time. With an angry click of his tongue Bunzō threw away the book, angrily leaned against his desk, angrily propped his head on his hand, angrily glared at nothing in particular. . . . Struck by a sudden thought he stood up, a look of resuscitation on his face.

"Maybe they'll call the whole thing off . . ." he murmured. But he came to himself at once and clamped his mouth shut in con-sternation. He felt surprised, bewildered, and finally desperate. "Damn you!" he said, shaking his fists in self-intimidation. But the mischievous worm within him again began to stir in his heart . . . perhaps, after all. . . .

Alas, no accident seemed to have occurred to Noboru, who appeared at about one o'clock. In honor of the occasion, he wore Japanese costume today—a brown silk kimono with a black twilled-silk coat. His sash was also of something chic: he was attired as usual in the height of fashion. He thundered up the staircase to Bunzō's room, and without a preliminary word of greeting plopped himself down. He gave Bunzō an extraordinarily supercilious look, as if he were examining his own nose, and at length enquired, "What's the matter? You look as if you've been drowned."

"I have a little headache."

"Is that so? The old lady hasn't by any chance been giving you a rough time, has she?"

This trivial conversation upset Bunzō. He felt somehow offended, but he was too diffident to say anything.

"How about it? Sure you won't go?"

"I don't think I will."

"Obstinate, aren't you? It's because you're so obstinate that you'd like me to plead with you to come, isn't it?" He laughed. "There's nothing I can do except laugh to myself. Nothing I say will have any effect on you." He barked a laugh.

After Noboru had spent a few minutes with Bunzō in this vague chatter which could be termed neither jest nor slander, Osei suddenly called up from downstairs. "Mr. Honda!"

"What is it?"

"The rickshaws have come, so if you're ready . . ."

"Let's go."

"Hurry then."

"Osei?"

"Yes?"

"I told them that it would be all right if the two of us rode together, and it's arranged that way. You don't mind, do you?"

There was no answer, only the sound of feet scampering away.

"It's charming how she runs off without answering, isn't it?" These words served as Noboru's final salutation to Bunzō, and with them he went downstairs. Bunzō, following him with his eyes, muttered bitterly, "The damned fool!" But even while his voice still wandered in a limbo of its own, he recalled how Osei looked in the spring when they had gone to see the cherry blossoms, and he sprang to his feet for no reason. After glaring in all directions, he finally directed his gaze at the fire pan. He collected his thoughts again and returned to where he had been sitting. Again he said bitterly, "The damned fool!" This time he referred to himself.

In the afternoon a light breeze sprang up, but the weather grew only the better. What with the fine weather and the fact that it was Sunday, the area around Dangosaka was so jammed with people out to see the chrysanthemums that it was scarcely possible to move on the roads. What a crowd! What a crowd! There were women with their hair done in foreign-style and in the *shimada*,[1] some in the double-loop coiffure and others in chignons, girls in the butter-fly bun and in bangs. There came Madame X, secretary to a certain learned society, but said to be really the spook of some old cat, and Miss Y, whose charmingly minute store of wisdom (of the size of a mustard seed) was concentrated in her feet, and whose very dreams were filled with jumping and prancing. There came wet nurses and scullery maids, fashionable ladies in semiforeign style, and women who looked like living proofs that polygamy was still being prac-ticed. What a crowd! What a crowd! Shaven-headed priests had come and long-haired men, men with half-shaven heads and men with topknots. And they too had come, those beloved of the gods, the darlings of destiny, the men among men and objects of universal esteem, those cynosures of envy—I mean they who in days of yore were called liegemen, but who now are our so-called officials, and who may in future generations be styled "public servants." Business-men came, and the meek and the humble. There came also exposed politicians, whose principle is not to look anyone in the face, and who, having forgotten themselves and their families, seem likely candidates for a prison cell. The whole world had come. All kinds of faces, hair-dos arranged to suit all kinds of fancies, costumes and scents of every conceivable description—but I have not the leisure to describe them all. Besides, the road is so narrow here that the con-gestion is quite unbelievable. And in the midst of all this there are some heartless individuals who ride through the crowd in their rickshaws two abreast!

[1] The *shimada* was the name of the hair style worn by young women.

The residents of the neighborhood who, in this glorious age, eke out a living from day to day by pasting together matchboxes, look up from their work only long enough to see the flower-viewers, and never do get to see any real chrysanthemums. When you stop to think of it, it really does take all sorts to make a world.

Dangosaka was in a state of the wildest confusion. Flower-sellers stood by the usual signboards waving the flags of their respective establishments in the attempt to lure in customers, and the cries of the barkers at every shop entrance got mingled quite unintelligibly in the autumn wind. In the midst of the turmoil all one could see were the feverishly shouting faces of the barkers, who were in the same frantic state no matter how often one looked at them. Not surprisingly, when one went inside the shops the confusion was exactly the same as outdoors.

If we may be permitted a generalization, the chrysanthemum is a flower which singly gives an impression of loneliness, but when in the thousands creates a very cheerful effect. Some claim that only when chrysanthemums are growing in their natural profusion are they worth seeing, and that to see them displayed on such a lavish scale as at Dangosaka is enough to dampen one's enthusiasm for chrysanthemums permanently. Here were massed, with no semblance of discrimination, yellow and white chrysanthemums, those flowers which faithfully bloom after all the rest of the fragrant species have departed. One or two visitors in a thousand might complain of the rather stiff appearance of the flowers, which looked like overstarched doll's clothes and rustled when you touched them, but there was not a single visitor who did not in fact seem more interested in food than in flowers—alas and alack.

To the Reader: The above is to be taken as the foolish reflections of a retired gentleman on viewing the chrysanthemums.

The Reader: What a bore!

To return to our story.

The two rickshaws raced up to Dangosaka and came smartly to a stop. From the rickshaws then emerged our old friend Noboru, Osei, and her mother.

Noboru's costume was as previously described.

Omasa wore a sash of black Chinese silk over her gray crepe kimono, underneath which was visible the border of her underrobe, of black crepe with a design of some sort sewn in glittering gold thread—a very sensible outfit.

Osei wore a yellow kimono with a sash of gray-blue damask filigreed with gold thread. Underneath, of course, was the customary full-length underrobe of scarlet crepe, and this was graced with a neckband of pale blue with a design sewn in gold. The cord of the sash was of pink crepe. In short, she was elegantly attired.

However, what caused people to stop and take notice was less Osei's clothing than her whole appearance. Although her hair was done up as usual in a European-style bun, it was so cunningly tied as to suggest that it might be some rare Japanese style of coiffure, and it was ornamented with a large hairpin in the shape of a rose. She wore only light make-up, preferring its simple neatness to the conventional cosmetics which, she said, went against Nature. Evidently she was all refinement, in character no less than appearance.

The envious sightseers who surrounded their party from time to time made quite audible comments: "They're sweethearts!" "No, husband and wife!" These speculations were accompanied by much gaping and pointing, and with each phrase that came his way Noboru looked the more pleased. Ostentatiously he paraded the two women through the various exhibits of chrysanthemums, never letting up his chatter for even an instant. That people nearby could overhear every word he spoke did not inhibit his usual flow of gossip.

Osei also seemed in unusually fine fettle today. There was something indefinably vivacious in her walk and her carriage and, of course, her conversation, which rather suggested a little bird who had escaped from its cage, and her ready wit was in evidence. She laughed ceaselessly, amused by Noboru's nonsense, but it was not necessarily because what he said was so funny. It seemed likely that she would have laughed just the same even had he remained silent, out of natural high spirits.

Omasa was exceedingly cool about the chrysanthemums, confining herself to an occasional "How pretty!" and a vague sweeping glance which made no attempt to focus on anything. On the other hand she studied with meticulous attention the appearance of every girl they passed who happened to be about the same age as Osei. First she would examine the face, then the clothes, the sash, the feet, and after the girl had gone by, Omasa would turn back for a final look at her appearance from behind—the sash again, and the hair. This accomplished, Omasa would dart a glance at Osei from the corner of her eyes and assume an air of serene composure.

Noboru's party visited last the florists' booths at the foot of the hill. After examining one after another of the displays, they stopped in front of one booth. Noboru declared that the face of the doll exhibited there looked extraordinarily like Bunzō yawning. Osei was highly amused, and delicately putting one sleeve to her face, leaned over the guardrail, convulsed with laughter. At this a student standing nearby wheeled around in her direction and stared through his glasses at Osei in amazement. Even her mother felt obliged to reprimand Osei for her unbecoming behavior.

At length Osei controlled her laughter. She lifted her face, still coquettishly graced with smiles, and looked beside her. Noboru was not there. Startled, she cast wild glances around her, her expression at once becoming quite serious.

Another glance sufficed to reveal to her Noboru, in front of a booth to the rear, busily engaged in bending his body quite horizontal in repeated obeisances directed at the back of a gentleman in Western clothes. The gentleman appeared utterly indifferent to Noboru, and continued for some time to face the opposite direction. At length, after having been the recipient of numerous unacknowledged bows, he deigned to turn his bushily bewhiskered, grumpy face and look at Noboru. Without a trace of a smile, without even removing his hat, he gave a perfunctory nod, to which Noboru responded by prostrating himself and making a series of deep reverences, continuing all the while to pour forth a stream of the usual tedious compliments.

Of the two ladies who appeared to be accompanying the gentleman, one sported a towering coiffure, and the other wore her hair
in an elegant, maidenly bun. They were both exceptionally beautiful and stylish women, and so well matched that one could not but
take them for sisters. Noboru bowed first to the lady in the lofty
chignon. He addressed himself next to the young lady in the bun,
who was so embarrassed that she averted her gaze when she
returned his bow, and blushed.

It was not possible for Osei to catch the conversation which
ensued, for the other party was at some distance from her and the
people about her were noisy. Whatever it was, a smile never deserted
Noboru's lips as he stood there chattering, occasionally punctuating
his discourse with gestures. Presently he seemed to have uttered
something amusing, for the gentleman suddenly opened his enormous mouth and began to laugh uproariously, with much shaking
of the shoulders. The lady in the chignon wrinkled the corners of
her mouth as she laughed. The young lady also started to titter, but
quickly hid her mouth with her sleeve. Only her eyes continued to
smile as she gazed demurely at Noboru's face. Noboru, conscious
of an honor too great for his station, permitted a smile of triumph
and contentment to suffuse his entire face. After waiting for the
gentleman's laughter to subside, he again began to chatter. Noboru
had apparently quite forgotten that Osei and her mother were
waiting.

Osei paid no attention either to the gentleman or to the distinguished lady, but she observed the girl in the bun with the minutest,
most unwavering, breathless attention, as if intent on drilling a hole
in her with her gaze. She did not respond even when her mother
addressed her.

Before long the gentleman's party gave indications of moving
towards where the women stood. Omasa noticed this and frantically
tugged at Osei's sleeve to rouse her from her trance. They quickly
stepped forward to the path to meet Noboru, who came up a few
minutes later with the gentleman. At the wicket he again bowed
slightly and, politely, affably, loquaciously, recited suitable farewells

to each of them. After they had departed he took two or three tentative steps by himself. An expression, as of sudden recollection, crossed his face, and he gazed around him in consternation.

"Mr. Honda, we're here."

Noboru, hearing Omasa's voice, hurried to the two ladies. "Sorry to have kept you waiting."

"Who was that?"

"That was the chief of my department," he answered smiling broadly, for whatever reason. "I didn't expect them to come today."

"Is the lady in the chignon his wife?"

"Yes, she is."

"And the one in the bun?"

"Oh, she? She's . . ." he began, turned back for another look, and added, "the younger sister of the department head's wife. She looks much prettier than when I saw her at their house."

"Yes, I suppose you might call her pretty, but it's all in the clothes, isn't it?"

"Today she's dressed up like a little lady, but when she's at home she wears the most nondescript clothes, and they treat her like a servant."

"Has she had an education?" Osei suddenly asked.

Noboru was perplexed. "I've never heard anything about that . . . but she may very well be educated, for all I know. She's only just come to live at my department head's house, and I really don't know very much about her yet."

At these words Osei turned around abruptly and, with a derisive expression in her eyes, stared at the young lady, who was about to enter a florist's booth halfway down the hill. Osei patted her sash in a moment of nervousness, but quickly regained her composure.

After they had got into rickshaws which were to take them next to Ueno Park, Omasa remarked to Osei, who rode with her, "You should have worn make-up like that girl."

"I hate it, all that heavy paint."

"But why?"

"It's so unpleasant."

"But you're still in your teens. It isn't the least unpleasant if you wear it. I can't tell you how much better it looks. It's so much more striking."

"If you like it so much, Mama, you should wear it yourself. It's funny the way you keep on saying how good it is when I tell you I hate it."

"All I meant to say is that I think it's nice, and I'm surprised you don't. You really are a funny girl to answer me back like that."

Osei appeared to have recognized that verbal attacks had already ceased to be necessary, and did not utter another word. Without being exactly dispirited or downcast, she had somehow become pensive. Her mother tried to patch together the fragments of the conversation, but Osei would not be her partner in this attempt. This odd situation lasted almost until they had reached Ueno Park, where Osei began to talk again and was more of her old self.

TRANSLATED BY DONALD KEENE

GROWING UP

[Takekurabe, 1895-1896] by Higuchi Ichiyō (1872-1896)

The prose of Higuchi Ichiyō, principal woman novelist of the Meiji period, contains strong echoes of Saikaku, and in a sense represents the last flowering of Tokugawa literature. Growing Up *tells of a group of precocious children who live just outside the Yoshiwara, the Tokyo licensed quarter, and in particular of Midori, whose sister is a prostitute in the quarter; of Nobu, the son of a priest; and of Shota, heir to a pawnshop. The translation is virtually complete.*

•

It is a long way around to the main gate of the Yoshiwara, the licensed quarter, to the willows with their trailing branches; but the Yoshiwara moat, dark like the smiles of the black-toothed beauties,[1] reflects the lights and the sport in the three-storied houses near enough to touch. Day and night the rickshaws come and go—who can guess what riches they tell of? The section is named for the Daionji Temple, but for all that its name reeks of Buddhism, it is a lively enough spot, people who live there say. And yet you know at once, when you turn in by the Mishima Shrine, that the profits are small. Nowhere a decent house, only rows of low tenements, ten and twenty to the row, their roof lines sagging, their front shutters carelessly left half open. One hears no rumors of rich men in these parts.

Everyone has something to do with the quarter. A husband bustles about in the doorway of one of the less elegant houses, bunches of coat checks jangling at his waist. In the evening he sets out for work, and his wife clicks flint stones after him for good luck. Any

[1] When this story was written, many women, and most courtesans, still blackened their teeth.

night could be his last. Ten bystanders slain. Blood flows as murder-suicide is foiled. A dangerous business to be in. Why then is there such a festive air about these gallant twilight departures?

A young girl goes through her course: a minor figure in the wake of some famous beauty, a maid tripping along with the lantern of a great house in her hand, and presently she graduates to—what? Strange that it should all seem so romantic. There she is now in her thirties, assured and trim, walking down the street in quick little steps with a bundle under her arm. No need to ask what it is. At the moat she stamps on the bridge. It's too far around to the gate—can't I leave it here? A seamstress for one of the beauties, presumably.

Fashions here are eccentric. Rarely is there a girl whose sash is pulled in with maidenly neatness. Rather you see wide, daring things thrown loosely around the waist. On an older woman the style is bad enough, but what about this cheeky thing here, certainly no more than fifteen or sixteen, whistling away like the celebrated ladies themselves? But that after all is the sort of neighborhood it is. That shopkeeper's wife—not long ago, when she still had a professional name in a cheap house by the quarter moat, she got to be friendly with one of the brave thugs you see about and the two of them went into business. When her savings are used up she can always go back to her old nest. Something in her manner tells of her past, and she is a great influence on all of the children.

In September comes the Yoshiwara carnival. With a precociousness that would astonish Mencius's mother, a boy of seven or eight goes about imitating this clown and that musician. "How about a round of the houses?" he says to his delighted audience. And presently you see him, the young gallant of the quarter, back from the bath with a towel slung over his shoulder, humming a mischievous song. His maturity at fifteen or sixteen is frightening. The school song has taken on the rhythms of the quarter, *gitchon-chon, gitchon-chon,* and at the athletic meets it threatens to turn into the tune all the beauties are singing. Education is never a simple matter, but think of the teacher who has to train these extraordinary children.

Not far from the quarter is the Ikueisha. It is not one of the

respected schools, and yet it has something of a name. Nearly a
thousand students elbow one another in its narrow rooms and halls.
Among them, Nobu of the Ryugeji Temple.[2] His thick black hair
will one day be shaved, and his child's clothes changed for the black
of the priest. . . . Perhaps it was by his own choice, perhaps he was
only reconciled to what had to be. In any case he was a student like
his father. Always quieter than the other boys, he had been the victim of many a bad joke. We hear it's your business; would you see
what you can do for this—and they would sling a dead cat at him.[3]
But that was all past. He was now fourteen. His appearance was in
no way unusual, and yet something about him, something of the
priest, singled him out from the rest.

2

The festival was to be the twentieth of August. Floats and wheeled
stages would push their way up the embankment, they might even
invade the quarter. Young blood raced at the thought of it. One
could never be sure what a half-overheard conversation might inspire these children to do, and the projects they had thought up were
bold indeed. Matched kimonos for each street were but a beginning.

The back-street gang, as it liked to call itself, had for its leader
Chokichi the son of the fire chief. Fifteen and violent, Chokichi had
been a little too sure of himself since the time he took his father's
place and helped police the Yoshiwara carnival. He wore his sash
low around his hips in the manner of the town braves, he answered
down his nose when he bothered to answer at all. "If that boy were
anyone but the chief's," muttered the wife of one of the firemen.

In Shota of the main street, however, Chokichi thought he saw
someone who could give him blow for blow. Shota was three years
younger, but he had money and he was an engaging lad no one
could dislike. He went to a scholastically distinguished school while
Chokichi had to do with the Ikueisha—even when the two schools
sang the same songs the Ikueisha somehow sounded apologetic, like

[2] The name Ryūgeji itself means "Ryūge Temple."
[3] As a priest it would be his business to recite prayers for the dead.

a poor relation. Last year, and the year before too, the main street
had blossomed more richly for the festival than the back street.
There had even been young men out watching over Shota and his
followers, and that had made it a little hard for the back street to
pick the fight it wanted. Another such year, Chokichi knew, and
his swagger—"Who do you think I am? I'm Chokichi, that's who
I am"—would come to seem a bit empty. He might not even be
able to put together a team for a decent water fight at the Benten
Ditch. If it was a matter only of muscles, Chokichi was of course
the stronger; but Shota had a deceptively mild air about him and
everyone was a little afraid of his learning. Two or three boys from
the back street even had quietly gone over to his side. That particularly annoyed Chokichi.

Two days to the festival. If it began to seem that Chokichi would
lose again, well, he would fight for what it was worth. What if he
lost an eye or a leg? It would be a small price to pay if he could give
Shota a few bruises too. Chokichi wouldn't be easy to beat with
Ushi the rickshawman's son on his side, and Bunji the barber's, and
Yasuke from the toyshop. But better than any of them—should have
thought of him before—Nobu from the Ryugeji Temple. If he could
get Nobu to help there would be a few brains on his side too.

Toward evening on the eighteenth, Chokichi stole up through the
bamboo groves to Nobu's room, furiously brushing the mosquitoes
from his face. "Nobu, Nobu. I want to talk to you.

"They say I'm tough. Well, maybe I am. But how about last year?
Listen to this, Nobu: that runt of Shota's swings on my little
brother, that's what. And then they all jump on him. How do you
like that, all of 'em jumping on my little brother. And that's not all,
either. The Moose from the Dangoya—he's so big he thinks he can
go around like a grownup—he starts calling me a pigtail. My father's
the chief, but I'm the tail end, that's what he says. How do you like
that? I'm off pulling the float myself, but I'm all for showing 'em
when I hear about it, only my father starts shouting at me and I
have to take it all. And what about the year before? You heard
about that, Nobu. All of them there in the paper store, and when I
come around for a look they say I can go have my own party. How

do you like that? There's nobody in the world but Shota, maybe? I don't care if he has money, he's just a broken-down loan shark, that's all he is. Be doing people a favor to kill him off. But this time I'll get even. How about it, Nobu? For a friend. You don't fight much, but how about it? For the street. You see the way he looks down his nose at us. Let's get back at him. I'm not very smart myself, but you go to the Ikueisha too. How about it? Just carry a lantern, that'll be plenty. If I don't get back at 'em this time I'll have to leave town. Come on, Nobu." Chokichi's heavy shoulders heaved with annoyance.

"But I'm no good at fighting."

"That's all right."

"I don't even know how to carry a lantern."

"That's all right."

"You don't care if we lose?"

"So we lose. All you have to do is go along. Let 'em know whose side you're on, that's all. I don't know much myself, but if they shout big words at us you can shout big words back at 'em. Give 'em a little Chinese. I feel better already. You're as good as all of 'em put together. Thanks, Nobu." Chokichi's tone was not usually so gentle.

The one with the rough sash and the flopping straw sandals of the workman, the other the small priest with his blue-black cloak and his purple sash—their ways of thinking were as different as their clothes, and it was seldom that they were not at cross-purposes. But Nobu's father, the reverend priest, and his mother too rather petted Chokichi ("Why the first squall he let out was right here in front of our gate"). The boys both went to the Ikueisha and suffered from the arrogance of the public schools. Then Chokichi was an unlikable boy quite without friends, while Shota had behind him even the young men of his street. There could be little doubt that Chokichi would lose again, and in all honesty one had to admit that much of the blame for the violence lay with Shota. Approached thus man to man, what could Nobu say?

"All right, I'll go along. I'll go along, but don't fight if you can help it. But if Shota starts something, why I can take care of him with my little finger." Nobu's timidity had somehow disappeared. He opened a drawer and took out a fine Kokaji knife that someone had brought him from Kyoto.

"You could really cut someone up with that," said Chokichi. Careful, careful—is one to brandish a Kokaji so?

3

Her hair—undone it would probably have stretched to her feet—was pulled up tight from the back. *Shaguma,* "red bear," a ferocious name for a girl's coiffure, but so fashionable that perhaps even the damsels in the fine houses had taken it up. Her skin was white, her nose well shaped. Her mouth was a little large, but closed it did not strike one as unattractive. Taken one by one her features were no doubt less than perfect. She had a soft, clear little voice, however, a bright manner and a winsome way of looking at one. I'd like to see her three years from now, young men on their way home from the quarter would say when they saw Midori of the Daikokuya, towel in hand, fresh from her morning bath, her throat white above an orange-red summer kimono gay with birds and butterflies, her black satin sash tied high at the waist, her colored sandals rather thicker than one usually sees in these parts. Midori was born in the south, and there was still a pleasant trace of the south in her speech.

What particularly won people was her straightforward generosity. Her income was remarkable for one her age. Her sister was prospering in the quarter, and some of the profits reached Midori herself. Attendants and satellites, hoping to win the proud lady's favor, would call Midori over. "Go buy yourself a doll," or, "It's only a little, hardly enough for a ball." No one took these gifts very seriously. For the ladies they were a sort of business expense, and Midori knew enough not to be too grateful. "Come on, I'll treat you all"—the matched rubber balls for twenty of her classmates were nothing. Once she pleased her friend the lady in the paper store by buying up all the shopworn games on the shelves. This opulence was a little extreme for Midori's age and station. Where would it all end? She had her parents, of course, but they had never been heard to utter a rough word to her. And if one was curious about the way she was petted by the owner of her sister's house, the Daikokuya, one found that Midori was not his adopted daughter, that she was not even a relation. When the gentleman came south to appraise the sister, the three of them, Midori and her mother and father, had given themselves up to his blandishments and packed their bags, and presently, whatever the understanding might have been, they were here keeping house for him. The mother took in sewing from the beauties, the father kept accounts somewhere in the quarter. The unwilling Midori was sent off to learn sewing and music and she went to school, but beyond that her time was her own: half the day in the streets, half the day in her sister's room, her ears filled with the sound of samisen and drums, in her eyes the reds and purples of the nightless city. When she first came to Tokyo she went out with a lavender neckpiece sewed to her kimono, and all the girls in the neighborhood laughed. "Farmer, farmer!" She cried over it for three days and three nights, but now it was she who laughed first. "Who showed you how to dress?" she would taunt, and no one could stand against her.

The festival was set for the twentieth. Midori's friends were showering her with suggestions.

"We'll do something together," said Midori. "Don't worry about money. I've got plenty. Just say what you want."

The friends, quicker than adults to see their opportunity, knew that they were not likely again to have a ruling lady so generous.

"How about a show? We'll use a store where everybody can see us."

"You call that an idea?" The boy already wore his headband in the rakish festival manner. "We'll get a *mikoshi*.[4] A real one. The heavier the better. *Yatchoi, yatchoi.*"

"Leave Midori out, and let you have all the fun? What do you want to do, Midori?" The girls would have Midori decide, but there

---

[4] The portable shrine around which most Japanese festivals center. *Yatchoi, yatchoi* is a childish variant of the chant with which *mikoshi*-bearers mark time. *Mikoshi* were, until very recently, carried only by men and boys; hence the resentment of the girl who speaks next.

was a suggestion in their manner that they would as soon forget the festival and go off to see a play.

"How about a magic lantern?" Shota's lively eyes moved from one to another. "I've got some pictures myself, and we can get Midori to buy the rest. We'll use the paper store. I can run the lantern, and maybe we can get Sangoro to do the talking. How about it, Midori?"

"Good, good. You have to laugh at Sangoro. We could put a picture of him in the lantern too."

The plans were made. Shota bustled about putting together what was needed.

By the nineteenth the news had reached the back street.

4

Nowhere hereabouts is one out of hearing of drum and samisen. Why then is a festival needed? But a festival is something special —only Otori day in November can rival it.

The main street and the back street each had matching kimonos, their street names worked into the patterns. Not as handsome as last year's, some grumbled. Sleeves were tied up with yellow bands, the showier the better. There were pear-shaped Daruma dolls, owls, papier-mâché dogs for those under thirteen or fourteen, and the child who could show the most was the proudest. Some had seven, nine, eleven dangling from their sleeves. Large and small bells jangling on backs, youngsters prancing about in stockinged feet— a contagious display of vitality.

Shota stood out from the crowd. His fair skin against a red-striped cloak and a dark-blue undershirt attracted one's attention immediately, and on looking closer one saw that his tight green sash was expensive crepe and the Chinese character on his cloak was a marvel of expert dyeing. He wore a festive flower in his headband and his sandals echoed the beat of the drums. But for all that, he kept apart from the noise-makers.

The festival eve had passed without incident, and now the great day itself was coming to a close. Twelve of them were gathered in the paper shop, only Midori was missing. She still lingered over her evening toilet.

"What's happened to her?" Shota went several times to the door. "Go see if you can hurry her, Sangoro. Have you ever been to Daikokuya's? Just call in from the garden. She'll hear you. Quick."

"You want me to go see? I'll leave the lantern here. But someone might take the candle—you watch it, Shota."

"Stingy—you could have called her and been back in the time it's taking you."

Sangoro did not seem to mind being scolded by a boy younger than he. "I'm off. Back before you know I'm gone." He bounded off—like the flying deva himself. One could understand why the girls giggled.

He was short and had a heavy head and almost no neck. His face, when he chanced to look over his shoulders at one, was like the pug-nosed mask the lion dancers wear, and it was not hard to see why he was called Buck-toothed Sangoro. He was dark, almost black, but what really caught one's eye was the expression on his face. Always laughing, he had an engaging dimple in each cheek, and his eyebrows were twisted as though someone had pinned them on blindfolded in a parlor game. Here, one said, was a child with no harm in him. Sangoro's rough kimono was not matched with the rest—too bad he had not had a little more time to get ready, he told friends who did not know the truth. His father had six children, Sangoro the oldest, and made his living in front of a rickshaw. There were steady customers in the teahouses, it was true, but no matter how briskly the wheel of the rickshaw turned the wheel of the family fortunes never seemed to keep up with it.

Sangoro had been sent off a couple of years before to a printing shop not far from Asakusa Park. Twelve was quite old enough to begin helping the family. He was by no means industrious, however, and he did not last ten days. There were a number of jobs after that, none of them for more than a month. From November until New Year he brought in a little money making shuttlecocks [5] at home, and in the summer, with his talent as a street hawker, he

5 For the traditional New Year game of battledore and shuttlecock.

helped the ice-seller by the medical station in the quarter. His friends
had not approved when they saw him pulling one of the wheeled
stages at the Yoshiwara carnival the year before—that was for the
low-class musicians and dancers from Mannenchō. "Mannenchō."
He had acquired a new nickname and even now it clung to him.
But everyone knew he was a clown and no one could dislike him.
That was Sangoro's one advantage in life.

The Tanakaya, Shota's family business, was all that kept Sangoro
and his family alive. The interest they paid was not low, of course,
but who could complain of the moneylender without whose services
one would starve?

Shota suggested once that Sangoro join his gang, and Sangoro
could not refuse. Still he was born in the back street and he had
grown up there, and the land he lived on belonged to the Ryugeji
Temple and the house he lived in to Chokichi's father. He could
not openly turn against the back street, but as quietly as he could
he went over to Shota and the main street. The accusing looks he
had to face were painful indeed.

Shota went back into the shop humming a favorite passage from
"Secret Meeting."

"Well," laughed the shopkeeper's wife. "I see we'll have to watch
you."

The boy's ears turned red. "Come on, everybody," he called out
in a voice louder than necessary. "Let's wait outside."

At the front gate he ran into his grandmother.

"So there you are. Why haven't you been home to eat? Too busy,
I suppose. You haven't heard me calling you all this time? —He'll
be back to play with you later." And to the shopkeeper's wife, "He
hasn't been too much of a nuisance, I hope."

There was little Shota could do but go with her.

How lonesome it seems when that child leaves. Almost as many
as before, and yet even we grownups feel it. He isn't a noisy child,
and he's not as good at clowning as Sangoro, but you won't find
many rich boys like him.

And did you see that nasty grandmother of his? She's sixty-three
if she's a day, and there she is done up like a young girl. It's a

wonder she doesn't put on rouge. She purrs like a cat, but even when someone's just died she's around collecting her money. Probably die with a bag of it in her arms, that's how fond she is of it. But we could use a little ourselves—why, we can't lift up our heads to her. They say she even has some lent out to the big houses in the quarter.

5

"The midnight hearth is cold to one who waits alone"—but are we concerned with love?

The wind was cool in the summer evening. Midori had been to the bath to wash away the sweat of the day, and now before a large mirror she was getting ready for the evening. Her mother personally saw to retouching the damaged coiffure. A beautiful child, she had to say—what if it was her own? Again and again she stepped back to look. Still not quite enough powder on the neck. Midori's kimono was a cool azure, and her straw-colored sash was embroidered in gold. Not for some time yet would they be able to think about the sandals she would wear.

"Still not ready?" Sangoro had walked around the block seven times, he had quite run out of yawns. The notorious mosquitoes attacked his neck savagely no matter how he tried to brush them away. His patience was very nearly exhausted when at last Midori appeared.

"Well, let's go."

He tugged at her sleeve, in too much of a hurry to answer.

"Stop it. I'm all out of breath. If you to have to run all the way you can just go ahead by yourself."

Sangoro arrived at the paper shop first, but Shota had already left. He was probably even then in the middle of his dinner.

"This is no fun, no fun at all. We can't start till he comes. Have you got any cutouts? Maybe fox-and-geese. Or anything you have. I need something to keep me busy." Midori was dejected.

Quickly as ordered the shopwife brought cutouts down from the shelf, and the girls set to work on them. The boys, with Sangoro at their head, launched into a performance of the dances from the Yoshiwara carnival.

> *"See how the north quarter* [6] *prospers,*
> *A light, a lantern at each door,*
> *And the Five Streets roar with life."*

So the chorus went. And on back to the dances of two and three years before, not a mistaken gesture or a false beat, ten performers and more quite carried away with themselves. A wall of curious onlookers grew up in the street outside.

A voice called in from the crowd. "Is Sangoro there? We want to see him—quick."

"Right with you." The unsuspecting Sangoro ran out the door, and a fist struck him square in the face.

"Double-crosser. Dirty the name of the back street, will you? Who do you think I am? I'm Chokichi, that's who I am. Play around with that crowd and you know what's coming to you."

Sangoro turned to run back into the shop, but someone from the back-street gang grabbed him by the hair and pulled him out again. "Kill him, kill him!" The attack roared up like the incoming tide. "Don't think the Moose from the Dangoya is going to get off either."

The paper lantern in front of the shop was smashed up in no time. "Watch out for the lamp. You're not to fight in front of the shop." But it was not likely that anyone was listening to the shop-wife's protests.

There were perhaps fourteen or fifteen in the attacking gang, each with a festive headband. Lanterns were swinging, arms flailing, let the blows fall where they might. Grimy sandals tramped in on the clean straw mats.

Shota, the real object of the attack, was not in sight. "Where's he hiding? Where's he run away to? You won't tell? You think we'll let you off?" They gathered in closer to kick and pound Sangoro.

[6] The Yoshiwara, the quarter of the story. The expression "Five Streets" also refers to the Yoshiwara.

"If you want to beat up Shota, why don't you? What have you got against Sangoro?" Midori was furious. She tried to shake off the shopkeeper's wife. "He hasn't run away and we haven't hidden him. He just isn't here. Can't you see? This is our place. You stay where you belong. Damn you, Chokichi—why are you hitting Sangoro?" There—they'd knocked Sangoro down. If they wanted to hit someone, let them hit her. She'd fight them. "Let me go, let me go." She tried to squirm loose.

"What's she howling about?" Chokichi knew all he needed to know about her—a tramp, going right after her sister. "Here's one for you." He stripped off his sandal. It landed with a splattering of mud on Midori's forehead.

Midori paled and started forward. "You'll only get hurt." The shopwife held her back.

"Look at 'em, look at 'em! Who do you think is on our side? Nobu, that's who. Any time you want to get even, just come around. Look at Sangoro, the sissy. Look at him—sissy, coward." Sangoro fell to the ground. "Watch out going home tonight. We'll be waiting."

There were footsteps at the gate. Someone had been to the police. Chokichi gave the warning, and Ushimatsu and Bunji and the rest melted off into the darkness, some of them possibly to hiding places up the alley.

"Damn you, damn you! Damn you, Chokichi! Damn you, Bunji! Damn you, Ushimatsu! Kill me! Come on, kill me! I'm Sangoro. I'm no girl. I'll come back and haunt you, I'll get you all. Don't you forget it. Damn you, Chokichi." Sangoro was sobbing, and hot tears streamed down his face. His kimono was torn, his hips and chest were covered with gravel. The others drew back at the violence of the outburst.

"There, now." As the wailing grew louder the wife of the shopkeeper ran to help him up. "There were so many of them and they were all so big." She patted his shoulder and brushed away the dirt. "We couldn't do anything ourselves, and what could you do? But it's lucky you weren't hurt. They might still be waiting for you somewhere. Suppose we ask the officer here to take you home. Then we'll all feel better. It's this way, officer . . ." she turned to the policeman who had just come up.

Sangoro drew back, suddenly quiet, as the policeman reached for his hand. "Thank you. You don't need to. I can go by myself."

"There's nothing to be afraid of. I'll just take you home. What are you worried about?" The policeman smiled and patted his head, but Sangoro only shrank back farther.

"My father won't like it when he hears I've been fighting. Our house belongs to Chokichi's father."

"Well, then, suppose I just take you as far as the door. I won't cause you any trouble."

The policeman led him off by the hand. The others sighed with relief as they watched them go off down the street, but at the corner Sangoro shook loose and scampered off into the darkness.

6

How strange. Like snow from a clear sky. Why should the child refuse to go to school? And she had no breakfast this morning. Possibly we should order something special for her? It is not a cold, she has no fever. Too big a day yesterday, I suppose . . . "Why don't you stay home this morning? I'll go to the shrine for you."

No, Midori had petitioned Tarō-sama for her sister's prosperity, and she would not feel right unless she went herself. "Give me some money for the collection. I'll be right back."

At the shrine, out in the paddy fields, she rang the bell, clapped her hands, and bowed. But what was really on her mind? She seemed pensive both on the way out and on the way back.

"I'm sorry about last night, Midori." Shota had recognized her in the distance.

"It wasn't your fault."

"But I was the one they were after. I wouldn't have left, only Grandmother came. And Sangoro wouldn't have gotten beat up. I went around to see him this morning, and he was crying, he was so mad. I got mad myself just listening to him. And you got hit in the face? Damn that Chokichi anyway. But you don't hold it against me, do you, Midori? I didn't run away. I didn't know a thing about it, honest I didn't. I ate in a hurry, and then just when I was on my way out Grandmother said she was going for a bath and I had to stay and watch the place. That must have been when it happened. I didn't know a thing about it." Shota apologized as though the crime had been his. He peered solicitously at Midori's forehead. "Does it hurt?"

"Hurt? That?" Midori smiled. "But listen, Shota. You aren't to talk about it. I'll get scolded if Mother hears. She's never laid a hand on me, and neither has Father, and now I get mud on my face from that Chokichi's foot . . ." Midori turned away.

"It was all my fault. I'm sorry. But don't be that way, Midori. Please." They had come to Shota's back gate. "Come on in. There's no one at home but me. Grandmother's out collecting the interest, and I don't like it here by myself. Come on in and I'll show you the prints I told you about. All sorts of prints." He pulled at her sleeve, and Midori nodded silently.

The wooden gate had taken on a pleasant coating of age. The garden was not large, but the arrangement of dwarf trees showed imagination. From the eaves hung a fern that Shota had bought at a summer market. An outsider might have raised an eyebrow on learning that this was the wealthiest house in the neighborhood— and that in it lived but an old woman and a child. The place could be watched perfectly by anyone in the tenement across the way, and it had never been broken into; but every chest and door had a chilly lock dangling from it.

Shota went in first and picked a spot where Midori could enjoy the breeze. Passing her a fan, motioning her to her place, he might have struck one as a little too mature for a twelve-year-old.

The color prints were family treasures, and Shota beamed when Midori praised them. Would she like to see an old battledore? [7] They had given it to his mother when she worked in the big house. Wasn't it funny? Feel—wasn't it heavy? And the face on it—people must have looked different in those days. . . . Shota was becoming

[7] In its simpler forms, used for the New Year game of battledore and shuttlecock, but often, as here, a heavily decorated display piece.

sentimental, rather against his will. If only his mother had lived. He was only three when she died. His father had gone back to the country,[8] and now there were only the two of them, he and his grandmother. "I wish I had a family like you, Midori."

"Stop it. Boys don't cry. And you'll get the pictures wet."

Did Midori think he was like a girl? Sometimes he got to thinking about things. Not now, especially, but on moonlit winter nights when he went down toward Tamachi collecting the interest. As he walked back up along the ditch, he would stop on the bank and cry. "It's happened lots of times. Not because of the cold. I don't mind the cold so much. I don't know why it is, but I just think about things. . . . What did you say?"

Yes, he had been making collections himself the last couple of years. His grandmother was getting old, and soon she would no longer be able to go out at night, and then her eyes were so bad that she had trouble with the papers. There used to be men around to help, but his grandmother had said that she could not get them to work. They were making a fool of her. "But when I get a little older I'm going to open the shop again. Not the way it used to be, maybe, but the Tanakaya sign will be up, anyway. I can hardly wait." People said his grandmother was selfish, but they shouldn't. She was doing it all for him. Some of the families she had to collect interest from were having a hard time, and they blamed everything on her. Shota would cry over that too sometimes. He was a sissy, there was no doubt about it. This morning at Sangoro's, for instance: so sore he could hardly move, Sangoro was out working just the same, afraid his father might find out about the fight; and Shota had not been able to say a word. "Boys aren't supposed to cry. That's why Chokichi thinks he can get away with it."

Now and then, artlessly, their eyes would meet.

"You looked better than anyone yesterday. You made me want to be a boy. That's the way I'd dress if I were a boy."

"I was good-looking—why, you were beautiful. Better looking than your sister, everyone said. I wish you were my sister. We'd go

---

[8] The father seems to have been adopted into his wife's family. Upon her death he returned to his own, but Shota, heir to the pawnshop, had to stay behind.

out together, and I'd brag and brag. It's no fun without brothers and sisters. I know. We'll have our picture taken together. I'll dress the way I was yesterday, and you can put on a striped kimono, and we'll go over to Kato's. Won't that Nobu be jealous? He'll burn when he sees it. He'll go white like a sheet, and he'll be boiling inside. But maybe he'll laugh—well, let him. We'll have a big one taken, and maybe Kato'll put it in his window. What's the matter, Midori? Don't you like the idea?"

"But what if I look funny in the picture? What will you do then?" Midori's clear laugh rang out, and her spirits seemed to be quite mended.

The morning coolness was giving way to the heat of the day. "Come over this evening, Shota," Midori called back as she left. "We'll float a lantern on the pond and chase fish. They've fixed the bridge."

Shota stood smiling after her. Wasn't she beautiful, though.

7

Nobu of the Ryugeji Temple and Midori of the Daikokuya went to the same school, the Ikueisha. It was at the last athletic meet, toward the end of April, when the cherries were past and the wistaria was blooming in the shade of the new leaves. Evening came on unobserved, so lively were the ball-throwing, the jumping, the tugging of ropes. Nobu seemed less in command of himself than usual. He tripped over the root of a pine by the lake and fell with one hand on the ground. His sleeve was a painful smear of red mud.

"Here, wipe it off with this." Midori, who happened to be passing by, offered him a scarlet silk handkerchief.

A jealous acquaintance saw them, and the gossip spread. "Did you see Nobu and his girl? A fine priest, smiling all over when he thanked her. Daikoku for the Ryugeji [9]—it was made to order."

[9] A priest's wife is called Daikoku, "god of the kitchen." Hence Midori of the Daikokuya should be ideal for Nobu of the Ryugeji Temple.

Nobu did not like gossip. He turned aside in disgust when anyone tried to pass along rumors about other people, and it was intolerable that he himself should now be the principal. He took fright
whenever he heard Midori's name. Please, not that story again. Still
it did not seem wise to go into a rage each time someone mentioned
Midori, and he did his best to feign indifference or to turn his
tormenters off with a stern look. But there Midori herself would
be, asking him a question, and he would feel a cold sweat breaking
out all over his body even though he could generally escape by
saying he did not know the answer.

Midori noticed none of this. She was friendly as ever. Once on the
way back from school she picked him out from a group of younger
boys he was walking with. "See that flower? I can't reach it, but I'll
bet you could. Would you break it off for me?"

Nobu could hardly walk off and leave her standing there. But he
was more and more sensitive to what people were saying. He
reached for the nearest branch—let others worry about whether the
blossoms were good or not—tore it off with the coldness of one who
performs an unpleasant duty, and almost threw it at her as he turned
to flee.

Midori was taken aback, and when similar incidents piled up she
came naturally to think that he was making a special effort to be
disagreeable. He was not rude to others, only to her. If she asked a
question he refused a decent answer, if she went up to him he ran
away, if she talked to him he became angry. He was stiff, sullen.
There was no possible way to please him. If he wanted to be difficult, to flare up as his moods took him, to insult her time after time
—well, he need be no friend of Midori's. Midori was rather hurt.
She saw no further need to speak to him. Unless there was something they had to discuss, the two of them passed silently in the
street. Neither thought of calling out a greeting to the other. A
broad river grew up between them, a river which boat or raft was
forbidden to cross. Each walked his own way along his own bank.

From the day after the festival Midori stopped going to school.
Her chagrin did not wash away so easily as that mud on her forehead. Children from the main street and children from the back

street sat side by side as usual, but there was a stubborn division between them.

It was cowardly of that Chokichi to single out a girl that night, a girl he knew could not fight back. Everyone knew that Chokichi himself was an ignoramus whose violence went to extremes, but he would probably not have stormed in on them with quite that enthusiasm if he had not had Nobu behind him. That Nobu, pretending to be so wise, so mild—if you could look backstage you would find he had managed everything. Very well: he was an upper classman, his marks were good, he was heir to the august temple; but Midori of the Daikokuya was not in his debt by so much as a scrap of paper, she need not submit to these insults.

Let the Ryugeji Temple have its illustrious followers, thought Midori. Her sister Omaki had well-placed followers too. For three years now she has had the steady company of good old Kawa the banker and Yone the stockbroker from Kabuto-chō; [10] and Tiny who sat in the Diet once even offered to pay off her debts and marry her, but Omaki did not much care for him. He's well thought of, too, people who ought to know will tell you. Just ask if you don't believe it. Why, if it weren't for Omaki the Daikokuya would be out of business today. That's why the gentleman who owns it is so good to her mother and father and to Midori herself. That porcelain statue of Daikoku he was so proud of and kept in the alcove—one day when Midori and a friend were playing battledore in the house they knocked over a vase and smashed the statue to bits. The gentleman was drinking sake in the next room when it happened. "Sometimes you're a little too lively, Midori," he said, and not another word. The girls at the Daikokuya couldn't get over it. Anyone else would have been scolded up one street and down the next.

All this kindness because of Omaki. Midori herself might be no more than a girl kept around to help in the house, but her sister was Omaki of the Daikokuya. Midori had no cause to feel inferior before the likes of Chokichi, and she had no intention of taking any insults from the reverend priest of the Ryugeji.

School would be no fun any more. Midori's inborn willfulness

10 Often called "the Wall Street of Tokyo."

came to the fore. She broke up her crayons, threw out her ink, and put away her books and abacus. She had no further need for them. Nothing would keep her now from playing with her good friends.

8

They fly impatiently up at night, and they leave sadly in the morning, carrying away memories of dawn farewells. Here a hat pulled low over the eyes, there a face deep in a scarf—it would be best not to look too closely. The delicious smart of her farewell slap sinks to his very bones, and that foolish smile makes one a little uncomfortable. Take care when you get to Sakamoto; you might be run down by the vegetable carts. To the corner of the Mishima Shrine it is well named the Street of the Lunatics. Carefully composed features somehow fall into disorder and—one has to admit it—he has the look of having been an easy victim for the ladies. He may be worth something over there, say the town wives who see him pass; but I wouldn't give two cents for him this morning.

One does not have to be reminded of the daughter of the Yang [11] who was loved by an emperor and celebrated in the "Ballad of the Everlasting Wrong" to know that there are times when daughters are more valuable than sons. Princesses enough have emerged from these back alleys. One beautiful lady, for instance, now removed to the heart of the city, is said to have noble friends. What sort of trees does rice grow on, she asks her newest friend, with all the guilelessness of the cloistered maiden; but for all that she grew up here, and she tied her sash as immodestly as the rest of them back in the days when she made playing cards to fill out the family income. But she has gone, and talk of her has given way to a newer success story. Kokichi, second daughter of the dyer, reigns over the house called New Ivy, and she is one of the attractions that bring people north of the park.

Talk of those who have succeeded has to do only with daughters. Sons are about as useful as the tail of the spotted mongrel nosing the

[11] Yang Kuei-fei, loved by the T'ang Emperor Hsüan Tsung. A poem by Po Chü-i describes the Emperor's grief after her death.

garbage there. Stout young fellows, glib and swaggering at sixteen, get together in groups called the Five and the Seven. Not yet complete gallants, not yet dandies with flutes tucked into their belts, they put themselves under leaders with brave names. Sporting emblazoned lanterns and matched headbands, they loiter before the gay houses. It will be a while yet before they are gambling with verve and bantering the ladies with complete assurance. Honest workers in the daytime, they come from the bath in the evening with dragging sandals and boldly cut kimonos and give their views on the latest topics. Have you seen the new one at the So-and-so? She looks like the girl at the thread store only her nose is twice as flat. Such are the things that are important. At each house they beg tobacco unblushingly, and each exchange of playful pinches and slaps is the honor of a lifetime. The heir of the stern, frugal family has changed his name to Roisterer and stands at the main gate picking fights.

The power of women. The prosperity of the Five Streets knows no spring and no autumn. Processions of great ladies are going out of fashion, but still the sandals of the servant girls and the singing and the dancing send out their insistent rhythm. What is it the throngs pour in to seek? Scarlet lining and swept-up hair, flowing skirts, dimpled cheek, and smiling eye. One would be hard put to say why, but the name of the prospering beauty commands respect hereabouts. You who live farther away may find it hard to understand.

It was not strange that Midori had caught the blight. She saw nothing in men to be afraid of, she saw nothing in her sister's calling to be ashamed of. The tearful farewell when that sister left for the city was a dream from the distant past, and now Midori rather envied the prosperous Omaki, able at the very peak of her profession to do so much for her mother and father. Midori knew nothing of Omaki's sorrows and struggles. Everything was so delightful—the little coaxing noises to tempt the passing townsman, the raps on the wall for good luck, the playful pinches and slaps for the departing guest. And—it was a little sad—she ran about town calmly using the special vocabulary of the quarter. She was thirteen. She caressed her doll just as the prince's daughter must caress hers, but courses in deportment and domestic management were for the classroom only, and what really commanded her attention was gossip about guests liked and unliked, fine dresses and cushions to advertise one's prosperity, tips for the teahouse that had introduced good customers. The flashy was good, the more restrained a failure. Midori thought she had reached the age of discretion, but that confidence was premature. She let her natural intractability lead her to whatever unformed schemes and aspirations it would. The flower before her eyes was still the best.

Street of the Lunatics, Street of the Late Sleepers. Presently here too the walks were swept and sprinkled. Then—down the street they came, each a performer with his one act, from Mannenchō and Yamabukichō and Shintanimachi where they had nested for the night. They too called themselves artists. Jugglers who hawked sweets, clowns, and umbrella dancers and lion dancers, their attire as varied as their talents, one in a smart summer kimono, another in faded cotton tied with a narrow black sash. Men and pretty women. Companies of six and seven and ten and a forlorn old man walking alone with a battered samisen under his arm. A girl of four or five with a bright red ribbon to tie up her sleeves had to dance to the *Kinokuni.*[12] Their goal was the quarter, where they would entertain guests who had stayed on for the day and dispel the sorrows of the ladies, the profits enough to keep those who had once tried their hand at the business from ever giving it up. The procession moved on with no thought for the small gains to be had in these outlying streets. Not even the beggar in tatters bothered to stop.

A lady minstrel walked by with the brim of her hat low over her face, and what one saw of her cheeks made one want to see more. She was famous for her voice and her playing. The wife at the paper shop would have liked to hear her just once.

"You want to hear her?" Midori, back from her morning bath, pushed her hair up with a wooden comb and ran out to stop the

[12] A popular song describing the tangerine boats from Kinokuni in southern Japan. Midori was born in Kinokuni, the present Wakayama Prefecture.

singer. One would guess, though Midori herself said nothing, that she pushed some money into the lady's sleeve. The song was a favorite of Midori's and it told of tragic love. The lady moved off with a gracious request for future patronage—knowing how little she could expect it.

What a thing to do—and a mere child, too. Midori drew more attention from the crowd than the lady.

It would be fun to stop the best of them, to make the street echo with flute and samisen and drum, to make people sing and dance, to do what no one else does.

9

"So did I hear it spoken," the sutra began. It was the august temple, and the chanting voice borne on the soft pine breeze should have cleaned the dust from one's heart.

Smoke rose from the roasting fish in the kitchen, and diapers had on occasion been seen drying over the tombstones. Nothing one could point to as violating the discipline,[13] indeed, and yet those who would make of the clergy so many sticks of wood might have found here signs of a turn too fleshly. The body of the reverend priest had filled out with his fortune. His stomach was a thing of beauty. And where would one find words to praise the luster of his complexion? Not the pale pink of the cherry blossom, nor yet the deeper pink of the peach. A fine coppery glow from the top of his shaven head down over his face to his neck, never a spot to mar it. When he raised his thick eyebrows, somewhat grizzled now, and broke into that laugh of his, one was a little uneasy lest Buddha in the main hall start up in surprise and tumble from his stand.

The wife of the temple was not many years past forty. Her skin was white and her hair was thin, done up in a slight little bun. Not notably unattractive, one could say of her. She was gracious to the devout, and even the sharp-tongued florist's wife in front of

---

[13] Buddhist priests were once, but for the most part are no longer, forbidden to marry and eat fish or meat.

the gate had nothing bad to say about her—the harvest of small favors, no doubt, handed-down kimonos and leftover tidbits.

She had been a member of the congregation, and she had been left a widow early. With nowhere to turn she had moved into the temple, where, if he would but give her a little to eat, she would serve as a maid. She took over the housework, from the laundry to the cooking, she even helped the men who tended the cemetery. The reverend priest thought the economics of the matter over carefully and presently deigned to favor her. She knew that the arrangement did not look as wholesome as it might. There was twenty years' difference in their ages. But where else could she go? She came to think of the temple as a good place to live and to die, and she learned not to worry too much about prying eyes. While to the faith-ful the situation was a little disconcerting, there was no harm in the woman and they could not find it in themselves to reproach her.

She was carrying her first child, O-hana, when a retired oil dealer named Sakamoto, fond of performing such services, intervened for the congregation to patch up appearances—it would be too much perhaps to say that he arranged the marriage.

She had two children, this O-hana and later Nobu. A pious, eccen-tric boy brooding in his room all day, and a winsome girl with a smooth skin and a round little jaw. O-hana was not a real beauty, but she was at her best age and she was much admired. It would be a shame not to use her talents, and yet it would hardly do to set up the daughter of a temple as a professional entertainer. While there may be worlds where the Buddha himself strums the samisen, in this world one did have to worry sometimes about what people thought. The reverend priest therefore opened a pretty little shop on a busy street in Tamachi to sell young tea, and he put O-hana behind the counter where she might make good use of her charms. Young men who knew little about measures and less about prices began to come in. There was hardly a day now when the place was empty before midnight.

The busy one was the reverend priest. Collecting bills, looking after the shop, officiating at funerals. There were sermons to be preached so many times a month, accounts to be kept, sutras to be

read. No telling how much longer he could keep it up, he would
sigh to himself as he took his flowered cushion out to the veranda in
the evening and sat fanning himself, half-naked, a glass of raw gin
before him. He liked fish, and most especially he liked broiled eels.
It was Nobu who would be sent out to the main street after them
—big oily coarse ones, please. Nobu, squirming with distaste for the
errand, would walk along looking at his feet. If the paper shop
across the way had its usual crowd of children, he would walk coolly
past the eelshop, afraid of being caught in an unpriestly performance, and from the corner he would turn back and dart into the
shop when no one was in sight. Never in his life would he eat fish
himself.

The reverend priest was a pragmatist to the core. He had acquired
something of a reputation for greed, but he was not so timid as to be
called off by malicious gossip. When he had a little spare time, he
thought, he might try making some rakes for Otori day himself.
He had early considered the possibility of setting up a stall in front
of the temple gate. He would have his good wife tie her hair up like
a shopkeeper, he decided, and sell hair ornaments guaranteed to be
particularly auspicious. At first the lady held back, but then she
heard of the vast profits being made by amateur shopkeepers all up
and down the street. There would be such a crowd, and no one
would be looking for her, and especially after sunset no one could
possibly notice. In the daytime she had the florist's wife take charge,
and when evening came she went out hawking hair ornaments herself. Might it be greed?—her shyness disappeared, and before she
knew it she was shouting with the best of them. "Everything cut-
rate, everything cut-rate." She would run out and tug at a customer's
sleeve. In the press of the crowd he would soon lose his eye for
quality and forget too that but a couple of days earlier he had
appeared at this same temple gate in quest of salvation. "Three for
seventy-five sen." Her price allowed for bargaining. "Too much.
Make it five for seventy-three."

There were no doubt all sorts of ways to make a shady profit,
Nobu thought. Even if word of the enterprise did not get to the
congregation, there was the matter of what the neighbors would

think. And might not his school friends hear about it, and whisper to each other that the Ryugeji had gone into the hair-ornament business and Nobu's good mother was out hawking with an enthusiasm near lunatic?

"Wouldn't it be better to stop?"

But the reverend priest laughed and laughed. "Quiet, quiet. You know nothing about it." There was no need to discuss the matter with Nobu.

Prayers in the morning, accounts in the evening. The reverend priest smiled happily as he did a sum on his abacus. Nobu watched with revulsion. What could have made the man become a priest?

Two parents and two children, a tranquil self-sufficient family. There was no reason for Nóbu's moodiness. He had always been a quiet child, and no one had ever paid the least attention to his suggestions. His father's enterprises, his mother's deportment, his sister's education, all seemed to him the most complete mistakes, but he knew that he would not be listened to, and he nursed his objections in silence. However perverse and haughty his acquaintances might think him, he was a weakling at heart. There was no help for it. He had not the courage to go out and protest when he heard that someone had maligned him. He could only shut himself in his room, too timid to face his detractor. His grades in school were good and his station was not a lowly one, and no one guessed his weakness. Nobu makes me nervous, someone complained; he's cold inside like a half-cooked dumpling.

10

Nobu was away on an errand to his sister's the night of the festival. He came home late and knew nothing of what had happened in the paper shop. When he heard the details the next morning from Ushimatsu and Bunji and the rest he was shocked afresh at Chokichi's violence, but there was after all no point in reproving him for what was past. Nobu did feel wronged, however, at the way his name had been used. He had had no part in the incident, and yet he seemed to carry a major share of the blame.

Chokichi perhaps sensed that he had gone too far, and for three or four days he avoided Nobu. Presently the furor seemed to have died down.

"I know what you're thinking. But it just happens this way. How are we to know Shota's not around? We don't have to pay any attention to that woman, maybe, and we don't have to beat up Sangoro. But here we are shaking our lanterns, see, and what can we do? We just want to show a little life. But I admit it. I always forget what you tell me. You won't let me down now, will you, Nobu? We've got something to go on, just having you with us, and you can't let us down now. I'll tell you what: you be chief of the gang. Even if you don't want to. We'll do better next time."

It's not for me, Nobu would have liked to say. But the apology was too abject, and his reproaches melted away. "Well, I'll do what I can. But you just hurt yourselves when you go around fighting people who can't fight back. Don't get excited about Midori and Sangoro. Take on Shota when he has his gang with him, don't go around picking fights with other people."

The innocent one was Sangoro. Kicked and beaten quite to the satisfaction of his attackers, he could hardly stand up for the next two or three days. In the evening when he had to take his father's empty rickshaw to the teahouse, his friend the caterer would stop him along the way. "What the devil's the matter with you, Sangoro? You look all beaten up." But his father was "Bowing Tetsu," who had never been known to lift his head to a superior. Tetsu was not one to protest the worst injustice, be it one of the gentlemen in the quarter who wronged him or the owner of his house or the land it stood on. Sangoro knew better than to go crying to his father. "They own this house, you know that well enough. I don't care if you were right and he was wrong, you don't fight with Chokichi. Go and apologize, go and apologize. I don't know what's to be done with you." There was nothing for it but to suffer in silence.

In a week or ten days, however, as the pain wore off, the resentment too vanished. Soon he was back tending Chokichi's baby brother, happy at the thought of the two sen it would bring him. "Go to sleep. That's right, that's right." He was fifteen, that most arrogant of ages, but he seemed not to mind the figure he cut with the baby strapped to his back. He even strolled out to the main street, there again to become the sport of Midori and Shota. "Sangoro's no man," they would laugh, but that never drove him away.

In the spring the cherries bloom and in the summer come the lanterns for the late Tamagiku.[14] In the autumn during the Yoshiwara carnival someone counted seventy-five rickshaws in ten minutes coming down this street alone. At the end of the carnival, when red dragonflies are darting over the paddy fields, the morning and evening winds are cold. Soon quail will be calling in the Yokobori Ditch. Mosquito incense in the shops gives way to charcoal for pocket warmers, the mortars have a sad ring to them, and in the quarter the clock on the Kadoebi[15] seems to have turned melancholy too. Fires glow at Nippori,[16] whatever the season, but it is now that one begins to notice them: "That is the smoke from the dead?" A samisen refrain drops down on the road behind the teahouses, and one looks up and listens. It is from the white hand of a geisha. The refrain itself is nothing—"Here, where we pass our night of love"—and yet it strikes the ear with a special poignancy. Guests who make their first visits to the quarter at this time of the year, a woman who used to be there says, are not the lighthearted roisterers of the summer. They are men with a deep seriousness about them.

It would be a chore to write down everything. This was the sort of thing they were talking about before the Daionji Temple. A blind masseuse, aged twenty, unhappy in love and despondent over her handicap, drowned herself in the lake at Mizunoya. Someone asked Kichigoro the grocery boy why Takichi the carpenter's apprentice did not seem to be around much any more. Taken in for this, said Kichigoro, shaking an imaginary dicebox. No one seemed to care

---

[14] Tamagiku was an eighteenth-century courtesan famous for her kind heart. Each July the Yoshiwara was decorated with lanterns in her honor.

[15] A very famous house in the Yoshiwara. It is still in business, almost the only house that makes any attempt to preserve Yoshiwara traditions.

[16] There was a crematorium at Nippori, just north of Ueno Park.

about the details. Out on the main street three or four little children played ring-around-a-rosy, and even their chanting voices seemed quiet, subdued. But the rickshaws on the way to the quarter moved by as briskly as ever.

It was the sort of melancholy night when there comes first a touch of autumn rain, and then, before one is ready for it, a sudden downpour pounding at the roof. Since the paper shop seldom attracted chance passers-by from the street, the front shutters had been closed since dark. Inside, playing marbles, were Midori and Shota as usual, and two or three small children.

"A customer? There's someone outside." Midori looked up.

"I didn't hear anything. But maybe someone's come to play with us." Shota stopped counting his winnings, two and four and six-eight-ten, and looked expectantly at the door. The footsteps stopped just outside.

II

"Boo!" Shota opened the door and poked his head out at whoever the friend might be. Someone was walking slowly off under the eaves two or three houses away. "Who is it, who is it? Come on in." He slipped the tips of his toes into Midori's sandals and ran out in the rain. "Oh, him." He turned back toward the shop. "He won't come even if you call him, Midori. It's him." Shota cupped his hand over his hair to suggest a priest's shaven head.

"Oh, him. Stuck-up priest. I can't stand him. I just can't stand him. He came to buy a pencil or something and heard us, and stood there listening and then left." Nasty, mean, conceited, stuttering, gap-toothed—come in and Midori would give him what he needed. Too bad he hadn't. Midori shivered as the rain from the eaves hit her forehead. She could see Nobu in the gaslight, four or five doors away now. He was hunched slightly forward, and he had a rough Japanese umbrella over his shoulder.

Midori looked after him and looked after him. Still she watched him trudge off down the street. "What's the matter, Midori?" Shota tapped her on the shoulder.

"Nothing," she answered absently, and turned to go back into the shop. "I can't stand him." She began counting her marbles. "He puts on that face, you'd think he never could get into a fight. You can't tell what he's up to. Don't you hate him, though? My mother says the best people are people who speak right out. That's what I don't like about him." He was always sulking, he was bad inside, if one could only see. Didn't Shota agree? Midori had trouble finding strong enough words.

"He knows something, though. He's not like that ignoramus Chokichi."

"Listen to the big words! We all know you're grown up, Shota. Come on, give us some more." She reached over and pinched his cheek. "Look at him. Just like a priest himself."

"I'll be grown up before long. And I'll wear maybe a long overcoat like the man at the Kabataya, and the gold watch Grandmother's been saving for me, and I'll have a ring made, and I'll smoke cigarettes. How do you think I'll look?"

"Fine!" Midori snorted. "You in a long overcoat. You'll look like a medicine bottle on skates."

"What do you mean—you think I'll always be this little? I'll grow up too."

"When will that be, Shota? Listen—the mice are laughing too." Mice were scampering back and forth in the hollow ceiling.

Everyone laughed but Shota. His eyes as always were dancing from one to another. "Midori's making fun of me. But I'll grow up. What's funny about it? And I'll get me a good-looking wife, and go out walking with her. I like people to be good-looking. Not like Chicken Pox at the bakery or Putty Face at the kindling store. If someone tried to give one of them to me I'd chase her back home." With emphasis he added that there was nothing he disliked more than pockmarks.

"Well, it's good of you to come here, then," the shopwife laughed. "You haven't noticed these of mine?"

"But you're old. I'm talking about people to marry. It doesn't matter about old people."

"I should have kept my mouth shut. . . . Let's see, now. They say the prettiest girls around here are O-roku from the florist's and Kii from the candy shop. Have you made up your mind, Shota? Which will you have? O-roku's pretty eyes, or Kii's pretty voice?"

"O-roku, Kii—what's good about them?" He flushed and backed away from the light.

"You like Midori, then? You have everything decided?"

Shota turned quickly away. "What's she talking about?" He broke into a school song, and tapped his accompaniment on the wall.

"Let's begin again." Midori gathered in the marbles. *She* was not blushing.

12

Nobu could have gone to his sister's some other way, but when he took the short cut he had to pass it: a latticed gate and inside it a stone lantern, a low fence, autumn shrubs, all disposed with a certain quiet charm. Reed blinds fluttered over the veranda, and one could almost imagine that behind the sliding doors a latter-day widow of the Azechi no Dainagon would be saying her beads, that a young Murasaki would appear with her hair cut in the childish bob of long ago.[17] It was the home of the gentleman who owned the Daikokuya.

Rain yesterday, rain again today. The winter under-kimono his sister had asked for was ready, and Nobu's mother was eager for her to have it at the earliest possible moment. "Even if you have to hurry a little, couldn't you take it to her on your way to school? She'll be waiting for it I know."

Nobu was never able to refuse. He slipped into a pair of rain clogs and hurried off with the bundle in his arm and an umbrella over his shoulder.

He turned at the corner of the moat and started down the lane he always took. At the Daikokuya gate a gust of wind lifted his umbrella. This would never do. He planted his feet and pulled

---

17 Murasaki was the great love of Prince Genji in the *Tale of Genji*. The widow of the Azechi no Dainagon was her grandmother.

back, and the thong of one of his clogs gave way. And it had seemed sound enough when he left home. His foot slipped into the mud—this was a far more serious problem than the umbrella.

There was no help for it. He bit his lip in annoyance. Laying the umbrella against the gate, he moved in out of the rain and turned to the job of repairing the thong. But what to do? He was a young gentleman, not used to working with his hands, and no matter how he hurried the repairing seemed no nearer finished. Hurry, hurry. He took out some foolscap he had drafted a composition on and tried twisting a strip of it into a paper cord. The perverse wind came up again and the umbrella sailed off into the mud. Damn it, damn it. As he reached to catch the umbrella O-hana's kimono rolled weakly off his knee. The wrapping was filthy, even his sleeve was splashed with mud.

Sad it is to be out in the rain without an umbrella, and incomparably sad to break one's sandal along the way. Midori saw it from afar through the door and the gate.

"Can I give him something to tie it with, Mother?" She rummaged through a drawer of the sewing table and snatched up a bit of printed silk. Almost too impatient to slip into her sandals, hardly bothering to take up an umbrella, she dashed out along the garden flagstones.

Her face turned scarlet as she came near enough to see who it was. Her heart pounded. Would anyone be watching?—she edged fearfully up to the gate. Nobu shot a quick glance over his shoulder. Cold sweat ran down his sides, and he felt a sudden urge to run off barefoot.

The Midori we have known would have pointed a teasing finger —look at him, would you. Just look at him. She would have laughed herself sick. She would have poured out all the abuse that came to her. It was good of you to see that they broke up our party the other night, and all because you were out to get Shota. You had them beat up Sangoro, and what did he ever do to you? You were behind it, you were lording it over all of them. Do you say you're sorry? You were the one that had the likes of Chokichi call me dirty names. What if I am like my sister? What's wrong with that? I don't owe you a thing, not a single cent. I have my mother and my father and the gentleman at the Daikokuya and my sister, and I don't need to ask favors of any broken-down priest. So let's not have any more of it. If you have anything to say to me say it out in the open, don't go talking behind my back. I'm here, any time you want to fight. Well, what about it?

She would have clutched at his sleeve and attacked with a violence that would have cut him low. But here she was, shrinking back in the shadow of the gate. Not a word out of her. And still she stood there squirming, unable to open her mouth and unable to walk off and leave him. This was indeed a different Midori.

13

Nobu always approached the Daikokuya gate with mounting terror, and he looked neither to the right nor to the left as he marched past. But the unlucky rain, the unlucky wind, and now this bungle. He stood under the gate trying to twist the paper cord. Already miserable enough, he felt as though someone had dashed ice water on him when he heard those steps. He trembled violently, his face changed color. Even without looking he knew it was Midori. He turned his back to her and pretended to be engrossed in the broken thong, but he was in such a panic that it was hard to see when the clog would be ready to wear again.

Midori stood watching. How clumsy he is! How does he expect to get it done that way? See, it comes undone even before he's finished twisting. And now he puts straw in. What good will that do? Doesn't he see he's getting muddy? There goes his umbrella. Why doesn't he shut it? Midori could hardly restrain herself. And yet she was silent. You can tie it with this—but something kept her from calling out to him. She stood in the shadow of the gate, heedless of the rain that wet her sleeves.

From the house came the voice of her mother, who could not see what was happening. "Midori, the fire for the iron is ready. Where is the child? Now what are you doing out there in the rain? You'll catch another cold, and you've just gotten over one."

"I'll be right in," Midori called back, wishing that somehow she could keep Nobu from hearing. Her heart raced. She could not open the gate, and yet she could not ignore the unfortunate. Turning over all the possibilities in her mind, she finally thrust her hand out through the lattice and tossed the cloth over to him. He ignored it. Ah, he's the same as ever. All Midori's resentment gathered in her eyes, tears of annoyance welled up. What does he have against me? Why doesn't he come out with it? There are plenty of things I would like to say too. He's impossible.

But there was her mother calling again. Midori took a step or two back from the gate, then collected herself with a start—what could she be thinking of, demeaning herself so—and marched firmly into the house.

Nobu was suddenly lonesome. He turned toward the gate. The tatter of silk, its red maple leaves shining in the rain, lay on the ground near his feet. He looked fondly at it in spite of himself, and yet, miserable though he was, he could not bring himself to reach over for it.

Clearly he was getting nowhere. He took the cord from his cloak and passed it several times around the clogs and over his instep in a most unpromising makeshift. That might do—he started out, but it was virtually impossible to walk. Could he ever get as far as Tamachi? No help for it. He started out again, the package at his side. He let his eye wander back to the maples on that bit of silk.

"What's the matter? Broke it, did you?" Someone came up behind him. "You won't get far that way."

It was the pugnacious Chokichi, evidently on his way home from the quarter. His sash was tied low on his hips in that swaggering manner he affected. He had on a brand-new cloak and carried a figured umbrella on his shoulder, and the shining lacquer on his rain clogs suggested that they had come from a shop case but that morning. A dashing figure indeed.

"I broke it and I can't think of anything to do," Nobu said weakly.

"I'll bet. You wouldn't know what to do. But it's all right. You can take mine. You won't break these."

"What will you do?"

"I'm used to going barefoot. Here we go." Chokichi hitched up his kimono skirt with aplomb and stepped out of his clogs. "You won't get anywhere with those."

"You're going barefoot? But I couldn't . . ."

"It's all right, I'm used to it. You'd cut your feet up, but mine are tough. Here, put 'em on." The beetle brows were pulled into a frown, but the words were remarkably friendly coming from one about as popular as the god of plagues himself. "Here. I'll toss yours in at your kitchen door. That'll do it. Come on, let's have 'em." The good turn done, Chokichi held out his hand for the broken clogs. "There you go. See you at school."

The one set out for his sister's, the other turned toward home, and the red maple leaves, a store of regrets, lay abandoned by the gate.

14

There were three Otori days this year.[18] The second one was spoiled by rain, but the others were fair and the crowds were immense. Not given to letting such chances pass, young men poured into the quarter from the back gate, so that with the main gate quiet, it was as if the directions had suddenly shifted. One trembled lest the pillars of heaven and the sinews of earth give way in the roar. Gangs pushed arm in arm across the drawbridges and into the Five Streets, plowing the crowds like boats plowing up the river. Music and dancing, shrill cries from the shabby little houses along the moat, and samisen in the more dignified heights, a delirious confusion of sounds that the crowds would not soon forget.

Shota had taken a holiday from collecting the interest. He went first to inquire after Sangoro, who was selling roast potatoes, and then to see how the Moose from the Dangoya was doing with the not very attractive sweets he offered.

"Making lots of money?"

18 The Otori fair is held on those days in November that fall under the zodiacal sign of the bird. Some years there are two, some years three.

"You came at the right time, Shota. I've run out. What'll I sell 'em now? I've put more on to cook, but they keep coming."

"You don't know much about your business, do you? Look in the pot. There's always some left around the edges. What you do is pour in some water and a little sugar, that's all, and you have enough for maybe ten or twenty people. Everybody does it. Who'll notice in this crowd? Go on, go on." Shota started for the sugar bowl himself.

"Aren't you the businessman, though." The Moose's one-eyed mother was filled with admiration. "I'm almost afraid of you."

"You don't have to be so good to know that much." He tossed her praise off lightly. "I just saw Fatty up the street do the same thing. . . . Has anyone seen Midori? I've been looking for her all day. Maybe over there?" He nodded toward the quarter.

"Oh, Midori. She went by a little while ago over the bridge. You should've seen her. Her hair done up like so." He swept his hands up grandly over his head to suggest the lines of the *shimada,* the coiffure a young girl adopts when she reaches adolescence. "She looked good. Good," he added, wiping his nose.

"Better than her sister, I bet. Maybe she'll turn out like her sister." Shota looked at the ground.

"Hope she does. Then we can go buy her. Next year I'll open a stall and make me some money." The Moose did not understand.

"Ha, ha. She wouldn't come near you."

"What do you mean, what do you mean?"

"She wouldn't, that's all. There are plenty of reasons." Shota laughed a little uncomfortably. "Well," he flung over his shoulder as he started for the door, "I'm going out and walk around a little. I'll be back after a while."

He sang in a strangely quavering voice,

> "Oh, once I was young and carefree,
> A flower, a butterfly . . .
> But now there is none who knows better
> How to suffer, how to sigh."

He hummed the refrain over again. His little figure soon disappeared in the crowd, the leather-soled sandals hitting the street as briskly as ever.

He pushed and elbowed his way to the corner of the moat, and there, coming toward him, was Midori. She was talking to a lady of the quarter. It was indeed Midori of the Daikokuya, but the Moose had not been wrong: a little shyly, she wore her hair in a fresh *shimada,* tied with a rich twist of ribbon. Her combs were tortoise shell, and little bunches of streamers hung shimmering from her hairpins. She was more brightly dressed than usual, the model Kyoto doll. Shota was speechless. Ordinarily he would have run over and taken her by the arm.

"Shota . . . you must have things to do, Otsuma. You needn't take me any farther. I'll go on with him." Midori bobbed her head in farewell.

"Well, Midori's found someone she likes better," laughed Otsuma. "She doesn't need me any more. I'll just go shopping." She tripped off in tiny little steps, and they watched her turn down a lane into the quarter.

"It looks wonderful." Shota pulled at Midori's sleeve. "When did you have it done? Yesterday? This morning?" And a little reproachfully, "Why didn't you tell me?"

"They did it this morning in Omaki's room. I hate it." Midori's tone was heavy, she looked down at the ground, she seemed shy of the passing crowds.

15

Praise sounded in her ears like taunts, and when passers-by turned to admire her, she felt as though they were jeering at her.

"I'm going home."

"Why? What's the matter? Did something happen? Did you have a fight with Omaki?"

Midori flushed. It was clear that he was still a child and could never understand. As they walked past the Dangoya, the Moose called out elaborately, "How well the lady and the gentleman seem to get on together."

Midori looked as if she wanted to weep. "Don't walk with me, Shota." She hurried off a step or two ahead.

She had promised to go to the Otori fair with him. Why then this change, why this hurry to go home? "Aren't you coming along? Why are you going that way? Listen to me." Shota was not used to being crossed. But Midori walked on ahead as though to shake him off. What possible reason could there be for it? Shota tugged at her sleeve to stop her, he looked inquiringly into her face.

She only flushed more deeply. "It's nothing," she said, but her tone suggested that the matter was not so simple.

Midori ducked in through her gate. Shota had been there often enough, and he saw no need to hold back. He followed her in from the veranda.

"It was good of you to come, Shota," Midori's mother greeted him. "She's been in a bad mood since this morning. We've had a terrible time with her. Do come in and entertain her."

"And what seems to be the matter?" Shota asked solemnly.

"She'll be over it before long." The mother smiled strangely. "She's just spoiled. I suppose you've been fighting with your friends too? A fine young lady!"

Midori did not answer. She lay face down under a quilt she had spread out in the back room.

Shota went timidly up to her, careful to keep his distance. "What's the matter, Midori? Aren't you feeling well? Tell me what's the matter."

Still Midori said nothing. She was sobbing quietly, her sleeves pressed to her face. There must be a reason, but what could it be? Shota was still a child. He could think of no way to comfort her. "But what's the matter? Have I done anything wrong? I can't remember anything." He knelt there bewildered, trying to get a glimpse of her face.

"You haven't done anything." Midori wiped her eyes.

"What's the matter, then?"

There were things Midori could not talk about. Sad thoughts

accumulated, vague thoughts that she could not define herself—
thoughts that would never have come to the Midori of yesterday.
How was she to describe the shame she felt? If only she could hide
in a dark room, speaking to no one and showing her face to no
one. She might have gloomy thoughts even then, but surely she
would not be driven to these extremes of depression if it were not
for the embarrassment of having to meet people. Ah, if she could
go on forever with her dolls and her cutouts, if she could go on
playing house, what a joy it would be. She hated it, hated it, she
hated growing up. Why did she have to grow old? If she could only
go back seven months, ten months, a year—it was as though she
were already an old woman.

And here was Shota nagging at her. Finally she lost control of
herself. "Go home, Shota. That's all I ask. I'll die if you stay. It
gives me a headache to listen to you, and it makes me dizzy to talk
to you. I don't want anyone to come near me, not anyone, and I
wish you would go home."

She had never turned on him before. Shota could not begin to
see what was wrong. It was as though he were groping his way
through a dense smoke. "You're hard to get along with, Midori.
You shouldn't talk that way." He spoke calmly, but there were
weak tears in his eyes.

Could that move Midori? "Go home, go home. If you don't go
home you're no friend of mine. I hate you."

"I'm going. Sorry to have bothered you." He ran off without saying good-bye to the mother, who had gone to look after the bath.

16

Dodging and ducking through the crowd, Shota hurried back to the
paper shop. Sangoro had closed up his potato stall and, with the
profits jingling in his pocket, was playing big brother to the rest of
his family. "I'll buy you whatever you want. Just name it."

Shota came hurtling into the shop in the midst of all this joy.

"Shota. I've been looking for you. I made myself a pile of money—
let me treat you."

"You think I'd let you treat me? You're too big for your size, that's what you are." This roughness was not like Shota. "I have other things on my mind," he added gloomily.

"A fight? Who with? Ryugeji? Chokichi? Where'd it start? Over there? By the shrine?" Sangoro shoved a half-eaten bun into his pocket. "It won't be like the other time. Give me a little warning and they won't whip me. I'll get in the first punch. Come on, Shota, let's go after 'em."

"Not so quick, not so quick. It's not a fight." But the matter was not an easy one for Shota to discuss. He pressed his lips tight together.

"When you came running in that way I thought sure it was a fight. But listen, Shota. If we don't get 'em tonight we won't have another chance! Chokichi's losing his right arm."

"What do you mean?"

"You haven't heard? I just heard myself. My father was talking to the woman at the Ryugeji. Nobu's going off somewhere to learn to be a priest. Can't have much of a fight when he puts on those clothes. Sleeves getting tangled up, hanging all the way down to here. But from next year you'll have both the main street and the back street. Nobody'll be able to stop you."

"Quiet, quiet. Give you two cents and you'll be off with Chokichi in a minute. A hundred like you wouldn't make me feel a bit better. Go ahead, see if I care whose side you're on. I wanted to take on Ryugeji myself, but if he's running off there's nothing I can do about it. I thought he'd wait till next year, after he graduates. Why did he make it so soon? The coward."

But he was not worried about Nobu. Instead he was turning Midori's odd behavior over in his mind, and his usual song failed to come. The crowds pouring past seemed muted and lonely. At Midori's, at the paper shop, Otori day was a mixed-up affair. All evening Shota lay sulking in the paper shop.

From that day on Midori was a changed girl. She went to her sister's room in the quarter when she had business, but she never so much as stopped to speak to anyone along the way. When her friends were lonesome and invited her out to play she put them off with endless promises, and even to Shota she was chilly, Shota who had been such a close friend. Her blush came too easily. It did not seem likely that the good days at the paper shop would ever come back.

Many were puzzled by the change. Some wondered if the girl might be ill, but her mother only smiled knowingly. "She'll be as saucy as ever before long. She's just having a vacation." Some praised Midori for having become so quiet and lady-like, some mourned the entertaining child who was gone. The gaiety disappeared from the main street like a fire put out. One seldom heard Shota's singing, but each night a lantern, somehow chilly, would go by on the embankment, and one would know that he was out collecting the interest. Only Sangoro's laughter, when occasionally the two of them went out together, was as it always had been.

Midori heard nothing of Nobu's plans. The old spirit was still put away somewhere, it was only that she had felt so unlike herself these last few weeks. She was shy, everything embarrassed her. One frosty morning someone left a paper narcissus at the gate. There was no message with it, but for reasons of her own Midori put it in a vase and sat looking fondly up at it. And then, she hardly knew where, she heard that the following day in a seminary Nobu had put on his dark robes.

TRANSLATED BY EDWARD SEIDENSTICKER

OLD GEN

[Gen Oji, 1897] by Kunikida Doppo (1871-1908)

"Old Gen" was the earliest of Doppo's many short stories and one of his most celebrated. It has a romantic, lyrical strain which gives it something of the quality of a long poem in prose. The influence of English literature, particularly the poetry of Wordsworth, is apparent in "Old Gen" and many others of Doppo's works.

•

Down from the capital once there came to Saeki a teacher of English named Kunikida. He arrived in the autumn and left around the middle of summer, but several months before he left he moved from downtown, which he hated, out to a place near the harbor. Kunikida was not a very congenial person and he seldom talked with anyone but the landlord of the new house where he was staying.

One rainy and windy summer evening when the waves were pounding the shore he came down from his room upstairs to the porch where the two old people of the family were enjoying the cool. They were talking in the dark and fanning away mosquitoes. Since the evening wind was still blowing the rain lightly this way and that, sometimes a drop or two would wet their faces, but they began to reminisce with one another, enjoying the occasional drops of rain.

That evening the landlord, among other things, told Kunikida about an old man named Gen. His life story was actually not very extraordinary, just the sort of thing one can hear all over Japan, but for one reason or another it impressed the teacher deeply. It seemed that he was, whenever he thought of it later, about to discover a secret. Gen seemed something like a box, containing some mystery or some answer, which no one could open any longer.

The old man spoke slowly.

"As you can see, even now there are only a few houses here near the harbor. The loneliness is always just as it is tonight. But think of when there was only old Gen's house on the shore! That old pine tree by his house which now stands near the road was right on the shore in those days. People who came from town to take Gen's ferry-boat used to sit there in the shade on the rocks by the shore. Now there are not even any more rocks there, thanks to dynamite!

"Well, Gen didn't always live alone. At first he had a pretty wife. Her name was Yuri and she was born out on the island. There are lots of stories about them, but this much is true, because one night when Gen was a little drunk he told me himself. When he was twenty-eight or so, late one spring night someone knocked on his door. Gen asked who it was. A young woman outside asked him to take her to the island. Looking out at her in the moonlight, he recognized her as a young girl named Yuri who lived on the island.

"At that time, although there were several boatmen along the coast, Gen was rather popular, because he was a fine young fellow and quite obliging. But there was another reason, too. I wish you could have heard him sing the way he used to sing in those days! Many people took his boat just for the music. It's funny but even at that time Gen didn't talk much more than he does today.

"Some people think the young girl from the island asked for his boat so late at night intentionally. . . . Anyway, I asked him what happened that night on the bay, but even when he was drunk, Gen spoke very little. He only smiled and two deep wrinkles formed on his forehead. To me the smile seemed a little sad, and well it might be, as things turned out.

"Well, they were married and for several years after the marriage he was happy as could be with his wife, but then when their boy Kōsuke was about seven years old she died during her second confinement. Several people offered to adopt Kōsuke and bring him up in their shop, but Gen refused, saying he couldn't give up his only son after he'd lost his wife.

"After this Gen seldom smiled and he never sang, unless he was slightly drunk. Then even his happiest song still sounded sad. Or perhaps people only thought so. But, no, really I think the death of his wife broke his heart.

"On misty days he used to take his son with him in the boat, saying it was bad to leave him alone in his lonely house. The passengers felt sorry for them, and women who had brought cakes and candies for their children at home used to give some of these to this lonely little boy. On such occasions Gen didn't express any thanks at all, as if he were not aware of their kindness. And yet nobody felt bad.

"Well, two years more passed. When the construction of this new harbor was about half-finished, my wife and I moved here from the island and built this house. The hill was cut back and a new road was constructed, but Gen's job remained just about the same.

"Then when Gen's boy Kōsuke was twelve, he was playing one day on the shore with some other children and somehow he drowned. The other children were afraid to tell their parents, so it was evening before anyone noticed that Kōsuke was gone and began to look for him. By that time of course it was already too late to do anything for him. Oddly enough, we found his poor little body just under his father's boat.

"After that Gen hardly sang at all. He stopped talking even with his best friends. He continued to run his ferryboat as before, but people began to forget his existence even when they used his boat. I myself only remember that he is still alive when I see him sometimes going by with his oar on his shoulder and with half-shut eyes.

"Anyway, you are the first person who has ever asked about him. Maybe if you invite him in sometime for a cup of wine you can get him to sing a song. But usually we can't understand what it says anymore. He never complains, but it's rather sad, don't you think? I feel sorry for him. . . ."

This was as much as the landlord said that night. Several weeks later Kunikida finished his teaching in Saeki and returned to Tokyo, but there he kept on thinking of Gen, especially when sitting by his desk at night listening to the rain fall. He pictured old Gen remembering the bygone pleasant spring nights with his eyes half-closed by the fire and thinking of his drowned son Kōsuke.

Thus the years passed and Kunikida remembered Gen sometimes and wondered how he was, long, in fact, after poor Gen, without the teacher's knowing it, was dead and gone to his grave.

One January day—it was the year following Kunikida's story—the sky was dull and it seemed about to snow. The main street of Saeki was not so crowded as usual, the shops were darkened, and in the narrow lanes the stones were frozen. From the foot of the castle the low and melancholy sound of a temple bell spread out slowly over the town like a water ring in a fishless pond and died away.

In the square children from poor families were standing about with ashen faces and playing unenthusiastic games. When a beggar came along, one of the children called, "Kishu! Kishu!", but Kishu passed without paying any attention to them. From his looks his age might be fifteen or thereabouts. His long, wild hair grew down his neck and his long face with its thin cheeks made his chin seem sharp. His eyes moved slowly and without any life. The bottom of his coat was wet and ragged and barely reached his knees. Through the torn seam of one sleeve there appeared an elbow thin like the legs of a grasshopper.

Just at this minute old Gen happened to come along also.

"Kishu!" the old man called to him in a low, strong voice. The young beggar looked up dully and saw old Gen. Each stood for a while looking at the other; then Gen took out his lunch box and offered a rice ball to the beggar, who took from his pocket a cup to receive it. Neither the one who gave nor the one who received said a word. Then Kishu passed on without once looking back, but Gen followed the beggar with his eyes until he had disappeared around the corner of a street. Looking up toward the sky, Gen noticed one or two flakes of snow. He sighed deeply and once again he looked where the beggar had disappeared. Trying not to laugh, the children poked their elbows at each other, but the old man took no notice.

In the evening Gen went back to his house. Despite the darkness, he did not light a lamp but sat in front of the fire with his face in his big thick hands. His shadow moved to and fro, huge, on the wall. Here a colored print, brought back by his wife from her parents' home when Kōsuke was five or six, had hung ever since, turning slowly black from smoke. Gen listened to the whispering sound of snow that enveloped the house and thought about Kishu.

One autumn several years before a woman beggar had appeared in Saeki. She brought with her a son about eight years old and whenever they came to a house together she usually got a good many things. As the charity of the people of this town seemed greater than that of other places, she must have thought that here was a good place to leave him behind, because she did the next spring. Later somebody who had been to Dazaifu said that he saw a beggarwoman very much like her in the company of a great big wrestler, begging at the gate of the shrine.

When they heard this story the people of the town despised the cold-hearted mother and felt more sympathy for the abandoned child than ever. Thus, at first, the mother's plan seemed to have worked. Some one taught him his ABC's for the fun of it; someone else taught him reading, and he could recite one or two pages from the standard grade school reader. He learned a song from hearing other children sing.

But the charity of the people of the town had its limit and it reached it pretty soon. While everyone felt sorry for the boy, no one wanted to take him in permanently. So sometimes people hired him to sweep the garden and were nice to him, but usually this, too, did not last long; other people began to say he couldn't remember things or that he was dirty or that he would steal. Anyway, they put him down as a *beggar* and kept him outside their world.

When he was young Kishu had played like other children, but, as the years passed and he grew older and the townspeople more hostile or indifferent, little by little his blighted heart withdrew, away, away to some desert island where the villagers never came and never wanted to come. He stopped thanking people. He ceased to smile or laugh. Seldom enough people saw him angry or saw him cry. If someone scared him with a stick just for fun, he moved away slowly with a kind of smiling face. He might make one think of a dog running away and wagging its tail when its master scolded.

Late that night Gen left the fire and took his boat lantern with him out into the snow. To and fro the beam ran over white ground, shining magically. The circle of light paused at one house after another. In the square a policeman, too, was out; he came up to shine his lantern in Gen's face. There appeared the deep wrinkles and thick nose of the tough old boatman.

"You're old Gen, aren't you?" the policeman said in surprise.

"Yes, sir," answered Gen in a hoarse voice.

"Who are you looking for so late at night?"

"Have you seen Kishu around here?"

"What do you want with Kishu?"

"It's so cold tonight I thought I'd ask him to stay at my house."

"All right. But nobody knows where he sleeps. . . . You had better not catch cold yourself." And so the policeman went his way.

Soon Gen came to the bridge and found footprints in the light of his lantern. They seemed quite new. Who else but Kishu would be walking barefooted in the snow?

The fact that old Gen wanted to take in Kishu became widely known in no time. The people who heard it did not at first believe it. They were surprised and then amused. Some people laughed and said they would like to see Kishu and Gen sitting down to dinner by themselves. But, anyway, the people of the town began to talk about old Gen again, who had become hardly more than a memory by that time.

A week or so after the snow Gen was about to untie his boat and set off one fine afternoon when two young men rushed up and boarded his boat, so that it was packed with people. Two girls who were going back to the island seemed to be sisters; they carried small packages and wore towels tied over their hair. There was an old couple with their grandchild, beside the two late-comers.

As the boat moved out they all repeated the town gossip. One of the young fellows mentioned a play being given in the town; the elder sister said that she had heard the costumes were particularly pretty. The old woman said the play was not very good, not even as good as last year's. One young fellow asked the sisters if it were true that the actor named Gorokume, who was said to be very handsome, was as popular among young girls on the island as he had heard. The sisters blushed and the old woman laughed out loud. But Gen kept his eyes fixed on the distant horizon and never joined in the conversation.

Then one of the boys said abruptly, "I heard you took Kishu in to live with you?"

"Yes, I did," Gen answered without a glance.

"Everybody is wondering what you're doing taking in a beggar boy like that and keeping him with you. What's the matter? Were you lonely living alone?"

"Yes."

"You could have easily found some nice child around here without taking *him*."

"That's true," said the old woman, looking up into Gen's face, but he looked away troubled and silent.

Gray smoke was rising quietly up from the hills in the west and glowing in the last of the evening sunlight.

"Kishu has no parents or brothers or home. I am an old man with no wife or child. If I take him as my son, he will take me as his father. Isn't that better for both of us?"

The people in the boat were surprised; they had never heard him talk this way before.

"Gen, how everything changes . . ." the old woman said. "It seems just like yesterday that I used to see your wife standing on the shore with the baby in her arms. How old would your boy have been now?"

"Perhaps a year or two older than Kishu."

"It's hard to guess how old that Kishu is, he's so dirty!"

The laughter lasted for a while.

"I don't know either. He said he is sixteen or seventeen. Nobody knows exactly, except maybe his mother. . . . But don't you feel sorry for him?" Gen said, looking at the child the old couple had with them.

"If a real feeling of love grows up between Gen and Kishu, then Gen's old age may be much happier. It would be nice to have him always there when Gen comes back in the evening," the old man said half-seriously.

"Sure, I think it would be fine," said Gen, full of pleasure.

"Aren't you planning to take Kishu to the play?" said one of the young men, less interested in teasing Gen than in seeing the sisters smile; but they smiled only a little, so as not to hurt Gen's feelings.

"That would be interesting!" the old woman said and banged the boat.

"I don't see any reason to take my boy to something like *The Tragedy of Awa no Jurobei* and have him cry," said Gen seriously.

"What do you mean 'my boy'?" said the old woman, pretending. "Your boy drowned over there, I heard," she added, pointing. Everyone looked at the place.

"Kishu, I mean," said Gen. Anger, shame, and joy filled his mind. Then only joy. Suddenly he began to sing and to row more stoutly than ever before. Neither the sea nor the mountains had heard that voice long since. It, too, spread out like a water ring over the sea at evening calm, touched shore, and echoed back faintly, faintly from thirty years ago.

Then the two girls got off at the island; the young men lay down on their backs and covered up with a blanket. In a low voice the old couple went on talking again about family and business; they gave some cakes to their grandchild.

Before the boat got back, the sun had already gone down behind the hills. The cooking smoke from evening meals lay over the village and along the shore. Old Gen was thinking that there was somebody waiting for him: Kishu might be drowsing in front of the fire. His stubbornness might soften. . . . Had he finished his supper or waited? When Gen had offered to teach him to row Kishu had seemed quite pleased. Surely even Kishu in time would be stout and healthy. How nice it would be to hear Kishu singing some of his songs. It might be that Kishu, too, would row his boat with just one girl in the moonlight.

When at last old Gen's boat reached the pier, he rolled up the straw mat and carried it under his arm and his oar on his back toward home.

"Son, I'm back," he called and put his oar in its usual place and went in. There was no light inside.

"What's the matter? I'm back. Kishu, where's the light? Kishu!" There was no answer.

"Kishu! Kishu!" a cricket repeated faintly.

Gen took a match from his pocket and lit it. No one was there, and the match burned out. Gloomy and cold the air came up from under the floor. He lit a small lantern and looked all about, calling and calling hoarsely, but the ash in the fireplace was white and cold; there was no sign of Kishu's supper. At last Gen lit his big boat lantern and left.

He asked at the blacksmith's. No one had seen Kishu. Finally, however, out on the edge of town on an old farm road with pine trees planted along it, he saw the figure of Kishu walking along with his hands in his pockets, his body bent forward.

"Kishu?" old Gen said, putting his hand on Kishu's shoulder. "Where are you going like this?" he went on in a tone of both relief and sorrow. Kishu looked back without surprise. "Kishu, don't you feel cold? Let's go back." Gen took his hand and they started back home; he explained he was sorry to be so late and he was sorry it was so lonely for Kishu at home.

Once they were back, Gen lit the fire and took out some food from the cupboard and fed Kishu. When Kishu finished his meal, Gen made his bed and covered him up with a blanket. He himself sat by the fire for a long, long time without moving, while the wood burned lower and lower. On his face, which had been exposed for fifty years to the sea winds, the faint reflections of the last flames moved. And the shining thing was probably a tear.

Next morning Gen got up early and fixed breakfast, but he himself ate little, saying he felt sick and thirsty. After a while he took Kishu's hand and put it to his forehead and asked him to tell

if he had any fever. Then Gen decided he had caught a cold and
went back to bed.

"Tomorrow I will be all right. Come over here, Kishu, and we can
talk. I will tell you some interesting stories," but he talked to him
as though to a child, this story and that. Had Kishu ever seen a real
live shark? At last he asked, "Don't you miss your mother?" but
Kishu did not understand him.

"You can stay here as long as you want to. Please think of me as
your father. I will take you to the play tomorrow. It's *Awa no
Jurobei* and then you can understand family love."

With that old Gen began to tell the plot of the play, which he had
once seen, years ago. He sang a song from the play and wept to
himself, the story was so sad. Kishu, however, seemed to be making
nothing of it at all.

"Well, maybe it is hard for you to get the idea from just hearing
the story, but tomorrow you'll see . . ." and finally Gen slept for a
while from fatigue at his own recitation. Then he seemed to wake
and to look about for Kishu; instead, he found a beggarwoman
who said Kishu was her son. She seemed to change into Gen's own
mother, telling him to look at a stage dazzlingly lit with many
candles, but he only took cakes, wondering why his mother wept
with her eyelids flushed. At last he fell asleep with his small head
on his mother's knees. After a long while it seemed his dream was
interrupted, as if his mother were shaking him. Old Gen raised his
head on the pillow and stared around. It was hard to separate dream
and reality.

"Kishu!" Kishu was gone.

Throwing off his blanket, Gen stood up suddenly, but his head
was pounding. In a moment he sank back dizzily into his bed and
pulled the covers up over his head.

That day the wind came up gradually, beginning in the morning.
None of the harbor people wanted to go to town and no one in
town wanted to go to the island. Thus the whole day passed; no one
called at old Gen's for his boat. By evening the sea had become so
much heavier that people began to think the pier might be destroyed.

Early in the morning of the following day, with the earliest light of dawn many of the harbor people came down to the pier with their lanterns and raincoats. Fortunately the pier was safe, but when they looked around and it was a little lighter they noticed a boat that had been driven up on the rocks and wrecked.

"Whose boat is *that*?" said the owner of one of the shops.

"It's Gen's, I'm almost sure," said one of the younger fellows. The men looked at each other without speaking for a while.

"Someone ought to tell him. . . ."

"All right, I will," said the same young fellow and started off at a run. He had not gone very far, however, before he noticed something strange hanging from the pine tree by the road. At first he thought it might be something blown there by the storm, but when he looked more closely it was a man. In fact, it was old Gen, dead, who had hanged himself there.

Kishu is much the same Kishu, taken for granted by the people of the town as a regular fixture of Saeki, and given as before to wandering the old city in the middle of the night like some ghost escaped from his grave. When somebody told him that old Gen had hanged himself, Kishu merely gave a vacant stare.

TRANSLATED BY SAM HOUSTON BROCK

Haru no hi ya
  hito nanimo senu
    komura kana

A day of spring:
  a hamlet where not anyone
    is doing anything.

Hibari-ha to
  kaeru-ha to uta no
    giron kana

On how to sing
  the frog school and the skylark school
    are arguing!

Kaerimireba
  yukiaishi hito
    kasumikeri

Backward I gaze
  but the one I met and passed
    is lost in haze!

Miyashiro ya
  niwabi ni tōki
    ukinedori

A shrine: —here, keeping
  far from garden lights, float
    wild birds, sleeping.

Kimi matsu yo
  mata kogarashi no
    ame ni naru

Night—and once again
  the while I wait for you cold wind
    turns into rain.

Wasureorishi
  hachi ni hana saku
    haru hi kana

A long forgotten thing:
  a pot where now a flower blooms—
    this day of spring!

Medieval Scene

Jūikki
  omote no furanu
    fubuki kana

Eleven of them go—
  horsemen who do not turn their heads
    through the whirling snow.

Kangetsu ya   Cold is the moonshine:
 sekitō no kage shadow of a stone pagoda
  matsu no kage   shadow of a pine.
        Masaoka Shiki (1867-1902)

Kaze ni kike   The winds that blow—
 izure ga saki ni ask them, which leaf on the tree
  chiru konoha will be next to go.
        Natsume Sōseki (1867-1916)

Hebi nigete   A snake! . . . and it passes—
 ware wo mishi me no but eyes that had glared at me
  kusa ni nokoru   stay in the grasses.

Ame harete   Clearing after showers—
 shibaraku bara no and for a little while the scent
  nioi kana   of hawthorn flowers.

Akikaze ya   The winds of fall—
 ganchū no mono and the things one looks upon
  mina haiku   are *haiku,* all!
        Takahama Kyoshi (born 1874)

TRANSLATED BY HAROLD G. HENDERSON

BOTCHAN

by Natsume Sōseki (1867-1916)

Natsume Sōseki is usually considered to have been the greatest novelist of the Meiji period, and he is also famous for his poetry in Chinese, his haiku, and his literary criticism. Before embarking on his career as a novelist in 1905, Natsume had been Professor of English Literature at Tokyo University; and the influence of English novels, particularly those of Meredith, was strong in some of his early works. Gradually, however, his novels acquired a philosophic tone which owed more to the East than to the West.

Botchan, published in 1906, was probably Natsume's most popular novel. It deals mainly with the experiences a Tokyo-bred young man has as a teacher in a country school on the island of Shikoku. The title is hard to translate: it is a familiar form of address for boys, something like "sonny." What follows is the first chapter of the novel.

•

From childhood I have suffered because of the reckless nature I inherited from my parents. When I was in elementary school I jumped out of the second story of the school building and lost the use of my legs for a week. Some people might ask why I did such a thing. I had no very profound reason. I was looking out of the second-floor window of the new schoolhouse when one of my classmates said as a joke that, for all my boasting, he bet I could not jump to the ground. He called me a coward. When the janitor carried me home on his back, my father looked at me sternly and said he did not think much of anyone who dislocated his back just by jumping from the second floor. I said next time I would show him I could do it without getting hurt.

One of my relatives gave me a penknife. I was showing some of my friends how nicely the blade would shine in the sun, when one of them said that the blade would shine all right, but it did not look as though it would cut. I replied that it would cut anything. He said that if that was so he would like to see me cut my finger. I said that a finger was no problem, and cut slantwise across the nail of my right thumb. Fortunately the knife was small and the bone hard, so that I still have the thumb, but the scar will remain until I die.

About twenty paces east of our yard there was a small vegetable garden on some high ground, and in the middle was a chestnut tree. This tree was more important to me than life. When the chestnuts were ripe, I would go out back as soon as I got up, pick up the ones that had fallen, and eat them at school. The west side of the vegetable garden adjoined the garden of the Yamashiroya Pawnshop. The son of the pawnshop-owner was thirteen or fourteen and a coward. But all the same, he would climb over the lattice fence and steal our chestnuts. One evening I hid behind the gate and caught him. When he realized that escape was cut off, he came flying at me. He was two years older than I and, coward though he was, very strong. He aimed his flat head at my chest and began pushing as hard as he could. Then his head slipped and went into the sleeve of my kimono. I could not use my hand because of his head, so I began waving my arm around wildly. His head wobbled back and forth with the sleeve until finally, unable to stand this any longer, he bit my arm. That hurt. I pushed him up against the fence, tripped him with my foot, and knocked him over. The yard of the pawnshop was about six feet lower than our vegetable garden, and as he fell he did a somersault, breaking down the fence, and landing with a grunt. In so doing he tore the sleeve off my kimono. When my mother went to the pawnshop that night to apologize, she got the sleeve back.

I got into a lot more trouble. The carpenter's son, the fishmonger's boy, and I once ruined a neighbor's carrots. The shoots were just coming up, and he had spread straw all over them. We held a wrestling match on the straw that lasted half a day, and all the new shoots were trampled down into the ground. Another time I caused a storm of complaint by stopping up a well that watered Mr. Furukawa's rice fields. The well consisted of a big bamboo pipe sunk deep into the ground from which the water bubbled up and flowed into the fields. At the time I did not understand how wells worked, so I stuffed the pipe full of stones and sticks, and when I had made sure that no more water came out of it, I went home. While I was eating supper, Mr. Furukawa came to our house, very excited and red in the face. I think my father settled by paying him some money.

My father had no use for me, and my mother generally favored my elder brother, who was disgustingly pale and liked to play theatre, especially if he could take the part of a female impersonator. "This boy," my father used to say whenever he saw me, "will never amount to anything." And my mother agreed. "He is so rowdy," she would say, "I worry about his future." They had reason to worry. I have never amounted to anything, as you can see. I have managed to stay out of jail and that is about all.

A few days before my mother died, I was turning somersaults in the kitchen and hit my side against the stove. It was very painful. My mother became angry and said she did not want to look at the likes of me, so I went to stay with some relatives. After a while I heard that she had died. I certainly did not think she would die so suddenly. If I'd known she was that sick, I thought when I returned home, I would have behaved better. My brother, in his usual way, said that I had been mean to Mother, and that that was why she had died so soon. I was mortified, and hit him in the face.

When my mother died there were only my father, my brother, and myself. My father never did anything. Whenever he met anyone, he always told him that he—the other person—was no damn good. I still don't know what my father found no damn good in other people. He was a peculiar father. My brother planned to become a businessman and studied English diligently. He was sly and effeminate and we were on poor terms; about once every ten days we had a quarrel. One day when we were playing chess he managed by foul means to maneuver me into a bad situation and then began to laugh. I got angry and hit him on the forehead with one of the chessmen I had in my hand. I cut his forehead a little and it began to bleed. He went and told my father, who said he was going to disinherit me.

At the time I thought that I could do nothing about it, and I had resigned myself to being disinherited, when Kiyo, who had been our maid for over ten years, tearfully apologized to my father for my behavior and finally managed to appease him. In spite of this I was not afraid of my father. I felt sorry instead that Kiyo had had to do such a thing. Kiyo, I had heard, came from a good family, but had lost everything at the time of the Restoration, and was finally reduced to working as a servant. By this time she was well on in years. This old woman, for what reason I do not know, was always extremely good to me. My father found me too much to handle and the neighborhood despised me as an incorrigible rough-neck; even my mother, a few days before her death, lost all patience with me; but this old woman continued to treat me with extravagant kindness. I had resigned myself to the fact that I did not have a lovable nature, and if I was treated like a block of wood I did not think it particularly strange. What puzzled me was Kiyo's attentive-ness. At times when there was no one else in the kitchen she would tell me that I had a fine, upright nature, but I never knew just what she meant. If I really had such a fine nature, other people besides Kiyo ought to treat me better, I thought. So whenever she said anything of the sort to me, I told her it was all flattery, and I did not like flattery. "That proves what a fine nature you have," she would say, gazing happily at my face. She had quite arbitrarily built up an image of me in which she took great pride. It made me feel uneasy.

After my mother's death Kiyo paid even greater attention to me. I often wondered why she was so partial to me, and thought how much better off she would be if she weren't, but her kindnesses continued. Sometimes she bought me cakes and biscuits with her own money. On cold winter nights she would suddenly appear, when I was already in bed, with a bowl of hot gruel made of buck-wheat flour that she had bought without telling anyone. And she not only gave me things to eat, but socks, pencils, and notebooks too. Once, though this was a good deal later, she even lent me three yen. I had not asked her to lend me the money. She simply brought it to my room, saying she thought I might be a little hard up for spending money. Of course I told her I did not need the money, but she insisted, and I finally accepted. I was very happy to have the money and put it into a purse and the purse into the breast of my kimono. But when I went to the toilet the purse fell down the hole. I emerged unhappily from the toilet and told Kiyo what had happened. She rushed to fetch a bamboo pole and said she would fish it out for me. In a little while I heard the sound of water splashing at the well. I went out to find her busily washing the purse, which dangled by its string from the end of the pole. When we opened it and removed the bills, they had turned brownish and the designs had faded. Kiyo dried them over the stove. "I think they are all right now," she said. When I complained that they smelled, she asked for them back and promised to exchange them. Somewhere, by some artifice, she changed the bills and brought back three yen in silver. I have forgotten how I spent the three yen. I assured her that I would return the money soon but I never did. Now, even though I would like to pay her back ten times the amount, it is no longer possible.

Kiyo gave me presents only when my father and brother were not around. This fact irritated me, for there was nothing I hated so much as enjoying something in secret. My brother and I, of course, were on bad terms, but I still did not like receiving cakes and colored pencils from Kiyo behind his back. Once I asked her why she only gave presents to me and never to my brother. She looked quite unconcerned, and replied that she saw no harm in it because my father bought things for my brother. This was rather unfair. My father was an obstinate man but he never stooped to favoritism. Yet it must have seemed that way to Kiyo, I suppose, because she was so fond of me. Although she may have been of good birth, she was quite without education, and nothing could be done to change her. Her partiality for me was really frightening. She was convinced that I was going to be a great success when I grew up. Likewise she had decided that my brother, who grew paler and paler over his books, would never amount to anything. You can do nothing with such a woman. Kiyo believed that anyone she was fond of was destined to be great, and anyone she disliked would surely come to a bad end. At the time I had no particular ambitions, but Kiyo kept saying that I would become this or that, until I began to feel that perhaps I would become famous after all. When I think of it now, it all seems so silly. Once I asked her exactly what sort of person she thought I would become, but she had no definite ideas. "I am sure that you will ride around in your own rickshaw and have a house with a fine big entrance," she said.

Kiyo's great wish was to live with me when I had become independent and had my own home. Again and again she would beg me to be sure to save a room for her. I somehow felt that I would one day have my own house, and I let the matter go with a reassurance that there would always be a place for her. But she had a very lively imagination, and would plan just how she would like things. "Do you think the suburbs would be nice, or would you prefer a house in the city? I hope you will have a swing in the garden. One Western-style room will be plenty, I think." At the time I had no desire for any kind of house, whether Western or Japanese, and I told her so. Then she praised me for having so few desires and being pure in heart. Whatever I said to Kiyo, she would praise me.

After the death of my mother I lived this way for five or six years: scolded by my father, fighting with my brother, receiving cakes and praise from Kiyo. I was quite content with things as they were, for I had no special ambitions. Other boys, I suppose, led about the same sort of lives. But Kiyo kept telling me that I was unfortunate and to be pitied, and I began to think that perhaps she was right. I suffered no real hardships. I was only annoyed that my father would not give me any spending money.

In January of the sixth year after my mother's death, my father died of a stroke. In March of the same year I was graduated from the middle school I had been attending, and in June my brother graduated from commercial school. He took a job with the Kyushu branch of a firm and had to leave Tokyo, but I was to stay there in order to continue my schooling. He suggested that he sell the house and dispose of the property before he left to take his position. I replied that whatever he wished to do would be all right with me. I certainly had no intention of becoming dependent on him. Any help that he gave me was sure to result in a quarrel, so it was natural that he should make such a suggestion. I felt that I would rather make a living by delivering milk than accept his half-hearted assistance and be under obligation to him. My brother called in a furniture dealer and disposed of the odds and ends that had accumulated in our family over the generations. Through the offices of a middleman he sold the house and lot to a wealthy family. I think he got a good price for them, though I know nothing of the details. A month before the sale I found lodgings elsewhere. I debated what to do next. Kiyo was very unhappy to see the house where she had lived for ten years pass into someone else's hands, but she was powerless to do anything about it, since the house was not hers. "If you were only a little older you could inherit the house," she said to me earnestly. If I could inherit the house when I was older I should have been able to inherit the house then. The old woman knew nothing of the law, and supposed that it was merely a matter of age that prevented me from acquiring my brother's house.

My brother and I could go our own ways without any trouble, but there was still the problem of where Kiyo was to go. My brother was of course in no position to take her with him—in any case she would not have had the slightest wish to trail along after him all the way to Kyushu—and I was living in a tiny room which I might have to vacate at any moment. There seemed to be nothing I could do. I asked Kiyo if she felt like working for someone else. She finally decided that she would stay at her cousin's house until I got married. Her cousin was a clerk in the law court; he was fairly well off, and had several times asked Kiyo to live in his home. She had always answered that she would rather stay in a place she was accustomed to, even if it meant being a maid. However, she seemed to prefer living with her cousin to taking a position with a strange family and having the trouble of getting used to new ways. But she advised me to get a house and a wife as soon as possible so that she could come and look after me. She liked me better than her cousin, I suppose.

Two days before he left for Kyushu, my brother came to see me and gave me six hundred yen. He told me that I might use the money to start in business or continue my schooling, as I pleased, but that from now on I was on my own. I could not help admiring the way he did it. I didn't absolutely need his six hundred yen, but the unaccustomed candor of his action impressed me, and I accepted the money with thanks. Then he gave me fifty yen to hand to Kiyo, which I promised to do. Two days later we parted at the Shimbashi Station, and I have never seen him since.

I lay in bed thinking of how to use the six hundred yen. Any kind of business would require a lot of trouble, and I did not think I could make a success of it. Anyway, I could hardly open much of a business with six hundred yen. Even if I did, with my lack of education I would certainly suffer in the long run. It was better to forget about using the money as capital, and think of it instead as money for my education. If I used only two hundred a year, I could study for three years, and in three years of hard study I could surely learn something. I decided that I would enter a school somewhere. I had never been fond of study of any kind. I was particularly bad in languages and literature; I could not understand one line out of twenty of poetry in the new style. But since I was sure to dislike whatever I studied, it did not make much difference what kind of school I entered. One day, as it happened, I was passing a school of physics when I noticed an advertisement calling for new students. I took this as a kind of stroke of fate, and went in to ask for a prospectus. I immediately filled out an entrance application. Now that I think of it, I imagine this mistake can also be attributed to my inherited recklessness.

For three years I worked at my studies about as hard as the average student, but I had no great aptitude, and it would have been easier to find my place in the class by counting from the bottom than from the top. Strangely enough, I managed to graduate at the end of the three years. This rather startled me, but having no cause to complain, I meekly accepted my degree.

Eight days after graduation the director of the school asked to see me. I went to his office wondering what he wanted. A middle school in Shikoku needed a mathematics teacher. The salary was forty yen a month. The director had sent for me to find out whether I would like to go. I had been studying for three years, but, to tell the truth, the thought of becoming a teacher, or of going off to the country, had never occurred to me. On the other hand, I had no other plan in mind, so when I heard the details I answered immediately that I would go. Again the curse of congenital recklessness.

Once I had accepted the position I had no choice but to go. For three years I had lived in my little room without having to listen to any complaints, without quarreling with anyone. It had been a comparatively carefree period of my life. But now the time had come when I must leave my room. I had been out of Tokyo only once in my life, when I went with some school friends on a picnic to Kamakura. Now it was no nearby Kamakura that I was going to but a really distant place. On the map it was only a dot on the seacoast, about the size of a pin point. It could hardly be a desirable place. I had no idea what sort of town it was or what sort of people lived there, but that didn't bother me. I would not worry about it— I would simply go. Of course leaving was somewhat of a nuisance.

I had gone to see Kiyo from time to time after we sold our house. Her cousin turned out to be an unusually nice person, and if he happened to be at home when I was there he would go out of his way to be kind to me. In my presence Kiyo would tell her cousin all about my good qualities. She announced that as soon as I graduated from school I was going to buy a house and go to work for the government. She made such decisions and pronouncements quite on her own while I sat in helpless embarrassment. I had this experience more than once: to my horror she even went so far as to tell stories about how I used to wet the bed when I was little. Kiyo was an old-fashioned woman, and she conceived of our relationship as a feudal one between lord and retainer. If I was her master, she decided, I must also be her cousin's master. This was rather hard on the cousin.

My position was definitely settled now, and a few days before the time to leave I went to see Kiyo. She was in bed with a cold, but when I arrived she quickly got up. "When are you getting your house, *botchan*?" she asked. One had only to graduate, she supposed, to have the money suddenly appear in one's pocket. It seemed more absurd than ever, if I were really such a great man, for her to keep on calling me *botchan* as if I were a child. I told her simply that, for the time being, I would have no house. When I added that I was going to the country, she looked utterly dejected, and kept straightening the strands of gray hair that had come out of place. I felt terribly sorry for her, and to cheer her up I said that I would be back very soon, certainly by summer vacation of next year. She still had a strange look on her face, so I asked her, "What shall I bring you for a present? What would you like?"

"I would like to eat some Echigo sugar cakes," she said. I had never heard of Echigo sugar cakes. To begin with, Echigo Province lies in an entirely different direction.

"I don't think they have any sugar cakes where I am going," I said.

"Then which way are you going?" she asked.

"Westward," I answered.

"This side of Hakone," she asked, "or beyond?" I did not know how to explain.

On the day of my departure she came in the morning and helped me with things. She put into my canvas bag some toothpaste, a toothbrush, and a towel that she had bought at a shop on the way. I told her that I did not need them, but she was insistent. We rode to the station in rickshaws and went up to the platform. When I had boarded the train she looked intently at my face.

"I may not see you again. Be sure to take good care of yourself," she said in a small voice. Her eyes were full of tears. I was not crying but I would have been with just a bit more. When the train finally got under way, I thought that everything would be all right now. I put my head out of the window and looked back. She was still standing there. She looked very small.

TRANSLATED BY BURTON WATSON

THE BROKEN COMMANDMENT

[Hakai, Chapter VII, 1906] by Shimazaki Tōson (1872-1943)

Shimazaki Tōson, whose first fame came as a poet, was also a major novelist. The Broken Commandment, *a pioneer Japanese problem novel, was published before the author had turned to the autobiographical fiction which was to be typical of him. It is the story of Ushimatsu, who at his father's command has concealed the fact that he is a member of the pariah* eta *class. The father's death, described here, comes at a time when circumstances are conspiring to make Ushimatsu reveal the secret of his birth. He eventually does, and emigrates to America. (For a further summary of this novel see* Keene, Japanese Literature, *pp. 99-101.)*

•

He would never forget the loneliness of that trip. He had been home two summers before, but this time, as he followed the river toward Nezu, it was as though he had become a different person. A little over two years, not a long time when he thought of it; but in those years violent changes had begun in his life. Some people may move naturally and gradually away from the world, not knowing when exactly the change came; but for Ushimatsu the spiritual unheaval was violent and profound.

There was no need here to hold himself in. He could breathe the dry air freely, he could give himself up to sorrow at his ill-starred birth and to astonishment at the changes in his life. The water, stirred to a yellow-green, flowing noiselessly toward the distant sea, the leafless willow branches seemed to cower over the bank—ah, the mountain river was just as it had always been.

Now and then he passed a party of mountain travelers. Some had the faces of the ruined and slunk by like famished dogs. Others, barefoot with dirty kimonos pulled about them, might have been looking for work. A sunburned father and son, bells in hand and voices raised in a sad canticle, had chosen the rigors of the pilgrim's way. A group of wandering performers in battered sunshades—they too seemed to be fleeing the world—would play a love tune as the mood took them and beg a penny along the way. Ushimatsu stared at them all, comparing them with himself. How he envied even them, free to wander as they would.

But presently he began to feel as though he too were moving into a freer world. Warmed by the brilliant sunlight, he walked the ash-colored earth of the old north country road, now up a hill, now past a mulberry patch, now and again through a town with its houses lining the road. He was sweating heavily, his throat was dry, his feet and ankles were gray with dust; and yet, strangely, he felt his spirits reviving. The branches of the persimmons bent low under their loads of yellow jewels, burrs hung from the chestnut trees, beans were swelling in their pods, and here and there the sprouting winter barley showed through the stubble in the fields. Songs of farmers near and far, birds—it was the "little June," the Indian summer of the mountains. Peaks towered clear in the distance, and volcanic smoke rose blue from the deep-shadowed valleys between. . . .

The mountains in the dying light of the evening changed from red to purple, purple to brown, and as the hills and the moors grew dark the shadows crept up from valley to valley, and the last sunlight shone from the peaks. In a corner of the sky wavered a brown cloud tinged with gold, the smoke from Mt. Asama it must have been.

His happiness, if such it was, did not last. He came to the edge of a wild valley, and there, strung out over the face of the mountain beyond, white walls and earthen walls in the evening sun, dark spots, possibly persimmons, between the roofs of the mountain houses—ah, it was Nezu. Even the songs of the farmers on their way home from work added to his agitation. As he thought of his father's life, how he had left the hamlet of outcasts at Komoro and come to this obscure mountain village to live out his days, the twilight scenery quite lost its charm. It was dark when he reached Nezu.

His father had died, not there but at the herdsman's hut in the West Mouth pasture. While Ushimatsu rested by the fire, his uncle, in that genial, unassertive way of his, talked of the dead man. The fire in the hearth was strong. Ushimatsu's aunt sniffled as she listened again to the story. His father had died from an accident at his post, so to speak, and not from illness or old age. It had not seemed possible that so experienced a herdsman could make a mistake with cattle. Life is unpredictable, however, and an unfortunate chain of circumstances had begun when a bull was unexpectedly added to the herd. The freedom of the wide pasture and the calls of the cows had set the animal wild, and in the end it had lost all traces of domestication and disappeared into the mountains. Three days, four days passed. Ushimatsu's father began searching through the tall grass, but found no trace of it.

He had set out again the day before. He always took along his lunch when he planned to go far, but this time for some reason he left without it. He did not come back when he should have. The young herdsman who helped him climbed to the corral to put out salt, and in with the herd gathered happily around was the bull, quite as though it had never been away. Its horns were stained with blood. The shocked herdsman called some passers-by to help tie the animal up—and perhaps because it was already exhausted, it offered little resistance. After a long search he found Ushimatsu's father moaning in a growth of dwarf bamboo and carried him back to the hut. The wound was beyond treating, but Ushimatsu's father was still fully conscious when the uncle arrived at the hut. He lived until ten that evening. The wake was to be tonight. Mourners were gathered at the hut now, waiting for Ushimatsu.

"And that is how it was." His uncle paused and looked at Ushimatsu. "I asked him if he had anything to say. He was in pain but his mind was clear. 'I'm a herdsman,' he said, 'and it's right I should die working with cattle. There's nothing much else to say. Ushimatsu, though—everything I've done has been for him. I made him give me a promise once. When he comes back tell him not to forget.' "

Ushimatsu listened with bowed head to his father's last message. His uncle went on. " 'And I want to be buried here in the pasture. Don't have the funeral in Nezu. Have it here if you can. And don't tell them at Komoro that I'm dead. Please.' I nodded and said I understood. He lay there smiling up at me, and after a while there were tears in his eyes. He didn't say anything more."

Ushimatsu was deeply moved. The desire to be buried in the pasture, the instructions against having the funeral in Nezu and sending word to Komoro, proved that to the end his father had been thinking of him. To the end he had shown the extreme caution that had governed his life, and the intense determination that had kept him from abandoning what he had once set out upon. His sternness with Ushimatsu had gone to the point of cruelty. Indeed Ushimatsu was afraid of his father, even now that he was dead.

Presently Ushimatsu and his uncle set out for the West Mouth pasture. The funeral arrangements were all made. The autopsy was over, the coffin had been bought, and an old priest from a temple in Nezu had already gone up for the wake. Ushimatsu had only to be present. It was a mile and a half over a lonely mountain road to the pasture. The darkness seemed to clutch at their faces, it was impossible to see even their feet. Ushimatsu went ahead, guiding his uncle by the light of a lantern. The path grew narrower as they walked out from the village, dwindling in the end to a faint line of footsteps through the fallen leaves. It was a path Ushimatsu as a boy had often traveled with his father.

The little hut was crowded with people. Light leaked through cracks in the walls, and the priest's wooden drum, echoing on the mountain air, blended with the murmuring of the brook to make the quiet seem yet more intense. The hut was no more than a shelter to keep off the rain and the dew. Except for travelers who went over the mountain to the hot springs beyond, there were few visitors here from outside. This was the harsh world of the forest ranger, the charcoal-maker, and the herdsman.

Ushimatsu put out the lantern and went into the hut with his uncle. The old priest, the village guildsmen who had come to help, and the farm men and women who had been friends of the dead man greeted Ushimatsu with appropriate words of consolation. Altar candles lighted the night through clouds of incense. The little room seemed cluttered, confused. The rough wooden coffin was draped in a white cloth, and before it stood a newly inscribed memorial tablet, offerings of water and sweets, and bunches of chrysanthemums and anise leaves. A pause came in the prayers. On a signal from the priest the mourners, tears streaming down their faces, went up in turn to take leave of the old herdsman. Ushimatsu, following his uncle, bowed slightly to look down at his father for the last time. In the dim candlelight the face seemed to say that the lonely herdsman's life was over and there remained but to lie deep in the earth of the pasture. Ushimatsu's uncle, faithful to the old way of doing things, had provided for the journey to the next world a sunshade and a pair of straw sandals. A knife to ward off devils lay on the lid of the coffin. The praying and the beating of the drum began again, and talk of the dead man, punctuated by artless laughter and the clatter of dishes, was sad and at the same time lively.

So the night passed. There had been those last instructions not to send word to Komoro, and it was seventeen years since the dead man had left the town. No message was sent, no one came from that hamlet of outcasts. Ushimatsu's uncle was on tenterhooks, even so, lest word somehow reach Komoro that the old "chief" was dead, and an embarrassing mission arrive for the funeral. Ushimatsu's father had long thought of being buried in the pasture, his uncle said. It might be that a temple funeral would be allowed to pass like any other farm funeral, but there was always a possibility that the body would be turned away. By custom members of the pariah class could not be buried in ordinary cemeteries. For Ushimatsu's sake his father had endured the privations of life in the mountains, and for Ushimatsu's sake he had chosen to rest here in the pasture.

The following afternoon the mourners gathered in and around the hut. The owner of the pasture, the dairyman who kept his cattle there, everyone who had heard of the death, came to pay respects.

The grave had been dug under a small pine tree atop a hill in the pasture. Presently the time came to commit the body, and the old herdsman was carried from the hut he had known so well. The priest followed the coffin with a pair of mischievous-looking acolytes behind him. Ushimatsu wore straw sandals like his uncle. The women all had white cloths around their heads. There were as many fashions of dress as there were mourners. Some wore formal cloaks, some homespun. The lack of display seemed in keeping with the rough life of the herdsman. There was no order to the procession, no ceremony. There was only the valedictory of honest hearts as the group moved quietly over the pasture.

The service at the hut, too, had been simple, and yet the plain rhythm of drum and bell and the mechanical chanting of the requiem had been a moving elegy to one caught up in memories.

The last of the late-blooming daisies had been trampled to the ground by the gravediggers. When each of the mourners had thrown down a handful of earth, making a little heap, it was shoveled roughly into the grave. It struck the lid of the coffin with a rumble as of an avalanche, sending out a pungent smell to call up thoughts almost unbearable. The grave filled, a mound grew up over it. Ushimatsu watched, sunk in thought, to the end. His uncle too was silent. Do not forget, his father had commanded with his dying words; and now his father was deep under the earth of the pasture.

Somehow they had come through safely. Leaving the owner of the pasture to look after the grave, and the young herdsman to take care of the hut, the mourners started back for the village. Ushimatsu thought of taking along the black cat his father had kept at the hut, but it was cold to his overtures. When he offered food, it refused to eat; when he called, it refused to come. They could hear it mewing forlornly under the veranda. Beast though it was, it seemed to miss its dead master. How would it live, they wondered, what would it find to eat when snow began to fall in the mountains? "Maybe the poor thing will go wild," said Ushimatsu's uncle.

One by one they started back. The young herdsman went along, carrying salt for the cattle, to see them as far as the corral. A wan

November sun made the West Mouth pasture seem lonelier than ever. Low pines grew here and there along the way. In the spring the hills were blanketed with mountain azalea, which the cattle refused to eat, but now there was only the withered grass. Everything brought memories to Ushimatsu of his father. He remembered how toward the end of May two years before he had visited his father in this pasture. He remembered that it had been the season when the horns of the cattle were itching and these withered azaleas were blooming in a wild profusion of reds and yellows. He remembered the children gathering spring herbs. He remembered the calls of the mountain doves. He remembered the pleasant breeze that had blown over the lilies of the valley and brought the scent of early summer. He remembered how his father had pointed to the new green on the hills and described the advantages of the West Mouth for grazing. He remembered the stories his father had told, of like animals that herded together, of jousts with horns when a new animal entered the herd, of the sanctions cattle apply to each other, of queens that had ruled the herd.

Ushimatsu's father had retired to the obscurity of the mountains, but all his life he had burned with a desire for fame and position. Quite unlike his genial brother, he had nursed a smoldering anger: his birth kept him from working his way ahead in the world; very well, he would withdraw to the mountains. And if he could not have the things he wanted for himself, he would have them for his children and his children's children. Even on the day the sun began coming up in the west that determination at least must not change. Go, fight, make your way in the world—his father's spirit lived in those words. As Ushimatsu thought over that lonely life, he felt more and more deeply the passion and the hope in the message his father had left behind. Death is mute, and yet it spoke now with the force of a thousand and ten thousand words to make Ushimatsu meditate on his life and destiny.

From the corral he could look back at the work his father had left. Cattle were scattered among the low pines, and in the corral itself were a number of still hornless calves. The young herdsman, mindful of his duties as host, started a fire from dead grass and went about gathering fuel. The mourners who were left had been up all the night before, and their labors today had been strenuous. Several of them half-dozed with the smell of burning leaves in their nostrils.

Ushimatsu's uncle put out little heaps of salt for the cattle, and Ushimatsu watched with a certain tenderness as he thought how near his father had been to the animals. The herd circled at a distance with quivering noses. A black cow flicked its tail, a white-faced red shook its ears, a brindle calf mooed. Two or three edged a little closer. They would as soon have their salt, but what of this uninvited audience? Ushimatsu's uncle laughed, Ushimatsu laughed too. With such entertaining companions it might indeed be possible to live in these remote mountains.

Presently they took their leave of the ground where Ushimatsu's father would rest forever. The high mountains fell away behind them. As they passed the Fuji Shrine Ushimatsu turned back to look again at his father's grave, but even the corral was out of sight. He could see, beyond that lonely pasture it would be, only a column of smoke trailing off into the sky.

TRANSLATED BY EDWARD SEIDENSTICKER

ONE SOLDIER

[Ippeisotsu, 1908] by Tayama Katai (1871-1930)

Tayama Katai was a pioneer in the movement in Japanese literature which stemmed from European Naturalism. His novel The Quilt *(*Futon, *1908) was an epoch-making work, describing in powerful and unadorned language the love affair between a married novelist and a young woman who studies under him.* One Soldier *is also in the naturalistic manner. It is clearly based on Tayama's own observations during his service with the army in the Russo-Japanese War of 1904-1905. It was at times considered too openly antimilitaristic, and was often reprinted with certain passages deleted.*

•

He started walking again.

The rifle was heavy, the pack was heavy, his legs were heavy. His aluminum canteen clanked noisily against his bayonet. The sound jarred horribly on his strained nerves, and he tried first one, and then another and another way of silencing it; but the clanking went on and on. He gave up.

The sickness had not really gone, and he breathed with difficulty. Shivering fits, spasms of heat and icy cold, passed incessantly through his frame. His head burned like fire, and his temples throbbed. What had made him leave the hospital, he wondered? Why—when the army doctor had asked him to stay—why had he left the hospital? He asked the question, but he felt no regrets over his decision. There had been fifteen of them there, sick and wounded, lying on bare boards in a small room, part of a dilapidated house which the re-treating enemy had abandoned. For twenty days he had endured the decay and the dirt, the moaning, the oppressive closeness, and the swarms of frightening flies. For food they had had rice-bran porridge with the merest pinch of salt, and he had often known the pangs of hunger. He felt sick even now as he recalled the latrine at the rear of the hospital. The pits were shallow, dug in haste, and the stench struck forcibly at your eyes and nostrils. Flies zoomed around you Dirty, and black as coal.

Anything was better than that. It was better to be here on this broad open plain. You could not imagine how much better. The plains of Manchuria were vast and deserted, endless fields of tall, ripening cane. But the air was fresh and clean. There was sunshine, there were clouds, there were mountains—he became suddenly aware of a dreadful clamor, and he stopped and turned in its direction. It was the same train that he had seen before, still over there on the track. Hundreds of Chinese coolies swarmed about the long, boiler-less, funnel-less monster, pushing frantically, like ants returning home with some gigantic prey.

The rays of the evening sun slanted across the scene, giving it the unreal clarity of a painting.

The noncommissioned officer he had noticed before was still riding on the train. There he was, the one standing aloft on the freight car with the tallest load of rice bales. He shouted to him.

"I'm sick. I can't walk. Can you give me a lift as far as Anshan?"

The fellow was laughing at him. "This train's not for soldiers. I don't know any regulation which says the infantry should ride on trains."

"I'm sick. Can't you see I'm sick? It's beriberi. If I can get to Anshan my unit will be there, I'm certain. Soldiers should help each other, you know. Give me a lift, please!"

He was imploring him, but the fellow would not listen. He only mocked. "Still a private, eh? Time you got yourself some stripes!"

The battles at Chin Chou and Têli-ssu had been won by common soldiers, hadn't they? Blockhead! Brute!

Suddenly a different train—the train in which he had set out for the war from the barracks at Toyohashi—passed before his mind's eye. The station was a mass of flags. Cheers resounded—banzai! banzai! Then, without warning, he was gazing into his wife's face. It was not the tear-stained face which had bade him good-bye at the gate, but a beautiful, smiling face from some moment—he could not remember the time or place exactly—when he had wondered at its loveliness with all his heart. His mother was shaking him by the shoulder now. It was time to get up, she was saying. He would be late for school. Somehow his mind had slipped back to his school-days. And now the evening sun was glistening on the bald pate of a ship's captain, in the bay at the back of the house. The captain was scolding a group of children, and one of those children was himself.

These shadows from the past and the painful, unpleasant realities of the present were clearly differentiated in his mind, but only a hairsbreadth separated them. The rifle was heavy, the pack was heavy, his legs were heavy. From the waist down he might have been another man, and he hardly knew whether it was he or someone else walking. The brown road—its parched mud surface deeply pocked and rutted by the boots, straw sandals, and gun-carriage wheels which had once sunk into it—stretched on and on before him. He had little love left for these Manchurian roads. How far must he go before the road came to an end? How far before he need walk no farther along it? The pebbled roads of his home district, the sandy roads along the seashore, wet after rain . . . how he longed for those smooth pleasant surfaces. This was a big broad highway, but there was not a smooth level patch to be seen. After a day's rain it would be as sticky as wet wall-plaster, and your boots, perhaps even the calves of your legs, would sink halfway into the mud. On the night before the battle at Ta-shih-ch'iao he had trudged in darkness through ten miles of oozy mire. Flecks of it had caked the back of his blouse and even the hair at the back of his head. That was the time when they were detailed to convoy the gun-carriages. The carriages had sunk into the mud and wouldn't budge an inch, and they had shoved and shoved to get them moving again. If the Third Regiment's artillery failed to move on ahead and take up their positions there could be no attack. And after working the night through there was that battle the next day. Endless streams of shells, theirs and the enemy's, passing overhead with a nasty, whining rush. The hot midday sun scorching down from directly above. Past four o'clock they came to close quarters with the enemy infantry. There was the sharp crackle of rifle fire, like beans popping in a frying pan. Now and again a shot had zipped close by his ear. Someone nearby in the line had gasped. He had looked around, startled, and seen the soldier topple forward, blood oozing slowly from a bullet wound in his stomach, glistening red in the warm evening sun. That soldier had been a good sort: cheerful, a nondrinker, at home in any company. After the landing they had gone out together on foraging duties, and they had rounded up pigs together. But that man was gone from the world of the living. It was somehow impossible to think it, but impossible to deny it.

Overtaking him, along the brown road, came a line of wagons loaded with army provisions. Some were drawn by donkeys, some by mules, and he listened to the strident shouts of their Chinese drivers—whoa, whoa, whee!—and to the cracking of the long whips, as they flashed in the evening sun. The road was so deeply pitted that the carts moved forward in a series of uneasy lurches, like ships crashing into waves. He felt weak. His breathing was as difficult as ever. He could go no farther like this. He started running after the wagons to ask for a lift.

The canteen went clank-clank. It jarred horribly. The odds and ends in his pack and the rounds in his ammunition pouches clattered noisily up and down. At times the butt of his rifle struck against his thigh, and he almost leapt in agony.

"Hi! Hi!"

They could not hear him.

"Hi! Hi!"

He put his body's whole strength behind his shouts. They had heard, of course, but not one of them turned to look. They must have guessed that there was no money in it. Momentarily he slackened his pace, but he ran forward again, and this time managed to draw level with the last wagon in the line.

The load of rice bales towered above him like a mountain. He saw the Chinaman glance behind. It was a plump, unpleasant face—but he gave the man no chance to say yes or no. He jumped on, and, gasping painfully for breath, settled himself among the bales. The

Chinaman urged on his mules, seemingly resigned to suffer the intrusion. The wagon bumped and lurched on its way.

His head reeled, and heaven and earth seemed to revolve about him. His chest was aching, his forehead throbbing. He was going to be sick. A sense of uneasiness and foreboding invaded every corner of his being with fearful insistence. And at the same time, while the dreadful lurching started again, all kinds of voices whispered inside his head and close around his ears. He had experienced similar bouts before, but none of them had been as bad as this.

They must have left the open plain and entered a village. A greenness of thick shady willows waved above him. The rays of the evening sun, piercing the greenness, clearly revealed each tiny leaf. He saw low shapeless roofs, and as he passed they seemed to be quivering as though shaken by a violent earthquake. Suddenly he realized that the cart had stopped.

They were on a stretch of road shaded by willows. He counted five carts, drawn up close one behind the other.

Someone grasped him by the shoulder.

It was a Japanese, a corporal.

"You there, what are you up to?"

He raised his aching body.

"What are you doing, riding on this cart?"

It was too much trouble to explain things. He had even lost the will to speak.

"You can't ride up there. Even if it was allowed, the load's already too heavy. You're from the Eighteenth Regiment, aren't you?"

He nodded in agreement.

"What's the matter?"

"I was in the hospital until yesterday."

"Are you better now?"

He nodded again, but without any particular meaning.

"It's hard luck your being sick, but you've got to get off this cart. We're in a hurry. The fighting's started at Liaoyang."

"Liaoyang!" The single word was enough to set his nerves on edge again. "Has it started already?"

"Can't you hear those guns?"

Some time back he had imagined that a kind of rumbling noise had begun over beyond the horizon, but he had told himself it could hardly be Liaoyang yet.

"Has Anshan fallen?"

"We took it the day before yesterday. Looks as if they'll put up some resistance this side of Liaoyang. It started at six this evening they say."

Yes, there was a faint, distant rumbling, and if you listened carefully there could be no mistake. They were guns. The old disagreeable noises moved through the air above his head. The infantry was attacking, weaving through the thick of it. Blood was flowing. As the thoughts flashed through his mind he experienced a strange mixture of panic and attraction. His comrades were in that battle. They were shedding their blood for the Japanese Empire.

He pictured the horrors of the battlefield and the scenes of triumph. But here, twenty miles away, here on the Manchurian plain all was at peace, only a sad autumn breeze blowing beneath the evening sun. The tide of great armies had swept over these villages and their peace was as if it had never been disturbed.

"It'll be a big battle, I suppose?"

"Certainly will."

"Not over in a day?"

"Of course not."

The corporal was speaking eagerly to him now, as one soldier to another, while the distant booming of the guns sounded in their ears. The drivers of the five heavily loaded wagons and the foremen of the Chinese coolies were squatting in a circle, jabbering noisily among themselves. The rays of the evening sun shone aslant the donkeys' long ears, and at times the air was rent with piercing brays. Over among the willows stood a row of five or six white-walled Chinese country houses, and in their gardens he could see tall pagoda trees. There were wells, too, and sheds. An old woman with bound feet hobbled by laboriously. Behind, visible through the leaves of the willows, was the vast empty plain. The corporal was pointing to a chain of brown hills. Beyond them rose a purple-tinged mountain. That was where the guns were firing.

The five wagons moved off.

He was left behind, alone again. He had been told that the next army supply depot was at Hsin-t'ai-tzu. That was another three miles, but there was nowhere to stay the night unless he reached there.

He made up his mind to go on, and he started walking again.

He moved with the utmost difficulty, he was so dog-tired, but somehow even walking was a relief after that wagon. The pain in his stomach was no better, but there was no sense in worrying about that now.

Again the same brown road ahead, the same fields of cane on either side, the same evening sunshine. The same train, even, was passing by on the track. This time it was returning, on the downgrade, and traveling at considerable speed. A train with a locomotive could not have traveled faster, and it made him giddy to watch the cars flashing in and out of the cuttings. The Japanese flag was fluttering on the last car, and he watched it appear and disappear a hundred times amid the cane fields. When it disappeared for a last time, only the noise of the train was left, and mingled with it, the insistent rumble of distant gunfire.

On the road itself there was not a village in sight, but to the west, discernible among gloomy clusters of willow trees, were the occasional brown or white shapes of cottages. There was no sign of inhabitants, but from the cottages rose thin threads of bluish smoke, lonely and cheerless.

The evening shadows had grown to great lengths. Those of the tall canes were darkening the whole breadth of the road, and had already begun to climb the canes opposite. Even the shadows of small weeds by the roadside were stretching enormous distances. In contrast, the hills to the east were now so sharply illuminated that they seemed to float in the air. With its indescribable strength of shadows the loneliness of evening came pressing in upon him.

He came to a break in the canes. Suddenly he saw his own shadow before him, amazingly long. The rifle on his shoulder was moving across the grass far out in the fields. He was stricken with a sense of his isolation.

Insects were singing in the grass. Their cries were strangely unlike those to which he had listened in the fields around his home. This foreignness, coupled with the immensity of the plain, sent a stab of pain through him. The flow of recollections, checked for more than an hour, came suddenly flooding in again.

The face of his mother, his wife, his brother, the faces of women he had known, passed before him in rapid succession as though they were pictures on a revolving paper lantern. The old house in the village, the warm security of his life at home, a fleeting image of himself—so very young he looked—setting out for Tokyo to earn his living. Tokyo. He saw the busy streets at night, the flower-shops, the magazine booths, the rows of newly published books, and— around the corner—the crowded vaudeville theatres and the reception houses: he heard the strumming of samisens, and the forced laughter of the women. Those were good times. The girl he liked best was in a house in Naka-chō, and he had gone there often. She had a round, winsome face, and even now he remembered her with affection. As the eldest son of a prosperous country household he had never known the lack of money, and life had been a series of pleasant experiences. His friends of those days had all gone out into the world now. Only a little while back he had run across one of them, an army captain of the Sixth Division. The fellow had a very high opinion of himself now.

Nothing was more cruel, he thought, than the narrow discipline of army life. But today, oddly enough, the thought roused in him none of the usual spirit of rebellion, not even a sense of martyrdom. He was gripped with fear. When he set out for the war he had dedicated himself body and soul to the service of his country and the Emperor. He had made a fine speech on the theme at his old school in the village. "I have no wish to return alive," he had said. He was in the prime of spirits and health, at that time. He had made that speech, but, of course, he had never expected to die. Beneath it all had been nothing but dreams of victory and glory. Now, for the first time, he was experiencing an uneasiness on the score of death. He really felt that it was possible that he might not, after all, return alive, and the thought filled him with terror. There was this sickness, this beriberi—and even if he recovered, the war itself was noth-ing but a vast prison from which, no matter how he struggled and craved for freedom, there was no escape. He recalled some words which his comrade who had been killed had once used to him.

"There's no way out of this hole. We have to be ready to die, and we have to put a good face on it."

And how on earth could he—a prey to fatigue, sickness, and fear—expect to escape from this dreadful inferno? Desertion? He would try even that if it were any good. The undying disgrace to his name would be bad enough, of course, but on top of that, on the dawn after his recapture, there was still the firing squad. The end was death again. But what were his prospects if he pressed on? He must be-come a man of the battlefields. A man of the battlefields must be resigned to annihilation. For the first time he marveled at his stu-pidity in leaving the hospital. It would have been so easy to have had himself invalided to the rear. . . .

It was too late now, he was trapped, there was no road of escape. Negative despair invaded his whole being, pressing upon him with irresistible strength. The will to walk was gone. Tears flowed uncon-trollably. If there are any gods in this life, help me, help me! Show me a way out! I shall bear every trial with patience after this! I shall do any amount of fine deeds! If I promise you anything I shall never go back on it!

He raised his voice, shouting and sobbing.

His breast heaved. He cried like a baby, the tears streaming down his cheeks. The thought that his body might perish was agonizing. In his breast, until this moment, passions of patriotism had often blazed. On the deck of the transport ship, joining with the others in the military songs, his imagination had been fired by notions of heroic death. If an enemy warship were to appear, he had thought, and sink their ship with a shot . . . if he were destined to be a corpse drifting among the weeds on the sea bottom, he would be proud to die in such a way. At the battle of Chin Chou, crouching low amid the death-dealing rattle of machine guns, he had gone bravely forward. Though there were times when he had been horri-fied at the bloodshed, the suffering of his comrades, he had felt that it was all for the motherland, all for honor. But the blood of his comrades was not his blood. Face to face with his own death the bravest soldier panicked.

His legs were heavy and weary. He felt sick. The thirty-mile journey—two days on the road, and a bitterly cold night in the open—had certainly played havoc with his already disordered system. The dysentery was gone, but the mild beriberi had become acute. He knew what that might mean . . . paralysis of the heart. He shuddered at the thought. Was there no way of escape at all? He wept aloud as he walked, his nerves on edge, his body shaking, his legs racked with cramp.

The plain was at peace. Now that the huge red sun was about to sink beneath the horizon one half of the sky was gold, the other a dark, deep blue. A speck of cloud, like a bird whose wings were tipped with gold, drifted across the sky. The shadows of the cane merged with the general shadow, and across the vast plain blew the autumn wind. Only a few minutes ago the guns from Liaoyang had been rumbling steadily and distinctly, but now they too had dwindled imperceptibly to silence.

Two privates were running up behind him.

They continued past for a dozen yards or so. Then one turned and started back.

He pulled himself together. He was ashamed to be seen like this, weeping aloud.

"Hi! What's the trouble?"

"Beriberi."

"That's hard luck. Is it bad?"

"It's pretty painful."

"You *are* in a mess. If beriberi affects your heart it's no joke. How far are you going?"

"My unit's over beyond Anshan, I think."

"You can't get that far today."

"I suppose not."

"Come along with us as far as Hsin-t'ai-tzu. We'll get a doctor to look at you."

"Is it a long way?"

"Just over there. You see that hill? This side of it there's the railroad. Where you see the flag flying, that's the Hsin-t'ai-tzu depot."

His spirits revived. He walked along behind the two of them. They were sorry for him, and they carried his rifle and pack. As they walked in front they talked of the day's fighting at Liaoyang.

"Plenty of reserves moving up, aren't there?"

"We're too few to attack. The enemy positions are pretty strong, I'm told."

"Do you think we'll win?"

"We're in for it if we lose."

"If only we could cut behind them for once."

"We'll do it properly this time. You'll see."

He listened intently to what they said. The guns opened up again in the distance.

The supply depot at Hsin-t'ai-tzu was a scene of tremendous activity and confusion. A regiment of the reserve had arrived, and in the shadow of the buildings above the railroad, alongside the stacks of provisions, were rows and rows of soldiers' caps, rifles, and swords. Five barrack buildings, formerly occupied by the enemy railway guard, flanked the rails. A flag fluttered above the building which now served as the supply depot headquarters, and there the confusion was at its worst. Soldiers were gathered outside it in a dense throng, and in and out, in endless succession, hurried officers with long swords hanging at their sides. Fires were lit beneath the depot's three large rice caldrons, and clouds of smoke curled upwards into the evening sky. In one the rice was already cooked, and the mess sergeant, bellowing commands at his subordinates, was supervising a hasty distribution of rations to the assembled soldiers. But since these three caldrons were obviously insufficient to meet the requirements of a whole regiment, the majority had been issued with a ration of hulled rice in their mess kits and were scattering to various parts of the field to prepare their suppers for themselves. The neighborhood was soon dotted with the flames of hundreds of cane fires.

Near one of the barrack buildings men were settling down to the nightlong labor of loading ammunition boxes on to freight trains bound for the front. Infantrymen and railway troops moved to and fro among the freight cars in feverish, ceaseless activity. A single noncommissioned officer directed their movements, issuing rapid words of command from a perch high on the load of a car.

The day was over, but the war went on. From beyond the dark saddle-shaped mountain of Anshan the sound of guns persisted.

Now that he had arrived he made inquiries about a doctor. But there was something incongruous about asking for a doctor here. This was no time or place for people to stop and concern themselves over the life or death of a single soldier. He managed, thanks to the efforts of his two friends, to get himself a small portion of boiled rice. That was all. We can't do much more now. Just wait a little longer. As soon as this regiment moves on we'll find the doctor and bring him to you. Take things easy and get a rest. If you go straight along the road from here, three or four hundred yards at most, you'll see a big house. You'll recognize it without any trouble—there's a sake stall in the entrance. Go right inside and get some sleep . . . that was all they could suggest.

He was sick to death of walking. He took back his rifle and pack, but when he placed them across his shoulders he almost collapsed beneath the weight. But it was impossible to give up here. If he were going to die, he must die in privacy. Yes, privacy . . . anywhere would do. He longed to enter some quiet place and sleep, and rest.

The dark road went on and on. Here and there he passed groups of soldiers. His mind returned suddenly to the barracks at Toyohashi. He had slipped away to a quiet bar and had drunk solidly. In his drunkenness he had struck a sergeant. They gave him a spell in detention. This really was a long road. There was no sign of anything resembling the house they had described. Three or four hundred yards, they had said. He must have come a thousand yards already. Perhaps he'd missed it. He turned and looked back—in the supply depot he could see the gleam of lamps and watchfires, and dark groups of soldiers moving uncertainly, as though they had lost their way. The shouts of the men at work on the ammunition trains reached him through the night air with startling clarity.

It was secluded here. Not a soul around. Suddenly he felt horribly

sick. Even if there was no house to hide himself in, he thought,
was a good place to die; and he sank to the ground in exhaus
Strangely enough he no longer felt as dejected and miserable as b
fore. No memories came back from the past. The shimmering light
of the stars shone into his eyes. He raised his head and glanced
casually around.

He was surprised to see that a little way before him, somehow
unnoticed till now, was a solitary Western-style house. Inside a lamp
was burning, and he could see a round, red paper lantern hanging
in the doorway. He heard voices.

Sure enough, in the entrance was something which might well be
a sake stall. It was difficult to be certain in the dark, but in one corner of the entrance there appeared to be an object like a stove, with
embers glowing red beneath it. A straggle of smoke curled up,
lightly enfolding the lantern. He could read the writing on the lantern: "Sweet Bean Soup. 5 Sen."

He moved forward to see better. In the darkness at one side of the
entrance he could make out a low stone step. This is the place, he
thought. His first reaction, on realizing that now he might rest, was
a feeling of unutterable content. Silently and stealthily he mounted
the stone step. It was dark inside. He could not be sure, but he
seemed to have entered a corridor. He pushed at what he thought
was the first door, but it would not open. Two or three steps farther
on was another door. He pushed, but again it would not open.

He went farther inside.

The corridor came to an end. There was no turning. Not knowing
what to do next he pressed against the wall on his right, and suddenly the darkness was broken. A door swung back. He could see
nothing inside the room, but stars were shining at him, and he knew
that in front was a glass window.

He set down his rifle, unhitched his pack, and dropped, suddenly,
full length to the floor. He drew a deep, laborious breath. He had
reached his haven of peace.

Beneath the feeling of satisfaction a new uneasiness was advancing
and taking possession of him. Something akin to fatigue, mental
exhaustion, and despair pressed heavily upon his whole being like a

weight of lead. Recollections came in disjointed fragments, sometimes flashing at lightning speed, sometimes growing slowly upon his consciousness with the ponderous insistence of a bullock's breathing.

There were throbbing pains in his calves like those of cramp. He writhed on the floor. His body was nearing the limit of its endurance. He tossed and turned, without knowing what he did.

The pain advanced on him like the tide. It raged with the ferocity of a great wind. He raised his legs and banged them on the hard wooden boards. He rolled his body to this side and to that. "This pain. . . !" Not thinking or knowing what he said he cried aloud.

In reality the pain did not yet seem unbearable. It was severe, but he told himself constantly that he must reserve his strength for the next great pain, and that helped, if only a little, to lessen the suffering of the moment.

He did not think so much how sad it was to die, but rather how best to conquer this pain. The weak, tearful, spiritless despair which gripped him was more than matched by this positive will to resist, which stemmed from his conviction, as a human being, that he had a right to live.

He was beyond knowing how much time had passed. He wished the doctor would come, but he had little leisure to dwell on the thought. New pains gripped him.

Nearby, beneath the floor boards, a cricket was singing. Even as he struggled in agony he said to himself that a cricket was singing. The insect's monotonous note of melancholy sank deep into him.

The cramp was returning. He writhed on the boards.

"This pain, this pain, this pain!"
He screamed the words at the top of his voice.
"This pain! Somebody . . . is there no one here?"
The powerful instinct to resist, to live, had fast dwindled, and he was not consciously calling for assistance. He was almost in a stupor. His outbursts were the rustling of leaves disturbed by forces of nature, the voices of waves, the cries of tragic humanity.
"This pain, this pain!"
His voice echoed startlingly in the silence of the room. In this

room, until a month ago, officers of the Russian railway guard had lived and slept. When Japanese soldiers first entered it they had found a soot-stained image of Christ nailed to the wall. Last winter those officers had looked out through this window at the incessant snowstorms sweeping across the Manchurian plain, and they had drunk vodka. Outside had stood sentries, muffled in furs. They had joked among themselves about the shortcomings of the Japanese army, and they had bragged. In this room, now, sounded the agonized cries of a dying soldier.

He lay still a moment. The cricket was singing the same melancholy, pleasing song. A late moon had risen over the broad Manchurian plain, the surroundings had grown clearer, and the moonlight already illuminated the ground outside the window.

He cried again. Moaning, despairing, he writhed on the floor. The buttons of his blouse were torn away, the flesh on his neck and chest was scratched and bloody, his army cap was crushed, the strap still about his chin, and one side of his face was smeared with vomit.

Suddenly a light shone into the room. In the doorway, like some statue in its niche, he saw a man, a candle in one hand. The man came silently into the room and held the candle above the sick soldier, where he lay twisting and turning on the floor. The soldier's face was colorless, like that of a dead man.

"What's the matter?"

"This pain, this pain!"

The man hesitated to touch the soldier. He stood by his side a while, looking down; then he placed the candle on the table, fixing it firmly in drops of molten wax, and hurried out of the room. Every object in the room stood clearly revealed in the candlelight. He saw that the untidy bundle in the corner of which he had been dimly aware was his own rifle and pack.

The flame on the candle flickered. The wax rolled down like tears.

After a while the man returned, bringing a soldier with him. He had roused one of a unit lodged for the night in a house across the way. The soldier looked at the sick man's face, and glanced around the room. Then he peered closely at the regimental markings on his shoulder.

The sick man could hear everything they said.

"He's from the Eighteenth Regiment."

"Is that so?"

"When did he come in here?"

"I've no idea. I woke about ten to hear someone screaming in pain. I couldn't make it out—there shouldn't have been anyone in the rest of the house. After I'd listened for a while I heard the cries again, getting louder, and I came here to see what was wrong. It's beriberi . . . a heart attack, too. There's nothing anyone can do about it."

"I suppose there's a doctor at the depot?"

"There is, but I doubt whether he'd come so late as this."

The two stood in silence.

The pain came flooding back again. He groaned. Cry followed cry, in unbearable crescendo.

"He's suffering terribly. Where's he from, I wonder?"

He felt the soldier searching in his breast pocket, removing his regimental paybook. He saw the man's dark, strong features, and he watched him walk close to the candle on the table to examine what he had found, his form dark against the light.

He heard the soldier read, every word reaching him distinctly. . . . Private Katō Heisuke, Fukue Village, Atsumi District, Province of Mikawa. Again images of home floated before his eyes. His mother's face, his wife's face, the great house standing amid camphor trees, the slippery rocks on the beach, the blue sea, the faces of the fishermen he had known so well.

The two watchers stood in silence. Their faces were white. From time to time they muttered words of sympathy. He knew now that he was going to die, but the knowledge did not carry with it any particular terror or sadness. He felt that the object which those two were regarding with such anxiety was not himself, but some inanimate thing in which he had no part. If only he could escape from this pain, this intolerable pain!

The candle flickered. The cricket sang on.

At dawn, when the doctor arrived from the depot, the soldier had been dead an hour. He died at about the time that loud cheering

from the depot workers announced the departure of the first ammunition train for Anshan, while the morning moon, pale and wan,
hung in the sky.

Soon the steady rumble of the guns was heard again. It was the
morning of the first of September, and the attack on Liaoyang had
begun.

TRANSLATED BY G. W. SARGENT

THE RIVER SUMIDA

[Sumidagawa, 1909] by Nagai Kafū (born 1879)

The River Sumida is a poetic evocation of Tokyo in 1890, at a time when the old city was gradually being destroyed by the new civilization from the West. Most of the people of the story have been left behind by the changes; Ragetsu, the professional haiku *poet, his sister Otoyo, a teacher of* tokiwazu *(a kind of dramatic recitation to music), and even the boy Chokichi, belong to the disappearing world of the old Tokyo. The author stated that he was stimulated to write* The River Sumida *by* Les Vacances d'un jeune homme sage *(1903), a novel by Henri de Régnier, but the resemblances between the two works are exceedingly slight. Régnier wrote of his book that it was built around little happenings of childhood which, when recollected in later years, "make us smile, as one smiles over the past, with regret and melancholy." This may have been Nagai Kafū's point of departure.*

•

The *haiku* master Ragetsu had decided to pay a summer visit to his younger sister, a teacher of *tokiwazu* in Imado, on the other side of Tokyo. He naturally did not propose to go out in the heat of the day, but when evening came he went to the bamboo fence overgrown with morning-glory by his kitchen door, and bathed himself by dashing a few bucketfuls of water over his body. Still stark naked, he poured himself a drink. By the time that he pushed his dinner tray from him the dusk of a summer evening had darkened into night, and a smoke of mosquito incense rose in all the little houses of the neighborhood. Through the blinds of his windows filled with pots of miniature trees could be heard the sounds of the street—the staccato clatter of geta, workmen humming as they went by, snatches of conversation. Ragetsu, warned by his wife that it was growing late, went out the door, fully intending to go at once to Imado, but being called to from the bench where the old men of the neighborhood were enjoying the cool, he sat down for a moment. Soon he was engaged, as every night, in the idle banter of those who love to talk when slightly drunk.

The days had become exceedingly short, just now when one was beginning to feel that the mornings and evenings were somewhat cooler and pleasanter. The morning-glories grew smaller with each day that passed, and when the western sun poured like burning flame into the little houses, the incessant shrilling of the cicadas dinned more frantically than ever. August was somewhat more than half-gone, and the rustle of the wind blowing through the maize fields behind the house could sometimes be mistaken for the autumn rain. Ragetsu, as a memento of the life of wild dissipation he had led when young, felt pain in the joints of his bones as soon as the seasons were about to change, and was always aware before anyone else of the approach of autumn. At the thought that autumn had come he would grow unaccountably excited.

After several false starts Ragetsu flew into a panic of fear that he might fail to visit his sister altogether, and one evening when the moon, still pure white but almost full, hung in the twilit sky, he set out on foot for Imado.

Following along the canal, he turned sharp left into a narrow lane so meandering that only a person born in the quarter could retain his bearings, circled around the Inari Shrine, and came to the bank of the River Sumida. In some of the filled-in rice fields along the lane stood rows of newly constructed tenements, still empty. In others were nurseries with large garden stones ranged outside the entrances; in others a scattering of thatched houses so rustic one could imagine oneself in the country. Through the cracks in the bamboo fences of some of these houses he could get a glimpse of women bathing themselves in the moonlight, and Ragetsu, whom the years had changed very little, stopped here and there for a peep, always with an innocent air of not looking. For the most part, however, he saw only unexciting housewives, and having looked he would hurry away, a disappointed expression on his face.

By the time he reached the banks of the river it was already growing dark under the cherry trees, and lamps flickered in the houses across the water. Yellow leaves caught in the river-wind were fluttering down in twos and threes. Ragetsu, at his destination at last after his long unbroken walk in the heat, heaved a sigh of relief and began to fan his bare chest. He saw a teashop which had not yet shut for the day, and hurried there. "A cup of cold sake, please," he said, sitting down. In the River Sumida little boats were plying to and fro, their sails swollen with the evening wind. As the surface of the water darkened with the twilight the wings of the seagulls seemed of an extraordinary whiteness.

Ragetsu drained the liquid that the waitress poured into the thick-rimmed glass, and went without further hesitation to board the ferry. Halfway across the river the combination of the cold sake and the rocking of the boat began gradually to affect him. The light of the evening moon as it first touched the leaves of the cherry trees seemed indescribably cool, and the smooth waters of the river in full tide flowed by with pleasant indolence. The *haiku* master shut his eyes and hummed to himself.

When he reached the opposite bank he suddenly remembered that he would have to buy a present, and he looked for a sweetshop in the neighborhood. He crossed Imado Bridge and went down the straight street that leads from it, feeling quite steady on his feet although he actually staggered a bit as he walked.

Here and there a shop sold Imado pottery, the only thing which distinguished, however slightly, this side street from similar ones in any part of the Tokyo suburbs, with their monotonous rows of little, squat houses. In the pale light of the lanterns hanging at the doorways the summer kimonos of people taking the evening cool shone white as they stood talking in the shadows of their houses or by the corners of the alleyways. The streets were hushed; somewhere a dog barked and a baby was crying. Ragetsu came in front of the Imado Hachiman Shrine, where a clump of trees stood tall against the Milky Way in the clear sky, and soon he recognized in the row of lanterns hanging before the houses along the street his sister's, with the words *Tokiwazu Motoji Toyo* written in old-fashioned script. Two or three people had stopped in the street in front of the house and were listening to the lesson going on inside.

The oil lamp, with a clouded glass and a wick turned three-quarters down, hung from a ceiling where mice occasionally scurried by, and shed its feeble light over the room, dimly illuminating the storage cupboard patched with advertisements for patent medicines and pictures of beautiful girls cut from the New Year's supplement of the newspapers, a chest of drawers aged amber in color, and old walls showing stains where the rain had leaked in. It was too dark to tell whether or not there might be a little garden beyond the shabby reed-blinds on the porch, but a bell hanging from the eaves tinkled sadly in the wind and insects hummed softly. Otoyo was seated with her back to an alcove, in which were displayed some potted plants, bought at a temple fair, and a hanging scroll. She held on her knee a samisen which she played, occasionally scratching her forehead with the plectrum. A man of about thirty, with the look of a businessman, was chanting in an alto voice, from a practice-book opened before him, the lovers' journey from *Koina Hambei*: "What shall we say? Now we are too much in love to call each other brother and sister."

Ragetsu sat on the porch twitching his fan, waiting for the lesson to end. Every now and then he would unconsciously begin singing between his teeth, in unison with the man having his lesson, no doubt because the sake had not yet entirely worn off. Sometimes he would shut his eyes and give forth an unrestrained belch, after which he would look innocently at Otoyo's face, lightly rocking his body from one side to the other. Otoyo must be over forty now, and the dim light of the hanging lamp made her thin little body look even older. At the sudden recollection that once, long ago, she had been the adored daughter of a well-to-do pawnbroker, it was not so much an actual emotion of sadness or nostalgia that Ragetsu experienced as an overwhelming astonishment. In those days, after all, he too had been young and handsome, was liked by women, and had led such a life of dissolution that he was eventually disinherited "for all eternity" by his family. The events of those days had now lost all reality and he could think of them only as dreams. His father, who had once struck Ragetsu's head with an abacus; the faithful old family clerk who had remonstrated with him, tears in his eyes; Otoyo's husband, who had discovered her in the pawnshop—all had scowled, laughed, wept, rejoiced, worked themselves into a sweat without complaining, and every one of them was dead now. Really, when one stopped to think of it, it did not make the least difference today whether these people had ever come into the world or not. They would be remembered only as long as he and Otoyo remained alive, and when, one of these days, they too had died, all would have disappeared completely, vanished into smoke.

Otoyo suddenly called to him, "You know, I'd been planning to visit you in a day or two."

After the man having his lesson had run through *Koina Hambei,* he rehearsed once or twice the recitatives from a similar piece and left. Ragetsu, a grave expression on his face, moved inside. He pensively beat his knee with his fan.

"As a matter of fact," Otoyo started again, "I hear the temple in Komagome is going to be torn down because of a change in city districts. That means we'll have to move Father's grave somewhere else. Four or five days ago a man came from the temple, and I was just thinking of coming over to discuss it with you."

"That's right," nodded Ragetsu, "you can't very well neglect a thing like that. Let's see, how many years has it been since the old man died. . . ?"

He leaned his head to one side in thought, but Otoyo relentlessly pursued the subject: how much the rent on a plot of land would be at the Somei cemetery, what sort of gratuity should be given to the temple. She concluded by saying that she would like Ragetsu, who was a man, to take care of everything and relieve her of the responsibility.

Ragetsu had started life as the heir to the Sagamiya, a prosperous pawnshop, but after his disinheritance had led the life of an idle young gentleman. With the death of Ragetsu's stubborn old father, the clerk (who had in the meantime married Otoyo) took over the shop and ran it responsibly. However, the changes that took place after the Meiji Restoration had brought a gradual decline in the family fortunes, and when a fire damaged the shop, the business collapsed. Ragetsu, who had devoted himself to refined pastimes, had no choice but to make a living with his *haiku;* and Otoyo, after the additional misfortune of the death of her husband, came to earn her living as a teacher of *tokiwazu,* thanks to a proficiency in that art which had brought her some celebrity in her girlhood days. Otoyo had an only son who was seventeen this year, and now that she had fallen on evil days, her sole pleasure in life was bound up with the hope of seeing him succeed in life. Bitter experience had taught her that disaster may lurk around the corner for one in business for himself. She had therefore decided that, even if it meant eating only two meals a day, she would some day put her son in a university and make a fine salaried man out of him.

Ragetsu drank the cold tea offered him and asked, "How is Chokichi?"

Otoyo answered with an air of pride, "His school has summer vacation now, but I thought it wouldn't do for him to waste his time, so I'm sending him to night school."

"He doesn't get back till late, I suppose."

"Yes. It's always past ten. There is a streetcar, but it's a long distance."

"Young people today really impress me—they're not at all the way I used to be." Ragetsu broke off this train of thought. "He's at middle school, isn't he? I don't know a thing about the schools nowadays, having no children of my own. Is he still a long way off from the university?"

"After he graduates next year he takes an examination. Then there's another big school before he can go to the university . . ." Otoyo was only too eager to explain everything, but being a woman quite ignorant of what was going on in the world, she faltered.

"It must be a terrible expense."

"Yes. I can tell you, it's all I can do to keep up with it. It's one yen a month for tuition alone, and what with books and all those examinations, you can't get by for less than two or three yen. And besides, he needs Western clothes, a summer suit and a winter suit both. Do you know he wears out two pairs of shoes a year?"

Otoyo, warming to her subject, laid heavy emphasis on her words as if to lend increased urgency to the description of her troubles. Ragetsu thought to himself, "If it's such a hardship, I should think Chokichi could find some way of making a living more in keeping with their means, even if she doesn't send him to the university." But he did not feel this strongly enough to voice it. He searched instead for some way of changing the subject, and naturally enough thought of Oito, the girl who had been Chokichi's playmate when he was a child.

"Let's see, Chokichi is seventeen—Oito must be a big girl now. Does she come to you for lessons?"

"No, she doesn't. She goes every day to Mr. Kineya down the street. I hear she'll soon be appearing in Yoshicho." Otoyo broke off as if she were thinking of something.

"Yoshicho? That's splendid. She was always a good girl, and very clever even when she was just a little thing. It'd be nice if she came over tonight. Wouldn't it, Otoyo?" The *haiku* master had grown more cheerful.

Otoyo knocked the ashes out of her pipe and answered, "It's different now. Chokichi, after all, is in the midst of his studies."

Ragetsu laughed. "You mean there mustn't be any mistakes? Yes, that's so. His is one career in which you can't afford to be careless."

"You're right." Otoyo thrust forward her chin. "It may only be a mother's prejudice, but to tell the truth I've been terribly worried about Chokichi."

"Well, then, you must tell me about it," Ragetsu said, striking his knees with lightly clenched fists. Otoyo had become very disturbed about Chokichi and Oito. The reason was, as she related, that Oito never failed to stop by every morning on her way back from her singing lesson, even when she had nothing to stop for. Chokichi would always wait for her, not budging from the window until she appeared. Moreover, when Oito was taken sick for ten days some time ago, Chokichi had behaved so distractedly that an outsider would have found him positively comical. All this Otoyo related without so much as pausing to draw breath.

Just as the clock in the next room was striking nine, the lattice door was flung open. Otoyo knew at once by the way the door was opened that Chokichi had returned. Abruptly breaking off her story, she called to him, "You're very early this evening."

"The teacher was sick and they let us go home an hour early."

"Your uncle has come."

His answer could not be heard, but from the next room came the sound of a parcel being thrown down, and a moment later Chokichi poked his gentle, weak, pallid face through the door.

2

For a while the late August sunset shone more intensely even than at the height of summer: the broad band of the river's surface was aflame, and the light was reflected dazzlingly from the white-painted boards of the university boathouse. Suddenly, as if a lamp had gone out, everything turned a dull gray, and only the sails of the cargo boats gliding over the swelling evening tide still glowed a pure white. Quickly, so quickly that there was not time to see, the early autumn twilight had become night, as though with the dropping of a curtain. In the harsh glare from the water the figures of the people aboard the ferryboat were dyed an inky black, with the bold relief of a monochrome. The long row of cherry trees on the opposite bank seemed of an almost terrifying blackness. The cargo boats which for a while had been plying to and fro in long chains, as if deliberately to create a charming effect, had disappeared all at once in the direction of the upper reaches of the river, and now there were only little fishing boats, back perhaps from the open sea, which floated here and there like leaves in the water. The River Sumida, as far as one could see, was again calm and lonely through all its expanse. Far off, in a corner of the sky upriver, a bank of cloud that still showed traces of summer was rising, and again and again lightning flashed in thin streaks.

Chokichi for the last hour or so had been wandering idly, now leaning on the railing of the Imado Bridge, now walking down from the stone embankment to the ferry slip, watching the river change from evening to dusk and from dusk to night. He had promised to meet Oito on the Imado Bridge tonight as soon as it was too dark to distinguish people's faces. Unfortunately, it happened to be a Sunday, which meant that he could not offer his mother the excuse of going to night school, and no sooner had he swallowed the last mouthful of dinner than he dashed out of the house, though the sun had not yet set. When he first arrived people were hurrying to and from the ferry, but now there was almost no one, and the lights of the cargo boats that anchor for the night under the bridge trembled in the water, just where the tall trees of a temple were reflected. A samisen could be heard from a newly built house that had a willow by its gate, and outside the lattice doors of the little houses along the water, the owners were beginning to come out, half-naked, to enjoy the cool. Chokichi stared intently over the bridge, thinking that it was time for Oito to be coming.

The first figure to cross the bridge was a priest in a black hempen robe. Then came a man in rolled-up trousers and rubber shoes, followed a few minutes later by a poorly dressed woman carrying an umbrella and a parcel, who strode by mannishly, kicking up the dust. Then, though he waited a long while, nobody at all. Chokichi, discouraged, turned his tired eyes to the river. The surface of the water was brighter now, and the unpleasant bank of clouds had entirely dissolved. He watched the big reddish moon rise from the trees over the embankment. The sky was clear as a mirror, making the embankment and trees that stood against it seem perfectly black. The evening star alone was visible; the light from the overbright sky blotted out the others. Broken pieces of clouds lay scattered horizontally the length of the sky, shining a translucent silver. Presently, as the full moon rose above the trees, its light was caught by the tile roofs along the river glistening with the night dew, by the stakes wet in the water, the strands of seaweed under the stone embankment lapped by the tide, the sides of the boats, the bamboo punting poles: the whole landscape gave off a pale glow. Chokichi was suddenly aware of how much more sharply now his own shadow was etched on the boards of the bridge. A man and a woman, street singers, passed by him exclaiming, "Just look at the moon!", and stopped for a moment. No sooner had they reached the row of houses on the other bank than they began to sing in insinuating tones, "A student sat on the rail of a bridge"; but realizing, apparently, that it would bring them no money, they hurried off without bothering to finish the song.

Chokichi felt not only the anxiety any lover experiences before a secret meeting and the irritation that comes from weary waiting, but a certain inexpressible sadness. What could the future be for Oito and himself? Leaving the distant future aside, what could their tomorrow be after they met tonight? It had been arranged that Oito should go tonight to a geisha house in Yoshicho to discuss plans, and she had promised Chokichi to walk there with him and talk on the way. If Oito were really to become a geisha now, they could no longer meet every day as they had. That was not the worst of it—he could not help feeling that everything was at an end, quite as if she were going off to some unknown, distant country from which she would never return. He would always remember the moon tonight. Chokichi was quite certain that one could not see such a moon twice in one lifetime. Many, many memories of every kind flashed through his mind like lightning. When they had attended elementary school they used at first to quarrel almost every day, but soon the other students were teasing them by linking their names on all the fences and walls of the neighborhood. His uncle would take them to see the circus; or they would throw crumbs to the carp in the pond.

Oito danced one year on the stage at the Sanja festival. She often danced too on the boats that took the neighborhood on the annual excursions to gather sea shells. On the way back from school they would meet almost daily in the grounds of a temple, and walk through the rice fields on the road they alone knew. . . . Ah, why should Oito become a geisha? He wanted to stop her; he had resolved to prevent her from becoming a geisha, by force if necessary, only to realize on second thought that he could by no stretch of the imagination show such authority towards Oito. He felt at once hopeless despair and resignation. Oito was fifteen, two years younger than

himself, but of late, and particularly today, Chokichi had been unable to shake off the feeling that she was far older. From the first
Oito had been stronger than Chokichi, and not nearly so cowardly.
Even when the other students had made fun of them by sketching
them together on the walls it had not bothered her in the least. She
had shouted back at those who teased her, "Yes, Chokichi is my husband!" It was Oito who last year had proposed that they meet every
day on the way back from school, and Oito who suggested that they
see a play together from the gallery. When they returned late at
night she was never afraid, and even when they lost their way on
some unfamiliar street, she would be the one to say, "Let's see how
far we can go. All we have to do is ask a policeman." She would
walk blithely on, as if it were a delightful adventure.

There was a loud clatter of geta on the wooden bridge as Oito
suddenly ran up. "I'm late, I'm sure. I don't like the way Mother's
done my hair." She straightened a side-lock disarranged by her running. "It looks funny, doesn't it?"

Chokichi could only stare at her in surprise. She looked high-
spirited and full of fun as always, but under the circumstances he
found this somehow displeasing. He was filled with things he
wanted to say—"don't you feel the least bit sorry at going away and
becoming a geisha"—but the words did not come from his mouth.
Oito, apparently oblivious to the crystalline moonlight shining in
the water of the river, began to walk briskly. "Let's hurry. Tonight
I'm rich. I'm going to buy a present."

"You'll come back for sure tomorrow, won't you?" Chokichi
blurted out, almost stammering in his distress.

"If not tomorrow then certainly the morning of the day after. I
have to go back home to get my clothes and all kinds of things."

They were passing through a narrow alley. She asked, "Why don't
you say something? What's the matter?"

"When you come back the day after tomorrow you'll be going off
again for good. Yes. You'll become one of them. You won't be able
to see me anymore."

"I'll come back sometimes to visit you. But I'll have to practice
very hard."

There was a slight cloudiness in her tone, but it was not pathetic enough to satisfy Chokichi. He said after a while, "Why are you becoming a geisha?"

"Oh, there you go asking that again. Don't be silly, Chokichi."

Oito repeated in great detail to Chokichi facts which he already knew only too well. He had known for two or three years that Oito would become a geisha—no, longer. It had all begun when Oito was seen by a certain lady maintained in a separate establishment in Hashiba. Oito's mother used to do sewing for her to help make ends meet, even while Oito's father, a carpenter, was still alive; and one day the lady said, "You must let me have Oito as my daughter. I will make a wonderful geisha out of her." The lady came, in fact, from a very distinguished geisha house in Yoshicho. At the time, however, Oito's family was not so pressed for money, and they found it too painful to part with their child just when she was at her most captivating age. They decided instead to have her taught music and the other necessary accomplishments while still keeping her under the parental roof. Later, when Oito's father died and her mother was for a time without means of support, the lady in Hashiba had given her the money to open the pastry-shop she now ran. It was thus not merely because of monetary obligation but out of real gratitude for the lady's kindness that it had been decided quite naturally, without anyone's having forced the issue, that Oito should go to Yoshicho. Chokichi was perfectly well acquainted with this whole history, and had not asked simply in order to hear it from Oito. He had hoped that she would adopt a slightly sadder tone in relating it, as if she were sorry to leave him—granted that she had no choice but to go. Chokichi was keenly aware that sooner or later differences of feelings would arise between them which could never be communicated, and this realization brought him an even deeper sadness.

His sadness became quite unbearable when Oito went into the shop arcade to buy a present. She suddenly stopped in the middle of the busy throng, out for the evening cool, and tugged at Chokichi's sleeve. "Chokichi," she murmured, "that's the way I'll be dressed soon, won't it? Gauzy crepe, just like that coat. . . ."

Chokichi turned around to see what she was referring to. A geisha went by, her hair piled high on her head. With her was a distinguished gentleman in crested black silks. Chokichi sighed—when Oito became a geisha, that was the kind of fine gentleman who would hold her hand as they walked together. How many years, he wondered, would it take him to become such a gentleman? His present schoolboy appearance filled him with inexpressible misery; at the same time, he felt that already he was disqualified even to be a simple friend to Oito.

By the time they reached the entrance to the street of Yoshicho with its row of hanging lanterns, Chokichi had lost even the strength necessary to reflect on how hopeless and tragic his situation was—all he could do was stand there absent-mindedly, looking in dumb dismay at the narrow dark street that twisted remotely and mysteriously out of sight.

"It's the first, second, third—fourth gas lamp. You can see, it says 'Matsubaya.' That's the house."

"Well, I'll be going now," Chokichi said, but did not move.

Oito held lightly to his sleeve. Suddenly she drew closer, as if to cajole him, and said, "Tomorrow or the day after. I'm sure we'll see each other when I get back home. Is that all right? I promise. Come to my house."

"Mmm."

Oito seemed to be entirely satisfied by this answer and went off, her geta clattering on the wooden sidewalk, without so much as turning back. Her footsteps sounded to Chokichi as if she were running away from him. A moment later he heard a bell tinkle at a lattice door. Chokichi unconsciously started to follow Oito down the street, but just then the door of the house nearest him opened. There were voices, and a man carrying a long paper lantern emerged. Nothing actually happened, but Chokichi quite lost heart, and he was so loath to be seen that he ran all the way to the main street. The round moon had become much smaller, and its clear light was pale; high above the roofs of the storehouses along the quiet narrow streets it climbed, in a sky full of stars.

3

Rising later and later, the moon every night grew steadily more luminous. One felt the dampness of the river wind ever more sharply, and it became unpleasantly chilly for a summer kimono. Before long the moon, rising too late, went unobserved. Morning, noon, and night, the sky was always full of clouds, which moved perpetually, in great heavy banks, sometimes covering the whole sky except for a few rifts of dark blue, which seemed deliberately left exposed. The weather turned oppressively humid, and a greasy clamminess clung to the skin. But even in such weather, a wind of uncertain strength and direction was quite likely to spring up, and rain fell intermittently, stopping only to start again. There was in this wind and rain a special mysterious power which transmitted a music never heard in spring or summer to the temple trees, to the reeds on the riverbanks, and to the shingled roofs of the slums stretching away to the edges of the city. Sunset came so early it was startling, and the long nights deepened at once into silence. The temple bell at eight or nine o'clock, which in summer often could not be heard for the clatter of people strolling in the evening cool, now brought a midnight hush to the vicinity. Crickets chirped frantically. The lamplight took on an unpleasant brightness. Autumn. Chokichi, for the first time, felt keenly that autumn was just as hateful as people said, that it really was unbearably lonely.

School had begun a few days before. Chokichi left the house early in the morning, his books wrapped together with the lunch packet his mother had prepared, but by the second or third day he lost the energy to walk all the way to Kanda. In previous years he had missed the schoolroom as the long summer vacation drew to a close, and had waited with some impatience for the beginning of classes. That boyish emotion now disappeared completely. What was the use of studying? School was not the place to give him the happiness he desired. Chokichi felt with an intuitive flash that school was something quite unrelated to his happiness.

On the morning of the fourth day of school Chokichi left the house before seven, as usual, and walked as far as the grounds of the

Kannon Temple. He sat heavily on a bench next to the main building, like an exhausted traveler on a wayside stone. No dirty scraps
of paper littered the dewy gravel walks; probably they had just been
swept; and instead of the usual bustle, the temple grounds seemed
wondrously spacious, silent, and holy in the early morning light.
Several shifty-looking men who appeared to have spent the night in
the temple corridors still sat there. One of them had untied the sash
of a filthy kimono and was nonchalantly adjusting his loincloth. The
sky was gray with low-hanging clouds, usual at this time of year,
and worm-eaten leaves, still green, kept drifting down from the trees.
Calls of crows and roosters and the beating of pigeon wings sounded
crisp and clear. The stone ablution basin, wet by overflowing water,
already seemed somehow cold in the shadow of the fluttering cloth
offerings. The men and women who came for morning worship
nevertheless stopped to wash their hands in the basin before climbing the steps to the temple. Among them Chokichi noticed a young
geisha with a pink handkerchief held in her mouth, who, as she
washed her white hands, apparently afraid of wetting her coat, held
them out so far that he could see her forearms. He heard one of the
students sitting on the next bench say, "Look! A *sänger*.[1] Not bad."

The slight figure with delicately sloping shoulders, the hair tied in
a *shimada,* the round face with its firm-set mouth, her fifteen or sixteen years—everything recalled Oito so much that Chokichi nearly
leapt from his bench. Oito had kept the promise she made the night
the moon was so lovely. She returned home two days later to fetch
her personal belongings, for she was now to reside permanently in
Yoshicho. Chokichi was amazed—Oito had changed so much that
she looked an entirely different person. Suddenly, in the space of a
single day, the girl in a plain sash of red muslin had blossomed into
a geisha, like the one he had just seen washing her hands. Already
she displayed a ring on her finger, and time and time again, quite
unnecessarily, she pulled her mirror and purse from her sash to
powder her face or smooth a vagrant wisp of hair into place. She
had kept a rickshaw waiting for her outside the door, and left after

[1] Then as now Japanese schoolboys were fond of using foreign words; *sänger* is used
to mean "geisha."

spending scarcely an hour with Chokichi, as if some extremely urgent business occupied her. Her parting words were to ask Chokichi to convey her regards to his mother. He did, it is true, hear her say in the tone he loved that she would come see him soon. Chokichi interpreted this not as a guileless promise, of the kind she had always made, but rather as the adroit flattery of an experienced woman. The girl Oito, his childhood sweetheart Oito, no longer breathed in this world. Behind her rickshaw, drawn so briskly that the dogs sleeping by the roadside were startled, lingered the scent of her face powder. It reached his nostrils with almost oppressive poignance.

The young geisha emerged from the temple after worshiping and lightly tripped towards the Nio Gate. Chokichi's eyes followed her, and he recalled that bitter moment when Oito's rickshaw had pulled away. He rose from the bench in anguish, as if incapable of enduring more. Mechanically he followed the girl to the end of the row of shops, where she disappeared into a side street. The shopkeepers were busy sweeping and arranging their merchandise. Chokichi, hardly knowing what he did, walked quickly in the direction of the Thunder Gate. It was not that he was hoping to find out where the young geisha had gone: he was pursuing an image of Oito which his eyes alone could detect. He had completely forgotten about school. After much wandering he saw at last in the distance the roof of the Meiji Theatre, and soon afterwards heard the distant whistle of a river steamboat. At that moment a terrible fatigue seized him. Not only was his forehead wet with perspiration under his school-cap, his whole body was soaked. But he could not bear to rest even for an instant, and at last he located the entrance to the street where he had been led the night of the moon.

One side of the street was lit by the morning sun, and Chokichi could now see the whole block from one end to the other. It did not consist entirely of little houses with latticework fronts; when seen by day there was also a quite surprising number of tall storehouses, and a board fence surmounted by spikes, above which pine branches were visible. He could also see the lime-sprinkled entrance of a public lavatory, boxes of rubbish neatly stacked for disposal, and cats wandering around the area. There was an unusually large number of people in the street, twisting away from one another as they passed on the narrow wooden sidewalks. A sound of talking intermingled with samisen practice, and he could also hear the splash of water from somebody's laundering. A short woman in a red undergarment with the skirt hitched up was sweeping the sidewalk with a grass broom, and another woman was energetically polishing the lattice-work in a door, spoke by spoke. Chokichi was taken aback by all these people and asked himself for the first time what he would do when once he had ventured into the street. He had thought of stealing by in front of the Matsubaya, and attempting to get a glimpse of Oito through the fence, but the spot was too exposed for him to escape notice. In that case, he wondered, should he continue to stand at the entrance to the street in the hope that Oito might go out on some errand? But this too was difficult—Chokichi felt as if the shop-keepers were all watching him, and he could not remain there even five minutes more. Just then an old peddler emerged from a side street, beating wooden clappers and trailed by the children of the neighborhood. Chokichi walked into the street from which the man had come. He needed some time to think.

Chokichi followed the street along its meandering course to the river. One thing was clear to him: it was most unlikely that he would meet Oito, no matter how long he waited. And it was too late now for him to go to school. If, on the other hand, he decided to take the day off, there was the problem of how and where to spend the time until three in the afternoon. His mother knew the school schedule by heart, and if Chokichi were to return an hour early or late, she would worry and immediately ask him bothersome questions. Chokichi was sure, of course, that he could easily talk his way out of the situation, but he found it extremely distasteful to suffer the pangs of conscience for such a minor offense. He was approaching the river now and could see the wooden bathhouses at the swimming place being dismantled and people fishing in the shade of the willow trees. Four or five passers-by had stopped and were idly watching the fishermen. Chokichi, thinking this was very opportune, went up to the men and pretended to be watching too.

He squatted down, lacking even the strength to stand, his back against the prop of a willow tree.

The sky had almost entirely cleared, and the humid autumn sun, shining with glaring brightness on the broad river, seemed intense enough to scorch the skin, despite the wind. There seemed to be a wonderful coolness to the shade from the thick cluster of branches that hung over the earthen wall along one side of the street, and an old man who sold sweet wine put down his gaily painted box and rested there. The tiled roofs of the rows of houses across the river, and everything else in the landscape, seemed depressingly dirty, no doubt because of the harsh intensity of the light. The rows of clouds hung motionless in layers, lower than the factory chimneys pouring forth volumes of smoke. The clock struck eleven in the little hut to the rear where they sold fishing equipment. As Chokichi counted the strokes he realized to his surprise how long a time he had spent walking. He felt relieved: at this rate it would not be difficult to pass the time until three o'clock. He noticed that one of the fishermen had begun to eat his lunch, and Chokichi opened his own packet. But he felt uneasy after he had opened it, as if someone were watching him. Fortunately, now that it was almost noon, no strollers remained on the river bank. Chokichi swallowed down the rice, the vegetables, and the rest as quickly as possible. The fishermen were silent as statues, and the man who sold wine dozed where he sat. In the hour after noon the riverside was stiller than ever. Even dogs ceased to stir. Why, Chokichi wondered, should he feel so bad and be such a coward? It seemed so ridiculous.

After taking a turn between Ryogoku Bridge and the New Bridge, Chokichi made up his mind finally to go back to Asakusa. He again approached the entrance to Yoshicho, drawn by a "perhaps" into which he put his whole heart. He was relieved to see that not so many people were in the street as in the morning, and, all fear and trembling, he steeled himself to walk by the Matsubaya. The interior of the house was extremely dark, and he could not even hear voices or the sound of a samisen. But simply having passed in front of his sweetheart's house, Chokichi felt such satisfaction at this almost unprecedented act that he ceased to regret the fatigue and suffering that all his wanderings had brought him.

4

Somehow or other Chokichi managed during the rest of the week to attend school, but the following Monday on his way there he suddenly got off the streetcar. He had not succeeded in solving a single one of the algebra problems which the teacher assigned. Nor had he prepared his Chinese classics or his English. Worst of all, and this was why he left the streetcar, today there was to be gymnastics, the thing which he loathed and dreaded most in the whole world. Such stunts as hanging upside down from an iron bar or leaping from a ledge higher than himself were quite impossible for Chokichi, however much the instructor, an ex-army sergeant, bullied him, however much the whole class mocked. Chokichi could not keep up with the other students in sports, whatever the variety, and he was compelled to endure their derisive hoots. Nobody in his class could approach Chokichi when it came to drawing or calligraphy, but he was by temperament inclined in a quite different direction from the world of parallel bars, jujitsu, and Japanese spirit. Ever since he was a small child he had loved to hear the samisen his mother played all day long to make her living, and he learned, without having studied how, to tune the strings. It was enough for him to hear a popular song once for him to memorize it. His uncle had been quick to recognize that the boy possessed the qualities necessary for becoming a master of the samisen, and had suggested to Otoyo that Chokichi be sent to study with some first-rate teacher. She had not only flatly refused, but vehemently prohibited Chokichi from ever touching a samisen again.

Had Chokichi been allowed to study the samisen, as his uncle Ragetsu had suggested, by now he certainly would have attained at least average proficiency, and he would have been spared the painful experience he was now undergoing. What had happened was truly irreparable. Chokichi felt that his whole life had been pointed in the wrong direction. Suddenly he felt a wave of hatred for his mother, and as his resentment for her mounted, he felt a longing for his uncle so strong that he would have liked to cling to him. Now that Chokichi had tasted the sufferings of love, he began to be able to interpret with a new meaning the stories which he had so often heard—and always with complete indifference—from his mother and even from his uncle himself about his uncle's career of debauchery. Chokichi recalled that his aunt, then a great courtesan had asked his uncle's help when the women of the Yoshiwara houses were released after the Meiji Restoration. His aunt had also been extremely fond of Chokichi when he was a little boy, but his mother did not seem to like her; Otoyo sometimes betrayed only too plainly that even to exchange greetings twice a year was a distasteful obligation. This recollection stirred up more unpleasant and resentful thoughts about his mother. Chokichi felt an unbearable constraint in a mother's love which seemed to keep such close watch over his every action. Once his aunt had said to Oito and himself in a voice filled with the warmest tenderness, "You must always stay friends." If only his mother were like her, she would quickly guess why he was suffering and show him sympathy. She would not force on him a kind of happiness which he did not in the least desire. Chokichi found himself comparing the attitudes of a respectable woman like his mother with those of a woman with a past like his aunt. He then compared his schoolteacher with his uncle Ragetsu.

These were the thoughts that filled Chokichi's head as he lay sprawled out in the park. Afterwards he took out the novel which he had hidden in his lunch packet and immersed himself in it. The thought occurred to him that he must somehow steal his mother's seal to affix to the excuse for absence he would have to offer at school the following day.

5

Weeks of virtually uninterrupted rain were followed by a few days of blue skies unmarked by a single cloud. When the clouds returned they were accompanied by a wind that would suddenly whirl through the dust on the streets. The wind and the cold grew sharper each day, and the doors and windows, shut tight now, began their incessant, gloomy rattling. Chokichi had to get up every morning by six at the latest in order to arrive on time at school, which began at seven. His six o'clock rising was in murkier darkness every day, and finally he had to use a lamp, just as if it were the middle of the night. The mere sight of the dull yellow flame of the lamp on an early winter's morning sufficed to infuse Chokichi with a sense of melancholy. His mother always got up earlier than Chokichi, apparently as a means of encouraging him, and shivering in her night clothes would prepare a hot breakfast. Chokichi appreciated her kindness, but it did not lessen his craving for more sleep. And if he attempted to linger an extra moment by the stove, his mother, who had eyes for nothing but the clock, would nag at him until he went grumbling out into the cold streets whipped by the river wind. Sometimes her excessive solicitude irritated him. He would deliberately untie his muffler because she had cautioned him about it, even if it meant catching a cold.

Chokichi dully compared this year's winter with last year's, and last year's with that of the year before. As he went back over the years, it came to him with startling clarity how much of happiness he had lost by growing up. When he was still a child, before he went to school, he could stay in bed as long as he wanted on cold mornings. Besides, he did not feel the cold so much. As a matter of fact, he used to jump out of bed joyfully when there was a cold wind or rain. But now that he was grown up, how disagreeable he found it to walk across Imado Bridge early in the morning when there was still white frost on the ground, and how sad the harsh red of the sun seemed as the sun sank early on winter afternoons behind old trees where the wind was always howling. What new sufferings would each year to come inflict on him? Never had the quick passing of the days seemed so melancholy as this December. The annual fair had already started at the Kannon Temple, and the bags of sugar which his mother's pupils brought her as New Year presents were stacking up. The mid-term examination was over, and a note from his teacher concerning Chokichi's bad marks had already reached his mother.

Chokichi had been resigned all along to receiving bad marks. He listened in silence, his head drooping, as his mother lectured him. It was her usual sentimental speech, the one she delivered apropos of anything at all: she and Chokichi had no one in the world to depend on but each other. It was the time of day when she had the most leisure for such lectures; the little girls who came for morning lessons had left, and there would be no other pupils until three in the afternoon, when girls returning from school would call. Along the windless streets the winter sun glittered on every window. They sat in silence. A girl's voice called from outside the lattice door in lively tones, "Good afternoon." Chokichi's mother stood in surprise. Almost at once the words came from the hall, "It's me. I've come to apologize for having neglected you so."

Chokichi trembled. It was Oito. She came in, unfastening her beautiful serge coat.

"Oh, Chokichi, you're here too. Today must be a holiday at school." She laughed, enchanted at the idea. Next she bowed politely to Otoyo, and murmured, "How have you been? It is really so difficult for me to get out nowadays. Otherwise I would never have been so neglectful."

Oito produced a box of cakes wrapped in a piece of silk. Chokichi stared dumbly at Oito, stupefied. His mother thanked Oito for the present in somewhat embarrassed tones, adding, "You've become so pretty. I hardly recognize you."

"I've aged terribly. Everybody says so." Oito gave a charming smile, and took from her sash a velvet cigarette case. "I smoke cigarettes now. Shocking of me, isn't it?" This time she laughed a little loudly.

"Come over next to me. It's cold," Otoyo said, taking the iron kettle off the brazier and putting in some tea. "When do you become a full-fledged geisha?"

"Not yet. Not till after I've been there quite a while."

"I'm sure you'll be popular. You're pretty and you've had good training."

"Thanks to you," Oito said. "They're very pleased with me. Some girls, even much bigger than I, don't know anything about music."

Otoyo took a cake dish from the cupboard, as if she had suddenly recalled something. "I'm sorry I haven't anything better to offer you, but these cakes are rather unusual." She picked one up with her chopsticks and offered it to Oito.

"Good afternoon, teacher," two little girls piped in a high-pitched monotone at the door.

"Please don't bother about me," said Oito.

Chokichi felt curiously ill at ease, and kept his eyes averted, but Oito whispered, as if nothing had changed between them, "Did you get my letter?"

In the next room the two little girls were singing something about the cherry blossoms of Omuro. Chokichi nodded and fidgeted in his place. Oito had sent him a letter a few weeks before, to say that she couldn't manage to leave the house. Chokichi had replied at once with a letter describing in detail everything that had happened to him since they parted. The kind of answer he had hoped for from Oito never came.

"Let's go to the fair at the Kannon Temple. I'm allowed to spend tonight at home."

Chokichi could not answer because his mother was in the next room. Oito, unperturbed, continued, "When you've eaten dinner, come call for me." Then, after a pause, "I suppose your mother will come along."

"Yes." Chokichi's voice had lost its strength.

Oito had a sudden recollection. "Do you remember how your uncle got drunk and had a fight with the old man who sold souvenirs? When was that? I was so frightened. I wish he could come tonight."

Oito took advantage of a break in the lesson to say good-bye to Otoyo. "I'll see you this evening. I'm sorry to have bothered you." So saying, she tripped off.

6

Chokichi caught a cold. Instead of taking proper care of it, he made an effort to attend school the first day after the winter vacation, and thereby caused his cold to develop into influenza, which was very prevalent. He spent the rest of January in bed.

The big drum of the First Horse Day festival at the Hachiman Shrine had been booming since early in the morning. Sometimes the shadow of a little bird skimming over the eaves twinkled over the front windows, where the warm, mild afternoon sunshine poured in. It was bright enough to see inside the dim Buddhist altar in the corner of the sitting-room. The plum blossoms in the alcove had already begun to scatter. Spring was paying its joyous visit to this dark, shut-up house.

Chokichi had been up and out of bed for two or three days, and felt strong enough to go for a walk in the sunshine. Now that he had recovered, the serious illness which had brought him twenty days of suffering seemed to Chokichi an absolute godsend. He had felt all along that he had no chance whatsoever of passing the examination the following month, and the enforced absence caused by his sickness furnished him now with a most plausible excuse to offer his mother if he failed.

He found himself walking behind Asakusa Park. Along the narrow street was a gaping ditch, beyond which he could see under sparse, wintry-looking trees the dirty row of the backs of the shooting galleries. Sinister-looking rickshaw coolies loitered about the street, always quick to cluster behind any passer-by whose appearance was the least prepossessing, with invitations to board their rickshaws. Chokichi walked as far as a crossroads where he could see the stone bridge where a policeman always stood, and all the way beyond to Awaji Temple. Some people had stopped in the street and were staring up at the Miyato Theatre. Chokichi also looked at the brightly illustrated signboards.

Just when Chokichi was beginning to think that he ought to look for some shelter from the cold wind—warm though the weather was, spring had after all only just begun—he noticed the narrow entrance to the gallery and went in. He climbed a staircase with broken steps. Halfway up, at the turning, it became dark, and a foul, tepid air descended from the crowd in the darker recesses above. There were frequent shouts from the audience acclaiming the actors, and

Chokichi, hearing them, felt the special pleasure and excitement that only a theatregoer who has grown up in a city can experience. He raced up the steps two or three at a time, and pressed his way into the crowd. The gallery, under the low sloping roof, was like the bowels of an ocean liner. The light given off by the naked gas lamps at the back of the theatre was cut off by the heads of the densely packed spectators. From the front rail of the gallery, where the standees were penned in like monkeys in a cage, the stage looked very small and remote because of the smoky, discolored air; the ceiling in contrast seemed extraordinarily big. The stage had just finished revolving, to the accompaniment of the beat of wooden clappers. Dirty cloths of a light blue were spread out under a platform on which stood a singularly angular stone fence. On the backdrop the lacquered gate of a daimyo's mansion was depicted in miniature. The whole expanse of sky above the gate was painted an unrelieved black in the almost painful attempt to convince the audience that the scene took place at night. Chokichi, convinced from his experience at the theatre that the combination of "night" and "river" certainly meant a murder scene, stood on tiptoe, his neck craned in youthful curiosity. Just as he expected, the dull rumble of the drum was suddenly punctuated by a rapping on the stage, and there emerged from the shadows around a hut to the left, loudly quarreling, a man dressed as a servant and a woman. The audience laughed. One of the actors, pretending to be searching for something he had dropped, picked up a sheet of paper, and suddenly assuming a quite different attitude, began to read the cast of characters of the play. It was entitled *The Evening Moon Amidst the Plum and Willow Trees*. The announcement was greeted by eager shouts from the audience. At a signal given by another light beating of the clappers, a man in black drew back a curtain to the right, revealing three chanters in formal costumes and two samisen players, crowded together on a little dais. The samisens began to play immediately, and then were joined by the voices of the chanters. Such music had been Chokichi's delight from childhood days, and not even the screams of a baby somewhere in the theatre or the voices of people shushing it could prevent him from catching perfectly the words that were chanted and the accents of the samisen.

"On a misty night when two or three stars are shining, and four or five times sounds the bell, should someone come pursuing me . . ."

Again there was a drumming. Every face in the audience was aglow with excitement now, and some spectators were carried away to the point of shouting. A courtesan in a red underrobe with a wide neckband of purple satin rushed out on the *hanamichi* [2] towards the stage, hunched over, and covered her face with a handkerchief.

"Down in front!" "Take off your hat!" "Damn you!" the shouts resounded.

"Fleeing, but she knows not where, pursued more closely than meshes in a fishing-net . . ."

The actor made up as a prostitute reached the end of the *hana-michi* and, looking back over his shoulder, recited some dialogue. Then followed a song.

"If you would come to me in secret, come by moonlight. Tonight no hindrance of a cloud will blot the moon. O tedious evening of waiting, all will be well, all will be well tonight. The fortuneteller said the clouds would swiftly pass away, and in the shining moonlight, face to face . . ."

The audience was again in an uproar. A lamp had been lit in an enormous round hole cut in the center of the black sky of the backdrop, and the cloud-shaped objects in the air were tugged out of sight on strings which were plainly visible to the audience. The moon was so excessively large and luminous that it seemed much nearer than the daimyo's mansion on the backdrop. But this did not in the least destroy the beautiful illusion for Chokichi or anyone else in the audience. When he remembered the big, round moon he had gazed at from Imado Bridge at the end of last summer while waiting for Oito, the stage was no longer a stage.

A haggard man in torn clothes and with disheveled hair walked out on the stage, his legs trembling as with exhaustion. He passed a woman, and turned to look at her face. "Izayoi, is it you?"

[2] A raised passageway which goes from the back of the theatre through the audience to the stage.

The woman clung to the man. "I have wanted so much to see you again!"

The spectators shouted, "Look at the two of them!" "Go to it!" "We're jealous!" Bursts of laughter. And, from more romantically inclined people, "Quiet!"

The stage revolved as the lovers leapt into the water, and the set reverted to that of the first scene. The woman had been saved by being caught in a fishing net, and the man was crawling up the embankment from the river, unable to yield himself to death. The plot was thickened with new complications. There were bawdy songs, expressions of envy for the rich and mighty and of joy to be still alive, examples of the curious workings of destiny, and a murder: with that the first act ended. A terrifyingly shrill voice screamed almost at Chokichi's ear, "Next show!" The audience began to move in surging waves towards the exits.

Chokichi walked quickly after leaving the theatre. It was still light, but the sun was no longer shining. The curtains and flags of the little shops were flapping wildly. Chokichi stooped and peeped into a shop to see the time, but inside the low-roofed building it was pitch dark. He walked ever faster, afraid of the night wind after his illness. But when he caught a glimpse of the expanse of the River Sumida spread out beyond Imado Bridge, he could not help pausing a moment. The surface of the river shone a melancholy gray, and a vapor misted over the opposite bank, hastening the close of the winter's day. A few seagulls glided in and out among the sails of the cargo boats. Chokichi thought there was something terribly sad about a flowing river. A lamp or two had been lighted on the opposite embankment. Withered trees, crumbling stone walls, dusty tile roofs—everything that met his eyes had a faded, cold color which brought back to him all the more vividly the bright figures on the stage. Chokichi envied the characters in the play so much that he almost hated them, and he bewailed his own fate. He was certain he would never attain such happiness. He thought that he would be better off dead, only to remember all the more bitterly that no one was willing to die with him.

As he started across Imado Bridge a wind from the river struck his face rudely, like a fist. He shivered with the cold, and this movement, to his surprise, brought from his throat a snatch of song which he could not remember having learned: *"To speak more were folly . . ."*

It was a phrase of a melodic beauty unique to the *kiyomoto* [3] style. Chokichi did not, of course, sing with the vigor of a chanter who throws his whole body into the music, nor as loud. The melody poured softly from his throat, and Chokichi felt as if it soothed a little the uncontrollable pangs in his heart. *"To speak more were folly . . ."* Chokichi kept repeating this phrase until he reached the front gate of his house.

7

He went again the following afternoon to the Miyato Theatre. Chokichi yearned for the intoxication of that sensation of pathos he had experienced for the first time the previous day when he saw the beautiful scene in which the two lovers, hand in hand, sighed out their love. He felt an almost intolerable longing for the excitement of the theatre itself, for the murky second balcony hemmed in by the blackened ceiling and walls, for the lights and the crowd. Chokichi felt at times a sadness and a loneliness which he could not explain, and it was not only occasioned by the lost Oito. He himself had not the least idea of the cause. He knew only that he was lonely, and spent every moment in a frantic search for an indefinable something which would console him in solitude and grief. He felt an overpowering urge to relate the vague sufferings hidden in his breast to a beautiful woman—it did not matter particularly which one—who would answer him in a gentle voice. He sometimes dreamt not of Oito but of some unknown woman he had brushed by in the street—a girl, a geisha, or even a housewife.

Chokichi watched the play for the second time with just as much interest as the previous day. But today he also looked at the people who sat in the boxes. "There are so many women in the world. Why, I wonder, do I never meet even one who is kind to me? Any

[3] A style of dramatic singing somewhat similar to the *tokiwazu* which Otoyo teaches.

one would do. If some woman would only address a kind word to me, I wouldn't brood so much about Oito." The more he thought about Oito the more he longed for something which would diminish his suffering. If he had that something he would not be despondent over his schoolwork and his future.

As he stood there in the crowd of standees, he was startled to have someone tap him on the shoulder. He turned around to face a young man in a felt hat, with thick eyebrows and wearing dark glasses. He was leaning down from the tier above.

"Is that you, Kitchan?"

Chokichi, having said that much, was at a loss to continue, so surprised was he at the great change in Kitchan's appearance. Kitchan was a friend from elementary school who always used to cut Chokichi's hair at his father's barbershop. Now he wore a jacket of Oshima pongee under his coat and a silk handkerchief around his throat. Chokichi caught a strong whiff of perfume as his friend leaned forward to whisper, "I'm an actor now."

Pressed as he was in the crowd, Chokichi could do no more than stand there in dumb astonishment. The scene soon shifted to the mimed action by the river, and the hero of the piece rushed off onto the *hanamichi,* the stolen money thrust into his kimono. At this point the wooden clappers sounded. The curtain started to close, and the same man as the previous day moved through the crowd of standees, shouting, "Next show!" By the time the crowd started to surge toward the narrow exits the curtain had been completely drawn, and a drum was rumbling somewhere backstage. Kitchan caught Chokichi by the sleeve. "Are you going? Why don't you stay for another act?"

A mean-looking man in theatrical livery came to collect the fee for the next act. Chokichi stayed where he was, although rather worried about the time.

Kitchan called, "There's room here. You can sit." He was in the empty back rows under the rear skylight. He waited until Chokichi was next to him before he began with a theatrical gesture to wipe his gold-rimmed glasses with his undersleeve of crepe silk. He said once more, "I'm an actor. I've changed, haven't I?"

"Yes, you have. I didn't recognize you at first."

"Were you surprised?" Kitchan laughed as if overjoyed. "Such as you behold me, I venture to call myself an actor! I'm a new star. I appear again the day after tomorrow. Come and see me, won't you? Go to the stage door and tell them to call Tamamizu."

"Tamamizu?"

"That's right. Tamamizu Saburo." He pulled out his wallet from an inside pocket and showed Chokichi a small visiting card. "You see? Tamamizu Saburo. My name is not Kitchan any more. I'm Tamamizu on the programs."

"It must be fun being an actor."

"Sometimes it's fun, sometimes it's hard work . . . but when it comes to women, I've got nothing to complain about!" Kitchan darted a sidelong glance at Chokichi's face. "Do you play around much with women?"

Chokichi did not answer, feeling it an insult to his manhood to say, "Not yet."

"Do you know a house called the Kajita Palace? It's the best in Tokyo. Let's go there tonight together. You needn't worry about anything. I don't mean to boast, but I'm not exactly a stranger there." Again Kitchan abandoned himself to foolish laughter.

Chokichi suddenly blurted out, "I suppose geishas are expensive, aren't they?"

"Do you like geishas? They're an extravagance." Kitchan, the new star, re-examined Chokichi's face in some surprise. He added more confidently, "They're not *really* so expensive, of course, but it's a little silly to pay money for a woman. I know a couple of geisha houses in the park. I'll take you along. Leave everything to me."

For the past few minutes people had been climbing up in threes and fours, and the gallery was now packed. Some of those who had stayed on from the previous act were bored with waiting and had begun to clap in impatience. Behind the curtains the wooden sticks were beaten occasionally, and gradually the intervals seemed to be shortening. Chokichi stood up. He was tired of sitting.

"We still have a long wait," Kitchan said, as if to himself, then added for Chokichi's benefit. "That was what we call 'turning' clappers. It's a signal to let the actors know that the props are ready. The act won't begin for a long time."

He lighted a cigarette with a debonair assurance. Chokichi murmured admiringly, "You don't say so?", and, still standing, surveyed the theatre. The members of the audience obviously did not know what the "turning" clappers meant, and were milling around on their way back to their seats after their stroll outside, afraid that the act would begin at any minute. Chokichi could see plainly the dust and tobacco smoke floating in the shaft of sunlight which slanted against the curtain from the side of the theatre. The late afternoon sunlight was strangely pathetic. Chokichi stared at the curtain patterned every now and then with waves by the blowing wind. An actor's name was written on the curtain, together with a list of geisha from Asakusa Park who had presented it to him.

After a while Chokichi asked, "Kitchan, do you know any of those geisha?"

"Of course! The park is the special domain of actors." Kitchan was probably rather humiliated. Truly or falsely, he began to narrate in great detail the career, appearance, and character of every last geisha whose name appeared on the curtain.

The clappers rang out twice. The song for the opening of the act and a samisen were heard, and the curtain was drawn aside to the rhythm of the steadily quickening beat of the sticks. From the gallery came already shouts calling the names of the actors. The bored chatter of the audience died out at once, and the theatre took on a brightness and an animation like the coming of the dawn.

8

It was not until Otoyo had walked as far as Imado Bridge that she realized for the first time that it was April, and spring was now in its full glory. She was kept so busy taking care of the household all by herself that she normally was aware of the change in seasons only when the sun reached her windows from the clear blue sky and buds sprouted on the willow at the entrance to the eelshop across the street. When she emerged from her low-lying alley, where the view was always blocked by the rows of tile roofs, and stepped onto the bridge, Otoyo (who in the course of a whole year only left her neighborhood two or three times) was so astonished by the sight of the River Sumida in April that she could scarcely believe her eyes. The flowing water sparkled under the pellucidly clear sky; rows of cherry trees were in blossom above the green grass on the banks; pennants of every shape and color flashed at the university boathouse; and the air was filled with near and faraway cries. A throng of people out to see the blossoms were boarding and disembarking from the ferries. The scene around her was almost too brilliantly colored for Otoyo's tired eyes. She started to go down to the ferry slip, but suddenly turned on her heels as if in fear, and hurried back to the street. She waited until the dirtiest rickshaw, and the one with the least prepossessing rickshawman, went by. She timidly called, "Rickshawman, how cheaply can you take me to Koume?"

Otoyo had more on her mind than cherry blossoms. She was at her wits' end. Chokichi, on whom all her hopes were founded, had not only failed his examinations but declared that he hated studying and no longer wanted to attend school. Otoyo, at a loss what to do, decided that the only course left her was to discuss the matter with her brother Ragetsu.

An old rickshaw coolie, the third man Otoyo bargained with, finally agreed to take her to Koume at her price. An immense crowd flowed over Azuma Bridge in the afternoon sunlight and the dust. The old coolie tottered along, steering his vehicle through the midst of the swiftly pulled rickshaws bearing young men and women in holiday finery to see the cherry blossoms. As soon as they crossed the bridge the excitement of the cherry blossoms was left behind. The only things which suggested spring in this neighborhood were the sunlight shining on the shabby roofs and the bright blue of the sky mirrored in the silent waters of the canals. The street was quite deserted except for clusters of children playing games and spinning tops. Ragetsu's wife, a former geisha, was fulling cloth on a board in front of her house. She had a towel under the neck of her cotton kimono as she worked, and the sun fell harshly on a face wrinkled by years of wearing heavy make-up.

When she saw the rickshaw pull up and Otoyo step from it, she rushed into the house, leaving the door wide open. "Guess who's here!" she cried, "Your sister's come from Imado!"

Her husband was sitting at a little desk on the veranda, grading *haiku* for a competition. Ragetsu took off his glasses and moved from his desk to the middle of the room. His wife entered with Otoyo. Since they were women of about the same age, they went through a long series of bows and compliments. From one exchange —"And how is Chokichi?" "He's well, but I simply don't know what to do with him."—Ragetsu learned more quickly than he had expected the reason for Otoyo's visit. He placidly knocked the ashes out of his pipe, and when his opinion was asked, held forth to the effect that every young man goes through a period of confusion; that while in this state, as he himself could well remember, the advice of parents is repugnant; that the best course was not to interfere but to let the boy have his way for the time. But there was no place in a mother's heart, filled with apprehension for the unknowable future, for the tolerant philosophy of a man of the world. In a hushed voice, and at immense length, Otoyo recounted the evil forebodings aroused in her for Chokichi's future when she discovered that he had often stolen her seal to forge excuses in her name for absences from school.

"When I ask him what he intends to do if he won't go to school, he says he thinks he'll become an actor. An actor! What shall I do? To think that Chokichi has gone bad that way—I feel so mortified I don't know what to do."

"He wants to become an actor?" Ragetsu recalled after a first moment of surprise how Chokichi as a boy of six or seven used to love to play with a samisen. "If that's what he really wants, there's nothing we can do about it. Still, it *is* a problem."

Otoyo went on to relate how misfortune had driven her to becoming the teacher of professional entertainers, but if she were to permit her son to take up so base a profession, it would be an unpardonable insult to the tombs of her ancestors. Ragetsu, at the allusion to the bankruptcy and collapse of the family, recalled—with such acute embarrassment that he wanted to scratch his bald head—

how his life of dissipation had led to his disinheritance. Having always had a great fondness for the world of entertainers, he would have liked to attack Otoyo's prejudiced views, but he feared that if she went on to a lengthy discussion of the "tombs of our ancestors" it would prove too much for him. He tried to think of some quick and painless way of calming Otoyo.

"I'll talk to him. Personally, I think it's better in the long run for a boy to be unsettled when he is young. But tell Chokichi to come and see me tonight or tomorrow. I'm sure I can get him to improve his conduct. You needn't worry so much. Things aren't as bad as your fears make them."

Otoyo begged him to do what he could and, declining her sister-in-law's invitation to stay longer, left the house. The spring sunset was reddening the sky beyond Azuma Bridge, throwing into sharp relief the crowds crossing the bridge on their way back from viewing the blossoms. Otoyo noticed a student, his school uniform glittering with gold buttons, making his way energetically through the crowd. She could not actually tell whether or not he was a university student, but seeing him awoke in her a quite unbearable grief that, after having struggled unaided for so many years to raise her son to be a fine student like that boy, the light of her hopes, which was her very life, had now been completely extinguished. Even though she had asked her brother's help, she still could not feel reassured, and this was not in the least because of his youthful indiscretions. The thought occurred to her that it did not lie within human powers to instill ambitions in Chokichi: she would have to ask help of the gods and Buddha. Acting on an impulse, Otoyo asked the rickshaw coolie to stop near the Kannon Temple. She hurried up to the sacred hall, quite unaware of the milling throngs. After murmuring a prayer, she bought a sacred fortune at a booth nearby. The scrap of yellowed paper she drew had been printed from a wood block.

No. 62   *Great Good Fortune*

Misfortunes steadily withdraw; good fortune will come your way.

> *Your fame and glory will grow throughout the land.*
> *Old things will change for the better; you will again*
>   *enjoy rewards.*
> *Success and prosperity will be yours.*
>
> *Your prayer will be answered. The sick person will recover.*
> *The lost object will be returned. The person you are waiting*
> *for will come. There is no obstacle to building a house or*
> *moving. The time is good for making a journey. All is*
> *propitious for marriages, coming of age ceremonies, and*
> *engaging servants.*

Otovo felt much relieved when she saw the words "Great Good Fortune," but she recalled then that "Great Good Fortune" is all too apt to change into misfortune and, again giving way to the imagining of fears of every sort, she returned home quite exhausted.

9

There was to be a meeting of *haiku* poets in the afternoon at the library of the Ryugan Temple. When Ragetsu and Chokichi (who had come that morning) finished eating lunch, they set out for the temple together, walking along the canal. The noon ebbtide revealed the black muddy bottom of the canal, and the warm April sunshine drew from the water a powerful stench of muck. The air was filled with flying cinders from a chimney somewhere, and the whir of machinery in a nearby factory could be heard. The houses along the street were built lower than the street itself, and as they passed they could plainly see the dark interiors where housewives, indifferent to the spring sunshine, were busily sewing to earn a few extra pennies. At the corners of these little houses, on dirty billboards were numerous posters calling for factory girls, as well as the usual advertisements of patent medicines and fortunetellers. Presently, however, the dreary street climbed a little in its meandering way, and its aspect was suddenly changed by the red-painted wall of the Myoken Temple on one side, and the pleasantly faded fence of a restaurant on the other. This marked the end of the poor district. Across the wooden bridge spanning the river, beyond the grass-covered bank, was a broad expanse of fields and trees, radiant in the colors of spring.

Ragetsu stopped. "I'm going to the temple across the river over there. You can see the roof by the pines, can't you?"

"Well," Chokichi said, all too quickly taking off his hat, "I think I'll be saying good-bye here."

"There's no hurry. I'm thirsty. How about resting for a minute or two?"

They followed the wooden fence to a teahouse sheltered with reed blinds, and there Ragetsu seated himself. The straight canal was dirty here too, but a delightful breeze blew from the distant fields, and on the opposite embankment, where a torii was visible, young leaves of the willows were fluttering. Sparrows and swallows kept up an endless chirping on the roof of the temple gate directly behind them. Here and there, it is true, columns of smoke were rising from factories, but one could still find pleasure in the peace of a spring afternoon far from the city. Ragetsu gazed at the surroundings, then glanced casually at Chokichi. He said, "You agreed, I take it, to what we were talking about before?"

Chokichi, who had just taken a sip of tea, could only nod.

"Be patient for another year. If you can manage to graduate from your present school. . . . Your mother is getting older now, and she can't remain so stubborn forever."

Chokichi nodded again, and stared vacantly into the distance. Two or three coolies were going back and forth carrying earth from a barge tied up in the canal to a factory on the other bank. Some rickshaws suddenly raced up from the bridge along the deserted nearer bank of the canal, and stopped before the temple gate. These were probably visitors who had come to pay their respects at the family graves. A woman got out of a rickshaw and went in the gate, holding by the hand a little girl.

Chokichi and his uncle parted on the bridge. Ragetsu turned with a worried expression for a final word. "Well," he said after a pause, "I know you must hate it, but for the time being please be patient. You'll never regret having been a good son."

Chokichi removed his hat and bowed slightly. He walked off

quickly, almost at a run, in the direction from which he had come. Ragetsu disappeared behind the weed-covered embankment. Nothing in all of his close to sixty years had ever bothered him quite so much and given him so painful an emotion as what had happened today. His sister's request had not been an unreasonable one, but at the same time he could not find it in himself to disapprove of Chokichi's ambition to enter the theatre. He was convinced that different people have different temperaments and that it was wrong to force them all into one mold, whatever the motive. Ragetsu, caught in a dilemma, was unable to side completely with either his sister or his nephew. He knew instinctively from his own past experiences exactly what lay at the very bottom of Chokichi's heart, even without asking. How painful and depressing he had found it when he was young to be compelled to waste a lovely spring day working in the darkness of the family pawnshop. How much more enjoyable it would have been to read an amusing book in a cheerful room overlooking the river than to sit under a dim lamp entering sums of money received and disbursed in the great ledger. Chokichi had said that he would rather make a living by something which he liked than become a punctilious functionary with a mustache. Both were possible ways to spend a lifetime. But Ragetsu, in his capacity as the boy's counselor, could not very well reveal his own feelings. The best he could do was to offer the temporizing comfort he had already given the boy's mother.

Chokichi walked aimlessly from one desolate street to another. He had no thought of taking a short cut which would lead him straight back home to Imado. Nor was he thinking of returning in a roundabout fashion, stopping off somewhere on the way. He was utterly overwhelmed by despair. Chokichi's only hope for support in his plan of becoming an actor had been to gain the sympathy of his kindly uncle. He had been sure that his uncle would help, but in this hope he had completely deceived himself. His uncle, it is true, had not voiced point-blank and violent opposition as his mother had, but, after citing the proverb, "A paradise on hearing, a hell at sight," Ragetsu had recounted at great length the difficulties of succeeding in a theatrical career, the hardships of stage life, the troublesome nature of the world of entertainers, and many similar things. He had gone on to urge Chokichi to show consideration for his mother, and had enjoined on him various things which Chokichi understood perfectly even without his uncle's advice. Chokichi had at last become aware of the convenient faculty that human beings possess for forgetting the sufferings and uneasiness of their youth when they grow old, so that they can with supreme indifference admonish and criticize young people of later generations. He felt with a stab of pain that there existed between the old and the young an unbridgeable gap.

The streets were narrow and the ground dark and dank wherever he walked. Most of the streets were mere alleys, so twisted that he wondered at times whether they might prove to be blind. The irregular rows of dismal little houses stretched on endlessly—shingled roofs covered with moss, foundations rotting, posts tottering, dirty boards, rags and diapers hanging out to dry, cheap sweets and pots and pans spread out for sale in the streets. Occasionally an unusually large entranceway could be seen: it invariably proved to be to a factory. The towering tiled roofs belonged to temples, usually utterly desolate; through the broken walls one could see all the way to the graveyards behind the temple buildings. Gravestones covered with moss stains and bundles of memorial tablets had fallen into the old ponds, which looked like vast, unbounded puddles. On the graves, it goes without saying, there was not a single fresh flower. Frogs could already be heard croaking in the ponds, and last year's withered grass rotted in the water.

Chokichi noticed by chance on one of the houses of the neighborhood a sign with the name of the street. He recalled at once that this was the very street mentioned in *The Calendar of Plum Blossoms,*[4] which he had avidly read not long before. Ah, he sighed, did those ill-starred lovers live in such a dark, sinister street? Some of the houses had bamboo fences exactly like the ones in the illustrations to the book. The bamboo was withered and the stalks were eaten at the

4 A romance written in 1832-1833 by Tamenaga Shunsui. The hero Tanjiro was for many years considered to be the great prototype of a passionate lover.

base by insects. Chokichi thought they would probably disintegrate if he poked them. An emaciated willow tree drooped its branches, barely touched with green, over the shingled roof of a gate. The geisha Yonehachi must have passed through just such a gate when, of a winter's afternoon, she secretly visited the sick Tanjiro. And it must have been in a room of such a house that the other hero, Hanjiro, telling ghost stories one rainy night, dared to take his sweetheart's hand for the first time. Chokichi experienced a strange fascination and sorrow. He wanted to be possessed by that sweet, gentle, suddenly cold and indifferent fate. As the wings of his fancy spread, the spring sky seemed bluer and wider than before. He caught from the distance the sound of the Korean flute of a sweet-seller. To hear the flute in this unexpected place, playing its curious low-pitched tune, produced in him a melancholy which words could not describe.

For a while Chokichi forgot the dissatisfaction with his uncle that had taken root in his breast. For a while he forgot the anguish of actuality.

10

There is a time between the end of spring and the beginning of summer, like the season when late summer turns to autumn, when heavy rains fall intermittently. This year, as usual, there was flooding, and Ragetsu, wondering how Otoyo's neighborhood had fared, decided to call one evening on his way back from an errand in that part of town. There had been no flooding there, but he was amazed by an even stranger calamity: Chokichi lay in a stretcher, and at the moment that Ragetsu arrived, noisy preparations were being made for sending him to the isolation hospital. Otoyo told him how Chokichi had gone out in his thin summer kimono to see the floods. He had walked around in the muddy water from evening until late at night, and had caught a cold which developed into typhoid fever. This was the doctor's explanation, and when Otoyo had finished recounting it, she followed the stretcher out, weeping. Ragetsu was obliged to look after the house until Otoyo's return.

After the confusion, like that of a spring cleaning or a moving, caused by the fumigation of the house by a man from the district office, there descended a loneliness devoid of all human feeling, rather like the atmosphere after a coffin has been sent off to a funeral. A strong wind sprang up at nightfall, and the shutters all began to rattle. The weather became unpleasantly chilly, and the wind which blew in now and again through holes in the battered kitchen door shook the flame in the dim hanging lamp in the sitting-room so violently as almost to extinguish it; each time the black oil smoke clouded the lamp chimney, and the shadows of the household furniture, set haphazardly around the room, moved on the dirty matting and the peeling wall. A voice in a nearby house somewhere began to intone the million invocations to the Buddha, and the sound fell plaintively on Ragetsu's ears. Time hung heavily now that he was alone. He was bored and rather lonely. At such a time, he thought, one needs a drink, and he wandered around the kitchen looking for some liquor. But in this household run by a woman there was not so much as a wine cup. He retraced his steps to the front window and, opening one of the shutters a crack, looked up and down the street. There was nothing resembling a wineshop in the houses on the opposite side. Most of the shops on the street were already shut although it was still early in the evening, and the gloomy voice intoning the million invocations could be heard all the more distinctly. The fierce wind from the river made the telegraph wires above the roofs sing, and this sound, together with the clearness of the stars, created an impression of coldness as if winter had suddenly returned this night.

Ragetsu closed the shutters and again sat vacantly under the hanging lamp. He smoked one pipe after another, and watched the hands of the grandfather clock move. Occasionally mice scurried inside the ceiling making a dreadful noise. It occurred to Ragetsu that there might be something to read in the room. He searched everywhere, on top of the chest of drawers, in the cupboard, but the only books he could find were singing-manuals and old almanacs. Taking the lamp in one hand, he climbed upstairs, where Chokichi's room was.

A number of books were piled on the desk, and there was also a bookcase. Ragetsu took out his spectacles and opened with curiosity one after another of Chokichi's books bound in Western style. Something fell out of one of them. He picked it up and discovered it was a photograph of Oito in the spring finery of a geisha. He continued idly leafing through the books, when this time he discovered a letter. The letter had apparently never been completed, and there were places where the words were lost because the paper had been torn. The general meaning, however, was clear from the words which were still legible. Chokichi and Oito were day by day growing further apart, even in their hearts, because of the difference in their circumstances; it seemed that in spite of their childhood friendship they were doomed finally to become utter strangers. Even supposing they occasionally exchanged letters, they would never be able to share the same feelings. He had decided to become an actor or an entertainer, but this ambition had been thwarted, and now he was condemned to the tedium of spending his days without purpose, vainly envying the happiness of Kitchan, the barber's son. At the moment he lacked the courage to kill himself, but would be very glad if he could take sick and die.

Ragetsu felt intuitively that Chokichi's illness after walking in the flood waters had resulted from a deliberate plan, and that all hope of his recovery was at an end. He was assailed by remorse as he wondered how he had been able to give Chokichi advice which was not really what he believed and thereby frustrate the boy's hopes. Ragetsu recalled once more how in his youth he had been driven from his parents' house because of his infatuation for a woman. He of all people should have shown himself Chokichi's ally. Unless he could make an actor out of Chokichi and give him Oito for a wife, it would render meaningless his own destruction of his father's business and his life of hardship. He felt dishonored in his pretensions of being a man of the world.

Another mouse suddenly raced over the ceiling. The wind was still blowing, and the flame in the hanging lamp quivered continually. Like some illustrator of romances thinking of pictures for a book, Ragetsu over and over drew in his mind the portraits of the two young, beautiful people—Chokichi with his fair skin, delicate face, and clear eyes; and Oito with her charming mouth and tilted eyes set in a round face. And he cried in his heart, "No matter how bad your fever is, don't die! Chokichi, there's nothing to worry about. I am with you."

TRANSLATED BY DONALD KEENE

Song on Traveling the Chikuma River

1

By the old castle of Komoro
In white clouds, a wanderer laments.
The green chickweed has not sprouted,
The grass has not yet laid its carpet;
The silver coverlet on the hills around
Melting in the sun, the light snow flows.

There is a warm light
But no scent to fill the fields;
Thinly the haze lies on the spring,
The color of the wheat is barely green.
Here and there little groups
Hurry along the road through the fields.
As it grows dark, even Asama cannot be seen,
A Saku reed pipe makes doleful music.
I entered an inn near the bank
Of the Chikuma River of hesitant waves,
Drank the cloudiness of cloudy sake
And rested myself for a while.

2

Yesterday again it was that way;
Today again it will be that way.
In this life, what do we fret about,
Worrying only over tomorrow?
How many times descending into the valley
Where lingers the dream of glory and decay,
Have I seen in the hesitation of river waves
The water mixed with sand swirl and return?

Ah, what does the old castle tell?
What do the waves on the banks reply?
Think calmly of the world that has passed,
A hundred years are as yesterday.

The willows of Chikuma River are misted,
The spring is shallow, the water has flowed.
All alone I walk around the rocks
And bind fast my sorrow to these banks.

Shimazaki Tōson (1872-1943)

TRANSLATED BY DONALD KEENE

My Songs

Because my songs are brief,
People think I hoarded words.
I have spared nothing in my songs.
There is nothing I can add.
Unlike a fish, my soul swims without gills.
I sing on one breath.

One Night

In every room
Light a brilliant light:
In every vase
Arrange poppy and rose:
Not to comfort
But to chastise.
For here a woman
   —Forgetting to praise,
     Forgetting to respond—
Suddenly wished to weep
Over a trifle.

A Mouse

In my attic dwells a mouse.
The creaking noise he makes
Reminds me of a sculptor who carves
An image all night long.

Again when he dances with his wife,
He whirls like a race horse, round.
Though the attic dirt and dust flutter down
On this paper as I write,
How would he know?
But I stop to think:
    I am living with mice.
    Let them have good food
    And a warm nest.
    Let them drill a hole in the ceiling and,
    From time to time, peep down on me.

                               Yosano Akiko (1878-1942)

Wake Not

There are some lives duller
Than dusty glass
Of windows, hot in the sun past noon.
Emptied of thought, senseless,
A young man sleeps, sweating, snoring.
Yellowish teeth protrude from his mouth.
The summer sun through the windowpane
Shines on his hairy leg,
And a flea crawls on it.

Wake not! wake not, till the sun goes down . . .
Till a cool still evening comes into your life.
    From somewhere the sensuous laugh of a woman.

A Fist

> Pitied by a richer friend than I,
> Taunted by a stronger one,
>> Flushed with wrath, I raised my fist,
>> When in a chink of my mad soul,
> I found a soul that was not mad
>> Crouching, blinking, meek, and guilty—
>> Miserable one!
>
> That distress!
> Who will you strike
> With that luckless fist—
>> Your friend? your self?
>> Or the innocent pillar at your side?

Ishikawa Takuboku (1885-1912)

TRANSLATED BY SHIO SAKANISHI

Secret Song of the Heretics

[*This poem is filled with curious old words dating back to the late sixteenth century, when Portuguese and Spanish priests propagated Christianity in Japan. The references in stanza two to the microscope and telescope are, of course, anachronistic. The magic lantern of stanza three is puzzling, as is the "white blood of marble": it seems likely that the poet was more interested in the exotic sound of the words than the meaning.*]

> •
>
> I believe in the heretical teachings of a degenerate age, the witchcraft of the Christian God,
> The captains of the black ships, the marvelous land of the Red Hairs,
> The scarlet glass, the sharp-scented carnation,
> The calico, arrack, and *vinho tinto* of the Southern Barbarians:

The blue-eyed Dominicans chanting the liturgy who tell me
    even in dreams
Of the God of the forbidden faith, or of the blood-stained
    Cross,
The cunning device that makes a mustard seed big as an apple,
The strange collapsible spyglass that looks even at Paradise.

They build their houses of stone, the white blood of marble
Overflows in crystal bowls; when night falls, they say, it bursts
    into flame.
That beautiful electrical dream is mixed with the incense of
    velvet
Reflecting the bird and beasts of the world of the moon.

I have heard their cosmetics are squeezed from the flowers of
    poisonous plants,
And the images of Mary are painted with oil from rotted
    stones;
The blue letters ranged sideways in Latin or Portuguese
Are filled with a beautiful sad music of heaven.

Oh, vouchsafe unto us, sainted padres of delusion,
Though our hundred years be shortened to an instant, though
    we die on the bloody cross,
It will not matter; we beg for the Secret, that strange dream
    of crimson:
Jesus, we pray this day, bodies and souls caught in the incense
    of longing.

One-sided Love

The acacia blossoms gold and red are falling,
In the dusky autumn light they fall.
My sorrow wears the thin flannel garb of one-sided love.
When I walk the towpath along the water

Your gentle sighs are falling,
The acacia blossoms gold and red are falling.

Kitahara Hakushū (1885-1943)

The Land of Netsuke

Cheekbones protruding, lips thick, eyes triangular,
Face like a netsuke carved by the great Shūzan,
Expression vacant as though the soul were removed,
Ignorant of himself, jumpy,
Cheap-lived,
Show-off,
Small-minded, self-satisfied,
Monkey-like, foxlike, squirrel-like, gudgeon-like,
　　Minnow-like, potsherd-like, gargoyle-faced
　　Japanese!

Winter Has Come

Suddenly, sharply, winter has come,
The white flowers of the *yatsude* have vanished
And the gingko trees have turned into brooms.

Whirling, the winter has come boring in.
Winter, that people hate,
Winter, that plants turn from, that insects flee, has come.

Winter!
Come to me, come to me.
I am the winter's strength; the winter is my food.

Soak through, thrust in,
Start conflagrations, bury in snow—
Winter like a knife has come.

Takamura Kōtarō (1883-1956)

TRANSLATED BY DONALD KEENE

Kimi kinu to You have come at last,
Itsutsu no yubi ni   And so I let go the dragonflies
Takuwaeshi Which I have held captive
Tombo hanachinu   In my five fingers
Aki no yūgure This autumn evening.

Kazu shiranu Of the numberless steps
Ware no kokoro no   Up to my heart,
Kizahashi wo He climbed perhaps
Hata futatsu mitsu   Only two or three.
Kare ya noborishi

                     Yosano Akiko (1878-1942)

Song of My Youth

[*The following sequence has been put together by the translator from a much larger number of* waka.]

Ishi hitotsu Like a stone
Saka wo kudaru ga   That rolls down a hill,
Gotoku ni mo   I have come to this day.
Ware kyō no hi ni
Itaritsukitaru

Ono ga na wo There is no way of returning
Honoka ni yobite   To the spring of my fourteenth year,
Namida seshi When, whispering my own name,
Jūshi no haru ni   I wept.
Kaeru sube nashi

Yoru nete mo	Even in sleep I whistled.
Kuchibue fukinu	Whistling indeed
Kuchibue wa	Was the song of my fifteenth year.
Jūgo no ware no	
Uta ni shi arikeri	

Uree aru	With the troubled eyes of a youth
Shōnen no me ni	I envied
Urayamiki	Birds flying—
Kotori no tobu wo	Flying they sang.
Tobite utau wo	

Akiya ni iri	Going into a vacant house once,
Tabako nomitaru	I smoked a cigarette,
Koto ariki	Only because I longed to be alone.
Aware tada hitori	
Itaki bakari ni	

Kagiri naki	Fearing I loved someone,
Chishiki no yoku ni	My sister pitied my eyes
Moyuru me wo	That were burning
Ane wa itamiki	With insatiable thirst for knowledge
Hito kouru ka to	

Kyōshitsu no	Running away
Mado yori nigete	From the window of a classroom,
Tada hitori	Alone,
Kano shiro-ato ni	I lay down among the ruins of a castle.
Ne ni yukishi ka na	

Hotobashiru	How pleasant
Pompu no mizu no	Is the water gushing from a pump!
Kokochi yosa yo	Awhile with the soul of a youth
Shibashi wa wakaki	I watch it.
Kokoro mote miru	

Nagaku nagaku
Wasureshi tomo ni
Au gotoki
Yorokobi wo mote
Mizu no oto kiku

With the joy of meeting
  A long-lost friend,
    I listen to the sound of water.

Yume samete
Futto kanashimu
Wa ga nemuri
Mukashi no gotoku
Yasukaranu kana

Awaking from a dream
  I grieve.
My sleep no more is so peaceful
  As in the olden days.

Ito kireshi
Tako no gotoku ni
Wakaki hi no
Kokoro karoku mo
Tobisarishi kana

Like a kite
  Cut from the string,
Lightly the soul of my youth
  Has taken flight.

Ishikawa Takuboku (1885-1912)

TRANSLATED BY SHIO SAKANISHI

Mono no yuki
Todomarame ya mo
Yamakai no
Sugi no taiboku no
Samusa no hibiki

The ultimate impasse!
From the immense gorge-choking cedar
Reverberations of the cold.

Furisosogu
Amatsu hikari ni
Me no mienu
Kuroki itodo wo
Oitsumenikeri

By the downflooding light of heaven
The invisible black cricket
Is driven and cornered.

Shimashi ware wa
Me wo tsumurinamu
Mahi ochite
Karasu nemuri ni
Yuku koe kikoyu

As I close my eyes
The high sun falls . . .
I hear crows cawing on their way to sleep.

Muragimo no   Straining my taut-stretched mind
Kokoro haritsume   For this moment I confront
Shimashiku wa   A man with hallucinations.
Genkaku o motsu
Otoko ni tai-su

Saitō Mokichi (1882-1953)

TRANSLATED BY HOWARD HIBBETT

THE ROMAJI DIARY

[Rōmaji Nikki] by Ishikawa Takuboku (1885-1912)

The Romaji Diary *was kept by Takuboku from April to June of 1909. For him to have written his diary in Roman letters (Romaji) instead of the usual mixture of ideographs and kana was as unusual for his day as a diary in Esperanto is today. The fact that he could be sure that no one would read his words permitted him to set down his feelings freely and fully. It is an amazing document, particularly when one considers that it was written a bare thirty years after the Meiji Restoration. It reveals a man of a depth, complexity, and modernity of thought and emotion that could not have been predicted from earlier literature. This diary was almost unknown until its full publication in 1954.*

Words in italics are in English in the original.

•

7th April 1909

This morning a violent west wind was roaring through the sky. The windows on the third floor were all rattling, and a dustlike sand from the street below came blowing in the cracks. But in spite of the wind the scattered clouds were motionless.

A springlike sunshine was warming the windowpanes. It was the sort of day when you might be sweating if it weren't for the wind. The old man from the lending library came in, wiping his nose with the palm of his hand. "Terrible wind," said he. "Still, the cherry blossoms all over Tokyo will be opening today. Wind or no wind, it's fine weather."

"Spring has come at last," I said, but of course he couldn't understand my feelings. "Eh! Eh!" answered the old man, "Spring, you know, is a loss as far as we're concerned. Lending books is finished for the season. All my customers would rather go out for a walk than read a book, and I can't say I blame them. The few people who do read books naturally take their time over it."

There is a five-yen bill in my wallet, the remains of what I borrowed yesterday of next month's pay from the company. All morning long I couldn't think about anything else. It must be the way people who normally have money feel when they are suddenly deprived of it. Both situations are funny, but though they're funny in quite the same way, there's a big difference in the happiness or grief involved!

Having nothing else to do, I tried to make a table of Romaji. From time to time the memory of my mother and my wife in Hokkaido leapt out of the middle of the table and took possession of me. "Spring has come. It's April! Spring! Spring! The blossoms are opening! It's already a year since I came to Tokyo. . . ! And still I haven't been able to make any arrangements to send for my family." That's the problem that keeps tormenting me, I don't know how many times a day.

Why did I decide to keep this diary in Romaji? Why? I love my wife, and it's precisely because I love her that I don't want her to read this diary. No, that's a lie! It's true that I love her, and it's true that I don't want her to read this, but the two facts are not necessarily related.

Am I a weakling then? No, my trouble comes entirely from the mistaken institution of marriage. Marriage! What an idiotic institution! What's to be done about it?

Today the members of the tennis team from Kyoto University, who are staying in the next room, are having their last day of play. They went off in high spirits.

After eating lunch I went by streetcar as usual to the office, where I corrected proofs with the old men in a corner of the editorial room. About five o'clock in the evening the proofs for the first edition were finished and I went back home: this is my daily stint to earn a living.

On the way back I walked along a street in Hongō, intending to do a little shopping. The cherry trees of the university campus had half-opened their blossoms in just one day.

The world is now completely given over to the spring.

The sound of the footsteps of the people going back and forth crowding the streets somehow exhilarated me. I couldn't help wondering where they had so suddenly appeared from, those beautiful people in beautiful clothes who were streaming by. It's spring, I thought. Then I thought of my wife and little Kyōko.

I had promised myself that I would send for them by April and I haven't—no, I can't.

Oh, my writing is my enemy, and my philosophy nothing but empty logic that I myself ridicule. I seem to desire so many things, but don't they boil down to one small one? Money!

When I got back after ten tonight there was a tremendous racket in the next room. One of the tennis players, having returned drunk from a dinner given in their honor, had smashed the light and was breaking up the frames of the sliding doors.

I met one of the students at the entrance to his room. He was a classmate of mine in high school and is now studying engineering in Kyoto. We carried on a childish conversation until about one in the morning. In the meantime the uproar in the next room had subsided. The spring night deepened, the night of a day which had opened the blossoms all over the city.

In the midst of a city quiet in sleep, I lay awake alone, and, counting the breaths of the calm spring night, I felt how dull and meaningless my life in this little room has been. What must I look like sleeping here all alone in this tiny room, overcome by an indescribable fatigue? The final discovery of human beings must be that the human being itself is not of the slightest importance.

I have lived a long time—over two hundred days—in this little room, filled with heavy uneasiness, and with the shallow hope that I may find something to interest me. How long will it last. . . ? No!

I read in bed the *Collected Stories of Turgenev*.

8th, Thursday

They probably forgot because they were all confused by the turmoil in the next room (but to be forgotten is already an insult, an insult natural enough in view of my present circumstances: thus thinking, I can laugh off anything at all). Two full hours after I got up and washed they still hadn't brought the breakfast tray.

I thought: up to now I have always kept quiet in such cases, and have never once got angry. But is that because I have an easygoing nature? Probably not. It's a mask, or, if not a mask, comes from some crueler idea. I thought; then I clapped my hands and called the maid.

The sky was calm and clear. There is something buoyant about the streets in blossomtime. Every now and then the wind scattered sand and fluttered the blossom-viewing kimonos of the passers-by.

On the way back from the office I met Hinosawa, the engineer. He is a real dandy. When he sat down in his newly tailored Western clothes next to me in a padded kimono with torn sleeves, I felt that I had to say something sarcastic. "Have you been to see the cherry blossoms?" "No, I haven't the time to look at cherry blossoms." "Really? That's fine," I said. What I said was extremely commonplace. It was something that anybody could say. I made that commonplace remark to that commonplace man because I thought it made for wonderful irony. Of course, there was no fear of Hinosawa's understanding my meaning: he is absolutely placid. That's what made it amusing.

There were two old women seated opposite us. "I dislike the Tokyo old women," I said. "Why's that?" "It gives me a bad feeling just to look at them. It really does. There's nothing motherly about them, like the ones in the country." Just then one of the old women glared at me from behind her dark glasses. The people around were also staring in my direction. I felt somehow pleased.

"Is that so?" said Hinosawa in as soft a voice as possible.

"Of course, when it comes to young women, there's no place like Tokyo. But once they get to be old, they all have a sour look on their faces."

"Ha, ha, ha, ha."

"I'm very fond of the motion pictures. Are you?"

"I haven't yet made the effort to go."

"They're really interesting. You should go have a look. One minute it's light, and the next minute it's dark. It's fun."

"It's bad for the eyes, isn't it?" I could already read an awkward embarrassment on my friend's face. I couldn't help feel a faint triumph.

"Ha, ha, ha!" This time it was I who laughed.

I went out about eight in the evening to buy a needle and thread to mend the holes in my kimono. The streets were full of the bustle of spring. Besides the usual night stalls there were many little shops selling plants.

Everybody was walking about happily, shoulders rubbing shoulders. I didn't buy the needle and thread. Although I could hear my heart shouting, "Don't! Don't!", I ended up by taking out my wallet and buying this notebook, socks, underwear, writing paper, and two bowls of pansies. Why is it that even when I am about to buy something necessary I always hear that voice say "Stop!"? "You'll be left without a penny," the voice says. "They're suffering in Hokkaido," the voice says.

9th, Friday

The cherry blossoms are almost in full bloom: it is a warm, calm, perfectly springlike day; the sky in the distance is veiled in mist.

On the tram going back this evening I saw a child who looked just as Kyōko did when I parted from her last spring. She was making a squeak with a toy flute, and as she did so she looked at me bashfully, hiding her laughing face. She was so adorable I felt like taking her in my arms.

The face of the child's mother looked the way I imagine my mother's did when she was young. The nose, the cheeks, the eyes—the whole face was like hers. It wasn't a very refined face!

It is a spring evening sweet as milk. In the distance a frog is croaking. The first frog of the year!

10th, Saturday

Last night I read until past three, and I got up today after ten. A wind from the south is blowing in the clear sky.

The fact that recent short stories have come to be no more than a kind of new form of sketches from life—no—the fact that we have stopped wanting to read them—in other words, the fact that we are dissatisfied with them—shows that the authority of Naturalistic philosophy as a view of life is gradually dying out.

How times change! It cannot be denied that Naturalism was the philosophy we sought out with the greatest eagerness. But before we knew it we had discovered the logical contradictions in it. Then when we had surmounted these contradictions and moved forward, the sword we held in our hands was no longer the sword of Naturalism. I for one am no longer able to content myself with an attitude of detachment. The attitude of the writer toward humanity cannot be one of detachment. He must be a critic. Or a planner for mankind.

The positive Naturalism I have reached is a new idealism. For a long time we despised the word "ideal." As a matter of fact, the kind of ideals we were then holding were, as we discovered, no more than pitiful illusions—no more than a *life illusion*. But we are alive and we must live. The ideal of destroying everything and then building anew with our own hands is no longer just a pitiful illusion. Even if the ideal itself is just a *life illusion,* we cannot live without it. If this deep internal need must also be discarded, there is nothing left for me to do but to die.

· ·

What I wrote this morning is a lie. At least in so far as I am concerned it is not a first principle. I do not consider that any human achievement, regardless of the field, is of consequence. I used to think that literature was more admirable and valuable than other things, but that was before I knew what "admirable" meant. Is it possible that anything done by a human being can be admirable? The human being itself is neither admirable nor valuable.

What I desire is peace of mind. I realized it this evening for the first time. Yes, it is exactly that, beyond any doubt.

I wonder what real assurance—the feeling that there is nothing to worry about—must be like. It has been such a long time since I experienced it—not since I became conscious of what was going on in the world—that I have forgotten.

Of late the most tranquil moments in my life have been the ones spent going back and forth to work on the streetcar. When I am at home doing nothing, I feel as if I should be doing something. But what? That's the problem. Read? Write? But there seems to be nothing to read or write. No, reading and writing are only a part of that "something." Is there anything else I can do besides read and write? That I don't know. But I feel, anyway, as though I should do something. Even when I am thinking of quite carefree things, I feel as if I am always being pursued by that "something." And as a result I can't seem to put my hand to anything.

At the office I wish the time would pass more quickly. It's not that there's anything I especially dislike about the work, or that the surroundings are disagreeable: when I return home early I am pursued by that feeling that I must do "something." I don't know what it is I should be doing, but I'm haunted by that compulsion.

I feel keenly the changing of the seasons. When I see the cherry trees in blossom, this simple fact strikes me sharp as an arrow. It is as if before my eyes I see the blossoms opening, and even as I watch the moment for them to scatter approaches. Whatever I see, whatever I hear, I feel exactly as if I were battling a stiff current. I don't have a moment of calm; I am not at peace. Am I being pushed from behind? Or am I being pulled from the front? Whichever it is I can't be calm. I feel I must dash out somewhere.

Then, what am I seeking? Fame? No, it's not that. Achievement? No, not that either. Love? No. Knowledge? No. Then, money perhaps? Yes, money. Not as an end, but as a means. What I am searching for with all my heart is peace of mind. Yes, that is it.

Does that mean I am tired?

The sort of revolution which took place within me at the end of last year progressed with tremendous force. Although I had no particular enemy in mind during those hundred days, I was always armed. Everyone, without distinction, seemed an enemy. Sometimes I thought that I would like to kill everyone I knew, starting with my closest friends. Anyone who was an intimate friend to me I hated because of his friendship. "Everything afresh" was the "new" hope which guided me each day. My "new world" was a world of the strong.

The Naturalism I held as my philosophy then abandoned its bastion of negativity, and charged out into the broad fields of Positivism. The strong had to strip themselves of all the shackles and the old armor of convention, and to fight boldly. They had to advance rapidly wherever their inclinations led them, their hearts like iron, unweeping, unsmiling, taking nothing into consideration. They had to discard as dust all the things which are said to be virtues of mankind, and then they must effortlessly perform deeds beyond human powers. And for what purpose? They themselves would not know—the very fact that it was their aim would make it the aim of all mankind.

The hundred days when I was armed were merely a period when I posed as a warrior. Whom did I defeat? How strong did I become?

In short, I'm tired. I'm tired without having fought.

One may cross the world by two paths and only two. *All or Nothing!* The one is to fight against everything. To win or else to die. The other is to fight against nothing. No triumphs, no defeats. There is a reassurance in never having been beaten. There is a vitality in always winning. And there is nothing to fear from either. . . . But even though I have these opinions they don't cheer me or give me the slightest strength.

My character is an unhappy character.

I am a weakling, a weakling with a marvelous sword inferior to none.

I can't stand it unless I fight, and yet I'm unable to win. That means that death is the only possible course for me. But I dislike the thought of death. I don't want to die! Then, how am I to live?

I want to live like a farmer, ignorant of everything. I'm far too clever.

I envy people who go crazy. I'm too healthy in mind and body.

I wish I could forget this, that, everything. But how?

Of late I have been tempted from time to time by the desire to go where there is no one else. A place with no one else—or at least where no voices are heard, where nothing can be heard which has the remotest connection with me, a place where there is no fear of anyone coming and looking at me—oh, I would like to go there all by myself for a week, ten days, no, even for a day, even for half a day.

I should like to rest my body as I please in a place where no matter what expression I have on my face, no matter what appearance I make, there is no fear of being noticed.

Sometimes, trying to forget this thought, I go to places where there are many people, like the motion pictures. And sometimes, on the other hand, I go when I feel a yearning for people—for young women. But I can't find any satisfaction there either. While I am watching the film, especially if it is the most stupid, childish kind, I do manage to return to the heart of a child, and I can forget everything; but as soon as the film is over and the lights flash on, and I see the countless swarming people, the desire to seek some gayer, more amusing place rises all the stronger within my breast. Sometimes I can smell right in front of my nose the fragrance of hair, or I can feel a warm hand in mine. But at such times my mind is calculating the contents of my pocketbook—or, rather, thinking of how to borrow some money! When I hold a warm hand or breathe the strong perfume of hair, I have the feeling not merely of holding a hand, but of taking in my arms a soft, warm, white body. And how lonely I feel when I return home without having done so! It is not just the loneliness that comes from having been unable to obtain sexual satisfaction: it is the deep terrible despair at not being able to get everything I want.

When I have had a little money I have without hesitation gone, filled with the voice of lust, to those narrow dirty streets.

Since last autumn I have gone thirteen or fourteen times, and I have bought about ten prostitutes. Mitsu, Masa, Kiyo, Mine, Tsuyu, Hana, Aki. . . . I have forgotten the names of some of them. What I sought was a warm, soft, white body: a pleasure in which my body and mind would melt. But those women, the old ones and the ones of fifteen who were still children, had all slept with hundreds or thousands of men.

There is no luster to their faces, their skin is cold and rough, they are so used to men that they feel no excitement. All it amounts to is that for a little while they hire out their private parts to men, and receive a pittance in exchange. Without even bothering to undo their sashes, they say "All right," and lie down just as they are, without the slightest embarrassment.

It doesn't make the least difference to them whether or not there is anyone on the other side of the partition who hears them. All it amounts to is that an excretory process has been effected with thousands of men. They have no desire to heal themselves with a pleasure in which the body and mind melt.

The nervous desire to seek strong excitement did not leave me even when I was receiving the excitement. I have spent the night three or four times.

It is no longer possible for me to go off somewhere all by myself, and yet I can obtain no satisfaction from people. I can't stand the agony of human life itself, but I can't do anything about it. Everything is in shackles, and there is heavy responsibility. What should I do? Hamlet said, *To be or not to be?* But in the present world the question of death has become more complicated than in Hamlet's time. Oh, Ilya! [1] Ilya's plan was the greatest plan that any human being could conceive. He tried to escape from life, no, he did escape, and then with all his strength he rushed from life—from this life of ours—into a limitless path of darkness. He dashed out his brains against a stone wall.

Ilya was a bachelor. I always think: how lucky Ilya was to have been a bachelor! There's the difference between the unhappy Ilya and myself.

I am worn out now. And I am seeking peace of mind. What sort of thing is "peace of mind?" Where is it? I can't return to the blank mind I had long ago before I knew pain, not if a hundred years were to elapse. Where is peace of mind?

I want to be sick. For a long time this desire has been lurking in my head. Sick! This word that other people hate sounds as sweet to

---

[1] Character in a Gorki story, "The Three of Them."

me as the name of the mountain where I was born. A free life, released from all responsibilities!

Sickness is the only way we have to obtain peace of mind.

I think: I wish they would all die. But nobody dies. I think: I wish they would all be my enemies. But nobody shows me any special enmity, and my friends all pity me.

Why am I loved? Why can't I hate anyone from the heart? To be loved is an insufferable insult.

But I am tired! I am a weakling!

> For just a year, for even a month,
> Even a week, even three days will do,
> God, if you exist, God!
> I have just one wish, that you
> Will break down my body somewhere.
> It doesn't matter if it hurts, make me sick
> Oh, make me sick.
>
> I want to sleep
> On pure white, soft, and
> Gently enveloping my whole body
> Cushions, where I feel as though I am sinking
> All the way into the bottom of a valley of peace, no
> On the worn mat of a home for the aged will do,
> Not thinking of anything (so that even if I die,
> I don't care) to sleep a long time.
> To sleep so soundly that I won't know
> If someone comes and steals my hands and feet.
>
> How's that for a feeling? Ah—
> Just the thought makes me sleepy.
>
> If I could tear off and throw away
> This garment I am wearing now,
> This heavy, heavy garment of obligation (ah, I grow drowsy).
> My body would become light as hydrogen,

And perhaps I would fly, high, high into the great sky,
And everyone below would say, perhaps, a lark!

Death! Death! My wish
Is for this alone.

Ah, will you really kill me? Wait just a bit,
Merciful God, oh, just a little while!

Just a bit, just enough to buy some bread,
Five, five cents will do,
If you have enough mercy to kill me!

A tepid wind heavy with rain is blowing this evening. In the distance the croaking of the frogs. At three in the morning the rain came splashing down.

11th, Sunday

Today I had to go to a poetry gathering at Yosano's house.[2] Naturally, there was no likelihood of anything amusing taking place. Hiraide was telling what a big success last night's "Devotees of Pan"[3] had been. Yoshii, who came in late, was saying, "Last night when I got drunk and pissed from Eitai Bridge, a policeman bawled me out." Everybody seems to have been drunk and had a wild time.

As usual we wrote poems on given themes. It must have been about nine o'clock when the selection of poems was completed. Recently I haven't felt like writing serious *uta,* and as usual turned out some mock verses. Here are a couple:

When I wear shoes
That make a squeak

[2] Yosano Tekkan (1873-1935), a leading poet of the day. For poetry by his wife Akiko, see pp. 202-3, 206.
[3] An artistic and literary club—1908-1912—led by the poets Kitahara Hakushū and Yoshii Isamu. The club stood for both European literature and the art of the Tokugawa period.

I feel unpleasant, as if
I tread upon a frog.

Your eyes must have
The mechanism of
A fountain pen—
You are always shedding tears.

The man
Whose hands tremble and voice breaks
At sight of a woman
No longer exists.

Akiko suggested that we sit up all night composing poetry. I
made some silly excuse and left.

Another precious day wasted. Suddenly a feeling of regret surged
up within me. If I was going to look at the cherry blossoms, why
didn't I go by myself and look at them as I wanted? A poetry
gathering! Of all the stupid things!

I am a person who delights in solitude, a born individualist. I feel
as if the time I have spent with others, at least when I haven't been
fighting with them, has been so much emptiness. It seems quite
natural that when I spend an hour with two or three or more people, the hour, or at least half of it, is so much emptiness.

I used to enjoy people's visits, and tried to send guests away as
happy as possible so that they would come again. What a stupid
thing to have done! Now I am not so pleased when people come.
The only ones I'm glad to see are those who are likely to lend me
money when I am broke. But I try not to borrow unless I have to.
How happy I would be if I could make a living without being
helped in anything because I am pitied! This doesn't necessarily refer
only to money. Then I could live without listening to anybody's talk.

I have thought what a pointless way I am living, but the thoughts
after that have frightened me. My desk is in a mess. I haven't anything to read. At the moment the most pressing thing is to write a
letter to my mother, but that also frightens me. I always think: I

wish I could comfort those poor people by writing them something, anything at all. And since the beginning of the year I've sent them exactly one letter and one postcard. This month, it was at the beginning of the month, I had a letter saying that they had only twenty sen to spend on Kyōko. I borrowed in advance even more than usual from the firm, with the intention of sending them fifteen yen. But I put it off from day to day, disliking to write a letter. Ah—

I fell asleep immediately.

12th, Monday

Today was just as beautiful as yesterday. The cherry blossoms, enjoying their three days of life under a windless sky, have yet to fall. The cherry tree under my window is sprouting pale leaves above the blossoms.

Down the hill on the right-hand side of the street, just at the corner of Tamachi, is a shoemaker's shop. When I passed there, suddenly a happy, gay voice entered my ears, as if from a fond memory. A wide grassy field floated up before my eyes—a skylark was singing in a cage at the shoemaker's. For a minute or so I remembered my dead cousin, with whom I used to go shooting in the fields near his house.

When I think of it, I have left my old—yes, old—friends, and the time has come for me to build a house for myself. The "old friends" I have are, or were, actually the newest friends I have made. Naturally I don't think of Yosano as an elder brother or as a father. He is simply a person who has helped me. The relations between one who helps and one who is helped can continue only while the former is more important a person than the latter, or while the two are traveling different roads, or if the former is no longer as great as the latter. When they are traveling the same road and there is rivalry between them, the friendship ends. I do not now have special respect for Yosano. We are both writers, but I somehow feel that we are traveling different roads.

I have no desire to be any closer to Yosano, but at the same time I do not feel any necessity of making a break with him. If an occasion comes, I should like to thank him for all he has done for me.

It is different with Akiko. I sometimes do think of her as an elder sister . . . the two of them are quite different.

Most of the other friends I have made through the New Poetry Society are very different from the Yosanos. I have already quarreled with Hirano. Yoshii is a second-rate lascivious daydreamer who frightens people by wearing a devil's mask—a pitiable second-rater. If their so-called literature is the same thing as my literature, I won't hesitate to throw away my pen forever. The others are not even worth mentioning.

No, such things have no use. However I think of it, they don't amount to anything.

To do only what I want, go where I want, follow all my own needs. . . .

Yes, I want to do as I please.

That is all! All of all!

Do not be loved by others, do not accept their charity, do not promise anything. Do nothing which entails asking forgiveness. Never talk to anyone about yourself. Always wear a mask. Always be ready for a fight—be able to hit the next man on the head at any time. Don't forget that when you make friends with someone you are sooner or later certain to break with him.

13th, Tuesday

Early this morning I opened my eyes, momentarily wakened by the noise of the maid opening the shutters. Hearing nothing else, I dozed off again, the unconscious sleep of spring. It is a cloudy calm day. All over the city the blossoms are gradually beginning to fall.

A sad letter came from my mother.

"Dear Mr. Ishikawa,

I was so happy with the letter you sent to Mr. Miyazaki. I have been waiting every day since, hoping word would come from you, and now it is April already. I am taking care of Kyōko and feeding her, which I have never done before. She is getting bigger every day, and is almost too much for me.

Can't you send for her? I beg the favor of a reply.[4] On the sixth and seventh there was a terrible rainstorm. The rain leaked in and we had nowhere to stay. Kyōko was so upset she couldn't sleep. She caught a cold on the second of April and is still not better. Setsuko [5] leaves for work every morning at eight o'clock and doesn't return until five or six. It's so hard for me when she is not here. There's no more household money left. Even one yen will be appreciated. I beg you kindly to send something soon. When do you think we will be able to go to Tokyo? Please let me know. If we don't get an answer from you, it's all over with us. We are all coming, so please make preparations.

                                                                Katsu"

My mother's letter, in shaky characters, full of spelling mistakes! I don't suppose very many people besides myself could read it. They say Mother was the best student at school when she was a girl. But in forty years of married life with my father, she probably never once wrote a letter. The first one I received from her was two summers ago. I had left Mother alone in Shibutami. She couldn't stand that dreadful town any longer, and she had written out of loneliness, searching in her memory for the completely forgotten characters. Today was the fifth letter I have received since coming to Tokyo. There are fewer mistakes, and the characters are better formed. How sad—my mother's letter!

                                                      14th, Wednesday
I decided to take off today and tomorrow, and started a story. I'm calling it "The Wooden Horse."

Inspiration in writing seems to be something like sexual desire. The man from the lending library came today and offered me some "unusual" books. Somehow I wanted to read them, and I borrowed two. One is called *The Misty Night in the Blossoms,* the other

[4] The letter is written in a combination of common, dialectal speech and old-fashioned phrases redolent of epistolary manuals.
[5] Takuboku's wife.

The Secrets of Love. I wasted three hours copying out in Romaji *The Misty Night.*

At night Nakajima came here, together with a minor poet named Uchiyama. Uchiyama's nose has the most extraordinary shape! It looks as if a deformed sweet potato had been stuck in the middle of his face, with a few parings and flattenings here and there. An endless flow of chatter comes from him: he's like one of those unshaven beggars one sees clowning in the streets. On top of everything else, he is practically a midget. I have never seen anyone quite so pathetic-looking. A truly pitiful, farcical innocent—excessively so, perhaps: I felt a strange impulse to smash him in the face. Every serious utterance he makes sounds funny, and when he says something humorous with a sniff of his grotesque nose, he looks as if he is crying.

It started to rain a little before ten. Nakajima professes to be a Socialist, but his is a very aristocratic socialism—he left in a rickshaw. Uchiyama—the poet is a real Socialist—went home under a borrowed umbrella. He really looked a poet.

I wrote three pages of "The Wooden Horse." I longed for Setsuko —not because of the lonely patter of the rain, but because I had been reading *The Misty Night in the Blossoms.*

                                                    15th, Thursday
No! Does my need for Setsuko arise simply out of sexual desire? No! No!

My love for her has cooled. That is a fact, a not surprising fact— regrettable but inescapable.

Love is only a part, not the entirety of human life, a diversion, something like a song. Everyone wants at times to sing and it is a pleasant thing to do. But man cannot spend his whole life in song, and to sing the same tune all the time, however joyous it may be, is sating.

My love has cooled; I am tired of singing that song—it's not that I dislike it. Setsuko is really a good woman. Is there in all the world another such good, gentle, sensible woman? I cannot imagine a better wife than Setsuko. Sometimes, even while I was actually sleeping with Setsuko, I have hungered for other women. But what has that to do with Setsuko? I was not dissatisfied with her. It is simply that men have complex desires.

I have not changed in my love for Setsuko. She was not the only woman I loved, but the one I loved most. Even now, especially during the last few days, I often think of her.

The present marriage system—the whole social system—is riddled with errors. Why must I be tied down because of parents, a wife, or a child? Why must they be victimized because of me? But that, naturally, is quite apart from the fact that I love my parents, Setsuko, and Kyōko.

16th, Friday

What an idiotic thing! Last night I stayed up until three copying in my notebook that pornographic old novel *The Misty Night in the Blossoms*. Ah, me!

I could not control my craving for that intense pleasure!

When I woke about ten this morning I felt a strange mental fatigue. I read the letter from Miyazaki.

Will they all please die, or must I? It's one or the other! I really thought that as I sat down to write an answer. I assured Miyazaki that I am now able to make a living, and said that all I need is the money to move from these lodgings, to rent a house, and to pay the traveling expenses for my family! When I finished writing, I wished I were dead.

I finally got off the one yen to my mother. Out of dislike for writing, out of fear, I have neglected to send it until today. I enclosed it in the letter to Miyazaki.

Tonight Kindaichi [6] came to my room. He talked about all kinds of things, hoping to stir up some literary inspiration in me. I didn't answer—instead, I indulged in a variety of absurd pranks which eventually drove Kindaichi away. I took up my pen immediately. Half an hour went by. I was obliged to give serious consideration again to my inability to write a novel and to the fact that my future

[6] Kindaichi Kyōsuke, the distinguished philologist and student of the Ainu, was a close friend of Takuboku's, and lived in the next room during this period.

is devoid of hope. I went to Kindaichi's room and performed my whole repertory of silly tricks. I painted a huge face on my chest and made all kinds of grimaces, whistled like a thrush, and, in conclusion, took out my knife and acted out the part of the murderer in a play. Kindaichi fled from the room! I certainly must have been thinking something horrible!

I had switched off the light in his room, and stood in the doorway brandishing my knife.

Later, back in my room, we looked at each other in dismay at what had happened. I thought that suicide could not frighten me.

Then, at night, what did I do? *Misty Night in the Blossoms!*

It is about two o'clock. Somewhere off beyond Koishigawa there is a fire, a single dull red line of smoke climbing perpendicularly into the black sky.

A fire!

17th, Saturday

I did not go to work today because I was sure I would be able to write—no, it was because I wanted to take the day off that I decided to write. I attempted to describe last night's thoughts about suicide. I wrote three pages and couldn't think of another line.

I tried to correct some poems, but just spreading out the paper was enough to make me sick.

I thought of writing a story about a man who is arrested by a policeman for sleeping in a vacant house, but couldn't find the energy to lift my pen.

I said to myself, "I positively will give up my literary career."

"If I give up literature, what shall I do?"

Death! That's the only answer.

Either I must have money or else be released from all responsibilities.

Probably this problem will haunt me until I die—I'll think about it in bed!

19th, Monday

The abominable treatment I receive at my lodgings has reached a limit. I got up about nine. No fire, even after I finished washing. I put away the bedding myself. While I impatiently smoked a cigarette, a child went by in the hall. I told him to get me fire and some hot water. Twenty minutes later they brought breakfast. Nothing to eat it with. I rang the bell. Nobody came. I rang again. Nobody came. After what seemed hours the maid brought a spoon, which she flung down without a word on the table. The soup had become stone cold.

Under my window an elderbush is in blossom. Long, long ago, when I was still living in Shibutami, I often used to make pipes from elder branches.

I always think when the maid and the others are rude to me, "Damn them! I can just imagine how they'll fawn on me when I pay the bill!" But, I wonder, will such a day ever come?

21st, Wednesday

The cherry trees are in full leaf. When I opened the window this morning, a smoky color of young leaves met my eyes. Yesterday I saw two people in summer hats. It's summer!

At nine o'clock I went to the public bath in Daimachi. I often used to go there when I first came to Tokyo last year. Nothing has changed, except that the seventeen-year-old girl-attendant, the one who seemed fond of me, is no longer there. I could see through the window the shadows of young leaves in the fresh morning sunlight. I returned to all my feelings of a year ago. Then the memory of the dreadful Tokyo summer came back with painful vividness, that summer I spent in lodgings. I was in terrible financial straits, but happy to be escaping even briefly the responsibility of providing for my family. Yes, I was enjoying the sensation of being a "semi-bachelor." I soon abandoned the woman with whom I was having an affair at the time. She's now a geisha in Asakusa. A great deal has changed. I have made a number of new friends and discarded them.

As I scrubbed my body, healthier than it was then, I lost myself in recollections—a year of terrible struggle! *The dreadful summer is coming again on me—the penniless novelist! The dreadful summer!*

alas! with great pains and deep sorrows of physical struggle, and, other young with the bottomless rapture of hand, Nihilist!

As I come out of the gate of the bathhouse, the expressful faced woman who sold me the soap yesterday said to me 'Good morning' with something calm and favourable gesture.

The bath and the memories bring me some hot and young lightness. I am young, and, at last, the life is not so dark and so painful. The sun shines, and moon is calm. If I do not send the money, or call up them to Tôkyô, they—my mother and wife will take other manner to eat. I am young, and young, and young: and I have the pen, the brain, the eyes, the heart and the mind. That is all. All of all. If the inn-master take me out of this room, I will go everywhere —where are many inns and hotels in this capital. To-day, I have only one piece of 5rin-dôkwa: [7] but what then? Nonsence! There are many, many writers in Tokyo. What is that to me? There is nothing. They are writing with their finger-bones and the brush: but I must write with the ink and the G pen! That is all. Ah, the burning summer and the green-coloured struggle!

TRANSLATED BY DONALD KEENE

[7] A small copper coin, half a sen.

THE WILD GOOSE

[*Gan, IX-XI, 1911-1913*] *by Mori Ōgai (1862-1922)*

Mori Ōgai was one of the leading literary figures of the early twentieth century. After his graduation from the Tokyo University Medical Department he spent several years studying in Germany, and returned to Japan to lead a double career as a writer and doctor. Some of his most famous works are translations from the German, and others describe his experiences in Europe as a young man.

Among Mori Ōgai's original writings the novel The Wild Goose, *published serially in 1911-1913, probably retains the greatest appeal. It is the story of Otama, a girl who, after a false marriage with a bigamous police officer, becomes the mistress of another man. Later in the novel she falls in love with a medical student who passes her house every day, but he leaves for Germany before she can confess her love. The following excerpts deal with her life immediately after she becomes the mistress of Suezō.*

•

Otama, who had never before been separated from her father, often thought of going to see how he was getting along. She was afraid, however, that Suezō, who came every day, might be annoyed if she were out when he called, and thus it was that her plan to visit her father was put off from one day to the next. Suezō never stayed until morning, and often he left as early as eleven. At other times, explaining that he had business that evening, he would stay only long enough for a moment's smoke by the fire. Yet there was no day on which Otama could be sure that he would not come. She might have gone to her father's in the daytime, but Ume, the maid, was such a child that it was impossible to trust her to do anything alone, and in any case, Otama did not wish to leave the house when the neighbors could see her. At first she had gone without thought to the public bath at the foot of the hill, but now she generally sent the maid down to make sure it was empty before quietly slipping out to take her bath.

On the third day after she moved, Otama, who was prone to take fright at almost anything, had had an experience that quite took her courage away. On the day of her arrival, men from the grocer's and the fish store had come with their order-books to request her patronage, but that morning the fishmonger failed to call, and she sent the maid out to buy a slice of fish for lunch. Otama had no desire to eat fresh fish every day; her father had always been satisfied with any sort of simple dinner, and she had become accustomed to making do with whatever happened to be in the house. But she had heard how people talk of "poverty-stricken neighbors who never eat fresh food," and she was afraid that the same thing might be said of her, bringing shame on a master who had been most generous. She accordingly sent the maid to the fish store at the foot of the hill, mainly so that she might be seen.

Ume found a shop and went in, only to discover that it was not the same one whose man had come for orders. The proprietor was out, and his wife was tending the counter. From the heaps of fish laid out on the racks, Ume selected a small mackerel that looked fresh, and asked the price. "I don't believe I've seen you before," said the fishwife. "Where do you come from?" Ume described the house on the hill in which she lived, whereupon the woman suddenly looked very displeased. "Indeed!" she said. "I'm sorry, then, but you had better run along. We have no fish here to sell to a moneylender's mistress!" With this she turned away and went on smoking, not deigning to pay any further attention to the girl. Ume, too upset to feel like going to any other shop, came running back and, looking very wretched, repeated in disconnected scraps what the fishwife had said.

As Otama listened her face turned pale, and for some time she stood silent. In the heart of the naive young woman a hundred confused emotions mingled in chaos, nor could she herself have untangled their knotted threads. A great weight pressed down upon her heart, to which now the blood from throughout her body flowed, leaving her face blanched and a cold sweat over her back. Her first conscious thought was that, after such an incident, Ume would no longer be able to remain in the house.

Ume gazed at the pale, bloodless face of her mistress, sensing merely that she was in great distress, without comprehending the cause. She had returned in anger from the store, but now she realized that there was still nothing for lunch, and she could hardly leave things as they were. The purse which her mistress had given her for the shopping remained thrust into the sash of her kimono. "I've never seen such a horrid old woman," she said in an effort to be comforting. "I don't know who would buy her fish, anyway! There's another store down by the Inari Shrine. I'll run down there and get something, shall I?" Otama felt a momentary joy that Ume had declared herself her ally, and her face reflected a weak smile as she nodded approval. Ume bounded off with a clatter.

Otama remained for a while without moving. Then her taut nerves began gradually to relax, and tears welled up in her eyes. She drew a handkerchief from her sleeve to press them back. In her heart was only one thought—how dreadful! Did she hate the fishwife for not selling her anything, or was she ashamed or unhappy that she was the sort of person that shops would not sell to? No, it was not that sort of feeling. Nor was it that she hated Suezō, the man to whom she had given herself and whom she now knew to be a moneylender. Nor indeed did she feel any particular shame or regret that she had given herself to such a man. She had heard from others that moneylenders were unpleasant, frightening people whom everybody detested; but her father had never borrowed money from one. He had always gone to the pawnshop, and even when the clerk had hardheartedly refused to give him as much as he asked for a pledge, the old man would never express any resentment over the clerk's unreasonableness, but would merely shake his head sadly. As a child fears ghosts or policemen, Otama counted moneylenders among the things to be afraid of, but with no vivid or personal emotion. What, then, upset her so?

In her mortification there was very little hatred for the world or for people. If one were to ask what in fact she resented, the answer was, perhaps, her own fate. Through no fault of her own she had been made to suffer persecution, and this was what she found so painful. She had first felt this mortification when she was deceived and abandoned by the police officer, and recently, again, when she realized that she must become someone's mistress. Now she learned that she was not only a mistress but the mistress of a despised money-lender, and her despair, that had been ground smooth between the teeth of time and washed of its color in the waters of resignation, assumed once more in her heart its stark and vivid outline.

After a while Otama got up, took from the cupboard a calico apron and, tying it on, went with a deep sigh into the kitchen. She was now quite calm again. Resignation was the mental process she had most often experienced, and if she directed her mind toward that goal, it operated with the accustomed smoothness of a well-oiled machine.

. .

At first when Suezō came in the evenings, Otama would spread a mat for him by the side of the large square brazier, where he would sit at his ease, smoking and gossiping. She herself, at a loss to know what to do with her hands, would sit on her side, drumming on the edge of the brazier or playing with the fire tongs, and answer him shyly. After they had chatted a while, she would become more voluble, speaking mostly of the minor joys and sorrows that she had known during the years with her father. Suezō paid little attention to the content of her discourse, but listened rather as to a cricket in a cage whose engaging chirps brought a smile to his face. Then Otama would suddenly become aware of her own garrulousness and, blushing, would break off her story and return to her former silence. Her words and actions were so guileless that to Suezō's ever observant eyes they appeared as transparent as clear water in a bowl. Her companionship brought a refreshing delight that to him was a totally new experience; in his visits to the house he was like a wild animal introduced for the first time to the ways of human society.

Some days later, when Suezō was sitting as usual before the brazier, he noticed that Otama, for no apparent reason, kept moving restlessly around the room without settling down. She had always been slow to answer and shy, but her behavior tonight had about it a new and unusual air.

"What are you thinking about?" he asked as he filled his pipe.

Otama pulled the drawer at the end of the brazier halfway out and, although she was not looking for anything, peered intently into it. "Nothing," she said, turning her large eyes to his face.

"What do you mean, 'nothing'? You're thinking, 'What shall I do, what shall I do?'—it's written all over your face," he retorted.

Otama flushed and for a moment remained silent while she considered what to say. The workings of the delicate apparatus of her mind became almost visible. "I've been thinking that I ought to go visit my father," she said. Tiny insects that must forever be escaping more powerful creatures have their protective coloring; women tell lies.

Suezō laughed and spoke in a scolding voice. "Come now! Your father living by the pond not ten minutes' walk from here, and you haven't gone to see him yet? You can go now if you like. Or, better still, tomorrow morning."

Otama, twirling the ashes with the fire tongs, stole a glance at Suezō. "I was just wondering whether it would be all right—"

"There's no need to worry about a thing like that. How long will you stay a child?" This time his voice was gentle.

Suezō was vaguely aware that there was still something in Otama's heart that she was hiding, but when he tried to discover what it was she had given him that childish, trivial answer. Still, as he left the house somewhat after eleven and walked slowly down the hill, he knew that there was something. She had been told something that had aroused in her a feeling of uneasiness, he surmised. But what she had heard, or from whom, he could not tell.

When Otama arrived at her father's house by the pond the next morning, he had just finished breakfast. Otama, who had hastened there without even taking time to put on any powder, wondered if she might not be too early; but the old man, accustomed to early rising, had already swept the gate and sprinkled water about to settle the dust. He was now just finishing his lonely morning meal.

The gates of the neighboring houses were still shut, and in the early morning the surroundings seemed unusually quiet. From the low windows of the house one could see through the pine boughs a weeping willow trembling in the breeze, and beyond, the lotus leaves that covered the surface of the pond. Here and there among their green shone the pink dots of blossoms newly opened in the morning sun.

From the time Otama was old enough to think for herself she had dreamt of all the things she would do for her father, should fortune ever come her way, and now, when she saw before her eyes the house that she had provided for him, she could not but feel joyful. Yet in her joy there was mingled a drop of bitterness. If it were not for that, how great her joy would be at meeting her father today, but, as she thought with irritation, one cannot have the world quite as one wishes it.

There had as yet been no visitors to the old man's house. When he heard the sound of someone at the gate, he put down the cup of tea he was drinking and glanced in surprise toward the entrance hall. Then, while she was still hidden by the hall screen, he heard Otama's voice calling, "Papa!" He restrained his impulse to jump up in greeting, and sat where he was, considering what to say. "It was so good of you to remember your old father," he thought of saying in spite, but when his beloved daughter suddenly appeared by his side, he could not utter the words. Disgruntled as he was, he only gazed in silence at her face. Against his will his expression softened.

Otama had thought only of how much she wanted to see her father again, but now was unable to find words for all the things she had planned to say.

The maid poked her head in from the kitchen and asked in her country dialect, "Shall I remove the tray?"

"Yes, take it away and bring some fresh tea. Use the green tea on the shelf," said the old man, pushing the tray away from him.

"Oh, please don't bother to make special tea!" Otama protested.

"Nonsense! I have some biscuits here, too." The old man rose and brought back some egg biscuits from a tin in the cupboard and put them on the table.

While the two drank their tea they chatted as if they had never been apart. Suddenly the old man asked in a rather embarrassed tone, "How are things coming along? Does your master come to see you sometimes?"

"Yes," said Otama, and for a moment she seemed unable to answer more. It was not "sometimes" that Suezō came, but every night without fail. Had she just been married, she might have replied with great cheerfulness to an inquiry as to whether she was getting along well with her husband, but in her present position the fact that her master came every night seemed almost shameful, and she found it difficult to mention. She thought for a moment, and then replied, "Things seem to be going all right, Papa. There is nothing at all for you to worry about."

"That's good," he said, though he felt at the same time a certain lack of assurance in his daughter's answer. An evasiveness had come into their speech. They who up until now had always spoken with complete freedom, who had never had the slightest secret from each other, found themselves forced, against their will, to address each other like strangers and to maintain a certain reserve. In the past, when they had been deceived by the fraudulent police officer, they had been ashamed before their neighbors, but they had both of them known in their hearts that the blame lay with him, and they had discussed the whole terrible affair without the slightest reserve. But now, when their plans had turned out successfully and they were comfortably established, a new shadow, a sadness, lay over their conversation.

The old man was anxious to have a more concrete answer. "What sort of man is he?" he began again.

"Well—" said Otama thoughtfully, inclining her head to one side and speaking as though to herself, "I surely don't think he is a *bad* person. We haven't been together very long, but so far he has never used any harsh language or anything like that."

"Oh?" said the old man with a look of dissatisfaction. "And is there any reason to suppose that he *is* a bad person?"

Otama looked quickly at her father and her heart began to pound. If she was to say what she had come to say, now was the time to say it. But the thought of inflicting a new blow on her father, now that she had at last brought him peace of mind, was too painful. She resolved to go away without revealing her secret, and at the crucial moment she turned the conversation in another direction. "They said he was a man who had done all sorts of things to build a fortune for himself. I didn't know what to expect, and I was rather worried. But he's—well, what would you say—chivalrous. Whether that is his real nature I can't say, but he is certainly making an effort to act that way. As long as he tries to be chivalrous, that's enough, don't you think, Papa?" She looked up at her father. For a woman, no matter how honest, to hide what is in her heart and talk of something else is not so difficult as it is for a man. It is possible that in such a situation the more volubly she speaks the more honest she really is.

"Perhaps you are right. But somehow you speak as though you don't trust the man," her father said.

Otama smiled. "I've grown up, Papa. From now on I don't intend to be made a fool of by others. I intend to be strong."

The old man, suddenly sensing that his daughter, usually so mild and submissive, was for once turning the point of her remarks at him, looked at her uneasily. "Well, it's true, as you know, that I've gone through life pretty consistently being made a fool of. But you will feel a good deal better in your heart if you are cheated by others than if you are always cheating them. Whatever business you are in, you must never be dishonest, and you must remember those who have been kind to you."

"Don't worry. You always used to say that I was an honest child, and I still am. But I've been thinking quite a bit lately. I want no more of being taken in by people."

"You mean that you don't trust what your master says?"

"Yes, that's it. He thinks I'm just a child. Compared to him, perhaps I am, but I am not as much of a child as he thinks."

"Has he told you anything that you've discovered to be untrue?"

"Indeed he has! You remember how the old go-between kept saying that his wife had died and left him with the children, and that if I accepted his favors it would be just as though I were a proper wife? She told us that it was just to keep up appearances that he couldn't let me live in his own home. It happens that he *has* a wife. He said so himself, just like that. I was so surprised that I didn't know what to do."

The father's eyes widened. "So, she was just trying to make it sound like a good match—"

"Of course, he has to keep everything about me a strict secret from his wife," Otama continued. "He tells her all kinds of lies, so I hardly expect him to speak nothing but the truth to me. I intend to take anything he says with a grain of salt."

The old man sat holding the burnt-out pipe he had been smoking, and looked blankly at his daughter. She seemed suddenly to have grown so much older and more serious. "I must be getting back," she said hurriedly, as though she had just remembered something. "Now that I've come and seen that everything is all right, I'll be visiting you every day. I had hesitated because I thought that I'd better get his permission first, but last night he finally told me I might come. Now I must run on and see how things are at home."

"If you got permission from him to come, why don't you stay for lunch?" the old man asked.

"No, I don't think I should. I'll come again very soon, Papa. Good-bye!" Otama got up to leave.

"Come again when you can," said the old man without rising, "and give my kindest regards to your master."

Otama pulled a little purse from her black satin sash, took out a few bills, and gave them to the maid. Then she went out to the gate. She had come intending to bare the bitterness in her breast and share her misfortune with her father, but to her own surprise she now found herself leaving almost in good spirits. With a cheerful face she walked along the edge of the pond. Although the sun, now risen high above Ueno Hill, was beating down fiercely, lighting the vermilion pillars of the Benten Shrine, Otama carried her little foreign-style parasol in her hand without bothering to put it up.

TRANSLATED BY BURTON WATSON

A TALE OF THREE WHO WERE BLIND

[*Sannin no Mekura no Hanashi, 1912*] *by Izumi Kyōka (1873-1939)*

Izumi Kyōka is known as a "romantic," and his best work derives from the erotic and fantastic literature of the Edo period. He is much admired as a stylist.

•

"One moment . . . you, sir."

At the voice, a chill shot down Sakagami's back—though not as at a voice he remembered and disliked. From the foot of the hill he had seen them creeping down toward him from Yotsuya, appearing and disappearing, floating up and falling back again, in the mist that huddled in motionless spirals halfway up the slope. He could hardly hear the sound of their feet; and then, as they passed, that voice.

They were nothing to him, and yet he knew that something must happen before he would be allowed to pass. They would call him, they would stop him—he was strangely sure that somehow he must hear a voice. It might be as when a traveler hears the cry of a raven or the scream of a night heron and cannot be sure, even if he is quite alone, that the call has been at him; but Sakagami knew that he would have to hear that unpleasant, that odious voice.

Three blind ones in single file.

In the center was a woman, perhaps in her middle years, white throated, thick haired, her shoulders thin and slight. The long sleeves, falling down from her folded arms, were of a darkness that seemed to sink through to the thin breasts beneath, and their trailing edges gave way to a like darkness in the obi. Was the slapping from her sandals?—but the long skirt brushed the ground and hid her feet.

The man in front wore a limp, loose garment, gray perhaps, in the darkness almost like the night mist itself spun and woven. His brimless cap shot into the air, a veritable miter. His gaunt body swayed as he drew near—and passed.

The other man, slender and of no more than medium height, clung to the woman as if he meant to hide in the shadow of her hair. Though Sakagami had had no clear view of any of them, the third had been the most obscure of all.

And yet Sakagami knew immediately that he had been stopped by this shadowy one.

"Are you speaking to me?" Sakagami looked back. His shoulders were hunched in the sudden chill, and his answer was like a curse flung at a barking dog.

"I am speaking to you." The voice was low. It was indeed the slight man in the rear. He seemed to straighten up as he spoke to Sakagami, who was two or three paces up the hill from him. He held his staff at an angle, an oar with which to row his way through the mist.

The other two—the long head in front; and the high Japanese coiffure (Sakagami could not be sure what style), like a wig on an actor's wig stand, suspended upside-down—stood diagonally down the slope with their backs to their companion.

Sakagami turned on his heels to stare at the man.

"And what do you want?"

"I should like to talk to you." Whether he was very sure of himself, or out of breath, his slowness seemed wrong in the cold of the late winter night.

2

"What is it?"

Coming toward him in the mist, they had seemed like two grave markers, a tall one and a low one, blown in by a last gust of the autumn winds from some cemetery on the moors, the dead tufts of grass white in the earth still clinging to their bases.

But his tone became more gentle as he saw that the three, groping their way along this shabby, deserted street as through the caves on the Musashino Plain, were only three blind ones who made their living by massaging and who had set out together, who would blow the flutes that were the sign of their trade, as thin and high in the winter night as the sound of a mosquito in January, and who would presently disappear behind the lantern of a poor rooming house.

"I have little to say. But I should like to know where you are going. Where? Where? Where?" There was a touch of derision in the nasal tone. His head cocked to one side, the man looked up at Sakagami. He raised his hand as if to scratch his ear, and tapped at the head of the staff.

"It makes no difference," said Sakagami testily. He was going to meet a woman who had been forbidden to see him. "Does it matter where I'm going?"

"It does. I am sorry, sir, but it does." There was a strength in the voice that kept Sakagami fixed to the spot.

"And why?" Sakagami turned and started down toward the man; but he pulled back as the mist clutched at his face.

"It is late." The voice was suddenly strong. The head bowed heavily toward the earth.

Long Head, in front, turned slowly to face the bank above the road.

The woman seemed to sink into the earth as she sat down disconsolately on her heels. The tip of her staff was white against the dark hair.

Seeing that the three meant to stay, Sakagami resigned himself to being delayed; but at the thought of what lay ahead his chest rose and fell violently, as if poison were being forced in through his mouth. A rising, a rush of blood, and a collapse with an angry tremor of the flesh.

Banks rose on both sides like mountain slopes. Against the sky, over the bank toward which Long Head faced, one or two barracks-style houses stood like tea huts on a mountain pass, tight and dark. Not a sliver of light escaped from them. On the bank, dead grass, blanketed by the mist as by a frost.

On the side of the road where the three had stopped, the bank had slid away, exposing the roots of trees and the retaining stakes.

Trees sent up their skeleton forms above. Here and there the mist clung to the branches like dirty moonlight. There were no stars. The bottom of a defile in Yotsuya, like the bottom of a mountain ravine, at one o'clock in the morning.

Only the racing in the chest. "Is it wrong to be so late?" The words themselves seemed to be weighted down by the heavy air.

"You were certain to say that." The man slapped the back of the hand that held the staff. "It is wrong, very wrong indeed."

"I am not to go on then?" Perhaps this oracle could tell him something of the meeting that was to come.

"If you will go on, whatever I say, let that be the end of it. But I must stop you for a moment. I alone—or that gentleman too."

Long Head coughed faintly as the other brought his staff upright.

3

"And what if I have to go?" Sakagami's breath came faster. "What if my father is dying, or a friend is ill? How can you know? You speak as though I were doing something wrong."

The man bent his head as though to rub his cheek against the staff, and laughed unpleasantly. "I know where you are going. And that gentleman says I must speak. . . . Shall I tell you? It will be no trouble. And you will tell me I am right. You go to meet a woman."

Sakagami did not answer.

"She has duties and ties. There are obstacles and complications. But you have pushed and slashed, and broken down fences and walls. . . . You have pressed her with an urgency that would tear her very breast open, and she will meet you at the risk of her life. You are on your way to meet her. I knew from your footsteps as you came up, and met us, and passed. I knew a man rushing along, out of his senses.

"Dew falls, frost falls. The moon clouds over, the stars are dark. In the wide skies too there are shadows. The shadows are gentle. But the breast is blocked and the breath is tight. See the lightning and the thunderclap after the darkness.

"In the heart of man, nothing is strange.

"I think as you do, I put myself in your place, and everything is clear, even to a blind man, as clear as this hand itself." The man brought his hand up to cover his face.

Sakagami could see in the dim light that the other two were nodding deeply, as if on a signal.

"You are fortunetellers, are you? I was in a hurry, and perhaps I was rude." Sakagami heaved a sigh. "She left home barefoot. . . . It is some distance from here, but she is waiting in the woods alone. She cannot move until I come.

"I had a telephone call from her just now, so short that it was no more than a signal, and I hardly know what I am about. Can I help going? Do you say I shouldn't go?"

"I thought as much. . . . No, you were right to admit everything like a man. It will be sad for both of you. But how very dangerous." The man clutched his staff to his chest with both hands, and stood in silence for a moment. "I shall ask you a question. Along this bank where we are gathered there is a row of gaslights. How many of them are lighted, and how many are dark? Tell me, please. Tell me." He nodded as he spoke, and his head fell to his chest.

Sakagami followed the line from the bottom of the hill behind the three. It was not the first time he had taken this road. Below the cliff, on one side, the gaslights stood at intervals of about two yards, put up by a nearby movie theatre for the safety of passers-by.

The lamps were white and cold as frost needles. The glass chambers, like windows in the face of the cliff, were dark as far as his eye reached. They drank at the mist and sucked it in, and at intervals spewed out an ashen breath.

Like a devil's death mask shaped from cotton wadding, the mist clung to the nearest lamp and became a great earth spider, sending out horrible threads on that ashen breath, into the sky and down to the ground. Was that why the mist seemed to clutch so at the face?

4

"They will all be out," the man said as Sakagami looked up and down the row.

"They are all out." The darkness of the night closed in more tightly.

"They will all be out. And now, you will see that one lamp up the hill from here is still burning. You see it? How many lamps away is it?"

"I see it." There was one feeble, wavering flame, about to float off on the mist. "But I can't tell you how many lamps away it is."

"Not far away. When the traveler sees a night crane in the pines along a lonely road, it is always in the fifth pine away. . . . The lamp will be the fifth up the hill from you.

"If I am wrong, that gentleman will tell me so. He says nothing. I am right. Count them for yourself, count them for yourself. One . . ." He tapped twice with his staff.

"One."

"Two." Tap, tap, tap.

"Three. Four. Five. It is the fifth."

"As I said."

"But why?"

"You see us, and this bank, and these dark lamps, all because oↄ that one light. But for it, you would not see me if I were to pinch your nose."

He did indeed see the dim figures by the light of that one lamp. By that faint light, even the row of dark lamps down the slope sent out an occasional flicker of light—and Sakagami stood dim and uncertain in the breathing mist.

"What does it mean?"

"And can you see nothing under the fifth lamp, the lamp that is burning?"

"I beg your pardon?" Sakagami's voice shook.

"And can you see nothing?"

"Nothing."

"Nothing?"

"Not a thing."

"That is not as it should be. If you will but go up and look, you will see. It is for that that I have stopped you. Listen, if you will."

He twisted and bent forward a little, and rattled his staff in the stones that lay at the base of a gas lamp. The sound was drunk up in the mist.

"Let me make the point clear: The gaslight under which we stand—it has moved not one step ahead of us and not one step behind us since I stopped you—is the nineteenth in the row from the bottom of the hill.

"If I am wrong, the master there will correct me.

"Three years ago, on a different night indeed, but in this same November, at this same hour, this happened to me too.

"I was not then the blind man you see now."

He turned squarely toward Sakagami, but his head was still bowed.

"I was going to meet a woman as you are, and I was climbing this hill.

"But I passed only one blind man. That is the whole of the difference."

Long Head faced squarely down the hill away from Sakagami, and started to walk off—and was still again.

5

And the woman: still sitting on her heels, she turned to hear the story. The knee of her kimono and the obi at her waist were folded one against the other. Her throat was white.

The man's voice was firm. "He called me from behind, as I called you, and, at the nineteenth lamp, the fifth below the lighted lamp, he said to me what I have said to you.

"I have but repeated it.

"And why should I not go to meet the woman, I retorted as you did. He answered. . . ."

Sakagami somehow knew that "he" was Long Head here.

" 'There is a strange creature under the fifth lamp ahead, the lamp that is still lighted. . . . A demon that takes the shadows of men, snatches them, devours them.

" 'He sucks at a shadow, and the man grows thin; licks the shadow with his tongue, and the man languishes; tramps on the shadow, and the man is ill; snuffs it quite away, and the man dies.

" 'The demon is always about, in the sunlight and the moonlight, to suck, to lick, to trample, and in time the man dies. Terrible though that is, it is more terrible when, under just such a light as we have here, he opens his mouth . . .' "

The blind man's gaping mouth.

" '. . . and swallows the shadow. That is all. The man dies. You are not to pass by here again.'

"That is what he said.

"But I was young and hotheaded. What was he talking about? I retorted. In the first place, what sort of monster was it? He did not smile. 'Very well, very well, I shall tell you. It is like a lizard with a fez. It is like a white dog spread-eagled, and on its head a biretta.'

"Seeing was quicker than hearing, I said. Let the thing have my shadow—I had believed nothing. I climbed to that fifth light, kicking up the gravel as I went. I found nothing there.

"The blind man, scraping at the gravel with his staff, sprang up the hill after me. 'Have you gone mad? You are too brave for your own good. It is no use talking to one who believes nothing I say, but the demon will not be after your shadow for a time.

" 'He has long been after the shadow of the woman, the woman you are going to meet. I tell her through you to be forever careful, not for a moment to be off her guard.'

"That is what he said."

6

"And why should he be giving advice—did he know the woman, I asked. 'A housewife in my block saw her just this evening. They were at the bath together. The skin like snow, patted and rounded —one wondered why it did not melt in the steam. Over it, scarlet satin, and a pale yellow sash—scarlet that seemed to glide and flow from the breasts. A kimono for good autumn weather, a latticework of indigo and dark-blue stripes. A black damask obi, and a scarlet cord. An azure ribbon to bind the hair. An ear, faint through hair aglow like falling dew. And the rich swell of the neck and shoulders. Woman though she was, the housewife I speak of stood fascinated. She moved around to the front, and stared at the back, and peered at the naked form in the mirror. And she described everything to me, down to the mole on the white skin at the base of the left breast.'

" 'It will be this woman you are going to see.'

"That is what he said."

Sakagami was trembling. Not only because the faint image of the woman, now looking away, came to him as that of the woman being described—the same kimono, the same obi.

But because of the woman he was going to meet tonight. He expected her to have on *that* obi, and *that* kimono—but what if she should have on the everyday black obi and the latticed kimono that had so become a part of his life?

His blood ran cold, and an instant later he flushed.

" 'Am I right? The kimono, the obi, the scarlet beneath . . . am I right about the woman you are going to meet?' It made no difference about the black damask, or about the indigo and blue, or about the white skin. But imagine, if you will, how it was to be told even of the mole on the breast.

"It was as though I could see before my eyes—fearsome thing— the figure lying naked, the kimono open, here in this Yotsuya Valley.

"The demon, said the blind man, was after the woman, to lick her shadow, to suck at it, to take it, to trample it, to devour it. 'Tell her, if you please, that she is to be careful.' But I was not listening. I flew off in a dark cloud. I was not to be stopped by iron gate or stone door, and I went to meet that small, defenseless woman.

"I had seen a demon that would take her shadow, would suck at her shadow, would lick at her shadow. I had seen it in the light of the gas lamp.

"The woman's house was very near here.

" 'It will be after you day and night. You are not looking well, your shadow is thin already. Watch for it.' That, sir, is what I said.

"An unhappy woman, whom labor and anguish had already so devastated that her obi, however tightly bound, could not be tight enough—into the head of this unhappy woman I drove my words as with a hammer.

"In my anger that she had shown herself naked to another. She fell upon my knee, and in a voice that trembled asked whom I had met and what I had heard along the way. Look to your own conscience—I said; and I did not tell her I had heard the story from a blind man.

"A tragic mistake. It was the blind man himself who clung to the woman like her very shadow. It was the blind man himself who might have been taken for a lizard in the gaslight, who hovered about the back fence, the well, the hedge, face livid, eyes red, lips pale and tight, waiting for the woman to come in or go out.

"Had she known it was the blind man, she would not have been so haunted by the story."

7

"Thereafter I saw the woman less often.

"She seemed to avoid me.

"I thought of killing her and myself; but presently, as I heard the details, I learned that she was avoiding everyone. She had a strange longing to be hidden.

"And finally, like the splittailed cat who has taken the shape of a beautiful woman, she came to hate the light of the sun. Whether it was night or day, she closed the doors and the shutters, and lay hidden behind two and three screens.

"I forced my way through, and saw her. Her very kimono seemed moldering and musty, and she only knelt looking at the floor, so slight and wraithlike that it seemed she must quite disappear.

"I raised her face. The eyes were destroyed. I beg your pardon? No, the woman's eyes, both the woman's eyes.

"I heard her story. She had not been able even for an instant to take her eyes from her shadow.

"If she went into the kitchen it was on the window, if she went to the veranda it was on the doorstep or behind her on the door, the wall, the screen.

"And wherever the shadow was, there was the demon, to suck at it, to lick, trample, rub, embrace, cover.

"In the light of the moon, the light of the sun, the light of the lamp, the faint light of the snow or of trees in blossom, there was always that shadow. And with the shadow: discomfort, revulsion—terror and loathing.

"Finally, darkness. But even when she could not see the palm of her own hand, there was the shadow. When all the lights were out.

"In the alcove, on the lintel, on the ceiling, on the doorframe, the floor, now here and now there—the shape of a lizard with something slapped down on its head, weirdly white, the body long, the legs writhing—now clinging, now curling into a ball, now crawling along stretched out its full length.

"She would scream when she saw it, and it would flit away—how quickly! But a moment later it would come creeping back again.

"She tried desperately not to see. But she saw because she had eyes. Lying back on her pillow, her hair pulled tightly back, she dropped medicine into her eyes, and was blind.

"Darkness, over the heart too. I took her hand, and for the first time told her that I had heard the story of the demon who eats shadows from a certain blind man halfway up the hill. I told her how old he seemed to be, and described his appearance, and the woman gasped as though her eyes had suddenly been opened, and began weeping bitterly.

"Frustrated in love, the blind man had put his curse on her.

"I clutched at the flesh of my face and wept tears of anger, chagrin, exation—and finally of pity. I determined that I would be with her, nd with this hand I drove a needle into both my eyes.

"A bond from one life lasts through three. Enlightenment has ome to us, and penitence, and release from the appetites of the world. We take our staffs, that blind man with us, and, ashamed of the daylight, go out into the night.

"We have met you along the way.

"I have troubled you; but as our sleeves brushed in the mist, I knew, and I spoke to you. It is for you to take my advice or throw it away.

"I have nothing more to say. If you will, I shall leave you."

Forlorn and graceful, the woman rose to her feet. Her weeping had sounded below the narrative.

Led by Long Head, the three of them groped their way down the hill. Three staffs, three phantoms in the fading gaslight.

The bit of silk pressed to the eyes by that white hand as the woman had arisen seemed to linger on, a scarlet butterfly cutting its way in and out of the mist.

TRANSLATED BY EDWARD SEIDENSTICKER

SANCTUARY

[from Gin no Saji, *1911-1912] by Naka Kansuke (born 1885)*

Naka Kansuke has spent his life outside the main stream of literary activity in Japan, and has never attained fame commensurate with his genius as a writer. His first novel, The Silver Spoon *(of which the concluding section is given here), is an extraordinarily beautiful evocation of the world of childhood, which retains its freshness today.*

•

The year I was sixteen I spent my vacation alone at a friend's summer house. Its heavily thatched roof was nestled in the foothills along the shore of a beautiful, lonely peninsula which I had once visited with my brother. An old woman who sold flowers came in to take care of the house. She was from the same province as my dead aunt, and somehow—if only in age and in the way she talked— reminded me of her. Since I knew the dialect too, and had heard a great deal about that part of the country, we were soon on very good terms. . . .

One afternoon as I was climbing toward a huge pine at the top of a mountain behind the house I lost my bearings and went off into a wild ravine. Elbowing blindly through the tall underbrush, lashed by dense branches and tripped by what looked like fan-vines, I clambered out of its choking depths up to a ridge. The ridge was shaped like an ox, its head thrust down the middle of a deep valley that opened out to the sea. I picked my way along its back toward the plump, bulging shoulders. Dried-up little pines were clinging desperately to places where reddish granite powder had hardened into a sharkskin-like crust; here and there lay the droppings of birds that had come to eat the pine cones. Clutching the coarse rock to keep from sliding down into the valley, I crawled up the hump that made the ox's shoulders. The sun leapt brilliantly into a sky full of dazzling light. Then I went along the gently sloping neck for about a hundred yards, as both sides of the ridge fell away more and more sharply and the valley became deeper and deeper, until at last, across a small level space that was the muzzle, I came to the edge of a sheer cliff.

I was on one of the many spurs reaching to the sea from the chain of rugged mountains, as high as two thousand feet, that extended seven or eight miles along this coast. Here, though, the middle one of three such spurs had been eroded at the base, so that it looked like a wedge driven between the other two. Screened in by the peak behind it and by the still higher rock cliffs on either side of the valley, under a vault of blue sky, it made a strange sanctuary. Now and then the hawks screeching shrilly overhead would swoop down, skim past my eyes, and soar into the sky again. Below, in the valley to my right, a road threaded the thick black forest, between the mountains, down toward the village on the other side. Through a narrow pass I could see mountain after mountain, red, pink, purple, faintly purple, with rows of clouds along them, going on in endless folds and layers. Full of joy and admiration, mingled with a kind of terror, I began to sing. An echo! My song was repeated as clearly as if someone hiding behind the mountain had mimicked it. Enticed by the unseen singer, I strained my voice to its highest pitch. The other voice, too, sang at that pitch. I spent the rest of the day singing there happily, with a primitive delight in that sure reply. By the time I reached our hedge gate the summer sun was sinking into the ocean.

I walked around to the bathroom to wash my feet, and then remembered the bath would be ready. The water was just right, so I got in the tub and soaked, stretching my tired legs luxuriously. Where the hot water circled my chest I felt as if I were lightly enlaced in threads. As I leaned back and held my buoyant body afloat, or breathed on my warm skin, I enjoyed the day's pleasures over again. I named the place Echo Peak. That I had found it by losing my way, which meant no one else knew about it, and that it could only be reached by scrambling across a dangerous ridge—these things made me all the more happy. Meanwhile I peered down through the shifting surface of the water . . . and noticed, barely visible, a pale oily glint. Had someone already taken a bath? Evidently another guest had come. I became extremely uneasy. To me, strangers were unbearable. Then, as I was feeling disappointed, my pleasure completely spoiled, the old woman hurried in to help me wash. She apologized for not having changed the water, and told me 'the young mistress from Tokyo' had arrived. It didn't sound like anyone in my friend's family. But I had heard of an elder sister in Kyoto who would be in Tokyo this summer—perhaps she was the one. In that case I would have to put up with it, I decided. Hopeless.

Lowering her voice dramatically, the old woman added, "Now there's a handsome young lady for you!" And she went out.

Later I slipped back to my own room like a fugitive, and sat leaning against the alcove pillar, utterly downcast. Meeting someone for the first time was an ordeal: the strain of being polite to an unfamiliar person bound me with invisible cords, till my forehead narrowed into a frown and my shoulders were burning hot. And now, it seemed, someone was in the guest cottage beyond the garden. The sister had not sounded too unpleasant; even so, I worried about what might be expected of me. Then I heard soft footsteps come down the veranda—to my door.

I left the pillar and went over to sit at my desk, just as a calm, gentle feminine voice asked, "May I trouble you for a moment?" As if impelled by that voice, the door slid smoothly open. "Oh dear," I heard, "you haven't been brought a lamp yet!" A white face was set in clear relief against the rectangle of dim light.

"How do you do?" She introduced herself as my friend's elder sister. "I'm afraid I'll be disturbing you for two or three days."

"Oh." I sat there like a criminal awaiting sentence.

"Do you suppose you'll like these?" Gracefully she offered me a dish of sweet-scented foreign confections . . . and all at once a grave, cool sculpture had become a beautiful woman, smiling shyly. Then, "I'll bring a lamp." And there was only the sculpture again, disappearing into the darkness.

I gave a sigh of relief. Filled with shame at my own wretchedness, I tried to remember how she had looked, but it was like groping for a dream. Yet when I shut my eyes tight, a sharp image drifted up as if I had suddenly gone out into a lighted place. A large round chignon in the style of a married woman. Black, black hair. Vivid black eyes sparkling under clear-cut eyebrows. So distinct was the entire outline that it gave me a curious feeling of coldness; even the somewhat pouting lips, which were painfully beautiful, seemed carved out of icy coral from the ocean depths. But when those lips curved up charmingly, parting to allow a glimpse of lovely teeth, that cool smile softened the whole image, and a tinge of color came into the white cheeks. The carved figure had turned into a beautiful woman.

After that I found myself trying to avoid her. Of course it was impossible not to meet now and then, though I would go off to Echo Peak in the morning and purposely come back too late for dinner. But when I went to the peak I refused to sing a note . . . like a bird out of season. And I stared vacantly at the deep colors of the mountains beyond the pass.

One evening, rather late, I was standing in the garden watching the moon rise over the mountain. Insects were singing everywhere, a fresh breeze carried the scent and murmur of the ocean across the fields. The round window of the guest cottage was still glowing, and in the lotus basin in front of it I could see the closed flowers, dimly white, and leaves beaded with moisture from a late afternoon shower. Sunk in the deepest and most obscure of all my thoughts, I stood there gazing at the moon, every night diminished a little further . . . and as I gazed I became aware that my friend's sister was standing beside me in the garden. The moon and flowers vanished—as the reflections in a pond vanish when a waterfowl sweeps down and alights on it, and there is only the white shape floating casually. . . .

In confusion I tried to say something. "The moon . . ." But she had discreetly begun to walk away. I flushed. It was my nature to be terribly ashamed of a trifle like that, of a little slip in speech or an awkwardness of any kind.

She went calmly on around the garden a little way, and then, as she was coming back to me, tactfully finished off my words: "It *is* beautiful, isn't it?" I was very grateful.

The next day I went to the cottage to return a newspaper, and found her combing her hair before a mirror. Her long hair was hanging loose, flowing smoothly down her back in rich waves. As I left, the hand that held the comb paused a moment, and the face in the mirror smiled. "I'll be going tomorrow," she said; "so I wondered if we couldn't have dinner together."

Again I went off to climb Echo Peak, and spent half the day, silent, in that sanctuary where only the soaring hawks could see me. The echo was silent too, but I thought of its friendly voice.

That evening the dinner table was spread with a pure white cloth; the old woman sat at one side, the sister and I facing each other. I felt shy, pleased, lonely, and sad, all at the same time.

"Won't you begin?" She bowed her head slightly. "The cook hasn't much experience, though. . . . I'm not sure you'll care for this." Smiling, she glanced over at my plate a little hesitantly. A square of homemade bean curd lay quivering there, so white it looked as if it would take up the indigo pattern of the plate. She grated citron for me, and I sprinkled on the pale-green powder. When I dipped the almost melting cake into its sauce, once, twice, it turned a reddish brown. Slowly I slipped it onto my tongue. There was the delicate savor of the citron, the sharp taste of soy sauce, and a cold, slippery feeling. I rolled it around in my mouth a few times and it was gone, leaving only a faint starchy flavor. Another dish held a neat row of tiny mackerel, their tails cocked up. The side-markings were chestnut-colored, the backs blue, the bellies a glittering silver—and there was the usual delicate aroma of this fish. When I pulled off a morsel of the firm flesh, dipped it in sauce, and ate it, it had a rich taste.

Later, fruit was served. The sister picked out a large, sweet-looking pear, and began to peel it. Setting the heavy fruit firmly in the circle of her long, arched fingers, she turned it round and round, as a strip of yellow peel curved over her pale hand and down in a loose spiral. Then she said she was not especially fond of pears, and put it, dripping with juice, on a dish for me. While I sliced and ate it, I watched her take a beautiful cherry, hold it lightly between her lips, and then glide it deftly in with the tip of her tongue. Her soft rounded chin moved deliciously.

She seemed unusually gay. The old woman became very jolly too, and announced she was going to guess how many teeth I had. So she hid her face like a child, pondered a long time, and declared: "Twenty-eight, not counting wisdom-teeth!"

"Everybody has twenty-eight."

But she wouldn't hear it. "What do you mean! Don't they say the Lord Buddha had forty odd?" Across the table I saw those lips part in a lovely smile.

After that our conversation somehow got around to birds. The old woman told us the mountains in her province were full of snowy herons. Wild geese and ducks came too, and flocks of cranes; a pair of white-naped cranes was sure to come every year, an event that had to be reported to the castle. Storks turned their heads to scream, and wove basket-like nests of twigs in the huge cedars of the local shrine. . . . On and on she went in her excitement, till we asked how long ago all that had been.

"When I was a child."

"Then they'd be gone now."

"But there were lots of them!" she insisted. "And they had little ones every year!" Again I saw that lovely smile.

My friend's sister was supposed to leave the next morning, but for some reason stayed till evening. When I came out of the bath at dusk, my room was dark and the old woman had gone off somewhere, so I decided to go out to the garden.

Just then I heard the sister call to me from the round window of the cottage. "I borrowed your lamp for a moment." And she came to say good-bye, bringing a tray of peaches.

"I hope you'll be all right. Do come to see us whenever you're in Kyoto."

I went down and sat in the garden by the flowers, and watched the stars wheeling on endlessly toward the ocean. There was only the sky, the cries of insects, the distant murmur of the waves. . . . The old woman came back with a rickshawman. I saw the sister, beautifully dressed and ready to leave, hurrying to my room to return the lamp. Finally, after her luggage had been taken out, she went down the veranda toward the entrance hall, and made a little bow to me as she passed.

"Good-bye!" she called. But I pretended not to hear.

"Good-bye! Good-bye!"

Silently I bowed my head there in the dark. The creak of the rickshaw died away, and I heard the gate being shut. Hidden among the flowers, I brushed at my streaming tears. Why had I kept silent? Why couldn't I have said good-bye? I stayed in the garden till I was cold, and at last, when the now slender moon hung over the mountain, went back to my room. Propping both elbows listlessly on the desk, I cupped my hands tenderly around a peach—a peach with a tinge of color, like a cheek, and with the smooth curve of a softly rounded chin—and pressed it to my lips. And as I sniffed the fragrance subtly diffused through its fine-textured skin, my tears began to fall once again.

TRANSLATED BY HOWARD HIBBETT

HAN'S CRIME

[Han no Hanzai, 1913] by Shiga Naoya (born 1883)

Shiga Naoya is one of the most important and influential writers of modern Japan. In his writings a style of exceptional beauty is joined to delicate perceptivity. Some of his stories are purely fictional, but his most characteristic works, such as At Kinosaki, *with its meditations on death, are largely autobiographical. Shiga's immense success encouraged many other writers to turn to the "I" novel, which occupies so prominent a place in twentieth-century Japanese literature.*

•.

Much to everyone's astonishment, the young Chinese juggler, Han, severed his wife's carotid artery with one of his heavy knives in the course of a performance. The young woman died on the spot. Han was immediately arrested.

At the scene of the event were the director of the theatre, Han's Chinese assistant, the announcer, and more than three hundred spectators. There was also a policeman who had been stationed behind the audience. Despite the presence of all these witnesses, it was a complete mystery whether the killing had been intentional or accidental.

Han's act was as follows: his wife would stand in front of a wooden board about the size of a door, and from a distance of approximately four yards, he would throw his large knives at her so that they stuck in the board about two inches apart, forming a contour around her body. As each knife left his hand, he would let out a staccato exclamation as if to punctuate his performance.

The examining judge first questioned the director of the theatre. "Would you say that this was a very difficult act?"

"No, Your Honor, it's not as difficult as all that for an experienced performer. But to do it properly, you need steady nerves and complete concentration."

"I see. Then assuming that what happened was an accident, it was an extremely unlikely type of accident?"

"Yes indeed, Your Honor. If accidents were not so very unlikely, I should never have allowed the act in my theatre."

"Well then, do you consider that this was done on purpose?"

"No, Your Honor, I do not. And for this reason: an act of this kind performed at a distance of twelve feet requires not only skill but at the same time a certain—well, intuitive sense. It is true that we all thought a mistake virtually out of the question, but after what has happened, I think we must admit that there was always the possibility of a mistake."

"Well then, which do you think it was—a mistake or on purpose?"

"That I simply cannot say, Your Honor."

The judge felt puzzled. Here was a clear case of homicide, but whether it was manslaughter or premeditated murder it was impossible to tell. If a murder, it was indeed a clever one, thought the judge.

Next the judge decided to question the Chinese assistant, who had worked with Han for many years past.

"What was Han's normal behavior?" he asked.

"He was always very correct, Your Honor; he didn't gamble or drink or run after women. Besides, last year he took up Christianity. He studied English and in his free time always seemed to be reading collections of sermons—the Bible and that sort of thing."

"And what about his wife's behavior?"

"Also very correct, Your Honor. Strolling players aren't always the most moral people, as you know. Mrs. Han was a pretty little woman and quite a few men used to make propositions to her, but she never paid the slightest attention to that kind of thing."

"And what sort of temperaments did they have?"

"Always very kind and gentle, sir. They were extremely good to all their friends and acquaintances and never quarreled with anyone. But . . ." He broke off and reflected a moment before continuing. "Your Honor, I'm afraid that if I tell you this, it may go badly for

Han. But to be quite truthful, these two people, who were so gentle and unselfish to others, were amazingly cruel in their relations to each other."

"Why was that?"

"I don't know, Your Honor."

"Was that the case ever since you first knew them?"

"No, Your Honor. About two years ago Mrs. Han was pregnant. The child was born prematurely and died after about three days. That marked a change in their relations. They began having terrible rows over the most trivial things, and Han's face used to turn white as a sheet. He always ended by suddenly growing silent. He never once raised his hand against her or anything like that—I suppose it would have gone against his principles. But when you looked at him, Your Honor, you could see the terrible anger in his eyes! It was quite frightening at times.

"One day I asked Han why he didn't separate from his wife, seeing that things were so bad between them. Well, he told me that he had no real grounds for divorce, even though his love for her had died. Of course, she felt this and gradually stopped loving him too. He told me all this himself. I think the reason he began reading the Bible and all those sermons was to calm the violence in his heart and stop himself from hating his wife, whom he had no real cause to hate. Mrs. Han was really a pathetic woman. She had been with Han nearly three years and had traveled all over the country with him as a strolling player. If she'd ever left Han and gone back home, I don't think she'd have found it easy to get married. How many men would trust a woman who'd spent all that time traveling about? I suppose that's why she stayed with Han, even though they got on so badly."

"And what do you really think about this killing?"

"You mean, Your Honor, do I think it was an accident or done on purpose?"

"That's right."

"Well, sir, I've been thinking about it from every angle since the day it happened. The more I think, the less I know what to make of it. I've talked about it with the announcer, and he also says he can't understand what happened."

"Very well. But tell me this: at the actual moment it did happen, did it occur to you to wonder whether it was accidental or on purpose?"

"Yes, sir, it did. I thought . . . I thought, 'He's gone and killed her.' "

"On purpose, you mean?"

"Yes, sir. However the announcer says that he thought, 'His hand's slipped.' "

"Yes, but he didn't know about their everyday relations as you did."

"That may be, Your Honor. But afterwards I wondered if it wasn't just because I did know about those relations that I thought, 'He's killed her.' "

"What were Han's reactions at the moment?"

"He cried out, 'Ha.' As soon as I heard that, I looked up and saw blood gushing from his wife's throat. For a few seconds she kept standing there, then her knees seemed to fold up under her and her body swayed forward. When the knife fell out, she collapsed on the floor, all crumpled in a heap. Of course there was nothing any of us could do—we just sat there petrified, staring at her. . . . As to Han, I really can't describe his reactions, for I wasn't looking at him. It was only when the thought struck me, 'He's finally gone and killed her,' that I glanced at him. His face was dead white and his eyes closed. The stage manager lowered the curtain. When they picked up Mrs. Han's body she was already dead. Han dropped to his knees then, and for a long time he went on praying in silence."

"Did he appear very upset?"

"Yes, sir, he was quite upset."

"Very well. If I have anything further to ask you, I shall call for you again."

The judge dismissed the Chinese assistant and now summoned Han himself to the stand. The juggler's intelligent face was drawn and pale; one could tell right away that he was in a state of nervous exhaustion.

"I have already questioned the director of the theatre and your assistant," said the judge when Han had taken his place in the witness box. "I now propose to examine you."

Han bowed his head.

"Tell me," said the judge, "did you at any time love your wife?"

"From the day of our marriage until the child was born I loved her with all my heart."

"And why did the birth of the child change things?"

"Because I knew it was not mine."

"Did you know who the other man was?"

"I had a very good idea. I think it was my wife's cousin."

"Did you know him personally?"

"He was a close friend. It was he who first suggested that we get married. It was he who urged me to marry her."

"I presume that his relations with her occurred prior to your marriage."

"Yes, sir. The child was born eight months after we were married."

"According to your assistant, it was a premature birth."

"That is what I told everyone."

"The child died very soon after birth, did it not? What was the cause of death?"

"He was smothered by his mother's breasts."

"Did your wife do that on purpose?"

"She said it was an accident."

The judge was silent and looked fixedly at Han's face. Han raised his head but kept his eyes lowered as he awaited the next question. The judge continued,

"Did your wife confess these relations to you?"

"She did not confess, nor did I ever ask her about them. The child's death seemed like retribution for everything and I decided that I should be as magnanimous as possible, but . . ."

"But in the end you were unable to be magnanimous?"

"That's right. I could not help thinking that the death of the child was insufficient retribution. When apart from my wife, I was able to reason calmly, but as soon as I saw her, something happened inside me. When I saw her body, my temper would begin to rise."

"Didn't divorce occur to you?"

"I often thought that I should like to have a divorce, but I never mentioned it to my wife. My wife used to say that if I left her she could no longer exist."

"Did she love you?"

"She did not love me."

"Then why did she say such things?"

"I think she was referring to the material means of existence. Her home had been ruined by her elder brother, and she knew that no serious man would want to marry a woman who had been the wife of a strolling player. Also her feet were too small for her to do any ordinary work."

"What were your physical relations?"

"I imagine about the same as with most couples."

"Did your wife have any real liking for you?"

"I do not think she really liked me. In fact, I think it must have been very painful for her to live with me as my wife. Still, she endured it. She endured it with a degree of patience almost unthinkable for a man. She used to observe me with a cold, cruel look in her eyes as my life gradually went to pieces. She never showed a flicker of sympathy as she saw me struggling in agony to escape into a better, truer sort of existence."

"Why could you not take some decisive action—have it out with her, or even leave her if necessary?"

"Because my mind was full of all sorts of ideals."

"What ideals?"

"I wanted to behave towards my wife in such a way that there would be no wrong on my side. . . . But in the end it didn't work."

"Did you never think of killing your wife?"

Han did not answer and the judge repeated his question. After a long pause, Han replied,

"Before the idea of killing her occurred to me, I often used to think it would be a good thing if she died."

"Well, in that case, if it had not been against the law, don't you think you might have killed her?"

"I wasn't thinking in terms of the law, sir. That's not what stopped me. It was just that I was weak. At the same time I had this overmastering desire to enter into a truer sort of life."

"Nevertheless you did think of killing your wife, did you not—later on, I mean?"

"I never made up my mind to do it. But, yes, it is correct to say that I did think about it once."

"How long was that before the event?"

"The previous night. . . . Or perhaps even the same morning."

"Had you been quarreling?"

"Yes, sir."

"What about?"

"About something so petty that it's hardly worth mentioning."

"Try telling me about it."

"It was a question of food. I get rather short-tempered when I haven't eaten for some time. Well, that evening my wife had been dawdling and our supper wasn't ready when it should have been. I got very angry."

"Were you more violent than usual?"

"No, but afterwards I still felt worked up, which was unusual. I suppose it was because I'd been worrying so much during those past weeks about making a better existence for myself, and realizing there was nothing I could do about it. I went to bed but couldn't get to sleep. All sorts of upsetting thoughts went through my mind. I began to feel that whatever I did, I should never be able to achieve the things I really wanted—that however hard I tried, I should never be able to escape from all the hateful aspects of my present life. This sad, hopeless state of affairs all seemed connected with my marriage. I desperately wanted to find a chink of light to lead me out of my darkness, but even this desire was gradually being extinguished. The hope of escape still flickered and sputtered within me, and I knew that if ever it should go out I would to all intents and purposes be a dead person.

"And then the ugly thought began flitting through my mind, 'If only she would die! If only she would die! Why should I not kill her?' The practical consequence of such a crime meant nothing to me any longer. No doubt I would go to prison, but life in prison could not be worse—could only be better—than this present existence. And yet somehow I had the feeling that killing my wife would solve nothing. It would have been a shirking of the issue, in the same way as suicide. I must go through each day's suffering as it came, I told myself; there was no way to circumvent that. That had become my true life: to suffer.

"As my mind raced along these tracks, I almost forgot that the cause of my suffering lay beside me. Utterly exhausted, I lay there unable to sleep. I fell into a blank state of stupefaction, and as my tortured mind turned numb, the idea of killing my wife gradually faded. Then I was overcome by the sad empty feeling that follows a nightmare. I thought of all my fine resolutions for a better life, and realized that I was too weakhearted to attain it. When dawn finally broke I saw that my wife also, had not been sleeping. . . ."

"When you got up, did you behave normally towards each other?"

"We did not say a single word to each other."

"But why didn't you think of leaving her, when things had come to this?"

"Do you mean, Your Honor, that that would have been a solution of my problem? No, no, that too would have been a shirking of the issue! As I told you, I was determined to behave towards my wife so that there would be no wrong on my side."

Han gazed earnestly at the judge, who nodded his head as a sign for him to continue.

"Next day I was physically exhausted and of course my nerves were ragged. It was agony for me to remain still, and as soon as I had got dressed I left the house and wandered aimlessly about the deserted parts of town. Constantly the thought kept returning that I must do something to solve my life, but the idea of killing no longer occurred to me. The truth is that there was a chasm between my thoughts of murder the night before and any actual decision to commit a crime! Indeed, I never even thought about that evening's performance. If I had, I certainly would have decided to leave out the knife-throwing act. There were dozens of other acts that could have been substituted.

"Well, the evening came and finally it was our turn to appear on the stage. I did not have the slightest premonition that anything out of the ordinary was to happen. As usual, I demonstrated to the audience the sharpness of my knives by slicing pieces of paper and throwing some of the knives at the floor boards. Presently my wife appeared, heavily made up and wearing an elaborate Chinese costume; after greeting the audience with her charming smile, she took up her position in front of the board. I picked up one of the knives and placed myself at the distance from her.

"That's when our eyes met for the first time since the previous evening. At once I understood the risk of having chosen this particular act for that night's performance! Obviously I would have to master my nerves, yet the exhaustion which had penetrated to the very marrow of my bones prevented me. I sensed that I could no longer trust my own arm. To calm myself I closed my eyes for a moment, and I sensed that my whole body was trembling.

"Now the time had come! I aimed my first knife above her head; it struck just one inch higher than usual. My wife raised her arms and I prepared to throw my next two knives under each of her arms. As the first one left the ends of my fingers, I felt as if something were holding it back; I no longer had the sense of being able to determine the exact destination of my knives. It was now really a matter of luck if the knife struck at the point intended; each of my movements had become deliberate and self-conscious.

"I threw one knife to the left of my wife's neck and was about to throw another to the right when I saw a strange expression in her eyes. She seemed to be seized by a paroxysm of fear! Did she have a presentiment that this knife, that in a matter of seconds would come hurtling towards her, was going to lodge in her throat? I felt dizzy, as if about to faint. Forcing the knife deliberately out of my hand, I as good as aimed it into space. . . ."

The judge was silent, peering intently at Han.

"All at once the thought came to me, 'I've killed her,'" said Han abruptly.

"On purpose, you mean?"

"Yes. Suddenly I felt that I had done it on purpose."

"After that I understand you knelt down beside your wife's body and prayed in silence."

"Yes, sir. That was a rather cunning device that occurred to me on the spur of the moment. I realized that everyone knew me as a believer in Christianity. But while I was making a pretense of praying, I was in fact carefully calculating what attitude to adopt."

"So you were absolutely convinced that what you had done was on purpose?"

"I was. But I realized at once that I should be able to pretend it had been an accident."

"And why did you think it had been on purpose?"

"I had lost all sense of judgment."

"Did you think you'd succeeded in giving the impression it was an accident?"

"Yes, though when I thought about it afterwards it made my flesh creep. I pretended as convincingly as I could to be grief-stricken, but if there'd been just one really sharp-witted person about, he'd have realized right away that I was only acting. Well, that evening I decided that there was no good reason why I should not be acquitted; I told myself very calmly that there wasn't a shred of material evidence against me. To be sure, everyone knew how badly I got on with my wife, but if I persisted in saying that it was an accident, no one could prove the contrary. Going over in my mind everything that had happened, I saw that my wife's death could be explained very plausibly as an accident.

"And then a strange question came to my mind: why did I myself believe that it had *not* been an accident? The previous night I had thought about killing her, but might it not be that very fact which now caused me to think of my act as deliberate? Gradually I came to the point that I myself did not know what actually had happened! At that I became very happy—almost unbearably happy. I wanted to shout at the top of my lungs."

"Because you had come to consider it an accident?"

"No, that I can't say: because I no longer had the slightest idea as to whether it had been intentional or not. So I decided that my best way of being acquitted would be to make a clean breast of everything. Rather than deceive myself and everyone else by saying it was an accident, why not be completely honest and say I did not know what happened? I cannot declare it was a mistake; on the other hand I can't admit it was intentional. In fact, I can plead neither 'guilty' nor 'not guilty.'"

Han was silent. The judge, too, remained silent for a long moment before saying softly, reflectively, "I believe that what you have told me is true. Just one more question: do you not feel the slightest sorrow for your wife's death?"

"None at all! Even when I hated my wife most bitterly in the past, I never could have imagined I would feel such happiness in talking about her death."

"Very well," said the judge. "You may stand down."

Han silently lowered his head and left the room. Feeling strangely moved, the judge reached for his pen. On the document which lay on the table before him he wrote down the words, "Not guilty."

TRANSLATED BY IVAN MORRIS

AT KINOSAKI

[Kinosaki ni te, 1917] by Shiga Naoya

•

I had been hit by a train on the Tokyo loop line and I went alone to Kinosaki hot spring to convalesce. If I developed tuberculosis of the spine it could be fatal, but the doctor did not think I would. I would be out of danger in two or three years, he said, and the important thing was to take care of myself; and so I made the trip. I thought I would stay three weeks and more—five weeks if I could stand it.

My head was still not clear. I had taken to forgetting things at an alarming rate. But I had a pleasant feeling of quiet and repose as I had not had in recent years. The weather was beautiful as the time came to begin harvesting the rice.

I was quite alone. I had no one to talk to. I could read or write, I could sit in the chair on the veranda and look out absently at the mountains or the street, and beyond that I could go for walks. A road that followed a little stream gradually up from the town was good for walking. Where the stream skirted the base of the mountain it formed a little pool, which was full of brook salmon. Sometimes, when I looked carefully, I could find a big river crab with hair on its claws, still as a stone. I liked to walk up the road just before dinner in the evening. More often than not I would be sunk in thought as I followed the blue little stream up that lonely mountain valley in the evening chill. My thoughts were melancholy ones. And yet I felt a pleasant repose. I thought often of my accident. But a little more and I would be lying face up under the ground in Aoyama cemetery. My face would be green and cold and hard, and the wounds on my face and my back would be as they were that day. The bodies of my grandfather and my mother would be beside me. Nothing would pass between us. —Those were the things I thought. Gloomy thoughts, but they held little terror. All this would come sometime. When would it be? —Much the same thoughts had come to me before, but that "when" had seemed distant then and beyond knowing. Now, however, I felt I really could not tell when it might be here. I had been saved this time, something had failed to kill me, there were things I must do. —I remembered reading in middle school how Lord Clive was stirred to new efforts by thoughts like these. I wanted to react so to the crisis I had been through. I even did. But my heart was strangely quiet. Something had made it friendly to death.

My room was on the second floor, a rather quiet room with no neighbors. Often when I was tired I would go out and sit on the veranda. The roof of the entranceway was to one side below me, and it joined the main building at a boarded wall. There seemed to be a beehive under the boards. When the weather was good the big tiger-striped bees would work from morning to dark. Pushing their way out from between the boards they would pause on the roof of the entranceway. Some would walk around for a moment after they had arranged their wings and feelers with their front and hind legs, and immediately they too would spread their slender wings taut and take off with a heavy droning. Once in the air they moved quickly away. They gathered around the late shrubs in the garden, just then coming into bloom. I would hang over the railing when I was bored and watch them come and go.

One morning I saw a dead bee on the roof. Its legs were doubled tight under it, its feelers dropped untidily over its head. The other bees seemed indifferent to it, quite untroubled as they crawled busily around it on their way in and out. The industrious living bees gave so completely a sense of life. The other beside them, rolled over with its legs under it, still in the same spot whenever I looked at it, morning, noon, night—how completely it gave a sense of death. For three days it lay there. It gave me a feeling of utter quietness. Of loneliness. It was lonely to see the dead body left there on the cold tile in the evening when the rest had gone inside. And at the same time it was tranquil, soothing.

In the night a fierce rain fell. The next morning it was clear, and the leaves of the trees, the ground, the roof were all washed clean. The body of the dead bee was gone. The others were busy again, but that one had probably washed down the eaves trough to the ground. It was likely somewhere covered with mud, unmoving, its legs still tight beneath it, its feelers still flat against its head. Probably it was lying quiet until a change in the world outside would move it again. Or perhaps ants were pulling it off. Even so, how quiet it must be—before only working and working, no longer moving now. I felt a certain nearness to that quiet. I had written a short story not long before called "Han's Crime." A Chinese named Han murdered his wife in his jealousy over her relations with a friend of his before they were married, the jealousy abetted by physical pressures in Han himself. I had written from the point of view of Han, but now I thought I wanted to write of the wife, to describe her murdered and quiet in her grave.

I thought of writing "The Murdered Wife of Han." I never did, but the urge was there. I was much disturbed that my way of thinking had become so different from that of the hero of a long novel I was writing.

It was shortly after the bee was washed away. I left the inn for a walk out to a park where I could look down on the Maruyama River and the Japan Sea into which it flows. From in front of the large bathhouse a little stream ran gently down the middle of the street and into the river. A noisy crowd was looking down into the water from one spot along its banks and from a bridge. A large rat had been thrown in and was swimming desperately to get away. A skewer some eight or ten inches long was thrust through the skin of its neck, so that it projected about three or four inches above the head and three or four below the throat. The rat tried to climb up the stone wall. Two or three children and a rickshawman forty years old or so were throwing stones at it. They were having trouble hitting their mark. The stones struck against the wall and bounced off. The spectators laughed loudly. The rat finally brought its front paws up into a hole in the wall. When it tried to climb in, the skewer caught on the rocks. The rat fell back into the stream, trying still to save itself somehow. One could tell nothing from its face, but from its actions one could see how desperate it was. It seemed to think that if it could find shelter somewhere it would be safe, and with the skewer still in its neck it turned off again into the stream. The children and the rickshawman, more and more taken with the sport, continued to throw stones. Two or three ducks bobbing for food in front of the laundry place stretched their necks out in surprise. The stones splashed into the water. The ducks looked alarmed and paddled off upstream, their necks still astretch.

I did not want to see the end. The sight of the rat, doomed to die and yet putting its whole strength into the search for an escape, lingered stubbornly in my mind. I felt lonely and unhappy. Here was the truth, I told myself. It was terrible to think that this suffering lay before the quiet I was after. Even if I did feel a certain nearness to that quiet after death, still the struggle on the way was terrible. Beasts that do not know suicide must continue the struggle until it is finally cut short by death. What would I do if what was happening to the rat were happening to me now? Would I not, after all, struggle as the rat was struggling? I could not help remembering how near I was to doing very much that at the time of my accident. I wanted to do what could be done. I decided on a hospital for myself. I told how I was to be taken there. I asked someone to telephone in advance because I was afraid the doctor might be out and they would not be ready to operate immediately. Even when I was but half-conscious my mind worked so well on what was most important that I was surprised at it afterward myself. The question of whether I would die or not was moreover very much mine, and yet, while I did consider the possibility that I might, I was surprised afterward too at how little I was troubled by fear of death. "Is it fatal? What did the doctor say?" I asked a friend who was at my side. "He says it isn't," I was told. With that my spirits rose. I became most animated in my excitement. What would I have done if I had been told it would be fatal? I had trouble imagining. I would have been upset. But I thought I would not have been assailed by the intense fear I had always imagined. And I thought that even then I would have gone on struggling, looking for a way out. I would have behaved but little differently indeed from the rat. Even now, I decided, it would be much the same—let it be. My mood at the moment, it was clear, could have little immediate effect. And the truth lay on both sides. It was very good if there was such an effect, and it was very good if there was none. That was all.

One evening, some time later, I started out alone from the town, climbing gradually up along the little river. The road grew narrow and steep after it crossed the railroad at the mouth of a tunnel, the stream grew rapid, the last houses disappeared. I kept thinking I would go back, but each time I went on to see what was around the next corner. Everything was a pale green, the touch of the air was chilly against the skin. The quiet made me strangely restless. There was a large mulberry tree beside the road. A leaf on one branch that protruded out over the road from the far side fluttered rhythmically back and forth. There was no wind, everything except the stream was sunk in silence, only that one leaf fluttered on. I thought it odd. I was a little afraid even, but I was curious. I went down and looked at it for a time. A breeze came up. The leaf stopped moving. I saw what was happening, and it came to me that I had known all this before.

It began to get dark. No matter how far I went there were still corners ahead. I decided to go back. I looked down at the stream. On a rock that sloped up perhaps a yard square from the water at the far bank there was a small dark object. A water lizard. It was still wet, a good color. It was quite still, its head facing down the incline as it looked into the stream. The water from its body ran dark an inch or two down the dry rock. I squatted down and looked at it absent-mindedly. I no longer disliked water lizards. I was rather fond of land lizards. I loathed the horny wall lizard more than anything else of its sort. Some ten years before, when I was staying in the mountains not far from Tokyo, I had seen water lizards gathered around a drain from the inn, and I had thought how I would hate to be a water lizard, what it would be like to be reborn one. I did not like to come on water lizards because they always brought back the same thought. But now I was no longer bothered by it. I wanted to startle the lizard into the water. I could see in my mind how it would run, clumsily twisting its body. Still crouched by the stream, I took up a stone the size of a small ball and threw it. I was not especially aiming at the lizard. My aim is so bad that I could not have hit it had I tried, and it never occurred to me that I might. The stone slapped against the rock and fell into the water. As it hit, the lizard seemed to jump five inches or so to the side. Its tail curled high in the air. I wondered what had happened. I did not think at first that the rock had struck home. The curved tail began quietly to fall back down of its own weight. The toes of the projecting front feet, braced against the slope with knee joints cut, turned under and the lizard fell forward, its strength gone. Its tail lay flat against the rock. It did not move. It was dead.

What had I done, I thought. I often enough kill lizards and such, but the thought that I had killed one without intending to filled me with a strange revulsion. I had done it, but from the beginning entirely by chance. For the lizard it was a completely unexpected death. I continued to squat there. I felt as if there were only the lizard and I, as if I had become the lizard and knew its feelings. I was filled with a sadness for the lizard, with a sense of the loneliness of the living creature. Quite by accident I had lived. Quite by accident the lizard had died. I was lonely, and presently I started back toward the inn down the road still visible at my feet. The lights at the outskirts of the town came into view. What had happened to the dead bee? Probably it was carried underground by that rain. And the rat? Swept off to sea, probably, and its body, bloated from the water, would be washing up now with the rubbish on a beach. And I who had not died was walking here. I knew I should be grateful. But the proper feeling of happiness refused to come. To be alive and to be dead were not two opposite extremes. There did not seem to be much difference between them. It was now fairly dark. My sense of sight took in only the distant lights, and the feel of my feet against the ground, cut off from my sight, seemed uncertain in the extreme. Only my head worked on as it would. It led me deeper and deeper into these fancies.

I left after about three weeks. It is more than three years now. I did not get spinal tuberculosis—that much I escaped.

TRANSLATED BY EDWARD SEIDENSTICKER

THE MADMAN ON THE ROOF

[*Okujō no Kyōjin, 1916*] *by Kikuchi Kan (1888-1948)*

●

Characters

KATSUSHIMA YOSHITARO, the madman, twenty-four years of age
KATSUSHIMA SUEJIRO, his brother, a seventeen-year-old high school student
KATSUSHIMA GISUKE, their father
KATSUSHIMA OYOSHI, their mother
TOSAKU, a neighbor
KICHIJI, a manservant, twenty years of age
A PRIESTESS, about fifty years of age

PLACE: A small island in the Inland Sea
TIME: 1900

The stage setting represents the backyard of the Katsushimas, who are the richest family on the island. A bamboo fence prevents one from seeing more of the house than the high roof, which stands out sharply against the rich greenish sky of the southern island summer. At the left of the stage one can catch a glimpse of the sea shining in the sunlight.

Yoshitaro, the elder son of the family, is sitting astride the ridge of the roof, and is looking out over the sea.

GISUKE (*speaking from within the house*): Yoshi is sitting on the roof again. He'll get a sunstroke—the sun's so terribly hot. (*Coming out.*) Kichiji! —Where is Kichiji?

KICHIJI (*appearing from the right*): Yes! What do you want?

GISUKE: Bring Yoshitaro down. He has no hat on, up there in the hot sun. He'll get a sunstroke. How did he get up there, anyway? From the barn? Didn't you put wires around the barn roof as I told you to the other day?

KICHIJI: Yes, I did exactly as you told me.

GISUKE (*coming through the gate to the center of the stage, and looking up to the roof*): I don't see how he can stand it, sitting on that hot slate roof. (*He calls.*) Yoshitaro! You'd better come down. If you stay up there you'll get a sunstroke, and maybe die.

KICHIJI: Young master! Come on down. You'll get sick if you stay there.

GISUKE: Yoshi! Come down quick! What are you doing up there, anyway? Come down, I say! (*He calls loudly.*) Yoshi!

YOSHITARO (*indifferently*): Wha-a-at?

GISUKE: No "whats"! Come down right away. If you don't come down, I'll get after you with a stick.

YOSHITARO (*protesting like a spoiled child*): No, I don't want to. There's something wonderful. The priest of the god Kompira is dancing in the clouds. Dancing with an angel in pink robes. They're calling to me to come. (*Crying out ecstatically.*) Wait! I'm coming!

GISUKE: If you talk like that you'll fall, just as you did once before. You're already crippled and insane—what will you do next to worry your parents? Come down, you fool!

KICHIJI: Master, don't get so angry. The young master will not obey you. You should get some fried bean cake; when he sees it he will come down, because he likes it.

GISUKE: No, you had better get the stick after him. Don't be afraid to give him a good shaking-up.

KICHIJI: That's too cruel. The young master doesn't understand anything. He's under the influence of evil spirits.

GISUKE: We may have to put bamboo guards on the roof to keep him down from there.

KICHIJI: Whatever you do won't keep him down. Why, he climbed the roof of the Honzen Temple without even a ladder; a low roof like this one is the easiest thing in the world for him. I tell you, it's the evil spirits that make him climb. Nothing can stop him.

GISUKE: You may be right, but he worries me to death. If we could only keep him in the house it wouldn't be so bad, even though he is crazy; but he's always climbing up to high places. Suejiro says that everybody as far as Takamatsu knows about Yoshitaro the Madman.

KICHIJI: People on the island all say he's under the influence of a fox-spirit, but I don't believe that. I never heard of a fox climbing trees.

GISUKE: You're right. I think I know the real reason. About the time Yoshitaro was born, I bought a very expensive imported rifle, and I shot every monkey on the island. I believe a monkey-spirit is now working in him.

KICHIJI: That's just what I think. Otherwise, how could he climb trees so well? He can climb anything without a ladder. Even Saku, who's a professional climber, admits that he's no match for Yoshitaro.

GISUKE (*with a bitter laugh*): Don't joke about it! It's no laughing matter, having a son who is always climbing on the roof. (*Calling again.*) Yoshitaro, come down! Yoshitaro! —When he's up there on the roof, he doesn't hear me at all—he's so engrossed. I cut down all the trees around the house so he couldn't climb them, but there's nothing I can do about the roof.

KICHIJI: When I was a boy I remember there was a gingko tree in front of the gate.

GISUKE: Yes, that was one of the biggest trees on the island. One day Yoshitaro climbed clear to the top. He sat out on a branch, at least ninety feet above the ground, dreaming away as usual. My wife and I never expected him to get down alive, but after a while, down he slid. We were all too astonished to speak.

KICHIJI: That was certainly a miracle.

GISUKE: That's why I say it's a monkey-spirit that's working in him. (*He calls again.*) Yoshi! Come down! (*Dropping his voice.*) Kichiji, you'd better go up and fetch him.

KICHIJI: But when anyone else climbs up there, the young master gets angry.

GISUKE: Never mind his getting angry. Pull him down.

KICHIJI: Yes, master.

(*Kichiji goes out after the ladder. Tosaku, the neighbor, enters.*)

TOSAKU: Good day, sir.

GISUKE: Good day. Fine weather. Catch anything with the nets you put out yesterday?

TOSAKU: No, not much. The season's over.

GISUKE: Maybe it *is* too late now.

TOSAKU (*looking up at Yoshitaro*): Your son's on the roof again.

GISUKE: Yes, as usual. I don't like it, but when I keep him locked in a room he's like a fish out of water. Then, when I take pity on him and let him out, back he goes up on the roof.

TOSAKU: But after all, he doesn't bother anybody.

GISUKE: He bothers us. We feel so ashamed when he climbs up there and shouts.

TOSAKU: But your younger son, Suejiro, has a fine record at school. That must be some consolation for you.

GISUKE: Yes, he's a good student, and that is a consolation to me. If both of them were crazy, I don't know how I could go on living.

TOSAKU: By the way, a Priestess has just come to the island. How would you like to have her pray for your son? —That's really what I came to see you about.

GISUKE: We've tried prayers before, but it's never done any good.

TOSAKU: This Priestess believes in the god Kompira. She works all kinds of miracles. People say the god inspires her, and that's why her prayers have more effect than those of ordinary priests. Why don't you try her once?

GISUKE: Well, we might. How much does she charge?

TOSAKU: She won't take any money unless the patient is cured. If he is cured, you pay her whatever you feel like.

GISUKE: Suejiro says he doesn't believe in prayers. . . . But there's no harm in letting her try.

(*Kichiji enters carrying the ladder and disappears behind the fence.*)

TOSAKU: I'll go and bring her here. In the meantime you get your son down off the roof.

GISUKE: Thanks for your trouble. (*After seeing that Tosaku has gone, he calls again.*) Yoshi! Be a good boy and come down.

KICHIJI (*who is up on the roof by this time*): Now then, young master, come down with me. If you stay up here any longer you'll have a fever tonight.

YOSHITARO (*drawing away from Kichiji as a Buddhist might from a heathen*): Don't touch me! The angels are beckoning to me. You're not supposed to come here. What do you want?

KICHIJI: Don't talk nonsense! Please come down.

YOSHITARO: If you touch me the demons will tear you apart.

(*Kichiji hurriedly catches Yoshitaro by the shoulder and pulls him to the ladder. Yoshitaro suddenly becomes submissive.*)

KICHIJI: Don't make any trouble now. If you do you'll fall and hurt yourself.

GISUKE: Be careful!

(*Yoshitaro comes down to the center of the stage, followed by Kichiji. Yoshitaro is lame in his right leg.*)

GISUKE (*calling*): Oyoshi! Come out here a minute.

OYOSHI (*from within*): What is it?

GISUKE: I've sent for a Priestess.

OYOSHI (*coming out*): That may help. You never can tell what will.

GISUKE: Yoshitaro says he talks with the god Kompira. Well, this Priestess is a follower of Kompira, so she ought to be able to help him.

YOSHITARO (*looking uneasy*): Father! Why did you bring me down? There was a beautiful cloud of five colors rolling down to fetch me.

GISUKE: Idiot! Once before you said there was a five-colored cloud, and you jumped off the roof. That's the way you became a cripple. A Priestess of the god Kompira is coming here today to drive the evil spirit out of you, so don't you go back up on the roof.

(*Tosaku enters, leading the Priestess. She has a crafty face.*)

TOSAKU: This is the Priestess I spoke to you about.

GISUKE: Ah, good afternoon. I'm glad you've come—this boy is really a disgrace to the whole family.

PRIESTESS (*casually*): You needn't worry any more about him. I'll cure him at once with the god's help. (*Looking at Yoshitaro.*) This is the one?

GISUKE: Yes. He's twenty-four years old, and the only thing he can do is climb up to high places.

PRIESTESS: How long has he been this way?

GISUKE: Ever since he was born. Even when he was a baby, he wanted to be climbing. When he was four or five years old, he climbed onto the low shrine, then onto the high shrine of Buddha, and finally onto a very high shelf. When he was seven he began climbing trees. At fifteen he climbed to the tops of mountains and stayed there all day long. He says he talks with demons and with the gods. What do you think is the matter with him?

PRIESTESS: There's no doubt but that it's a fox-spirit. I will pray for him. (*Looking at Yoshitaro.*) Listen now! I am the messenger of the god Kompira. All that I say comes from the god.

YOSHITARO (*uneasily*): You say the god Kompira? Have you ever seen him?

PRIESTESS (*staring at him*): Don't say such sacrilegious things! The god cannot be seen.

YOSHITARO (*exultantly*): I have seen him many times! He's an old man with white robes and a golden crown. He's my best friend.

PRIESTESS (*taken aback at this assertion, and speaking to Gisuke*): This is a fox-spirit, all right, and a very extreme case. I will address the god.

(*She chants a prayer in a weird manner. Yoshitaro, held fast by Kichiji, watches the Priestess blankly. She works herself into a frenzy, and falls to the ground in a faint. Presently she rises to her feet and looks about her strangely.*)

PRIESTESS (*in a changed voice*): I am the god Kompira!

(*All except Yoshitaro fall to their knees with exclamations of reverence.*)

PRIESTESS (*with affected dignity*): The elder son of this family is under the influence of a fox-spirit. Hang him up on the branch of a tree and purify him with the smoke of green pine needles. If you fail to do what I say, you will all be punished!

(*She faints again. There are more exclamations of astonishment.*)

PRIESTESS (*rising and looking about her as though unconscious of what has taken place*): What has happened? Did the god speak?

GISUKE: It was a miracle.

PRIESTESS: You must do at once whatever the god told you, or you'll be punished. I warn you for your own sake.

GISUKE (*hesitating somewhat*): Kichiji, go and get some green pine needles.

OYOSHI: No! It's too cruel, even if it is the god's command.

PRIESTESS: He will not suffer, only the fox-spirit within him. The boy himself will not suffer at all. Hurry! (*Looking fixedly at Yoshitaro.*) Did you hear the god's command? He told the spirit to leave your body before it hurt.

YOSHITARO: That was not Kompira's voice. He wouldn't talk to a priestess like you.

PRIESTESS (*insulted*): I'll get even with you. Just wait! Don't talk back to the god like that, you horrid fox!

(*Kichiji enters with an armful of green pine boughs. Oyoshi is frightened.*)

PRIESTESS: Respect the god or be punished!

(*Gisuke and Kichiji reluctantly set fire to the pine needles, then bring Yoshitaro to the fire. He struggles against being held in the smoke.*)

YOSHITARO: Father! What are you doing to me? I don't like it! I don't like it!

PRIESTESS: That's not his own voice speaking. It's the fox within him. Only the fox is suffering.

OYOSHI: But it's cruel!

(*Gisuke and Kichiji attempt to press Yoshitaro's face into the smoke. Suddenly Suejiro's voice is heard calling within the house, and presently he appears. He stands amazed at the scene before him.*)

SUEJIRO: What's happening here? What's the smoke for?

YOSHITARO (*coughing from the smoke, and looking at his brother as at a savior*): Father and Kichiji are putting me in the smoke.

SUEJIRO (*angrily*): Father! What foolish thing are you doing now? Haven't I told you time and time again about this sort of business?

GISUKE: But the god inspired the miraculous Priestess . . .

SUEJIRO (*interrupting*): What nonsense is that? You do these insane things merely because he is so helpless.

(*With a contemptuous look at the Priestess he stamps the fire out.*)

PRIESTESS: Wait! That fire was made at the command of the god!
(*Suejiro sneeringly puts out the last spark.*)

GISUKE (*more courageously*): Suejiro, I have no education, and you
have, so I am always willing to listen to you. But this fire was
made at the god's command, and you shouldn't have stamped
on it.

SUEJIRO: Smoke won't cure him. People will laugh at you if they
hear you've been trying to drive out a fox. All the gods in the
country together couldn't even cure a cold. This Priestess is a
fraud. All she wants is the money.

GISUKE: But the doctors can't cure him.

SUEJIRO: If the doctors can't, nobody can. I've told you before that he
doesn't suffer. If he did, we'd have to do something for him. But
as long as he can climb up on the roof, he is happy. Nobody in the
whole country is as happy as he is—perhaps nobody in the world.
Besides, if you cure him now, what can he do? He's twenty-four
years old and he knows nothing, not even the alphabet. He's had
no practical experience. If he were cured, he would be conscious of
being crippled, and he'd be the most miserable man alive. Is that
what you want to see? It's all because you want to make him
normal. But wouldn't it be foolish to become normal merely to
suffer? (*Looking sidewise at the Priestess.*) Tosaku, if you brought
her here, you had better take her away.

PRIESTESS (*angry and insulted*): You disbelieve the oracle of the god.
You will be punished! (*She starts her chant as before. She faints,
rises, and speaks in a changed voice.*) I am the great god Kompira!
What the brother of the patient says springs from his own selfishness. He knows if his sick brother is cured, he'll get the family
estate. Doubt not this oracle!

SUEJIRO (*excitedly knocking the Priestess down*): That's a damned
lie, you old fool.
(*He kicks her.*)

PRIESTESS (*getting to her feet and resuming her ordinary voice*):
You've hurt me! You savage!

SUEJIRO: You fraud! You swindler!

TOSAKU (*coming between them*): Wait, young man! Don't get in such a frenzy.

SUEJIRO (*still excited*): You liar! A woman like you can't understand brotherly love!

TOSAKU: We'll leave now. It was my mistake to have brought her.

GISUKE (*giving Tosaku some money*): I hope you'll excuse him. He's young and has such a temper.

PRIESTESS: You kicked me when I was inspired by the god. You'll be lucky to survive until tonight.

SUEJIRO: Liar!

OYOSHI (*soothing Suejiro*): Be still now. (*To the Priestess*): I'm sorry this has happened.

PRIESTESS (*leaving with Tosaku*): The foot you kicked me with will rot off!

(*The Priestess and Tosaku go out.*)

GISUKE (*to Suejiro*): Aren't you afraid of being punished for what you've done?

SUEJIRO: A god never inspires a woman like that old swindler. She lies about everything.

OYOSHI: I suspected her from the very first. She wouldn't do such cruel things if a real god inspired her.

GISUKE (*without any insistence*): Maybe so. But, Suejiro, your brother will be a burden to you all your life.

SUEJIRO: It will be no burden at all. When I become successful, I'll build a tower for him on top of a mountain.

GISUKE (*suddenly*): But where's Yoshitaro gone?

KICHIJI (*pointing at the roof*): He's up there.

GISUKE (*having to smile*): As usual.

(*During the preceding excitement, Yoshitaro has slipped away and climbed back up on the roof. The four persons below look at each other and smile.*)

SUEJIRO: A normal person would be angry with you for having put him in the smoke, but you see, he's forgotten everything. (*He calls.*) Yoshitaro!

YOSHITARO (*for all his madness there is affection for his brother*): Suejiro! I asked Kompira and he says he doesn't know her!

SUEJIRO (*smiling*): You're right. The god will inspire you, not a priestess like her.

(*Through a rift in the clouds, the golden light of the sunset strikes the roof.*)

SUEJIRO (*exclaiming*): What a beautiful sunset!

YOSHITARO (*his face lighted by the sun's reflection*): Suejiro, look! Can't you see a golden palace in that cloud over there? There! Can't you see? Just look! How beautiful!

SUEJIRO (*as he feels the sorrow of sanity*): Yes, I see. I see it, too. Wonderful.

YOSHITARO (*filled with joy*): There! I hear music coming from the palace. Flutes, what I love best of all. Isn't it beautiful?

(*The parents have gone into the house. The mad brother on the roof and the sane brother on the ground remain looking at the golden sunset.*)

TRANSLATED BY YOZAN T. IWASAKI AND GLENN HUGHES

THE TIGER

[*Tora, 1918*] *by Kume Masao (1891-1952)*

•

As was his custom, Fukai Yasuke, the Shimpa [1] actor, did not awaken until it was nearly noon. With a rather theatrical blink of his sleep-laden eyes, he looked out at the blue sky of a cloudless autumn day, and surrendered himself to a huge, deliberate stretch. But, with a sudden realization that this performance was somewhat overdone, even for him, he darted a furtive glance about the room and smiled sheepishly at the thought of how much a part of him the grandiose gestures of the stage had become. He was, even for an actor, a born exaggerator: the very essence of his acting style lay in his ability to create farcical effects through the overuse of the bombastic and the grandiloquent. He was the best known comic actor of the Shimpa.

Fukai had started life as the dashing young man of a fish market down by the river; but when he heard that Kawakami, the founder of the Shimpa Theatre, was rounding up a collection of bit-players, Fukai had gone at once to apply for a job, ignoring the caustic comments of his friends. When it at last came Fukai's turn to undergo his stage test, Kawakami had taken one hard look at the young fishmonger with his close-cropped head, and said in tones of undisguised contempt, "You'll never make an actor, I can see."

Fukai had poured forth in his defense every argument he could muster, but Kawakami only smiled and paid him no further attention. Even this experience did not chasten Fukai. The next time he shaved every last hair from his head, and went in disguise to take another test. It so happened that one theatre needed a large number of players, and Fukai, by mingling in with the other applicants evaded Kawakami's watchful eye long enough to get himself hired.

[1] The "New School," a late nineteenth-century development in Kabuki, founded by Kawakami Otojirō.

Once he entered the company, however, Kawakami noticed him immediately.

"So! You've finally wormed your way in!" Kawakami said in considerable surprise.

"That's right. I'm a thickheaded fellow," Fukai replied, knocking on his shaven pate.

Kawakami laughed. "It can't be helped, I suppose. Now that you're in, let's see you buckle down and work hard." It had occurred to him that such a man might possibly have his uses, and there was no reason not to let him into the company gracefully.

Such was Fukai's initiation into the theatre. Since then he had become an outstanding player of comic parts, and having weathered the various vicissitudes of Shimpa, he had eventually succeeded in making himself indispensable. His salary was quite a handsome one; he would every now and then, in true actor's fashion, take up with some woman; there was no doubt but that he had made quite a success of himself.

That did not mean, however, that he was satisfied with his present lot. He was already over thirty-five. Had he followed one of the more usual vocations, at this time of life he would have been at the height of his powers and his capacity to work, but as things stood with him now, his sole function was to play the clown on the stage. He had never had a single straight part. He served merely to give the audience a good laugh, or to liven them to the proper pitch for some other actor. It was obvious even to Fukai that this was no better than being the comic assistant in some juggler's act. Obvious, but there was nothing he could do about it. At the prime of life, he was still continuing in the same old way.

Fukai had a son nearly eight years old. Last year the boy had made his debut on the stage, and like his father—or rather, with much more confidence than his father—could look forward to a future as a Shimpa actor. Fukai had no intention of letting his son play comic parts. No, he was determined to see to it that, unlike himself, the boy was given the chance to play serious roles.

At the moment Fukai still lay indolently in bed, thinking about the part he had been assigned the day before. Yesterday at the

Kabuki Theatre there had been a reading of the script of the forth-coming production *The Foster Child,* and he had been assigned the part of "the tiger." This was not the name of a character: it was the beast itself, and *that* was his whole part.

Play a tiger! He was disgusted at the thought, but it had struck him as so amusing that he could not bring himself to complain. He had played a cat once. He had also pranced around in front of the curtain in the role of a dog. People had dubbed him "the animal actor." What, then, was so strange in his being cast as a tiger? On the contrary, it would have been really hard to understand if the part had *not* devolved upon him.

Still it saddened him a little to think that there was nothing un-usual about his playing a tiger. Long years of experience had accus-tomed him to this disappointment: he knew it was the way he earned his living, and he was, after all, a comedian. And yet it seemed as if the "humanity" in him were being affronted. He even felt a moment of anger.

At the reading of the script the day before, all eyes had auto-matically turned his way when the author paused and said, with a glance that took in the whole company, "I thought I'd change the old plot here a bit, and bring out Tamae's extravagance by having him keep a tiger on his front porch. The tiger's a savage brute from Malaya, and at the end of the scene he goes wild and turns on Tamae. How does that strike you?"

"Sounds all right to me," the head of the company had answered. "That gives us a chance to fit in a part for Fukai here. I take it he won't turn it down?"

Once more everyone had looked his way, and this time Fukai could sense in their expressions a kind of mocking contempt. Never-theless, when Kawahara, the leading actor of female roles, remarked, "It's a sure hit! That act will be devoured by Fukai's tiger!", he too had joined in the laughter. He had even felt a glow of pride.

"Well, anyhow," he thought, still lying in bed, "I've got to play the part of the tiger, and play it well. It's nothing to be ashamed of. . . . Just so long as you do a part well, whether it's a beast or a bird, you're a good actor. Besides, when all's said and done, I'm the only actor in the whole of Japan that can play a tiger. I'll do a tiger for them that'll make the audience stand up and shout. And I'll give the other actors a good kicking around. If I'm to go on making my living, that's the only thing I *can* do."

He jumped out of bed, called to his wife downstairs, and got dressed. This accomplished, he went down with a cheerful countenance. His late morning meal was waiting for him on a tray covered with a yellow cloth. After a cursory brushing of his teeth, he applied himself eagerly to the food.

His son Wataru was lying on the veranda, idly leafing through the pages of an old issue of *Theatre Arts Illustrated,* no doubt an issue—one of the very rare ones—with a tiny photograph of Fukai on the first page, printed out of pity for him. He felt—it was nothing new—an embarrassment before his son. What kind of image of him as an actor was reflected in his son's eyes? And to what extent did this conflict with the boy's impression of him as a father? —These were some of the vague thoughts that ran through his head as he mechanically ate his meal.

Wataru called to him, "Father! Haven't you a rehearsal today?"

"No—at least I don't have to go to the theatre."

As he said this, his chagrin at being cast as a tiger, without a single word of dialogue to memorize, returned to him in full force. This time there was no necessity even for working out his cues with the other actors. All he had to do was decide in his own mind the most tiger-like manner in which to jump around the stage.

But come to think of it, just how *did* a tiger spring upon its victim? He had seen paintings of tigers, of course, and knew how tigers were represented in old-fashioned plays. But he had only the haziest notion what real tigers were like. When it actually came to playing the part of one, even Fukai, "animal actor" that he was, was ignorant of their special qualities. One thing was sure—they belonged to the cat family. He probably could not go too far wrong if he thought of them as huge, powerful cats. Still, if he failed to do any better than behave like a cat in one of those cat fights of the old plays, some malicious critic might say that Fukai had literally come on a tiger and exited a cat, which would be very irritating indeed.

"Do you have to go see anybody about anything?" Wataru, unaware of his father's troubled thoughts, persisted with his interrogation, his voice taking on that wheedling tone that children affect when they want to get something out of their parents.

"Let's see. No, I suppose not. But what are you asking me for, anyway?"

"I thought if you hadn't anything to do, maybe you'd take me to Ueno today. It's such a nice day. Please take me."

"Why do you want to go to Ueno? There's nothing to interest you. A kid your age wouldn't get anything out of the art museum. . . ."

"But I want to go to the zoo! I haven't been there once since last year!"

"The zoo?" Fukai repeated the word mechanically. Various ideas fluttered through his mind. Ought he to regard his child's words as a kind of divine revelation and be duly thankful? Or should he take them as an irony of fate, to which the proper response was a bitter smile? It was hard to know how to react. But even assuming that the gods were manifesting their contempt for him through the child, his long professional experience told him that his first concern should be to make good use of this opportunity for finding out how a tiger really behaves.

"They've got a hippopotamus at the zoo now, Father! Come on, take me, please."

He turned to his wife and said, as if in self-explanation, "Shall Wataru and I go to see the hippopotamus and the tiger?"

"Why don't you, if you haven't anything else to attend to? You never can tell—it might prove more of a distraction than going somewhere else," agreed his wife, showing by the special emphasis she placed on the words "somewhere else" that her mind was on quite a different subject than the tiger.

He was by no means impervious to the irony of her remark, but knew how to parry the thrust by taking it lightly. "I see. I suppose that would give you less to worry about than if I went to see a 'cat' somewhere!" His laugh was intentionally loud.

"Let's get started, Father, shall we?"

"All right! All right!"

Unashamedly he had leapt at this Heaven-sent opportunity, but somewhere deep inside him there still lurked an uneasiness which made him feel embarrassed before the child. However, he told himself, it was, after all, his job; cheered by this thought, he lightheartedly abandoned all compunctions. He had become once more the true son of Tokyo, who consoles himself by laughing at his own expense.

Less than half an hour later, he and Wataru boarded a streetcar headed for Ueno. Like most actors, he hoped when on a streetcar or in some other public place, to enjoy by turns the pleasure of elaborate efforts to remain unrecognized, and the agreeable sensation of being noticed and pointed out, despite his precautions. Decked out in a kimono of a pattern garish enough to attract anyone's attention, and with Wataru dressed in one of those kimonos with extra-long sleeves that are the mark of a child actor, Fukai sat down in a corner of the car, his elbows close to his sides, as if to appear as inconspicuous as possible. True, he did not especially wish to have any of his acquaintances catch sight of him on the way to the zoo; still, it would be amusing to meet someone unexpectedly and tell him with a straight face about his strange errand, making the whole business into a good joke.

At Suda-chō a man got on who filled the bill to perfection: the drama critic from the J newspaper, with whom Fukai had a casual acquaintance. Fukai recognized him instantly from under the felt hat pulled low over his brow, and sat with bated breath, waiting for it to dawn on the other man who he was. The critic presently discovered him and came over. With a conspiratorial, friendly air, he tapped Fukai silently on the shoulder.

Fukai looked up eagerly. "Is that you, sir? What an unexpected place to run into you!"

"I seem to be sharing the same car with a strange fellow! That's what makes riding these spark-wagons such an adventure."

"Where are you heading for? Are you on the way to her house or on your way back?"

"Which answer should I choose, I wonder? You might say I was on my way there, and then again you might say I was on my way back."

"That's because you've reached the point where you don't remember anymore where your real home is, I suppose."

"I'm not so much of a man about town as all that! But what about you? Where are you off to?"

"Me? Oh, a really fashionable place! —Look for yourself! I'm with my little millstone." He pointed with his chin at the child, whom the critic had not noticed up to this point.

"Is that you, Wataru? So you're keeping your father company today, are you? Or is your father keeping *you* company?"

"That's it, that's what makes me so stylish today—I'm being dragged off to Ueno by the kid!"

"What? To the exhibition at the art museum? Sounds pretty impressive!"

"Oh no, we wouldn't go to such an unrefined place. It's the zoo for us," he said, adding hastily, "to see the hippopotamus."

"The zoo?" The drama critic raised his eyebrows. Then his face lighted into a broad smile, and he slapped his knee. "I get it! But I'll bet it's not the hippopotamus you're going to see! You're off to see the tiger. I've heard all about the plot of the new play. They say the big boss himself thought up that idea. He's a smart man."

"Is that right? It's news to me. Here I've been furious at the leading man all along, thinking it was one of his tricks. I see I had better take the part more seriously. I've got to keep on the good side of the boss, you know."

"Now you've confessed it! But if you want to see a tiger, you needn't go to all the trouble of making a trip to the zoo."

"You mean a couple of quarts will make anybody a tiger?" [2]

"How about it? What do you say we have a look at one of those tigers?"

"No, can't do it. After all, I can't just ditch this fellow here," said Fukai, glancing once more at the child.

[2] In Japanese slang a boisterous drunken man is called a "tiger."

"You're getting old, aren't you?" the critic said casually, looking fixedly at Wataru.

At these words, like cold water dashed in his face, Fukai became serious again. He felt moreover profoundly ashamed that he had carried on this tiresome prattle without the least regard for his son's feelings. But his whole training had been much too frivolous for him to let the conversation drop, even at this juncture.

"I may be getting along in years, but they still treat me like a child as far as my parts are concerned. A tiger is more than even I can put up with."

"The other parts are just as bad. Who knows? The tiger may in the long run bring you more credit. It could easily turn out to be the hit of the show."

"That's what I keep telling myself, and that's why I have every intention of doing my best."

"Of course you will! We're all looking forward to your tiger."

"You overwhelm me!" Fukai smiled ironically, but secretly derived considerable solace from the critic's words.

The streetcar by this time had arrived at Ueno, and prodded impatiently by his son, Fukai hurriedly got off, taking an unceremonious leave of the critic.

The trees in Ueno Park had turned their bright autumn colors, and streams of people were moving along the broad gravel walks, with here and there a parasol floating in their midst. For Fukai, who was used to being indoors all the time, to be out under the blue sky at once raised his spirits. They made straight for the zoo.

Once inside the wicket, Wataru started to skip off happily. Fukai restrained him. "I'll be looking at the tiger, and after you've seen everything, come back and meet me there."

Wataru was in too much of a hurry to ask why his father was so interested in the tiger. Rejoicing in this release from parental authority, he bounded off gaily, and was soon lost in the crowd of children before the monkeys' cage.

Fukai for his part was also glad to be free of the child. Relying on his vague memories of the layout of the zoo from a previous visit years ago, he slowly walked in search of the cages where they kept the dangerous animals. He found the tiger almost immediately.

He had a queer feeling as he stopped in front of the cage. Inside the steel bars crouched the tiger that he sought, its forelegs stretched out indolently. When Fukai first noticed its dirty coat and lack-luster eyes, glimmering like two leaden suns, he felt a certain disappointment—it was too unlike the fierce power of the beast he had hitherto imagined. But as he intently observed the tiger, a feeling of sympathy gradually came over him. He felt pity for the tiger, but that was not all—a strange affection welled up. Shut up in a dank cage on this brilliant autumn day, robbed of all its savage powers, forced to crouch there dully, not so much as twitching under the curious stares of people: Fukai felt the wild beast's circumstances much resembled his own. But just wherein the resemblance lay was not clear, even to himself.

Deeply moved by these emotions, which remained nevertheless vague and unformulated, he stood in rapt contemplation before the cage, forgetting that he was to play the part of this tiger, forgetting to note the tiger's posture or the position of the legs.

The tiger and Fukai were both absolutely motionless. For a long time the man and the beast stared at each other. In the end, Fukai felt as if he were experiencing the same feelings as the tiger, as if he were thinking the tiger's thoughts.

Suddenly the tiger contorted its face strangely. At the same instant, it opened its jaws ringed with bright silver whiskers, and gave vent to an enormous yawn. The inside of its gaping mouth was a brilliant scarlet, rather like a peony, or rather, a rose in full bloom. This action took less than a minute, after which the tiger lapsed back into its silent apathy.

Startled out of his trance, Fukai summoned back to mind the nearly forgotten purpose on which he had come. The tiger, after demonstrating only that single yawn, remained immovable as a tree in some primeval forest, but Fukai was content. It seemed to him that, having penetrated this far into the tiger's feelings, he would be able to improvise the pouncing and roaring and all the rest.

"Yes, I'll really do the tiger! I can understand a tiger's feelings a whole lot better than those of a philandering man about town," he cried to himself.

Presently his son rejoined him, and taking the boy's hand, Fukai walked out the gate of the zoo, with a lighter step than when he had come.

The following day he happened to glance at the gossip column called "A Night at the Theatre" in the J newspaper. There, in unadorned terms, appeared the following paragraph:

> *Fukai Yasuke, well known as a popular actor of animal roles, has recently severed the last of his few tenuous connections with the human species. He devours his lunch in seclusion, emitting weird meows and grunts. He is still intent enough on getting his salary to stand up on his hind legs and beg for it, but now that he finally seems to have won a part in the forthcoming production at the Kabuki Theatre, he is so pleased with his role as a tiger that he spends his days going back and forth to the zoo to study.*

This was the drama critic he had met the day before, giving free rein to his pen. A feeling of resentment rose up in Fukai when he read the article. However, that quickly vanished, and an embarrassed smile took its place, to be followed in turn by an expression of contentment. "After all, that's what my popularity depends on."

Viewed in that light, it seemed more important than ever that he should make a success with the role of the tiger. Now, whether smoking a cigarette or eating his lunch or lying in bed, his thoughts were completely absorbed with the actions of tigers.

Opening day arrived at last. The play developed through its various scenes, and soon it was time for the third act, in which he was to appear as the tiger. There was no trace of a smile on his features as he put on the tiger costume. He stretched out on the balcony of Tamae's villa, just as the wooden clappers announced the beginning of the act

The curtains parted. No one else was on stage. The tiger raised itself slightly, as if it had finally awakened from its long midday slumber, and uttered a few low growls. At that moment five or six voices called out, "Fukai! Fukai!", from up in the top gallery. Fukai felt considerable gratification.

The principal actor and Kawahara, the female impersonator, came on stage. But the shouts of recognition from the gallery when they made their entrances were certainly no more enthusiastic than those that had greeted him. "Look at that!" he thought, feeling more and more pleased with himself.

The play advanced. As he listened to the dialogue, he was waiting only for the instant when he would spring into action. The play reached its climax. The moment for him to act was here at last.

He stretched himself once, with a movement that might have been that of a cat just as well as a tiger. He growled lazily once or twice. Then, as Tamae began to tease him, he made a sudden savage lunge straight at Tamae's chest. The chain by which he was fastened sprang taut with a snap as he bounded fiercely about.

The audience was in an uproar. "Fukai! Fukai!" voices shouted all over the theatre. Fukai was almost beside himself as he pounced and leapt. He had no complaints now. Nor any resentment. His depression and shame had vanished. All that remained in his ecstatic heart was an indescribable joy.

The curtains closed just as he was executing the most daring and savage leap of all. The applause of the audience echoed through the theatre. He was utterly content. Still dressed in his costume, he withdrew triumphantly. In the dark shadows of the wings someone unexpectedly caught his hand. He turned his head, somewhat startled, and looked through the peepholes in his mask. There stood his son, Wataru. "Father!" he said.

With sickening suddenness, Fukai plunged from the heights of pride to the depths of shame. He blushed as he stood before his son. But when he looked down once more into the boy's eyes, there was no hint of reproach in them for the role his father had played. Their expression was tearful, as if he could have wept in sympathy with his father.

"Wataru!" exclaimed Fukai, clasping the boy tightly in his arms.

The tears fell in big drops and trickled along the stripes in the tiger costume. . . .

Thus the tiger and the human child stood for a while, weeping together in the shadows of the dark scenery.

TRANSLATED BY ROBERT H. BROWER

KESA AND MORITŌ

[Kesa to Moritō, 1918] by Akutagawa Ryūnosuke (1892-1927)

*The reinterpretations of traditional Japanese tales, chiefly of those
contained in the thirteenth-century* Tales from the Uji Collection, *form the most brilliant part of the writings of Akutagawa Ryūno-suke. In this unusual presentation of the affair between the lady
Kesa and the soldier Moritō—treated also by Kikuchi Kan in his
"Gate of Hell"—Akutagawa's particular genius for the macabre is
splendidly displayed.*

●

*Night. Moritō gazes at the new-risen moon, as he walks through
dead leaves lying outside a wall. He is lost in thought.*

There's the moon. I used to wait for it, but now its brightness fills
me with horror. When I think that I'll be a murderer before the
night is over, I can't help trembling. Imagine these two hands red
with blood! How evil I'll seem to myself then! Yet if I had to kill
a hated enemy, my conscience wouldn't trouble me this way. Tonight I must kill a man I do not hate.

I've known him by sight for a long time . . . Wataru Saemon-
no-jō. Though his name's still new to me, I can't remember how
many years ago I first saw that fair, slightly too handsome face. Of
course I was jealous when I found he was Kesa's husband, but my
jealousy has completely disappeared. So even if he's a rival in love,
I don't feel any hatred or resentment toward him. No, you might say
I'm sympathetic. When Koromogawa told me how hard he worked
to win Kesa, I actually thought very kindly of him. Didn't he go so
far as to take lessons in writing poetry, merely to help his courtship?
I find myself smiling a little to think of the love poems written by
that simple, honest samurai. Not a scornful smile: it seems rather

touching that he went to such lengths to please her. Perhaps his passionate eagerness to please the woman I love gives me, her lover, a kind of satisfaction.

But can I really say that I love Kesa? Our love affair has had two phases: past and present. I was already in love with her before she married Wataru. Or I thought I was. Now that I recall, my feelings were scarcely pure. What did I want from Kesa, at that time when I'd never had a woman? Obviously I wanted her body. I'm not far wrong in saying my love was only a sentimental embellishment of that desire. For example, it's true I didn't forget her during the three years after we broke off—but would I have stayed in love if I'd already slept with her? I admit I haven't the courage to say yes. A good deal of my later love was regret that I'd never had her. So I brooded on my discontent, till at last I fell into this relationship that I'd feared, and yet longed for. And now? Let me ask myself again. Do I really love Kesa?

When I happened to see her three years later at the dedication of the Watanabe Bridge, I began trying everything I could think of to meet her in secret. And after about half a year I succeeded. Not only that, I made love to her just as I'd dreamed. Yet what dominated me then was not the regret that I hadn't slept with her. Meeting Kesa there in Koromogawa's house, I noticed my regret had already faded. No doubt it was weakened because I'd had other women—but the real reason is that she was no longer beautiful. What had become of the Kesa of three years ago? Now her skin was lusterless; her smooth cheeks and neck had withered; only those clear, proud, black eyes . . . and there were dark rings around them. The change in her had a crushing effect on my desire. I remember how shocked I was: face to face with her at last, I had to look away.

Then why did I make love to a woman who seemed so unattractive? In the first place, I felt a strange urge to make a conquest of her. There sat Kesa, deliberately exaggerating how much she loved her husband. But to me it had only a hollow ring. She's vain of him, I thought. Or again: She's afraid I'll pity her. Every moment I became more anxious to expose her lies. Why did I think she was lying? If anyone told me conceit had something to do with my suspicion, I couldn't very well deny it. Nevertheless, I believed she was lying. I still believe it.

But it wasn't only the urge to conquer her that possessed me. Even more—and I feel myself blush to think of it—I was driven by sheer lust. Not the regret that I'd never slept with her. It was a coarse lust-for-lust's-sake that might have been satisfied by any woman. A man taking a prostitute wouldn't have been so gross.

Anyway, out of such motives I finally made love to Kesa. Or rather I forced myself on her. And now when I come back to my first question—no, there's no need for me to go on wondering whether or not I love her. Sometimes I hate her. Especially when it was all over and she lay there crying . . . as I pulled her up to me she seemed more disgusting than I was. Tangled hair, sweat-smeared make-up—everything showed her ugliness of mind and body. If I'd been in love with her till then, that was the day love vanished for-ever. Or, if I hadn't, it was the day a new hatred entered my heart. To think that tonight, for the sake of a woman I don't love, I'm going to murder a man I don't hate!

And, really, I have only myself to blame. I boldly suggested it. "Let's kill Wataru!" . . . When I think of whispering those words into her ear, I begin to doubt my own sanity! But I whispered them, though I knew I shouldn't have, and set my teeth against it. Why did I want to? Looking back at it now, I can't imagine. If I have to decide, I suppose the more I despised and hated her, the more I felt I had to bring her some kind of shame. What could be better than saying we should kill Wataru—that husband she made so much of—and forcing her to consent? And so, like a man in a nightmare, I pressed her to agree to this murder I didn't want to commit. If that's not a sufficient motive, I can only say that some unknown power—call it an evil spirit—lured me astray. Anyhow, I grimly went on whispering the same thing over and over into Kesa's ear.

After a little while she looked up at me—and meekly consented. But it wasn't just how easily I'd persuaded her that surprised me. Then, for the first time, I saw a curious gleam in her eye. . . . Adulteress! A sudden despair awakened me to the horror of my dilemma. How I detested that foul, repulsive creature! I wanted to

ᵗake back my promise. I wanted to thrust that treacherous woman
down into the depths of shame. Then, even if I'd satisfied myself
with her, my conscience could have hidden behind a display of
indignation. But it was impossible. While she looked into my eyes
her expression changed, as if she knew exactly what I was thinking
. . . I confess it frankly: the reason I found myself fixing the day
and hour to kill Wataru was the fear that, if I refused, Kesa would
have her revenge. Yes, and this fear still holds its relentless grip on
me. Never mind those who would laugh at my cowardice—they
didn't see Kesa at that moment! In despair I watched her dry-eyed
weeping, and thought: If I don't kill him she'll make sure I'm the
victim somehow, so I'll kill him and get it over with. And after I
made the vow, didn't I see her pale face dimple with a smile as she
lowered her gaze?

Now, because of this evil promise I'm going to add murder to all
my other crimes! If I break this promise that hangs over my head
tonight. . . . But I can't. For one thing, there's my vow. For another, I said I was afraid of her revenge. And that's certainly true.
But there's something more. . . . What? What is the power that
drives me, a coward like me, to murder an innocent man? I don't
know. I don't know, though possibly. . . . But that couldn't be. I
despise the woman. I'm afraid of her. I detest her. And yet . . . perhaps it's because I love her.

*Moritō wanders on, silent. Moonlight. A voice is heard singing a
ballad.*

> *Darkness enshrouds the human heart*
> *In an illimitable night;*
> *Only the fires of earthly passion*
> *Blaze and die with life.*

2

*Night. Kesa sits outside gauze bed curtains, her back to a lamp. She
nibbles at her sleeve, lost in thought.*

Will he come or not, I wonder. Surely he will, yet the moon is already sinking and there isn't a footstep. He may have changed his mind. If he doesn't come. . . . Oh, I'll have to lift up my wicked face to the sun again, like any prostitute. How could I be so brazen? I'd be like a corpse left by the roadside—humiliated, trampled on, and then shamelessly exposed to light. And I'd have to keep silent. If that happened, even my death wouldn't be the end of it. But no, he'll come. When I looked into his eyes before we parted that day, I knew he would. He's afraid of me. He hates and despises me, and yet he's afraid of me. Of course, if I had to rely only on myself, I couldn't be sure he'd come. But I rely on him. I rely on his selfishness. Yes, I rely on the disgusting fear that his selfishness creates. And so I can be sure of him. He'll come stealing in . . .

But what a pitiful thing I am, now that I've lost confidence in myself! Three years ago I depended above all on my own beauty Perhaps it would be truer to say till that day—the day I met him at my aunt's house. One glance into his eyes and I saw my ugliness mirrored in them. He pretended I hadn't changed, and talked as seductively as if he really wanted me. But how can such words console a woman, once she knows her own ugliness? I was bitter . . . frightened . . . wretched. How much worse, even, than the ominous uneasiness I felt as a child in my nurse's arms when I saw the moon eclipsed! He had destroyed all my dreams. And then loneliness enveloped me like a gray, rainy dawn. Shivering with that loneliness, at last I yielded my corpselike body to the man—to a man I don't even love, a lecherous man who hates and despises me! Couldn't I bear the loneliness of mourning my lost beauty? Was I trying to shut it out that delirious moment when I buried my face in his arms? Or, if not, was I myself stirred by his kind of filthy lust? Even to think so is shameful to me! shameful! shameful! Especially when he let me go, and my body was free again, how loathsome I felt!

I tried not to weep, but loneliness and anger kept the tears welling to my eyes. I wasn't just miserable because I'd been unfaithful. I had been unfaithful, but worst of all I was despised, I was hated and tormented like a leprous dog. What did I do then? I have only a vague, distant memory. I recall that, as I was sobbing, I thought his mustache grazed my ear . . . and with his hot breath came the soft whispered words: "Let's kill Wataru!" Hearing them I felt an odd exhilaration, such as I'd never known before. Exhilaration? If moonlight may be called bright, I felt exhilarated—but it was far from an exhilaration like strong sunlight. Yet didn't those dreadful words comfort me, after all? Oh, to me—to a woman—is there still joy in being loved even if it means killing your own husband?

I went on crying for a while, out of my strange, moonlit-night feelings of loneliness and exhilaration. And after that? When did I finally promise to help him in this murder? Only then did I think of my husband. Yes, only then. Until that instant I was obsessed with my own shame. And then the thought of my husband, my gentle, reserved husband . . . no, it wasn't the thought of him, but the vivid image of his smiling face—smiling as he told me something. In that instant the plan occurred to me. I was ready to die . . . and I was happy.

But when I stopped crying and looked up into *his* eyes, my ugliness was still mirrored in them. I felt the happiness dissolve away . . . again I think of the darkness of that eclipse I saw with my nurse . . . it was as if all the evil spirits lurking beneath my joy had been set free at once. Was it really because I love my husband that I wanted to die in his place? No, it was a pretext—I wanted to make up for the sin of giving my body to that man. I haven't the courage to commit suicide, and I'm miserably worried about what people will think. All this might still be forgiven, but it's even more disgusting—much more ugly. On the pretext of sacrificing myself for my husband, didn't I really want revenge for the man's hatred of me, for his scorn, for his blind, evil lust? Yes, I'm sure of it. Looking into his face I lost that queer moonlight exhilaration and my heart froze with grief. I'll not die for my husband—I'll die for myself. I'll die from bitterness for my wounded feelings, from resentment for my tainted body. Oh, I didn't even have a decent cause for dying!

Yet how much better to die that unworthy death than to go on living! So I forced a smile and promised over and over to help kill my husband. He's clever enough to guess what I'll do if he fails me.

He even swore to it, so he'll surely come stealing in. . . . Is that the wind? When I think all these torments will end tonight, I feel an immense relief. Tomorrow the chilly light of dawn will fall on my headless corpse. When he sees it, my husband—no, I don't want to think of him. He loves me but I can't return his love. I have loved only one man, and tonight my lover will kill me. Even the lamplight is dazzling . . . in this last sweet torture.

Kesa blows out the light. Soon, the faint sound of a shutter open-ing. And a shaft of pale moonlight strikes the curtains.

TRANSLATED BY HOWARD HIBBETT

HELL SCREEN

[Jigokuhen, 1918] by Akutagawa Ryūnosuke

•

I doubt whether there will ever be another man like the Lord of
Horikawa. Certainly there has been no one like him till now. Some
say that a Guardian King appeared to her ladyship his mother in a
dream before he was born; at least it is true that from the day he
was born he was a most extraordinary person. Nothing he did was
commonplace; he was constantly startling people. You have only
to glance at a plan of Horikawa to perceive its grandeur. No
ordinary person would ever have dreamt of the boldness and daring
with which it was conceived.

But it certainly was not his lordship's intention merely to glorify
himself; he was generous, he did not forget the lower classes; he
wanted the whole country to enjoy itself when he did.

There is the story about the famous Kawara Palace at Higashi
Sanjō. It was said that the ghost of Tōru, Minister of the Left,
appeared there night after night until his lordship exorcised it by
rebuking it. Such was his prestige in the capital that everyone, man,
woman, and child, regarded him, with good reason, as a god in-
carnate. Once, as he was returning in his carriage from the Feast of
the Plum Blossoms, his ox got loose and injured an old man who
happened to be passing. But the latter, they say, put his hands together in reverence and was actually grateful that he had been
knocked over by an ox of his lordship.

Thus, there are the makings of many good stories in the life of
his lordship. At a certain banquet he made a presentation of thirty
white horses; another time he gave a favorite boy to be the human
pillar of Nagara Bridge. There would be no end if I started to tell
them all. Numerous as these anecdotes are, I doubt if there are any
that match in horror the story of the making of the Hell Screen,
one of the most valuable treasures in the house. His lordship is not

easily upset, but that time he seemed to be startled. How much more terrified, then, were we who served him; we feared for our very souls. As for me, I had served him for twenty years, but when I witnessed that dreadful spectacle I felt that such a thing could never have happened before. But in order to tell this story, I must first tell about Yoshihide, who painted the Hell Screen.

2

Yoshihide is, I expect, remembered by many even today. In his time he was a famous painter surpassed by no contemporary. He would be about fifty then, I imagine. He was cross-grained, and not much to look at: short of stature, a bag of skin and bones, and his youthful red lips made him seem even more evil, as though he were some sort of animal. Some said it was because he put his reddened paint brush to his lips, but I doubt this. Others, more unkind, said that his appearance and movements suggested a monkey. And that reminds me of this story. Yoshihide's only daughter, Yūzuki, a charming girl of fifteen, quite unlike her father, was at that time a maid in Horikawa. Probably owing to the fact that her mother had died while she was still very small, Yūzuki was sympathetic and intelligent beyond her years, and greatly petted by her ladyship and her attendants in consequence.

About that time it happened that someone presented a tame monkey from Tamba. The mischievous young lord called it Yoshihide. The monkey was a comical-looking beast, anyway; with this name, nobody in the mansion could resist laughing at him. But they did more than that. If he climbed the pine tree in the garden, or soiled the mats, whatever he did they teased him, shouting, "Yoshihide, Yoshihide."

One day Yūzuki was passing along one of the long halls with a note in a twig of red winter plum blossom when the monkey appeared from behind a sliding door, fleeing as fast as he could. Apparently he had dislocated a leg, for he limped, unable, it seemed, to climb a post with his usual agility. After him came the young lord, waving a switch, shouting, "Stop thief! Orange thief!" Yūzuki hesitated a moment, but it gave the fleeing monkey a chance to cling to her skirt, crying most piteously. Suddenly she felt she could not restrain her pity. With one hand she still held the plum branch, with the other, the sleeve of her mauve kimono sweeping in a half-circle, she picked the monkey up gently. Then bending before the young lord, she said sweetly, "I crave your pardon. He is only an animal. Be kind enough to pardon him, my lord."

But he had come running with his temper up; he frowned and stamped his foot two or three times. "Why do you protect him? He has stolen some oranges."

"But he is only an animal." She repeated it; then after a little, smiling sadly, "And since you call him Yoshihide, it is as if my father were being punished. I couldn't bear to see it," she said boldly. This defeated the young lord.

"Well, if you're pleading for your father's skin, I'll pardon him," he said reluctantly, "against my better judgment." Dropping the switch, he turned and went back through the sliding door through which he had come.

3

Yūzuki and the monkey were devoted to each other from that day. She hung a golden bell that she had received from the Princess by a bright red cord around the monkey's neck, and the monkey would hardly let her out of his sight. Once, for instance, when she caught cold and took to her bed, the monkey, apparently much depressed, sat immovable by her pillow, gnawing his nails.

Another strange thing was that from that time the monkey was not teased as badly as before. On the contrary, they began to pet him, and even the young lord would occasionally toss him a persimmon or a chestnut. Once he got quite angry when he caught a samurai kicking the monkey. As for his lordship, they say that when he heard his son was protecting the monkey from abuse, he had Yūzuki appear before him with the monkey in her arms. On this occasion he must have heard why she had made a pet of the monkey.

"You're a filial girl. I'll reward you for it," he said, and gave her a crimson ceremonial kimono. Whereupon the monkey with the greatest deference mimicked her acceptance of the kimono. That greatly tickled his lordship. Thus the girl who befriended the monkey became a favorite of his lordship, because he admired her filial piety —not, as rumor had it, because he was too fond of her. There may have been some grounds for this rumor, but of that I shall tell later. It should be enough to say that the Lord of Horikawa was not the sort of person to fall in love with an artist's daughter, no matter how beautiful she was.

Thus honored, Yoshihide's daughter withdrew from his presence. Since she was wise and good, the other maids were not jealous of her. Rather she and her monkey became more popular than ever, particularly, they say, with the Princess, from whom she was hardly ever separated. She invariably accompanied her in her pleasure carriage.

However, we must leave the daughter a while and turn to the father. Though the monkey was soon being petted by everybody, they all disliked the great Yoshihide. This was not limited to the mansion folk only. The Abbot of Yokogawa hated him, and if Yoshihide were mentioned would change color as though he had encountered a devil. (That was after Yoshihide had drawn a caricature of the Abbot, according to the gossip of the domestics, which, after all, may have been nothing more than gossip.) Anyhow, the man was unpopular with anyone you met. If there were some who did not speak badly of him, they were but two or three fellow-artists or people who knew his pictures, but not the man.

Yoshihide was not only very repellent in appearance: people disliked him more because of his habits. No one was to blame for his unpopularity except himself.

4

He was stingy, he was bad-tempered, he was shameless, he was lazy, he was greedy, but worst of all, he was arrogant and contemptuous, certain that he was the greatest artist in the country.

If he had been proud only of his work it would not have been so bad, but he despised everything, even the customs and amenities of society.

It was in character, therefore, that when he was making a picture of the Goddess of Beauty he should paint the face of a common harlot, and that for Fudō [1] he should paint a villainous ex-convict. The models he chose were shocking. When he was taken to task for it, he said coolly, "It would be strange if the gods and buddhas I have given life with my brush should punish me."

His apprentices were appalled when they thought of the dreadful fate in store for him, and many left his studio. It was pride—he imagined himself to be the greatest man in Japan.

In short, though exceptionally gifted, he behaved much above his station. Among artists who were not on good terms with him, many maintained that he was a charlatan, because his brushwork and coloring were so unusual. Look at the door-paintings of the famous artists of the past! You can almost smell the perfume of the plum blossom on a moonlit night; you can almost hear some courtier on a screen playing his flute. That is how they gained their reputation for surpassing beauty. Yoshihide's pictures were reputed to be always weird or unpleasant. For instance, he painted the "Five Aspects of Life and Death" on Ryugai Temple gate, and they say if you pass the gate at night you can hear the sighing and sobbing of the divinities he depicted there. Others say you can smell rotting corpses. Or when, at the command of his lordship, he painted the portraits of some of his household women, within three years everyone of them sickened as though her spirit had left her, and died. Those who spoke ill of Yoshihide regarded this as certain proof that his pictures were done by means of the black art.

Yoshihide delighted in his reputation for perversity. Once, when his lordship said to him jokingly, "You seem to like the ugly," Yoshihide's unnaturally red lips curled in an evil laugh. "I do. Daubers usually cannot understand the beauty of ugly things," he said contemptuously.

[1] The third of the Five Great Kings, guarding the center. In his right hand he holds a sword to strike the demons, in his left, a cord to bind them.

But Yoshihide, the unspeakably unscrupulous Yoshihide, had one tender human trait.

5

And that was his affection for his only child, whom he loved passionately. As I said before, Yūzuki was gentle, and deeply devoted to her father, but his love for her was not inferior to her devotion to him. Does it not seem incredible that the man who never gave a donation to a temple could have provided such kimono and hairpins for his daughter with reckless disregard of cost?

But Yoshihide's affection for Yūzuki was nothing more than the emotion. He gave no thought, for instance, to finding her a good husband. Yet he certainly would have hired roughs to assassinate anyone who made improper advances to her. Therefore, when she became a maid at Horikawa, at the command of his lordship, Yoshihide took it very badly; and even when he appeared before the daimyo, he sulked for a while. The rumor that, attracted by her beauty, his lordship had tasted her delights in spite of her father, was largely the guess of those who noted Yoshihide's displeasure.

Of course, even if the rumor were false it was clear that the intensity of his affection made Yoshihide long to have his daughter come down from among his lordship's women. When Yoshihide was commanded to paint Monju, the God of Wisdom, he took as his model his lordship's favorite page, and the Lord of Horikawa, highly pleased—for it was a beautiful thing—said graciously, "I will give you whatever you wish as a reward. Now what would you like?" Yoshihide acknowledged the tribute; but what do you think was the bold request that he made? That his daughter should leave his lordship's service! It would be presumptuous to ask that one's daughter be taken in; who but Yoshihide would have asked for his daughter's release, no matter how much he loved her! At this even the genial daimyo seemed ruffled, and he silently watched Yoshihide's face for a long moment.

"No," he spat out, and stood up suddenly. This happened again on four or five different occasions, and as I recall it now, with each repetition, the eye with which his lordship regarded Yoshihide grew colder. Possibly it was on account of this that Yūzuki was concerned for her father's safety, for often, biting her sleeves, she sobbed when she was in her room. Without doubt it was this that made the rumors that his lordship had fallen in love with Yoshihide's daughter become widely current. One of them had it that the very existence of the Hell Screen was owing to the fact that she would not comply with his wishes, but of course this could not have been true.

We believe his lordship did not dismiss her simply because he pitied her. He felt sorry for her situation, and rather than leave her with her hardened father he wanted her in the mansion where there would be no inconvenience for her. It was nothing but kindness on his part. It was quite obvious that the girl received his favors, but it would have been an exaggeration to say that she was his mistress. No, that would have been a completely unfounded lie.

Be that as it may, owing to his request about his daughter, Yoshihide came to be disliked by his lordship. Then suddenly the Lord of Horikawa summoned Yoshihide, whatever may have been his reason, and bade him paint a screen of the circles of hell.

6

When I say screen of the circles of hell, the scenes of those frightful paintings seem to come floating before my very eyes. Other painters have done Hell Screens, but from the first sketch Yoshihide's was different. In one corner of the first leaf he painted the Ten Kings [2] and their households in small scale, the rest was an awful whirlpool of fire around the Forest of Swords which likewise seemed ready to burst into flames. In fact, except for the robes of the hellish officials, which were dotted yellows and blues, all was a flame color, and in the center leapt and danced pitch-black smoke and sparks like flying charcoal.

The brushwork of this alone was enough to astonish one, but the

[2] Judges of the underworld.

treatment of the sinners rolling over and over in the avenging fire was unlike that of any ordinary picture of hell. From the highest noble to the lowest beggar every conceivable sort of person was to be seen there. Courtiers in formal attire, alluring young maidens of the court in palace robes, priests droning over their prayer beads, scholars on high wooden clogs, little girls in white shifts, diviners flourishing their papered wands—I won't name them all. There they all were, enveloped in flame and smoke, tormented by bull- and horse-headed jailers: blown and scattered in all directions like fallen leaves in a gale, they fled hither and yon. There were female fortunetellers, their hair caught in forks, their limbs trussed tighter than spiders' legs. Young princes hung inverted like bats, their breasts pierced with javelins. They were beaten with iron whips, they were crushed with mighty weights of adamant, they were pecked by weird birds, they were devoured by poisonous dragons. I don't know how many sinners were depicted, nor can I list all their torments.

But I must mention one dreadful scene that stood out from the rest. Grazing the tops of the sword trees, that were as sharp as an animal's fangs—there were several souls on them, spitted two or three deep—came falling through space an ox-carriage. Its blinds were blown open by the winds of hell and in it an emperor's favorite, gorgeously attired, her long black hair fluttering in the flames, bent her white neck and writhed in agony. Nothing made the fiery torments of hell more realistic than the appearance of that woman in her burning carriage. The horror of the whole picture was concentrated in this one scene. So inspired an accomplishment was it that those who looked at her thought they heard dreadful cries in their ears.

Ah, it was for this, it was for this picture that that dreadful event occurred! Without it how could even Yoshihide have expressed so vividly the agonies of hell? It was to finish this screen that Yoshihide met a destiny so cruel that he took his own life. For this hell he pictured was the hell that he, the greatest painter in the country, was one day to fall into. . . .

I may be telling the strange story of the Hell Screen too hastily;

I may have told the wrong end of the story first. Let me return to Yoshihide, bidden by his lordship to paint a picture of hell.

7

For five or six months Yoshihide was so busy working on the screen that he was not seen at the mansion at all. Was it not remarkable that with all his affection, when he became absorbed in his painting, he did not even want to see his daughter? The apprentice to whom I have already referred said that when Yoshihide was engaged on a piece of work it was as though he had been bewitched by a fox. According to the stories that circulated at that time Yoshihide had achieved fame with the assistance of the black art because of a vow he had made to some great god of fortune. And the proof of it was that if you went to his studio and peered at him unbeknownst you could see the ghostly foxes swarming all around him. Thus it was that when once he had taken up his brushes everything was forgotten till he had finished the picture. Day and night he would shut himself up in one room, scarcely seeing the light of day. And when he painted the Hell Screen this absorption was complete.

The shutters were kept down during the day and he mixed his secret colors by the light of a tripod lamp. He had his apprentices dress in all sorts of finery, and painted each with great care. It did not take the Hell Screen to make him behave like that: he demanded it for every picture he painted. At the time he was painting the "Five Aspects of Life and Death" at Ryugaiji, he chanced to see a corpse lying beside the road. Any ordinary person would have averted his face, but Yoshihide stepped out of the crowd, squatted down, and at his leisure painted the half-decayed face and limbs exactly as they looked.

How can I convey his violent concentration? Some of you will still fail to grasp it. Since I cannot tell it in detail, I shall relate it broadly.

The apprentice, then, was one day mixing paints. Suddenly Yoshihide appeared. "I'd like to take a short nap," he said. "But I've been bothered a lot by bad dreams recently."

Since this was not extraordinary the apprentice answered briefly but politely, "Indeed, sir," without lifting his hand from his work. Whereupon the artist said, with a loneliness and diffidence that were strange to him, "I mean I would like to have you sit by my pillow while I rest." The apprentice thought it unusual that he should be troubled so badly by dreams, but the request was a simple one and he assented readily. Yoshihide, still anxious, asked him to come back in at once. "And if another apprentice comes, don't let him enter the room while I am sleeping," he said hesitantly. By "room" he meant the room where he was painting the screen. In that room the doors were shut fast as if it were night, and a light was usually left burning. The screen stood around the sides of the room; only the charcoal sketch of the design was completed. Yoshihide put his elbow on the pillow like a man completely exhausted and quietly fell asleep. But before an hour was out an indescribably unpleasant voice began to sound in the apprentice's ears.

8

At first it was nothing more than a voice, but presently there were clear words, as of a drowning man moaning in the water. "What . . . you are calling me? Where? Where to . . . to hell? To the hell of fire . . . Who is it? Who is your honor? Who is your honor? If I knew who . . ."

Unconsciously the apprentice stopped mixing the colors; feeling that he was intruding on privacy he looked at the artist's face. That wrinkled face was pale; great drops of sweat stood out on it, the lips were dry, and the mouth with its scanty teeth was wide open, as though it gasped for air. And that thing that moved so dizzily as if on a thread, was that his tongue!

"If I knew who . . . Oh, it is your honor, is it? I thought it was. What! You have come to meet me. So I am to come. I am to go to hell! My daughter awaits me in hell!"

At that moment a strange, hazy shadow seemed to descend over the face of the screen, so uncanny did the apprentice feel. Immediately, of course, he shook the master with all his might, but Yoshihide, still in the clutch of the nightmare, continued his monologue, unable, apparently, to wake out of it. Thereupon the apprentice boldly took the water that stood at hand for his brushes and poured it over Yoshihide's face.

"It is waiting: get in this carriage. Get in this carriage and go down to hell." As he said these words Yoshihide's voice changed, he sounded like a man being strangled, and at length he opened his eyes. Terrified, he leapt up like one pierced with needles: the weird things of his dream must still have been with him. His expression was dreadful, his mouth gaped, he stared into space. Presently he seemed to have recovered himself. "It's all right now. You may leave," he said curtly.

As the apprentice would have been badly scolded had he disobeyed, he promptly left the room. When he saw the good light of day, he sighed with relief like one awakening from a bad dream.

But this was not the worst. A month later another apprentice was called into the back room. As usual Yoshihide was gnawing his brushes in the dim light of the oil lamp. Suddenly he turned to the apprentice. "I want you to strip again."

Since he had been asked to do this several times before, the apprentice obeyed immediately. But when that unspeakable man saw him stark naked before him, his face became strangely distorted. "I want to see a man bound with a chain. I want you to do as I tell you for a little while," he said coldly and unsympathetically. The apprentice was a sturdy fellow who had formerly thought that swinging a sword was better than handling a brush, but this request astonished him. As he often said afterwards, "I began to wonder if the master hadn't gone crazy and wasn't going to kill me." Yoshihide, however, growing impatient with the other's hesitation, produced from somewhere a light iron chain a-rattle in his hand; and without giving him the opportunity of obeying or refusing, sprang on the apprentice, sat on his back, twisted up his arms and bound him around and around. The pain was almost intolerable, for he pulled the end of the chain brutally, so that the apprentice fell loudly sideways and lay there extended.

9

He said that he lay there like a wine jar rolled over on its side. Because his hands and feet were cruelly bent and twisted he could move only his head. He was fat, and with his circulation impeded, the blood gathered not only in his trunk and face but everywhere under his skin. This, however, did not trouble Yoshihide at all; he walked all around him, "a wine jar," making sketch after sketch. I do not need to elaborate on the apprentice's sufferings.

Had nothing occurred, doubtless the torture would have been protracted longer. Fortunately—or maybe unfortunately—something like black oil, a thin streak, came flowing sinuously from behind a jar in the corner of the room. At first it moved slowly like a sticky substance, but then it slid more smoothly until, as he watched it, it moved gleaming up to his nose. He drew in his breath involuntarily. "A snake! A snake!" he screamed. It seemed that all the blood in his body would freeze at once, nor was it surprising. A little more and the snake would actually have touched with its cold tongue his head into which the chains were biting. Even the unscrupulous Yoshihide must have been startled at this. He dropped his brush, bent down like a flash, deftly caught the snake by its tail and lifted it up, head downward. The snake raised its head, coiled itself in circles, twisted its body, but could not reach Yoshihide's hand.

"You have made me botch a stroke." Complaining offensively, Yoshihide dropped the snake into the jar in the corner of the room and reluctantly loosed the chain that bound the apprentice. All he did was to loose him; not a word of thanks did the long-suffering fellow get. Obviously Yoshihide was vexed that he had botched a stroke instead of letting his apprentice be bitten by the snake. Afterwards they heard that he kept the snake there as a model.

This story should give you some idea of Yoshihide's madness, his sinister absorption. However, I should like to describe one more dreadful experience that almost cost a young apprentice his life. He was thirteen or fourteen at the time, a girlish, fair-complexioned lad. One night he was suddenly called to his master's room. In the lamplight he saw Yoshihide feeding a strange bird, about the size of an ordinary cat, with a bloody piece of meat which he held in his hand. It had large, round, amber-colored eyes and feather-like ears that stuck out on either side of its head. It was extraordinarily like a cat.

10

Yoshihide always disliked anyone sticking his nose into what he was doing. As was the case with the snake, his apprentices never knew what he had in his room. Therefore sometimes silver bowls, sometimes a skull, or one-stemmed lacquer stands—various odd things, models for what he was painting—would be set out on his table. But nobody knew where he kept these things. The rumor that some great god of fortune lent him divine help certainly arose from these circumstances.

Then the apprentice, seeing the strange bird on the table and imagining it to be something needed for the Hell Screen, bowed to the artist and said respectfully, "What do you wish, sir?" Yoshihide, as if he had not heard him, licked his red lips and jerked his chin towards the bird. "Isn't it tame!"

While he was saying this the apprentice was staring with an uncanny feeling at that catlike bird with ears. Yoshihide answered with his sneer, "What! Never seen a bird like this? That's the trouble with people who live in the capital. It's a horned owl. A hunter gave it to me two or three days ago. But I'll warrant there aren't many as tame as this."

As he said this he slowly raised his hand and stroked the back of the bird, which had just finished eating the meat, the wrong way. The owl let out a short piercing screech, flew up from the table, extended its claws, and pounced at the face of the apprentice. Panic-stricken, the latter raised his sleeve to shield his face. Had he not done so he undoubtedly would have been badly slashed. As he cried out he shook his sleeve to drive off the owl, but it screeched and, taking advantage of his weakness, attacked again. Forgetting the master's presence, the lad fled distracted up and down the narrow room; standing, he tried to ward it off, sitting, to drive it away. The sinister bird wheeled high and low after its prey, darting at his eyes, watching for an opening. The noisy threshing of its wings seemed to evoke something uncanny like the smell of dead leaves, or the spray of a waterfall. It was dreadful, revolting. The apprentice had the feeling that the dim oil lamp was the vague light of the moon, and the room a valley shut in the ill-omened air of some remote mountain.

But the apprentice's horror was due not so much to the attack of the horned owl. What made his hair stand on end was the sight of the artist Yoshihide. The latter watched the commotion coolly, unrolled his paper deliberately, and began to paint the fantastic picture of a girlish boy being mangled by a horrible bird. When the apprentice saw this out of the corner of his eye, he was overwhelmed with an inexpressible horror, for he thought that he really was going to be killed for the artist.

II

You could not say that this was impossible to believe. Yoshihide had called the apprentice deliberately that night in order to set the owl after him and paint him trying to escape. Therefore the apprentice, when he saw what the master was up to, involuntarily hid his head in his sleeves, began screaming he knew not what, and huddled down in the corner of the room by the sliding door. Then Yoshihide shouted as though he were a little flustered and got to his feet, but immediately the beating of the owl's wings became louder and there was the startling noise of things being torn or knocked down. Though he was badly shaken, the apprentice involuntarily lifted his head to see. The room had become as black as night, and out of it came Yoshihide's voice harshly calling for his apprentices.

Presently one of them answered from a distance, and in a minute came running in with a light. By its sooty illumination he saw the tripod lamp overturned and the owl fluttering painfully with one wing on mats that were swimming in oil. Yoshihide was in a half-sitting position beyond the table. He seemed aghast and was muttering words unintelligible to mortals. This is no exaggeration. A snake as black as the pit was coiling itself rapidly around the owl, encircling its neck and one wing. Apparently in crouching down the apprentice had knocked over the jar, the snake had crawled out, and the owl had made a feeble attempt to pounce on it. It was this which had caused the clatter and commotion. The two apprentices exchanged glances and simply stood dumbfounded, eying that remarkable spectacle. Then without a word they bowed to Yoshihide and withdrew. Nobody discovered what happened to the owl and the snake.

This sort of thing was matched by many other incidents. I forgot to say that it was in the early autumn that Yoshihide received orders to paint the screen. From then until the end of the winter his apprentices were in a constant state of terror because of his weird behavior. But towards the end of the winter something about the picture seemed to trouble Yoshihide; he became even more saturnine than usual and spoke more harshly. The sketch of the screen, eight-tenths completed, did not progress. In fact, there did not seem to be any chance that the outlines would ever be painted in and finished.

Nobody knew what it was that hindered the work on the screen and nobody tried to find out. Hitherto the apprentices had been fascinated by everything that happened. They had felt that they were caged with a wolf or a tiger, but from this time they contrived to keep away from their master as much as possible.

12

Accordingly, there is not much that is worth telling about this period. But if one had to say something, it would be that the stubborn old man was, for some strange reason, easily moved to tears, and was often found weeping, they say, when he thought no one was by. One day, for instance, an apprentice went into the garden on an errand. Yoshihide was standing absently in the corridor, gazing at the sky with its promise of spring, his eyes full of tears. The apprentice felt embarrassed and withdrew stealthily without saying a word. Was it not remarkable that the arrogant man who had used a decaying corpse as model for the "Five Aspects of Life and Death" should weep so childishly?

While Yoshihide painted the screen in a frenzy incomprehensible to the sane, it began to be noticed that his daughter was very despondent and often appeared to be holding back tears. When this happens to a girl with a pale modest face, her eyelashes become heavy, shadows appear around her eyes, and her face grows still sadder. At first they said that she was suffering from a love affair, or blamed her father, but soon it got around that the Lord of Horikawa wanted to have his way with her. Then suddenly all talk about the girl ceased as if everybody had forgotten her.

It was about that time that late one night I happened to be passing along a corridor. Suddenly the monkey Yoshihide sprang out from somewhere and began pulling the hem of my skirt insistently. As I remember it, the night was warm, there was a pale moon shining, and the plum blossoms were already fragrant. The monkey bared his white teeth, wrinkled the tip of his nose, and shrieked wildly in the moonlight as though he were demented. I felt upset and very angry that my new skirts should be pulled about. Kicking the monkey loose, I was about to walk on when I recalled that a samurai had earned the young lord's displeasure by chastising the monkey. Besides his behavior did seem most unusual. So at last I walked a dozen yards in the direction he was pulling me.

There the corridor turned, showing the water of the pond, pale white in the night light, beyond a pine tree with gently bending branches. At that point what sounded like people quarreling fell on my ears, weird and startling, from a room nearby. Except for this everything around was sunk in silence. In the half-light that was neither haze nor moonlight I heard no other voices. There was nothing but the sound of the fish jumping in the pond. With that din in my ears, I stopped instinctively. My first thought was "Some ruffians," and I approached the sliding door quietly, holding my breath, ready to show them my mettle.

13

But the monkey must have thought me too hesitant. He ran around me two or three times, impatiently, crying out as though he were being strangled, then leapt straight up from the floor to my shoulder. I jerked back my head so as not to be clawed, but he clung to my sleeve to keep from falling to the floor. Staggering back two or three steps, I banged heavily into the sliding door. After that there was no cause for hesitation. I opened the door immediately and was about to advance into the inner part of the room where the moonlight did not fall. But just then something passed before my eyes— what was this?—a girl came running out from the back of the room as though released from a spring. She barely missed running into me, passed me, and half-fell outside the room, where she knelt gasping, looking up at my face, and shuddering as though she still saw some horror.

Do I need to say she was Yūzuki? That night she appeared vivid, she seemed to be a different person. Her big eyes shone, her cheeks flamed red. Her disordered kimono and skirt gave her a fascination she did not ordinarily possess. Was this really that shrinking daughter of Yoshihide's? I leaned against the sliding door and stared at her beautiful figure in the moonlight. Then, indicating the direction where the alarmed footsteps had died away, "What was it?", I asked with my eyes.

But she only bit her lips, shook her head, and said nothing. She seemed unusually mortified. Then I bent over her, put my mouth to her ear, and asked, "Who was it?" in a whisper. But the girl still shook her head; tears filled her eyes and hung on her long lashes; she bit her lips harder than ever.

I have always been a stupid person and unless something is absolutely plain I cannot grasp it. I did not know what to say and stood motionless for a moment, as though listening to the beating of her heart. But this was because I felt I ought not to question her too closely.

I don't know how long it lasted. At length I closed the door I had left open and, looking back at the girl, who seemed to have recovered from her agitation, said as gently as possible, "You had better go back to your room." Then, troubled with the uncomfortable feeling that I had seen something I should not have, embarrassed though no one was near, I quietly returned to where I had come from. But before I had gone ten steps, something again plucked the hem of my skirt, timidly this time. Astonished, I stopped and turned around. What do you think it was? The monkey Yoshihid' his gold bell jingling, his hands together like a human, was bowin most politely to me, again and again.

14

About two weeks later Yoshihide came to the mansion and asked for an immediate audience with the Lord of Horikawa. He belonged to the lower classes but he had always been in favor, and his lordship, ordinarily difficult of access, granted Yoshihide an audience at once. The latter prostrated himself before the daimyo deferentially and presently began to speak in his hoarse voice.

"Some time ago, my lord, you ordered a Hell Screen. Day and night have I labored, taking great pains, and now the result can be seen: the design has almost been completed."

"Congratulations. I am content." But in his lordship's voice there was a strange lack of conviction, of interest.

"No, congratulations are not in order." With his eyes firmly lowered Yoshihide answered almost as if he were becoming angry. "It is nearly finished, but there is just one part I cannot paint—now."

"What! You cannot paint part of it!"

"No, my lord. I cannot paint anything for which a model is lacking. Even if I try, the pictures lack conviction. And isn't that the same as being unable to paint it?"

When he heard this a sneering sort of smile passed over his lordship's face. "Then in order to paint this Hell Screen, you must see hell, eh?"

"Yes, my lord. Some years ago in a great fire I saw flames close up that resembled the raging fires of hell. The flames in my painting are what I then saw. Your lordship is acquainted with that picture, I believe."

"What about criminals? You haven't seen jailers, have you?" He spoke as though he had not heard Yoshihide, his words following the artist's without pause.

"I have seen men bound in iron chains. I have copied in detail men attacked by strange birds. So I cannot say I have not seen the sufferings of criminals under torture. As for jailers—" Yoshihide smiled repulsively, "I have seen them before me many times in my dreams. Cows' heads, horses' heads, three-faced six-armed demons, clapping hands that make no noise, voiceless mouths agape—they all come to torment me. I am not exaggerating when I say that I see them every day and every night. What I wish to paint and cannot are not things like that."

His lordship must have been thoroughly astonished. For a long moment he stared at Yoshihide irritably; then he arched his eyebrows sharply. "What is it you cannot paint?"

15

"In the middle of the screen I want to paint a carriage falling down through the sky," said Yoshihide, and for the first time he looked sharply at his lordship's face. When Yoshihide spoke of pictures I have heard that he looked insane. He certainly seemed insane when he said this. "In the carriage an exquisite court lady, her hair disordered in the raging fire, writhes in agony. Her face is contorted with smoke, her eyebrows are drawn; she looks up at the roof of the carriage. As she plucks at the bamboo blinds she tries to ward off the sparks that shower down. And strange birds of prey, ten or twenty, fly around the carriage with shrill cries. Ah, that beauty in the carriage. I cannot possibly paint her."

"Well, what else?"

For some reason his lordship took strange pleasure in urging Yoshihide on. But the artist's red lips moved feverishly, and when he spoke it was like a man in a dream. "No," he repeated, "I cannot paint it." Then suddenly he almost snarled, "Burn a carriage for me. If only you could . . ."

His lordship's face darkened, then he burst out laughing with startling abruptness. "I'll do entirely as you wish," he said, almost choking with the violence of his laughter. "And all discussion as to whether it is possible or not is beside the point."

When I heard this I felt a strange thrill of horror. Maybe it was a premonition. His lordship, as though infected with Yoshihide's madness, changed, foam gathered white on his lips, and like lightning the terror flashed in the corners of his eyes. He stopped abruptly, and then a great laugh burst from his throat. "I'll fire a carriage for you. And there'll be an exquisite beauty in the robes of a fine lady in it. Attacked by flames and black smoke the woman will die in agony. The man who thought of painting that must be the greatest artist in Japan. I'll praise him. Oh, I'll praise him!"

When he heard his lordship's words, Yoshihide became pale and moved his lips as though he were gasping. But soon his body relaxed, and placing both hands on the mats, he bowed politely. "How kind a destiny," he said, so low that he could scarcely be heard. Probably this was because the daimyo's words had brought the frightfulness of his plan vividly before his eyes. That was the only time in my life that I pitied Yoshihide.

16

Two or three days after this his lordship told Yoshihide that he was ready to fulfill his promise. Of course the carriage was not to be burned at Horikawa, but rather at a country house outside the capital, which the common people called Yukige. Though it had formerly been the residence of his lordship's younger sister, no one had occupied Yukige for many years. It had a large garden that had been allowed to run wild. People attributed its neglect to many causes: for instance, they said that on moonless nights the daimyo's dead sister, wearing a strange scarlet skirt, still walked along the corridors without touching the floor. The mansion was desolate enough by day, but at night, with the plashing sounds of the invisible brook and the monstrous shapes of the night herons flying through the starlight, it was entirely eerie.

As it happened, that night was moonless and pitch black. The light of the oil lamps shone on his lordship, clad in pale yellow robes and a dark purple skirt embroidered with crests, sitting on the veranda on a plaited straw cushion with a white silk embroidered hem. I need not add that before and behind, to the left and to the right of him, five or six attendants stood respectfully. The choice of one was significant—he was a powerful samurai who had eaten human flesh to stay his hunger at the Battle of Michinoku, and since then, they say, he has been able to tear apart the horns of a live deer. His long sword sticking out behind like a gull's tail, he stood, a forbidding figure, beneath the veranda. The flickering light of the lamps, now bright, now dark, shone on the scene. So dreadful a horror was on us that we scarcely knew whether we dreamed or waked.

They had drawn the carriage into the garden. There it stood, its heavy roof weighing down the darkness. There were no oxen harnessed to it, and the end of its black tongue rested on a stand. When we saw its gold metalwork glittering like stars, we felt chilly in spite of the spring night. The carriage was heavily closed with blue blinds edged with embroidery, so that we could not know what was inside. Around it stood attendants with torches in their hands, worrying over the smoke that drifted towards the veranda and waiting significantly.

Yoshihide knelt facing the veranda, a little distance off. He seemed smaller and shabbier than usual, the starry sky seemed to oppress him. The man who squatted behind him was doubtless an apprentice. The two of them were at some distance from me and below the veranda so that I could not be sure of the color of their clothes.

17

It must have been near midnight. The darkness that enveloped the brook seemed to watch our very breathing. In it was only the faint stir of the night wind that carried the sooty smell of the pine torches to us. For some time his lordship watched the scene in silence, motionless. Presently he moved forward a little and called sharply, "Yoshihide."

The latter must have made some sort of reply, though what I heard sounded more like a groan.

"Yoshihide, tonight in accordance with your request I am going to burn this carriage for you."

His lordship glanced sidelong at those around him and seemed to exchange a meaningful smile with one or two, though I may have only imagined it. Yoshihide raised his head fearfully and looked up at the veranda, but said nothing and did not move from where he squatted.

"Look. That is the carriage I have always used. You recognize it, don't you? I am going to burn it and show you blazing hell itself."

Again his lordship paused and winked at his attendants. Suddenly his tone became unpleasant. "In that carriage, by my command, is a female malefactor. Therefore, when it is fired her flesh will be roasted, her bones burnt, she will die in extreme agony. Never again will you find such a model for the completion of your screen. Do not flinch from looking at snow-white skin inflamed with fire. Look well at her black hair dancing up in sparks."

His lordship ceased speaking for the third time. I don't know what thoughts were in his mind, but his shoulders shook with silent laughter. "Posterity will never see anything like it. I'll watch it from here. Come, come, lift up the blinds and show Yoshihide the woman inside."

At the daimyo's word one of the attendants, holding high his pine torch in one hand, walked up to the carriage without more ado, stretched out his free hand, and raised the blind. The flickering torch burned with a sharp crackling noise. It brightly lit up the narrow interior of the carriage, showing a woman on its couch, cruelly bound with chains. Who was she? Ah, it could not be! She was clad in a gorgeously embroidered cherry-patterned mantle; her black hair, alluringly loosened, hung straight down; the golden hairpins set at different angles gleamed beautifully, but there was a gag over her mouth tied behind her neck. The small slight body, the modest profile—the attire only was different—it was Yūzuki. I nearly cried aloud.

At that moment the samurai opposite me got to his feet hastily and put his hand on his sword. It must have been Yoshihide that he glared at. Startled I glanced at the artist. He seemed half-stunned by what he now saw. Suddenly he leapt up, stretched out both his arms before him, and forgetting everything else, began to run toward the carriage. Unfortunately, as I have already said, he was at some distance in the shadow, and I could not see the expression on his face. But that was momentary, for now I saw that it was absolutely colorless. His whole form cleaving the darkness appeared vividly before our eyes in the half-light—he was held in space, it seemed, by some invisible power that lifted him from the ground. Then, at his lordship's command, "Set fire," the carriage with its passenger, bathed in the light of the torches that were tossed on to it, burst into flames.

18

As we watched, the flames enveloped the carriage. The purple tassels that hung from the roof corners swung as though in a wind, while from below them the smoke swirled white against the blackness of the night. So frightful was it that the bamboo blinds, the hangings, the metal ornaments in the roof, seemed to be flying in the leaping shower of sparks. The tongues of flame that licked up from beneath the blinds, those serried flames that shot up into the sky, seemed to be celestial flames of the sun fallen to the earth. I had almost shouted before, but now I felt completely overwhelmed and dumbfounded; mouth agape, I could do nothing but watch the dreadful spectacle. But the father—Yoshihide. . . .

I still remember the expression on his face. He had started involuntarily toward the carriage, but when the fire blazed up he stopped, arms outstretched, and with piercing eyes watched the smoke and fire that enveloped the carriage as though he would be drawn into it. The blaze lit his wrinkled face so clearly that even the hairs of his head could be seen distinctly: in the depths of his wide staring eyes, in his drawn distorted lips, in his twitching cheeks, the grief, dread, and bewilderment that passed through his soul were clearly inscribed. A robber, guilty of unspeakable crimes and about to be beheaded, or dragged before the court of the Ten Kings, could hardly have looked more agonized. Even that gigantic samurai changed color and looked fearfully at the Lord of Horikawa.

But the latter, without taking his eyes off the carriage, merely bit his lips or laughed unpleasantly from time to time. As for the carriage and its passenger, that girl—I am not brave enough to tell you all that I saw. Her white face, choking in the smoke, looked upward; her long loosened hair fluttered in the smoke, her cherry-patterned mantle—how beautiful it all was! What a terrible spectacle! But when the night wind dropped and the smoke was drawn away to the other side, where gold dust seemed to be scattered above the red flames, when the girl gnawed her gag, writhing so that it seemed the chains must burst, I, and even the gigantic samurai, wondered whether we were not spectators of the torments of hell itself, and our flesh crept.

Then once more we thought the night wind stirred in the treetops of the garden. As that sound passed over the sky, something black that neither touched ground nor flew through the sky, dancing like a ball, leaped from the roof of the house into the blazing carriage. Into the crumbling blinds, cinnabar-stained, he fell, and putting his arms around the straining girl, he cried shrill and long into the smoke, a cry that sounded like tearing silk. He repeated it two or three times, then we forgot ourselves and shouted out together. Against the transparent curtain of flames, clinging to the girl's shoulder, was Yoshihide, Yoshihide the monkey, that had been left tied at the mansion.

19

But we saw him only for a moment. Like gold leaf on a brown screen the sparks climbed into the sky. The monkey and Yūzuki were hidden in black smoke while the carriage blazed away with a dreadful noise in the garden. It was a pillar of fire—those awful flames stabbed the very sky.

In front of that pillar Yoshihide stood rooted. Then, wonderful to say, over the wrinkled face of this Yoshihide, who had seemed to suffer on a previous occasion the tortures of hell, over his face the light of an inexpressible ecstasy passed, and forgetful even of his lordship's presence he folded his arms and stood watching. It was almost as if he did not see his daughter dying in agony. Rather he seemed to delight in the beautiful color of the flames and the form of a woman in torment.

What was most remarkable was not that he was joyfully watching the death of his daughter. It was rather that in him seemed to be a sternness not human, like the wrath of a kingly lion seen in a dream. Surprised by the fire, flocks of night birds that cried and clamored seemed thicker—though it may have been my imagination—around Yoshihide's cap. Maybe those soulless birds seemed to see a weird glory like a halo around that man's head. If the birds were attracted, how much more were we, the servants, filled with a strange feeling of worship as we watched Yoshihide. We quaked within, we held our breath, we watched him like a Buddha unveiled. The roaring of the fire that filled the air, and Yoshihide, his soul taken captive by it, standing there motionless—what awe we felt, what intense pleasure at this spectacle. Only his lordship sat on the veranda as though he were a different sort of being. He grew pale, foam gathered on his lips, he clutched his purple-skirted knee with both hands, he panted like some thirsty animal. . . .

20

It got around that his lordship had burnt a carriage at Yukige that night—though of course nobody said anything—and a great variety of opinions were expressed. The first and most prevalent rumor was that he had burnt Yoshihide's daughter to death in resentment over thwarted love. But there was no doubt that it was the daimyo's purpose to punish the perversity of the artist, who was painting the Hell Screen, even if he had to kill someone to do so. In fact, his lordship himself told me this.

Then there was much talk about the stony-heartedness of Yoshihide, who saw his daughter die in flames before his eyes and yet wanted to paint the screen. Some called him a beast of prey in human form, rendered incapable of human love by a picture. The

Abbot of Yokogawa often said, "A man's genius may be very great, great his art, but only an understanding of the Five Virtues [3] will save him from hell."

However, about a month later the Hell Screen was completed. Yoshihide immediately took it to the mansion and showed it with great deference to the Lord of Horikawa. The Abbot happened to be visiting his lordship at the time, and when he looked at it he must have been properly startled by the storm of fire that rages across the firmament on one of the leaves. He pulled a wry face, stared hard at Yoshihide, but said, "Well done," in spite of himself. I still remember the forced laugh with which his lordship greeted this.

From that time on, there was none that spoke badly of Yoshihide, at least in the mansion. And anyone who saw the screen, even if he had hated the artist before, was struck solemn, because he felt that he was experiencing hell's most exquisite tortures.

But by that time Yoshihide was no longer among the living. The night after the screen was finished he hanged himself from a beam in his studio. With his only daughter preceding him he felt, no doubt, that he could not bear to live on in idleness. His remains still lie within the ruins of his house. The rains and winds of many decades have bleached the little stone that marked his grave, and the moss has covered it in oblivion.

TRANSLATED BY W. H. H. NORMAN

[3] The Five Virtues of Confucius: Humanity, Justice, Propriety, Wisdom and Fidelity.

THE CANNERY BOAT

[Kani Kōsen, 1929] by Kobayashi Takiji (1903-1933)

The Cannery Boat *is the story of the voyage of a floating cannery in the waters off Kamchatka. The ship is manned by rough sailors, students from the universities, who have been tricked into believing the work is a desirable summer job, and boys from the farms of northern Japan. The descriptions of the life aboard ship are powerful and convincing, but what gives this book its characteristic flavor is the Marxist philosophy underlying it. The boss, Asakawa, is a fiend, and he represents an organization of cold-blooded monsters to whom the loss of sailors' lives means nothing. The only cheerful moments come when, in the extract given here, some sailors hear of the deliverance afforded by communism.* The Cannery Boat, *for all its gross imperfections, is considered to be the masterpiece of the "proletarian literature" movement. The author later died in prison of torture.*

•

In the afternoon the sky changed. There was a mist so light as to seem almost unreal. Myriads of three-cornered waves sprang up across the great cloth of sea. Suddenly the wind began to howl through the masts. The bottoms of the tarpaulins covering the cargo flapped against the deck.

The crests of the triangular waves were soon flinging their white spray over the whole surface of the sea, for all the world like thousands of rabbits scampering over a vast plain. This was the herald of one of Kamchatka's sudden storms. All at once the tide began to ebb quickly.

The ship started to swing round on herself. Kamchatka, which until now had been visible on the starboard side, suddenly appeared on the port side. There was great excitement among fishermen and sailors. Above their heads sounded an alarm whistle. They all stood looking up at the sky. The funnel shook and rattled. Maybe because they were standing directly under it, it seemed incredibly wide, like a huge bathtub, sloping away out backwards. The piercing note from the alarm whistle had something tragic in it. Warned by its prolonged blowing, the boats out fishing far from the main ship returned home through the storm.

Early that morning the boss had received warning of the storm from another ship which was anchored about ten miles away. The message also stated that if the boats were out they should be recalled immediately. Asakawa had said, "If we're going to take notice of every little thing that comes along, do you think we'll ever get finished with this job we came all the way to Kamchatka to do?" This information had leaked out through the radio operator.

The first sailor to hear this had started to roar at the operator as if he had been Asakawa. "What does he think human lives are, anyway?"

"Human lives?"

"Yes."

"But Asakawa never thinks of us as human beings."

Toward evening there was a great shouting from the bridge. The men below rushed up the companionway two steps at a time. Two boats had been sighted, drawing near. They had been lashed together with ropes. They came very close, but, just as if they were at one end of a seesaw with the ship at the other, the big waves lifted them up and down by turns. One after another immense roaring waves rose up between them. Although so near, they made no progress. Everyone felt the tension. A rope was thrown from the deck, but it did not reach. It only fell on the water with a vain splashing. Then, twisting like a water snake, it was hauled back. This was repeated several times. From the ship all shouted in one voice, but no answer came. Faces were like masks, with eyes immobile. The whole scene, with its unbearable grimness, seared every heart.

By dusk all the boats except two had got safely back. As soon as the fishermen came on deck they lost consciousness. One of the boats, having become full of water, had been anchored and its crew transferred to another boat. The other one together with its crew was missing.

The boss was fuming with rage. He kept on going down into the fishermen's cabin and then up again. The men cast sullen glances at him throughout this performance.

The next day, partly to search for the missing boat, partly to follow up the crabs, it was decided that the ship should move on. The loss of the carcasses of five or six men was nothing, but it would be a pity to lose the boat. . . .

When the lost boat did not return, the fishermen gathered together the belongings of the missing men, looking for the addresses of their families and getting everything ready in case worse came to worst. It wasn't the pleasantest of jobs. As they worked they had the feeling that they were examining their own remains. Various parcels and letters addressed to women relatives were discovered in the missing men's baggage. Among one man's things there was a letter written in crudely formed script, obviously with a frequently licked pencil. This was passed from one rough sailor's hand to another's. Each one spelled the words out to himself laboriously, but with intense interest, and shaking his head passed it on to his neighbor. It was a letter from the man's child.

One man raised his head from the page and whispered, "It's all because of Asakawa. When we know for sure this poor fellow is dead we'll revenge him." The speaker was a big, hefty man who had a past behind him. In a still lower voice one young round-shouldered fisherman said, "I expect we could beat up Asakawa."

"Ah, that letter was no good; it's made me homesick," said another man.

"Look here," the first speaker said, "if we don't look out the swine will get us. We've got to look out for ourselves."

One man who had been sitting in the corner with his knees up, biting his thumbnails and listening to every word, remarked, "Leave it to me. When the time comes, I'll lay into the swine!"

They were all silent, but they felt relieved.

Three days later the *Hakkō Maru* returned to her original position and the missing boat came back. Everyone on board was safe and sound.

Because of the storm they had lost control of their boat. They were more helpless than babes strung up by the neck, and were all prepared for death. Fishermen must always be ready for death.

Their boat had been washed up on the coast of Kamchatka, and they were rescued by some Russians living near. The Russians were a family of four. Thirsty as they were for a "home" with women and children in it, this place held an indescribable attraction for the sailors. Added to that, everyone was kind, offering all kinds of help. Still, at first the fact that their rescuers were foreigners, with different colored hair and eyes, using incomprehensible words, made the sailors feel rather strange. The thought soon occurred to them, however, that after all these were just human beings like themselves.

Hearing of the wreck, many people from the village gathered. The place was a long way off from the Japanese fishing waters.

They stayed there two days recovering and then started back. "We didn't want to come back. Who would, to a hell like this?"

Their story didn't end there. There was another interesting thing which they were hiding.

Just on the day they were to leave, as they were standing round the stove, putting on their clothes and talking, four or five Russians entered, and with them was a Chinese. One Russian, with a large face and a short brown beard, burst into a flood of loud talking and gesticulations. In order to let him know that they could not understand Russian the sailors waved their hands in front of their faces. Then the Russian said a single sentence and the Chinese, who was watching his lips, started to speak in Japanese. It was strange Japanese, with the order of the words all mixed up. Word after word came reeling out drunkenly.

"You, for sure, have no money."

"That's right."

"You are poor men."

"That's right too."

"So you proletarians. Understand?"

"Yes."

The Russian, smiling, started to walk around. Sometimes he would stop and look over at them.

"Rich man, he do this to you" (gripping his throat). "Rich man become fatter and fatter" (swelling out his stomach). "You no good at all, you become poor. Understand? Japan no good. Workers like this" (pulling a long face and making himself look like a sick man). "Men that don't work like this" (walking about haughtily).

The young fishermen were very amused at him. "That's right, that's right," they said and laughed.

"Workers like this. Men that don't work like this" (repeating the same gestures). "Like that no good. Workers like this!" (this time just the opposite, swelling out his chest and walking proudly). "Men that don't work like this!" (looking like a decrepit beggar). "That very good. Understand? That country, Russia. Only workers like this!" (proud). "Russia. We have no men who don't work. No cunning men. No men who seize your throat. Understand? Russia not at all terrible country. What everyone says only lies."

They were all vaguely wondering whether this wasn't what was called "terrible" and "Red." But even if it was "Red" one part of them couldn't help feeling that it sounded very right.

"Understand? Really understand?"

Two or three of the Russians started to jabber something among themselves. The Chinese listened to them. Then in a stuttering kind of way he began to speak again in Japanese: "Among men who no work, many make profit. Proletariat always like this" (a gesture of being gripped by the throat). "This no good! You proletarians, one, two, three, a hundred, a thousand, fifty thousand, a hundred thousand, all of you, all like this" (swinging his hands like children do when walking together). "Then become strong. It safe" (tapping the muscles of his arm). "You no lose. Understand?"

"Yes."

"Japan no good yet. Workers like this" (bending and cringing). "Men who no work like this" (pretending to punch and knock over his neighbor). "That no good! Workers like this" (straightening up his body in a threatening way and advancing; then pretending to knock his neighbor down and kick him). "Men who no work like this" (running away). "Japan only workers. Fine country. Proletarians' country! Understand?"

"Yes, yes, we understand."

The Russian raised a strange voice and began a kind of dance.

"Japan workers, act!" (straightening himself and making to attack). "Very glad. Russia all glad. Banzai! . . . You go back to ship. In your ship men who no work like this" (proud). "You, proletariat, do this!" (pretending to box, then swinging hands as before, and then advancing). "Very safe. You win! Understand?"

"We understand." The young fishermen, who before they knew it had become very much excited, suddenly shook the Chinese's hand. "We'll do it . . . we'll certainly do it."

The head sailor thought all this was "Red," that they were being egged on to do terrible things. Like this, by such tricks, Russia was making a complete fool of Japan, he thought.

When the Russian had finished he shouted something and then pressed their hands with all his might. He embraced them and pressed his bristly face to theirs. The flustered Japanese, with their heads pushed back, did not know what to do.

The sailors in the hold listening to this story were eager to hear more, in spite of occasional glances toward the door. The fishermen went on telling them many other things about the Russians. Their minds lapped it all up as if they were blotting paper.

"Hey, there, that's about enough!" The head sailor, seeing how impressed they all were by these tales, tapped the shoulder of one young fisherman, who was talking for all he was worth.

TRANSLATED ANONYMOUSLY

TIME

[*Jikan, 1931*] *by Yokomitsu Riichi (1898-1947)*

Yokomitsu Riichi was one of the most brilliantly gifted of modern Japanese writers. His name is associated with a number of literary schools of the twenties and thirties, but he was essentially an independent. He disagreed both with the advocates of "proletarian" literature and the writers of autobiographical fiction, affirming his own belief in the purely artistic values of literature. European influences are detectable in his works, but in "Time" and some of his other stories we find not only the psychological insights characteristic of European writing, but an essentially Buddhist concern with the hell that man creates for himself on earth.

•

The manager of our troupe failed to return for a whole week after stepping out one evening. Takagi decided to open the suitcase he had left behind. It was empty. Then we were really at our wits' end. When the truth dawned on us—our manager had run off, leaving us without a penny—we were all too dumbfounded to make any suggestion as to how to deal with the room and board bill. I was finally chosen as delegate for the group to face the landlord. I asked him please to allow us to continue as we were for the time being, and assured him that remittances would be forthcoming from our families. I earned us thus a temporary reprieve. Two or three money orders did in fact come, and each time we acclaimed them with joyous shouts. What happened, however, was that the money which arrived was the exclusive possession of the man receiving it, and it simply led to his making off immediately with whichever actress of the company he liked best.

Finally there were twelve of us left—eight men and four women:

six-feet tall, amply built Takagi, who assumed as a matter of course that women had eyes for no one but him; Kinoshita, who liked gambling better than three meals a day and whose every thought was directed towards inventing a means of seeing dice through the box; pale, gentle Sasa, whom everyone called Buddha, and who, mysteriously enough, licked the windowpanes when he was drunk; Yagi, who was a little peculiar, and collected women's underwear; Matsugi, a champion at hand and foot wrestling, always on the look-out for billiard parlors in whatever town we went to; Kurigi, who was forever forgetting and mislaying his belongings, and whose only talent was for losing whatever came into his hands; Yashima, who, miser that he was, hated to return borrowed articles; and my-self—eight men, plus the four women, Namiko, Shinako, Kikue, and Yukiko. In our cases it was not so much that remittances were unconscionably slow in arriving, as that little or no possibility existed of any money coming to us. Knowing this all along, we had placed our hopes on the money of others more likely to receive it.

The landlord's looks turned unfriendly, as he too began to doubt whether he would see his money, however much longer he waited. His surveillance over the remaining twelve of us was eagle-eyed, to say the least. For our part, we each felt that it was preferable for no money to arrive at all than to have some come to any one of us—whoever received it was sure to sneak off by himself, and make the burden on those who remained all the heavier. Our suspicions grew so strong that soon we were spying on one another secretly, wondering who would be the next to run off. But it was only at the beginning that we could afford the luxury of this mutual spying. Before long we had more pressing matters on our minds than who would be the next to escape—the landlord stopped giving us even one meal a day. We gradually turned pallid and unwell, and our days were spent drinking water to fill our stomachs and discussing interminably what we should do. At length we reached agreement: we would all escape together. If, as we reasoned, we escaped in a group, we would have little to worry about even if a couple of men were sent in pursuit of us. There lurked also in our minds the specter of the fate which lay in store for anyone who happened by

mischance to be the last left behind. These considerations led us to
swear up and down to make a joint escape. However, if we were
mply to make a wild break for it, or in any way attract the atten-
n of the local bullies in the landlord's employ, we would have
chance of success. We decided therefore to take advantage of our
sits to the public bath, the one freedom we were allowed, and some
ainy night when the watch over us was least strict to make our
escape. We would have to follow the road along the coast rather
than an easier route, for unless the way we took was the most
difficult and unlikely, we were certain to be caught. With these
matters settled by way of preliminaries, we resolved to await a rainy
night.

In the room next to the one where our escape plans were being
discussed, Namiko lay all alone. She had suffered a severe attack of
some female sickness during a performance, and was still unable to
move from her bed. Whenever the question of what to do with her
arose, we all fell silent. On this one topic, no one had a word to say.
It was quite clearly—if tacitly—understood that we had no alternative but to abandon her. As a matter of fact, I was also of the opinion
that we would have to sacrifice Namiko for the sake of the eleven
others of us, but after we had finished our discussion I happened to
pass through her room. She suddenly thrust out her arms and seized
my foot. She begged me in tears to take her along, insisting that
she must escape when we did. I managed eventually to extricate
my foot by promising to discuss the matter with the others.

I called everyone together again to reopen our discussion. They
were all perfectly aware of my reason for summoning them. In their
eyes flashed repeated warnings not to propose anything foolish. I
asked if they would not consent to taking Namiko along. First of
all, I explained, she was passionately anxious to escape with the
rest of us. There was also the sentimental consideration that, after
all, she had shared rice from the same pot with us for such a long
time. Yukiko, who was standing next to me, capitulated first. She
declared that she didn't feel right about leaving Namiko behind.
She had once received a pair of stockings from her. Shinako remembered that she had been given some lace cuffs, and Kikue had

been given a comb. The women thus were at least not opposed to taking Namiko along. Not one of the men spoke openly. Instead, one after another they took me aside to urge that I drop the subject. "Come on," I said, in an attempt to persuade them, "let's take her. Something good is bound to come of it." They began for the first time to come around to my point of view, and finally agreed that we might as well take her.

When we actually reached the point of making our escape, we faced the necessity of following a trail over the cliffs along the sea for some fifteen or twenty miles before we could get through the pass. The thought of carrying a sick woman on our backs loomed as a staggering undertaking. In order to fool that scoundrel of a landlord we would have to leave the rooming house one by one, swinging our towels as part of the pretense of visiting the public bath in a storm. If we took too much time over our departure we would have no chance to eat, and would be obliged to set out with empty stomachs. In that case we would have no choice but to risk making our way, under cover of darkness, to the next station.

I asked Namiko to try and stand, as a test of her ability to walk. She made an effort, but immediately collapsed limply over the bedding, moaning that her eyes felt as if they were swimming in her head. She seemed utterly without bones. I, who in a moment of sympathy had urged the others to take Namiko along, now could not help thinking that in her condition it would be best for all of us to leave her behind. "Wouldn't you really prefer to remain here by yourself?" I said. "I can't imagine that the landlord would do anything bad to a sick person like yourself. We promise to send you money." Namiko burst into tears. "I'd rather you killed me than left me here alone." She persisted, and I could do nothing to change her mind. After having convinced the others to take Namiko along, I could not bring myself to be so irresponsible as to propose now that we abandon her. So, I too began to wait for the next rainy night. I made no mention of Namiko again. But even waiting for the rain was not easy for us. Anyone who went to the public bath would always pawn an article of clothing and buy buns to be shared with the rest of us. We realized, however, at this rate we might use up the money needed for our train fare, and then face real disaster. We stopped smoking altogether, and limited ourselves to only one bun a day. The whole time was spent lolling around, drinking water to keep ourselves going. There was nothing else to do. Fortunately, the autumn rains began to fall a few mornings later, and by late afternoon an increasingly violent storm had developed. We determined to stage our escape that night, and each of us completed whatever preparations were necessary. We waited for the dark. One thought obsessed me—assuming that we all managed to reach the railway station safely, which man would eventually go off with which woman. The fact that eight men had remained behind with the four women was not only because they had no money. Each of the women had had relations with two or even three of the men, I rather suspected, which made separation extremely difficult. I felt certain that sooner or later, somewhere, there would be trouble. However, no one betrayed any presentiment of this as night approached and the time set for our escape drew upon us. Soon, one or two at a time, the members of the troupe began going out, towels in hand. It crossed my mind that, unknown to me, the matter of which man would go with which woman had already been decided. My share of the escape preparations consisted merely of bundling together changes of clothes for all of us and throwing the bundles over the wall to the others waiting on the opposite side. I was conscious of the danger that, if I was the last to leave, since it had been my idea to take Namiko along, I might well be left to figure out an escape for the two of us. Were such a proposal to be made, the others were only too likely to agree with it. I therefore contrived that Takagi should be the last to leave. With my towel slung over my shoulder I took Namiko on my back and set out in the rain for the bamboo thicket where I was to join the others.

There were about ten of us huddled together in the thicket, protected only by three oil-paper umbrellas. We waited for the others. Kinoshita, who had taken our bundles to the pawnshop, did not appear. No one actually voiced anything, but an expression of uneasiness gradually crept over our faces, as much as to say, "Kinoshita has run off with the money." We stood in silence, staring at each other. Soon, Kinoshita returned with ten yen in his hand. Our next problem was to eat before we started. Takagi was the last to arrive and suggested we all go together to a restaurant. Matsugi pointed out that it would be best to go one at a time, since we were sure to be discovered if we went in a crowd. We agreed to this. We decided to divide the money, but all we had was a ten yen bill. We could have sent someone to change it, but the unspoken fear that anyone who went for change might run off with the money prevented us from letting the money out of our sight. Someone said, "Having the money is just the same as not having it. What are we going to do?" For a while there was silence, then another remarked that if we delayed any longer people from the rooming house would catch up with us. And still another voice: "What could we do if they really came after us? I'm too hungry to move." When we reached this impasse Yashima suggested that the money be turned over to me, since I was the one person who could not run away or hide, what with a sick woman on my back. To this everyone assented. However, I knew that if I were entrusted with the money the others would constantly be spying on me, and this would be extremely disagreeable. I thought it would be better if in front of everybody I gave the money to Namiko. As guardian of our money, she would certainly, at least for the time being, be carefully protected. I thrust the bill into her kimono. With this, the sick woman, who up until now had been treated as a disgusting nuisance, suddenly became an object of value, a reassuringly dependable safe-deposit vault. Automatically we began to formulate regulations around her. First of all, the men in the group were to take turns carrying Namiko on their back, each one taking a hundred steps. The women were not required to carry the burden, but to take turns counting. Next we settled the order of carrying her, while the women laughingly watched and backed one or another of us in our choosing games. Those of us who were to go in front began to walk out of the bamboo thicket.

There were only three umbrellas for the twelve of us, and the rain whipped by a gale beat headlong into our faces. We struggled forward in single file, four to an umbrella, and drenched by the rain. In the middle was Namiko, guarded like a holy image in procession, immediately behind her the women, and farther back some of the men. Sasa, who was near the middle, suddenly called out, "We seem to have forgotten all about eating." There were cries of assent, and again the column came to a halt. But there was hardly time now for eating: if we were overtaken we would be finished. Several favored making a desperate attempt to cross the pass tonight in the hope that tomorrow would be safe, and by tacit consent our column began to wriggle caterpillar-like ahead in the darkness. The starch had drained from the women's felt hats, which began to make a loud spattering noise. At first we thought in terror that it might be the sound of pursuers. From time to time, as if by a prearranged signal, we all would turn to look behind us. But as Kurigi said, even supposing that the landlord discovered what had happened and sent people out after us, they would never choose this terrible road at first. This observation was reassuring, but the fact remained that none of us had ever traveled on the road before. We had not the least idea what lay ahead, not even whether we were to pass through cultivated land or barren desolation. The road, from which the sand had been washed by the rain to expose frequently the raised heads of stones, was only dimly visible at our feet. Uneasiness akin to desperation mounted steadily within us. Only Kinoshita, who chattered on with his usual socialistic talk, displayed any energy. "The next time I meet that damned manager who's responsible for all our suffering, I will really give him a beating," he swore, and at his words the hatred of the group for the already half-forgotten manager suddenly flared up again. "Beat him? I'll shove him in the ocean!" shouted someone else; and another voice chimed in, "The ocean's too good for him! I'll split his head open with a rock." "I'll stick burning hot prongs down his throat!" "Burning hot prongs are too good for him," another man was saying when the sick woman, who up until that moment had not uttered a sound, suddenly burst into loud wails. Yagi, who was carrying her on his back, stopped in his tracks. There were cries from behind. "What's the matter? Can't you move any faster?" Namiko was weeping convulsively, and she began now to beg us to go on without her. At first we were at a loss to tell what had caused this outburst, when we discovered that she was losing blood. We stood there in the rain, bewildered and helpless. I suggested that the women be left to deal with this female disorder, and one of the women thereupon said that a dry cloth was needed immediately. I felt obliged to offer my undershirt. The sick woman felt sorry for us, and all the while that Matsugi, whose turn was next, was carrying her, she begged him in tears again and again to go on without her. Matsugi finally lost his temper and threatened to leave her then and there if she kept whining, and this only made her wail all the more hysterically. Uppermost in our minds, however, was the fear of being overtaken. Finally we reached a point where even that ceased to worry us, when thoughts of our hunger assailed us. "Tomorrow," began one of us, "when we get to a town the first thing I'm going to do is eat pork cutlets." "I'll take fish." "I'd rather have eels than fish." "I'd like a steak." Then we all started to talk about food, not listening to what anyone else had to say, but elaborating on what we liked to eat and places where we had once had a good meal. We were becoming like voracious beasts.

I was as desperate as the others, at least as far as hunger was concerned. I looked for something to eat along the road, but ever since we had emerged from the bamboo thicket we had not passed a single cultivated field. There was hardly much point in searching here: to the right was a wall of sheer rock, and to the left, at the foot of a cliff that dropped several hundred feet, we could hear the sound of waves. It was all we could do to avoid a misstep from the path, which was a bare four feet wide. We lurched ahead tied to one another with our belts, following whichever way the umbrella in front led. The road twisted up and down. Sometimes the rain unexpectedly swept up on us from below, and before we knew it we would be pasted against the edge of the rock face. Our column staggered ahead over the endless cliff, now stretching out, now contracting, and we began to collide with each other: we obviously could not allow stories of food to dull our faculties. Presently the pleasant remembrances of food turned into grim reminders of the fact that we had nothing to eat. One after another of us dropped out of the discussion. Then we were silent, and all that could be heard between the roar of the waves and the sound of the wind was the monotonous voice of the woman counting the number of paces. There were no sighs now, nor even so much as a cough. The silence which pressed on every one of us, the mute fear of what would happen if things continued this way much longer, was almost tangible enough to touch. At this juncture Namiko's losses of blood became severe. The confusion of removing our undershirts and the wailing of Namiko restored our animation, and with it talk about food. Some protested that so much talk about food worked up our appetites all the more, but the others answered that talk was now the only means at our disposal for blunting our hunger. Water was better than nothing, and some began to lick the drops of rain which trickled from the umbrellas, or else to chew on pine needles pulled from the stunted trees along our way. We looked like so many ravenous demons, but this occasioned no laughter. My clothes were soaked through and through, but my throat was parched. When the rain blew against me I would turn my head away from the umbrella into the rain with my mouth open. And when it came my turn to carry Namiko again, however much I tried to remind myself that the weight on my back was a woman, I was so hungry that I could scarcely keep my feet moving. Everything grew misty before my eyes as I ran more and more out of breath. My arms became numb, and my legs trembled under me. I could go on only by biting my tongue and leaning my head into the back of the man in front of me who carried the umbrella. By the time that the woman had counted up to about ninety, I felt like tossing Namiko over the edge, but I steeled myself against betraying any emotion, for I knew that if she detected it she would start her screeching again. My eyelids became so stiff that when I opened them I heard a click. Even though the burden was eventually shifted to the next man, it came back every eight hundred yards, after each man had performed his stint, and there was pitiful little time to recuperate from the strain. To make matters worse, every minute increased my hunger, and with it the sick woman on my back became heavier. This was unbearable enough, but Namiko took it into her head to insist that we carry her at the front of the column because she couldn't bear being sandwiched in the middle. This was probably more agreeable to Namiko, for it reduced her fear of being abandoned, but we who were doing the carrying were additionally fatigued by the constant pushing from behind. I recalled that everyone was being made to suffer simply because I had brought the sick woman along, and I resolved that if ever we became so exhausted as to reach the verge of collapse, I would either hurl Namiko into the ocean or remain with her and ask the others to go on without us.

But in point of fact we had already reached the "verge of collapse" and such thoughts obviously served no useful purpose. Our faces were livid and stained with a greasy sweat, our eyes had begun to glaze, and there were some who after protracted yawns would suddenly let out strange, unnerving cries. When one of us, as if broken by the wind, collapsed over a projecting ledge of the rock wall, Namiko again began to weep and beg us to leave her there. Water was streaming from the women's hair and clothes, and they walked like specters, with their wet hair plastered over their faces. The color of their underwear had seeped through and stained their kimonos. By the time water had soaked their compacts and purses, a heavy calm fell over them. Kikue said, "We're going to die soon, anyway; I wish it were all over." "Why don't you jump over the edge then? It'd be perfectly simple," snapped Yagi. This crude joke apparently got on the nerves of Kurigi, who was already at the end of his tether. He snarled, "What do you mean by joking when people are suffering?" and closed in on Yagi. Yagi drew himself up, as if startled at being so unexpectedly threatened, and blurted out, "You needn't get so angry, no matter how much I joke with Kikue. You may be in love with her, but you haven't got a chance —I've seen her with Takagi myself." Gentle Sasa, who up to now had kept absolutely silent, suddenly pulled a knife from his pocket and lunged at Takagi. Takagi deftly avoided the point of Sasa's knife, and made a headlong dash along the cliff. Sasa ran in pursuit, lurching heavily. Kurigi, who for a while had remained dumbfounded by this development, now realizing that his enemy was actually not Yagi but rather Takagi and Sasa, ran off after them.

Dimly visible through the dark beside me, I could see and hear Kikue, sobbing that it was all her fault. "Go at once," I said, "and stop the fight." But she answered, "Unless you go too I can't stop them." Then, and this came as an entirely unexpected event, Namiko suddenly thrust out her arms and, fastening herself on the neck of the weeping Kikue, began to gnash her teeth. Apparently she had realized for the first time that her lover—whichever one of the three he was—had been taken from her. Soon even Yagi, who had caused the quarrel, was in a rage, and I was amazed to see him drag Shinako to the ground and demand that she reveal her lover's name. It was obvious that the fight could soon involve us all, and if anyone got hurt and could not proceed farther, we were all without question doomed. I was appalled at our horrible plight; my only comfort came from the fact that nobody around me had a weapon. But one of the men up the road had a knife, and I could not very well leave things at that. Shaking all over, I ran along the black cliff, shouting again and again, "Wait! Wait!" When I had gone about two hundred yards I saw the three of them lying motionless by the side of the road, flat on their backs. I thought that they must be dead, but I noticed then that they were all staring at my face, their eyes popping from their sockets. I asked what had happened. "We decided that to get hurt fighting over a woman in a place like this wouldn't do us any good, and we stopped. But don't make us talk for a while—we're so exhausted that breathing is painful."

"You are very wise," I said, and returned to the sick woman. There the fight seemed just beginning. Yagi and Kinoshita were grappling and snarling on the road near the shrieking Namiko. Even the women had evidently lost all track of who had stolen their man and whose man they themselves had stolen. They were in such a state of bewilderment that they did not even bother to ask me what had happened in the fight up the road. The fights had not actually come as a great surprise to me, but I never imagined that they would explode with such violence here. The detached calm with which I had contemplated the quarrels was now rudely shattered by the realization that our progress might be halted because of them. Yagi and Kinoshita had long been on bad terms and rivals in love.

There was not much likelihood therefore that they would separate even if I tried to force my way in and stop the fight. In any case, it was certainly pleasanter for them to be lying on the ground hitting each other than to be on their feet walking and obliged to carry a sick woman. They seemed in fact to be hitting each other merely in order to rest their grappling legs. I thought that the best plan was to let them fight all they could, as long as they did not cause each other any real harm. I sat on the ground to rest myself while the two of them continued to wrestle weakly. As I watched, suddenly both Yagi and Kinoshita ceased moving altogether, both apparently utterly exhausted, and capable now only of panting furiously. This, I thought, was a good point to intervene. I said, "You can't go on lying there indefinitely. If you want to fight, go ahead and fight. If you've had enough, break it up now, and let's get moving again. The three of them up the road have had the sense to realize that nothing is so stupid as fighting over a woman, and now they've made up." Yagi and Kinoshita slowly got to their feet and began to walk.

When our procession joined the three men up the road, the sick woman was shifted to another back. There were no more undershirts left among us to wipe her bleeding, and now as we walked along peacefully, our shorts one by one were used. In spite of the fact that the result of the immorality of the women had been to excite violent quarrels among the men, when the various relations had become so excessively complicated as to upset all judgments, a balance was restored, and a kind of calm monotony ensued. This to me was at once fascinating and terrifying. But soon afterwards, as hunger began to assail us more fiercely than ever, our peace was turned into a bestial stupor from which all individuality had been stripped. I became incapable of speech. The skin of my abdomen stuck to my spine. There was no saliva left in my mouth. Sour juices welled up from my stomach, bringing with them a griping pain. The rims of my eyes burned. My incessant yawns reeked of bitter tobacco. No doubt as a result of our exhaustion from the scuffles, not a word was said as we proceeded in the soaking rain, with our heads down. Our helplessness was so manifest, that Namiko, now weeping quietly to herself, began to appear the strongest of us. We were plunged into despair and doubted we could ever manage to cross the cliff which extended limitlessly before us in the dark. We could no longer think in terms so remote as hope or a happier future. Our heads held no other thoughts but of the moments of time that kept pressing in on us, one after another: what would our hunger be like in another two minutes, how could we last out another minute. The time which I could conceive of came to be filled entirely with sensations of hunger, and I began to feel as if what was trudging forward in the endless darkness was not myself but only a stomach. I could feel already that time as far as I was concerned was nothing but a measure of my stomach.

We must have walked ten or twelve miles since nightfall. Just about when the men were turning over the last of their under-clothes to the sick woman, we discovered a small hut on the rock face somewhat above the road. Those who were in the lead could not be sure at first whether it was a boulder or a hut. While they were still arguing, we saw that it was an abandoned water mill. We decided that it would be a good idea to rest there a bit, if only to escape from the rain, and we went in. It was evident that no human being had made his way here for a very long time: cobwebs that crisscrossed the hut clung to our faces. There was space enough to shelter us from the rain, a musty little room into which the twelve of us squeezed. "There must be water somewhere, this is a mill. I'm going to look," Yagi said, and wandered outside the hut. But the pipes which should have carried water had rotted into pieces, and the blades of the water wheel were covered with white mold. It was impossible to find any water here. The sweat on our skins turned icy, and the dampness in our clothes made us shiver. To our fatigue and hunger now was added the biting cold of the late autumn night, so sharp that anyone who separated himself from the others could not have endured it. We wished to make a fire, but no one had matches. The best we could do was remove our coats, spread them out on the floor, and arrange ourselves together so as to share one another's warmth. The sick woman was placed in the center with the three other women around her, and the men spread their arms around the women making an effect something like an artichoke. But such measures did not suffice. The cold assaulted us even more keenly. Then our teeth began to chatter so badly that we could not form words but only stammer. Tears came but not a sound from the lips. We were shaking like jellyfish in the water. Soon the sick woman in the center lost even the strength to shiver, and in the midst of our trembling she lay shrunken and motionless. One of the women moaned, "When I die, please cut off my hair and send it to my mother. I can't stand any more." Then another voice cried, "I'm finished too. When I die, cut off my thumb and send it home." "Send back my glasses." Even while they spoke our knees grew numb, our thighs grew numb, and soon the pain reached our heads. Kurigi suddenly burst out, "I'm being punished now because when I was a boy I threw stones at the village god." And Takagi said, "I'm being punished for having deceived so many women," a remark which seemed to transfix men and women alike. They joined in with affirmative exclamations amidst their tears. The extreme mercilessness they all displayed rather amused me, but at the same time I could not detach myself from the conviction that we would die there. I was sitting on a wooden support next to the millstone, and I wondered when the next disaster would strike us. It proved to be something which we might have foreseen: an insidious drowsiness began to overtake us. Our shivering imperceptibly had died away. I realized with a shock that if we once permitted ourselves to fall asleep the end would come. I began to shout, to shake people's heads, to strike them. I told them if we fell asleep we were finished; I urged them to hit at once anyone who dozed. What made our struggle so difficult against the strange enemy was that the very consciousness we were losing was the only weapon we could employ in our defense. Even as I exhorted the others, I felt myself growing increasingly drowsy, and my thoughts wandered to reveries on the nature of sleep. I dimly realized that soon I too would be dropping off. But that thought itself made me leap up, ready to kick that thing, whatever it was, that was trying to steal my consciousness. Then I came face to face with something even stranger—in the midst of this frantic shuttling between life and death I sensed time, milder than ever I had experienced it, and I felt that I should like to go that one step further and peep at the instant of time when my consciousness was extinguished. Abruptly I opened my eyes and looked around me. In front the others were all dropping off to sleep, their heads hanging lifelessly.

I rushed from one to another, striking violently, and shouting warnings to wake up. Each opened his vacant eyes, some only again to lean senselessly against the person next to them, others, aware suddenly of the mortal danger threatening them, gazed around in bewilderment, blinking their eyes. Still others thought that having been struck by me gave them the right to hit anyone else who was asleep, and there soon began a wild melee. At each slight letup sleep crept back to suck up all consciousness. I pulled each by the hair, I shook their heads wildly, I slapped them so hard on the cheeks that the imprint of my fingers remained. But even if I had struck so hard that they tasted the bones of my fist, even if I had had a fist of iron, no sooner would my violent actions stop for a moment than all would plummet towards death. Even while I went on pummeling the eleven others, watching intently their every move-ment, I felt suddenly buoyed up by the infinite pleasure into which my consciousness was melting. Pleasure—indeed there is nothing to compare with the gaiety and transparency of the pleasure before death. The heart begins to choke from its extremity of pleasure, as if it were licking some luscious piece of fruit. It holds no melan-choly, like a forgetting of the self. What is this thing between life and death, this wave which surges up in ever shifting colors with a vapor joyous as the sky? I wonder if it is not the face of that dreadful monster no human being has ever seen—time? It gave me pleasure to think that when I died and disappeared every other man in the whole world would vanish at the same time with me. This temptation to kill every human being, this game with death enticed me, and I wavered on the point of yielding myself without further struggle to sleep. And yet, when I observed the others I would pound them with both hands, scarcely caring where I struck. To fight to keep others from death—why should such a harmful act prove beneficial? Even supposing that we managed to escape death now, it was impossible to imagine that when we were dying at some future time we could do so without the least worry, so neatly and so pleasantly as now. And yet I seemed to want them to live again. I pulled the women by the hair and beat them, kicked the men over and over. Could that be called love, I wonder? Or was it more properly to be termed habit? I was so painfully aware of the unhappy future that awaited us all that I felt like strangling each to death, and yet I was compelled by helping them to prolong their sufferings. And was this action to be called salvation? —My lips formed the words, "Go ahead and die!", but I continued to tear frantically through their sleep as though struggling with some misfortune from long years past which had never ceased in its depredations. Gradually they awakened and then, with exactly the expression of "Which one of you has destroyed my happiness?", fell to hitting those around them more savagely than ever. It seemed impossible that anyone could now sleep undisturbed. Some kept moving even while asleep, with only their hands flailing the air in motions of striking. The others, even as they were stamping, kicking, hitting, wildly pounding one another in this scene of inferno, began to fall asleep again. What at first had been round and gathered together steadily disintegrated as heads dropped between legs and trunks became interlocked. In this coagulating, amorphous mass, it was no longer possible to tell whom one struck or where the blow fell. I ranged over as large an area as I could, furiously striking everyone, for I knew that anyone who escaped would die. But lethargy is filled with a submerged terror that attacks with a ferocity only second to that of brute violence; an instant, it would seem, after arousing someone I would open my eyes to find him striking my head or thrusting his knee into my groin. Each time I awoke I would wriggle my way among the bodies around me and sink into them. Thus we moved again and again from sleep to waking.

Outside the hut changes had also been taking place. The rain had stopped, and in the moonlight streaming in through holes in the crumbling walls we could see the spider webs etched with absolute clarity. We tried to make our way outside in the hope of shaking off our drowsiness, but our legs refused to move. So we crawled out on our bellies and stared at the mountains and the sea illuminated by moonlight. Then Sasa, who was beside me, wordlessly tugged at my sleeve and pointed dementedly at a place down the cliff. I looked, my mind a blank—a thin stream of water was flowing from the rocks, making a faint splashing sound as it sparkled in the moonlight. I tried to shout "Water!" but I had no voice. Sasa went down the cliff, rubbing his knees painfully. After a few minutes he reached the spring and began to drink. His spirits were suddenly restored, and he shouted "Water! Water!" I too faintly called out at the same time.

We were saved. The others, incapable as they were of moving their legs, crawled out of the hut, each man for himself, and headed for the spring. One after another, their pale cobweb-covered faces exposed by the moonlight, they pressed their noses into the rock. The clear water filled with the smell of the rock soaked through from the throat to the stomach and down to the toes, with the sharpness of a knife. Then, as the force of life first began to operate, we all let out cries of wonder at the moon, as if we felt that this is what it meant to be really alive, and we pressed our mouths again to the rock. Suddenly I remembered the sick woman in the hut. I wondered if she might not have fallen asleep and died already. I asked the others to think of some way of getting water to her. Takagi had the idea of carrying water in a hat. We filled his soft hat with water, but after taking a few steps the water leaked out of it. Then we tried putting five hats together, one inside the other, and filled them with water. This time it did not leak noticeably, but it was obvious that by the time we got the hat to Namiko the water would be gone. "Wouldn't the quickest way," Sasa suggested, "be to pass the hat along in a relay?" The eleven of us distributed ourselves in the moonlight at intervals of about twenty feet apart. I was chosen to be the last in line, the one to give the water to Namiko. While I waited for the hat to be passed up, I kept shaking the sick woman. Although her skin still bore red marks where she had been struck, her body was crumbling into sleep under my shaking, and she showed no signs of returning to consciousness. I took her by the hair and shook her head violently. Her eyes opened, but it was no more than that, for they remained fixed in a dull stare. Just then the hat arrived, with almost all the water gone. I poured into her mouth the few remaining drops, and for the first time she seemed to open her eyes of her own volition. She placed her hand on my knee and looked around the hut. I said, "It's water. You must drink it or you'll die." I lay her over my knee and waited for the next hat. Another came and again I poured the drops into her mouth. As I repeated this over and over I seemed to see the others, shouting as they scrambled one after another back up the steep cliff from the spring, their weary bodies caught in the moonlight, and exactly as though I were pouring distilled moonlight I poured the drops of water into the sick woman's mouth.

TRANSLATED BY DONALD KEENE

EARTH AND SOLDIERS

[Tsuchi to Heitai, 1938] by Hino Ashihei (born 1907)

The most famous literary products of the "China Incidents" of the thirties were the diaries written by Hino Ashihei, an official correspondent attached to the troops. The reading public of the time found such absorbing interest in the descriptions of the fighting, with its scenes of pathos and heroism, that, in the old phrase, "the price of paper rose." Hino has been denounced for his lack of a more critical attitude toward these wars of aggression, but it is undeniable that he accomplished brilliantly the task of making reportage into a work of artistry.

•

October 28, 1937
Aboard the (Censored) Maru.

Dear Brother:

Again today, there is the blue sky and the blue water. And here I am writing this while lying on the upper deck of the same boat. I wish this were being written at the front, but not yet. All I can tell you is about the soldiers, lolling about the boat, the pine groves and the winding, peaceful line of the Japanese coast. What will be our fate? Nobody knows. The speculation about our point of disembarkation is still going on. Rumors that we are bound for Manchukuo are gaining strength.

Besides, there is a well-founded report that on the Shanghai front, where there has been a stalemate, our troops attacked and fought a ferocious battle. The story is that two days ago they advanced in force and rolled back the line for several miles, taking two important Chinese cities. They say that big lantern parades are swirling through the streets of Tokyo, in celebration. So the war is over! And we are to be returned, like victorious troops. That would be funny, in our case, but anyway, we are to be sent home soon!

Of course, this is nonsense, some absolutely ridiculous story. Yet we cannot avoid listening when someone talks in this vein. We cannot believe it and yet we do not wish to convince ourselves that it is not true.

This sort of life, while it is bad for the men because it is too easy, is even worse for the war horses, down in the hatch. They have been stabled below decks, in a dark and unhealthy hole. Sometimes, you can see them, clear down in the hold, standing patiently in the darkness. Some have not survived so well. They have lost weight. Their ribs are showing and they look sickly.

They have the best in food and water. Actually, they get better care than the men. Does it surprise you to know that, in war, a horse may be much more valuable than a man? For example, the horses get all the water they need. On the other hand, the supply of water for the men is limited, barely enough for washing, let alone the daily bath to which we are accustomed.

From that standpoint, the horses are much better off than we are. But the poor creatures have no opportunity for exercising, breathing fresh air, and feeling the sunlight. They are growing weaker. With my own eyes, I have seen a number of them collapse.

I never looked at a war horse, without thinking of poor Yoshida Uhei, who lives on the hillside, back of our town. In my memory, they are always together, just as they were before the war ever came. It is impossible to disassociate one from the other.

Perhaps you do not remember Uhei. He was a carter. He had a wagon, with which he did hauling jobs. His horse, Kichizo, drew it.

In all my life, I have never known such affection between man and animal. Kichizo was a big, fine chestnut, with great, wide shoulders and chest, and a coat like velvet. It used to shimmer in the sun and you could see the muscles rippling underneath the skin. Uhei cared for Kichizo like a mother with a baby.

I suppose this can be explained, at least in part, by the fact that Uhei had no children. He was already past forty, but his wife had never conceived. Undoubtedly, Uhei long ago gave up hope of having a child. So all his affection turned toward Kichizo, the horse. You have heard fathers brag about their sons? In a way, he did the same thing about Kichizo. "What strength!" he would say, "and yet how gentle he can be. He's a dear fellow, that Kichizo, even though he is so big and strong."

Then the war came. It came clear down to our little town, into the nooks and corners of the country, taking men and horses. Kichizo was commandeered by the army.

When he heard the news, Uhei was speechless with surprise for a while. I remember it very well. "The army needs your horse, Uhei," someone told him. "It is for the nation." Uhei looked at the speaker with dumb disbelief in his face. His eyes were frozen, uncomprehending. "Don't worry," they told him, "Kichizo will be all right. He isn't a cavalry horse. He won't be in any danger. They'll use him behind the lines, to pull wagons. It won't be anything different than what he does here. And the army takes good care of its horses. They're very important. Don't you worry about him."

Uhei turned away without speaking and began to run toward his home. He broke into a dead run, like a crazy man, and we saw him disappear behind the bend in the road. "He'll be all right," somebody said, "after all, it's only a horse."

That same afternoon, Uhei came back to town. He looked different then. He was smiling and his eyes were shining, and he swaggered around the streets. "Have you heard the news?" he kept saying, "Kichizo, my horse, is going to the war. They need big strong fellows for the army, so of course Kichizo was the first horse they thought about. They know what they're doing, those fellows. They know a real horse when they see one."

He went to the flagmaker and ordered a long banner, exactly like the ones people have when a soldier is called to the war.

"Congratulations to Kichizo on his entry into the army," this banner said, in large, vivid characters. Uhei posted a long pole in front of his house, high on the hillside, and attached this banner. It streamed out in the wind, where everyone could see. Uhei was bursting with pride. As soon as the banner was up, he took Kichizo out from the field and pointed up to where it floated gracefully above the house. "You see that, Kichizo," he said. "That's for you. You're a hero. You've brought honor to this village."

Meanwhile, Uhei's wife, O-shin, was carrying this human symbolism even further. She bought a huge piece of cloth and began preparing a "thousand-stitches belt" for the horse.[1]

This cloth that O-shin bought was big enough to cover four or five men. When she stood in the street, asking passers-by to sew a stitch, they all laughed, but they did it. She had a needle that she borrowed from a matmaker to do such a big piece of work. When the stitches were all in, she herself worked all through one night, finishing the belt. It was very difficult, with such a big needle, but she finished it.

They put the good-luck belt around Kichizo's middle, just as though he were a soldier. At the same time, Uhei visited a number of different shrines in the neighborhood and bought lucky articles. O-shin sewed them into the belt.

And finally, he gave a farewell party and invited all the neighbors. Uhei was not a rich man and he couldn't afford it. If he had any savings, they were all spent that night. I was among those he invited. I took, as a gift, a bottle of wine.

Most of the guests were already there, in Uhei's neat little house, by the time I arrived. They were in good humor, laughing and drinking. Uhei was excited and bustling around, seeing to everything. His eyes were glistening. "Yes, it's rare to find such a wonderful horse," he said. "You seldom find a horse with so much spirit and intelligence and at the same time so strong and vigorous. Oh, he'll show them! I'm so happy. Have a drink! Have many cups of wine for this happy occasion!"

There were tears rolling down his cheeks as he spoke and the bitter salt mingled with the wine he was drinking. Everyone was making a noise, laughing and talking and roaring jokes. O-shin kept

[1] The "thousand-stitches belt" is a talisman, with red threads sewn by well-wishers for a Japanese soldier when he leaves for the front. It is supposed to protect him from wounds.

hustling in and out of the kitchen, bringing hot food and warming the wine. She was a plain little thing, drab, I used to think. But that night, smiling and exuberant, she seemed transformed and almost beautiful.

When the party was at its height, Uhei suddenly jumped up from the table and ran outside. We heard the heavy clomp-clomp of a horse, walking through the front yard. And then, through an open window, Kichizo's long graceful neck came in. His head stretched all the way to the banquet table. He looked at us gravely; I again had the feeling that he knew all about this occasion, and knew it was for him, and what it meant.

Uhei ran into the room again and threw his arms around the horse's neck, and gave him boiled lobster and some octopus, and poured the ceremonial wine into his mouth. "To Kichizo," he cried. "Dear, brave Kichizo!" We all stood and drank and roared "Banzai!" three times. It must have seemed a little silly and sentimental. Yet, Uhei had inoculated us all with something of the love he had for that horse and it seemed natural enough to us.

In the later afternoon of the next day, I saw Uhei at Hospital Hill, returning from the army station. He had delivered Kichizo to them. I spoke to him, but he seemed not to recognize me, nor to have heard my voice, for he walked on a few paces. Then he turned and acknowledged the greeting in a distant, absent-minded sort of way. He looked haggard and sickly, as though he had lost his strength, and he left me hurriedly. All he said was "Kichizo has gone."

Later, someone told me how he brought the horse to the station. It was a terribly warm day. So Uhei took his own grass hat, cut two holes in the side for Kichizo's ears, and put it on the horse's head. Poor Kichizo, that heavy "thousand-stitches belt" must have been very warm and uncomfortable in such weather. Besides, Uhei had decorated him with national flags, so that he looked like some sacred animal on the way to dedication at a shrine. I suppose he felt just that way about him.

O-shin accompanied them, holding the reins, as they walked to the station. It was a curious and sad little trio, the man and woman with that great sleek horse in its strange attire, walking slowly down the hillside, through the village and up the other side. Everyone watched silently. No one laughed.

At the army station, a good many other horses were already gathered together in the yard. They had been examined by the army veterinarians before being accepted. Now they were merely waiting to be taken away on the train. No one knew just when it would come.

O-shin left immediately, but Uhei stayed and stayed beside Kichizo, patting its hip and running his fingers through its mane. At first, the soldiers laughed, just as the people in the village had done. But they soon saw how Uhei felt about his horse and then they told him, kindly. "Don't cry, Uncle. It's a great promotion for your horse, isn't it? He's going to serve the nation now, instead of pulling a cart around the village. That's something, isn't it? Well, then, cheer up. Besides, he'll get better care in the army than you could ever give him. Don't you worry. He's going to be all right." So they tried to console Uhei. Nevertheless, he stayed until dark.

Early the next day, he was back at the army station, fussing over Kichizo. Of course, there was nothing to be done. The army grooms had already cared for and fed and watered the horses, but the poor man wanted to see for himself. He clucked around Kichizo like a hen with its chicks. Not that day, nor for several days afterward, did the train come to take the horses away.

It was quite a distance from Uhei's house to the army station, but he came every day, faithfully. He came early and stayed until dusk.

At last the fatal day came. All the horses were loaded on the train and taken to the harbor, where they went aboard the transports. Uhei went along. He went as far as they would let him and then the grooms again told him not to worry, and promised they would take good care of Kichizo. He bowed, eyes brimming with tears. He bowed and bowed, and could only mumble, "Thanks, thanks, very much."

As the boat moved out of the harbor, he ran up to a bridge overlooking the water. It was high above the water and he stayed there until the very smoke from the steamer had vanished beneath the horizon. He waved his flag and shouted, "Kichizo," until he was hardly able to speak. And he kept his eyes riveted on the spot where the ship had disappeared.

This is all I know about the story. When I was called to the front, he was the first to come and wish me luck and help me with my preparations. On the day I left, he came again to the harbor and begged me to look out for Kichizo. "You know him," he said, eagerly. "You couldn't miss him among a thousand horses. Anyway, he has a small white spot on his left side and, on the opposite hip, the character 'Kichi' is branded. You couldn't miss him."

"If I see him, I'll be sure and write to you," I said.

"Remember, he's a beautiful reddish chestnut," Uhei continued. "Yes, tell me if you see him. And please say something to him about me. That would seem strange to you, wouldn't it, talking to a horse? All right, but just pat him on the nose, once or twice."

It seems cold and unkind of me, but only once have I asked about Kichizo since I came aboard this boat. The groom said he had not seen any such horse. Nor have I, although I have not tried to examine all the horses. But when I see one of them fall sick and die, and then go over the side to the small boat, I cannot help but recall Uhei. For his sake, I hope nothing like this has happened to Kichizo.

Speaking of the "thousand-stitches belt" reminds me of a recent episode that may give you a clear insight into our minds and hearts, these days.

As you know, there is not a man aboard ship without one of these belts. They encircle every waist and each stitch carries a prayer for safety. Mine is of white silk and has a number of charms sewn into it. I do not understand the symbolism connected with each. Some are Buddhist and others Shinto. It makes no difference, of course. All are supposed to afford protection from wounds.

Mother gave me an embroidered charm bag, which contains a talisman of the "Eight Myriads of Deities," and a "Buddha from Three Thousand Worlds." In addition to those, I have an image of the Buddha, three inches in height, of exquisite workmanship. This was a present from Watabe, who lives on the hillside. When he gave it to me, he said it had been through three wars. "No bullet ever touched the man who wore it," he said. "It is a wonderful charm." Three different soldiers had carried it in the Boxer Rebellion, the first Sino-Japanese War, and the Russo-Japanese War. According to his story, they came through without a scratch.

All the men on this ship are loaded with tokens and amulets and belts and mementoes from their family and friends. On warm days, when we take off our shirts, these articles are seen everywhere. I do not mean to scorn them, but it would be interesting to study them all, with the superstitions they embody. However, one cannot disregard the heartfelt sentiment connected with them.

There was one man who did scoff at them, and in no uncertain terms, either. He no longer does so. This man, Corporal Tachibana, is quite a character. He says he is an atheist. He likes to talk about his ideas and he deliberately provokes arguments, in which he stoutly defends the materialistic point of view. In these, he employs big, pedantic words that so puzzle the men that they cannot reply. Personally, I doubt that he himself understands the meaning of all the words he uses.

Particularly when he has had a little wine, Corporal Tachibana used to like to ridicule the men about their charms and talismans. "Absurd," he would say. "Absolutely ridiculous! If we could really protect ourselves with such things, there never would be anyone killed in war. The Chinese would use them, too, and so would every other kind of soldier. Then what kind of a war could you have, if nobody was killed? It is nonsense, and it is not befitting a member of the imperial army to do such things."

Of course, this was perfectly true and the men knew it. But still they believed in their pitiful little articles, the luck charms. To me, it seemed cruel and heartless of him. If he himself preferred not to place any stock in these ideas, very well. But why should he shake the faith of simple men who did? Strangely enough, however, he himself had a "thousand-stitches belt" around his middle.

One day recently, when it was very hot, we were all on the upper deck, lying in the shade. Suddenly, without a word, Corporal Tachibana jumped over the side and landed with a magnificent splash. He is not a good swimmer, and when the foam and spray disappeared, we saw him sink. Then he reappeared, churning the water with his arms and legs. Immediately, two of the men stripped and dived in after him. At the cry, "Man overboard," a boat was lowered.

They pulled him into the boat and finally brought him up on deck again. His dripping hair was hanging over his face and his stomach heaved. In his right hand was his "thousand-stitches belt"!

As soon as he caught his breath, he explained that when he pulled off his shirt, his belt came with it and the wind blew it into the sea. When he saw it fluttering into the water, he jumped after it.

"Not because I was afraid of being shot, if I lost it," he said, grinning. "I don't believe it can protect me in war. But my folks were so sincere about it that I couldn't just lose it in the ocean, this way. So I had to get it."

He must have thought we did not believe him, for he added, "The prayers of my people, reflecting on my brain, made me do it." Men who had been listening to him, with sly smiles on their faces, suddenly grew serious. The joking stopped. Inadvertently, it seemed to me, he had denied his own arguments and revealed a belief little different from that of the other men. Unconsciously, I put my hand on my own belt.

So much for today, I will write again soon.

TRANSLATED BY BARONESS SHIDZUÉ ISHIMOTO

THE MOLE

[*Hokuro no Tegami, 1940*] by *Kawabata Yasunari (born 1899)*

'The Mole" is a product of Kawabata's period of full maturity, and reveals the mastery of the psychology of women which is perhaps the outstanding feature of his writings.

•

Last night I dreamed about that mole.

I need only write the word for you to know what I mean. That mole—how many times have I been scolded by you because of it.

It is on my right shoulder, or perhaps I should say high on my back.

"It's already bigger than a bean. Go on playing with it and it will be sending out shoots one of these days."

You used to tease me about it. But as you said, it was large for a mole, large and wonderfully round and swollen.

As a child I used to lie in bed and play with that mole. How ashamed I was when you first noticed it.

I even wept, and I remember your surprise.

"Stop it, Sayoko. The more you touch it the bigger it will get." My mother scolded me too. I was still a child, probably not yet thirteen, and afterwards I kept the habit to myself. It persisted after I had all but forgotten about it.

When you first noticed it, I was still more child than wife. I wonder if you, a man, can imagine how ashamed I was. But it was more than shame. This is dreadful, I thought to myself. Marriage seemed at that moment a fearful thing indeed.

I felt as though all my secrets had been discovered—as though you had bared secret after secret of which I was not even conscious myself—as though I had no refuge left.

You went off happily to sleep, and sometimes I felt relieved, and a little lonely, and sometimes I pulled myself up with a start as my hand traveled to the mole again.

"I can't even touch my mole any more," I thought of writing to my mother, but even as I thought of it I felt my face go fiery red.

"But what nonsense to worry about a mole," you once said. I was happy, and I nodded, but looking back now, I wonder if it would not have been better if you had been able to love that wretched habit of mine a little more.

I did not worry so very much about the mole. Surely people do not go about looking down women's necks for moles. Sometimes the expression "unspoiled as a locked room" is used to describe a deformed girl. But a mole, no matter how large it is, can hardly be called a deformity.

Why do you suppose I fell into the habit of playing with that mole?

And why did the habit annoy you so?

"Stop it," you would say. "Stop it." I do not know how many hundred times you scolded me.

"Do you have to use your left hand?" you asked once in a fit of irritation.

"My left hand?" I was startled by the question.

It was true. I had not noticed before, but I always used my left hand.

"It's on your right shoulder. Your right hand should be better."

"Oh?" I raised my right hand. "But it's strange."

"It's not a bit strange."

"But it's more natural with my left hand."

"The right hand is nearer."

"It's backwards with my right hand."

"Backwards?"

"Yes, it's a choice between bringing my arm in front of my neck or reaching around in back like this." I was no longer agreeing meekly with everything you said. Even as I answered you, though, it came to me that when I brought my left arm around in front of me it was as though I were warding you off, as though I were embracing myself. I have been cruel to him, I thought.

I asked quietly, "But what is wrong with using my left hand?"

"Left hand or right hand, it's a bad habit."

"I know."

"Haven't I told you time and time again to go to a doctor and have the thing removed?"

"But I couldn't. I'd be ashamed to."

"It would be a very simple matter."

"Who would go to a doctor to have a mole removed?"

"A great many people seem to."

"For moles in the middle of the face, maybe. I doubt if anyone goes to have a mole removed from the neck. The doctor would laugh. He would know I was there because my husband had complained."

"You could tell him it was because you had a habit of playing with it."

"Really. . . . Something as insignificant as a mole, in a place where you can't even see it. I should think you could stand at least that much."

"I wouldn't mind the mole if you wouldn't play with it."

"I don't mean to."

"You are stubborn, though. No matter what I say, you make no attempt to change yourself."

"I do try. I even tried wearing a high-necked nightgown so that I wouldn't touch it."

"Not for long."

"But is it so wrong for me to touch it?" I suppose I must have seemed to be fighting back.

"It's not wrong, especially. I only ask you to stop because I don't like it."

"But why do you dislike it so?"

"There's no need to go into the reasons. You don't need to play with that mole, and it's a bad habit, and I wish you would stop."

"I've never said I won't stop."

"And when you touch it you always get that strange, absent-minded expression on your face. That's what I really hate."

You're probably right—something made the remark go straight to my heart, and I wanted to nod my agreement.

"Next time you see me doing it, slap my hand. Slap my face even."

"But doesn't it bother you that even though you've been trying for two or three years you haven't been able to cure a trivial little habit like that by yourself?"

I did not answer. I was thinking of your words, "That's what I really hate."

That pose, with my left arm drawn up around my neck—it must look somehow dreary, forlorn. I would hesitate to use a grand word like "solitary." Shabby, rather, and mean, the pose of a woman concerned only with protecting her own small self. And the expression on my face must be just as you described it, "strange, absent-minded."

Did it seem a sign that I had not really given myself to you, as though a space lay between us? And did my true feelings come out on my face when I touched the mole and lost myself in reverie, as I had done since I was a child?

But it must have been because you were already dissatisfied with me that you made so much of that one small habit. If you had been pleased with me you would have smiled and thought no more about it.

That was the frightening thought. I trembled when it came to me of a sudden that there might be men who would find the habit charming.

It was your love for me that first made you notice. I do not doubt that even now. But it is just this sort of small annoyance, as it grows and becomes distorted, that drives its roots down into a marriage. To a real husband and wife personal eccentricities have stopped mattering, and I suppose that on the other hand there are husbands and wives who find themselves at odds on everything. I do not say that those who accommodate themselves to each other necessarily love each other, and that those who constantly disagree hate each other. I do think, though, and I cannot get over thinking, that it would have been better if you could have brought yourself to overlook my habit of playing with the mole.

You actually came to beat me and to kick me. I wept and asked why you could not be a little less violent, why I had to suffer so because I touched my mole. That was only surface. "How can we cure it?" you said, your voice trembling, and I quite understood how you felt and did not resent what you did. If I had told anyone of this, no doubt you would have seemed a violent husband. But since we had reached a point where the most trivial matter added to the tension between us, your hitting me actually brought a sudden feeling of release.

"I will never get over it, never. Tie up my hands." I brought my hands together and thrust them at your chest, as though I were giving myself, all of myself, to you.

You looked confused, your anger seemed to have left you limp and drained of emotion. You took the cord from my sash and tied my hands with it.

I was happy when I saw the look in your eyes, watching me try to smooth my hair with my bound hands. This time the long habit might be cured, I thought.

Even then, however, it was dangerous for anyone to brush against the mole.

And was it because afterwards the habit came back that the last of your affection for me finally died? Did you mean to tell me that you had given up and that I could very well do as I pleased? When I played with the mole, you pretended you did not see, and you said nothing.

Then a strange thing happened. Presently the habit which scolding and beating had done nothing to cure—was it not gone? None of the extreme remedies worked. It simply left of its own accord.

"What do you know—I'm not playing with the mole any more." I said it as though I had only that moment noticed. You grunted, and looked as if you did not care.

If it mattered so little to you, why did you have to scold me so, I wanted to ask; and I suppose you for your part wanted to ask why, if the habit was to be cured so easily, I had not been able to cure it earlier. But you would not even talk to me.

A habit that makes no difference, that is neither medicine nor poison—go ahead and indulge yourself all day long if it pleases you. That is what the expression on your face seemed to say. I felt dejected. Just to annoy you, I thought of touching the mole again there in front of you, but, strangely, my hand refused to move.

I felt lonely. And I felt angry.

I thought too of touching it when you were not around. But somehow that seemed shameful, repulsive, and again my hand refused to move.

I looked at the floor, and I bit my lip.

"What's happened to your mole?" I was waiting for you to say, but after that the word "mole" disappeared from our conversation.

And perhaps many other things disappeared with it.

Why could I do nothing in the days when I was being scolded by you? What a worthless woman I am.

Back at home again, I took a bath with my mother.

"You're not as good-looking as you once were, Sayoko," she said. "You can't fight age, I suppose."

I looked at her, startled. She was as she had always been, plump and fresh-skinned.

"And that mole used to be rather attractive."

I have really suffered because of that mole—but I could not say that to my mother. What I did say was: "They say it's no trouble for a doctor to remove a mole."

"Oh? For a doctor . . . but there would be a scar." How calm and easygoing my mother is! "We used to laugh about it. We said that Sayoko was probably still playing with that mole even now that she was married."

"I was playing with it."

"We thought you would be."

"It was a bad habit. When did I start?"

"When do children begin to have moles, I wonder. You don't seem to see them on babies."

"My children have none."

"Oh? But they begin to come out as you grow up, and they never disappear. It's not often you see one this size, though. You must have had it when you were very small." My mother looked at my shoulder and laughed.

I remembered how, when I was very young, my mother and my sisters sometimes poked at the mole, a charming little spot then. And was that not why I had fallen into the habit of playing with it myself?

I lay in bed fingering the mole and trying to remember how it was when I was a child and a young woman.

It was a very long time since I had last played with it. How many years, I wonder.

Back in the house where I was born, away from you, I could play with it as I liked. No one would stop me.

But it was no good.

As my finger touched the mole, cold tears came to my eyes.

I meant to think of long ago, when I was young, but when I touched the mole all I thought of was you.

I have been damned as a bad wife, and perhaps I shall be divorced; but it would not have occurred to me that here in bed at home again I should have only these thoughts of you.

I turned over my damp pillow—and I even dreamed of the mole.

I could not tell after I awoke where the room might have been, but you were there, and some other woman seemed to be with us. I had been drinking. Indeed I was drunk. I kept pleading with you about something.

My bad habit came out again. I reached around with my left hand, my arm across my breast as always. But the mole—did it not come right off between my fingers? It came off painlessly, quite as though that were the most natural thing in the world. Between my fingers it felt exactly like the skin of a roast bean.

Like a spoiled child I asked you to put my mole in the pit of that mole beside your nose.

I pushed my mole at you. I cried and clamored, I clutched at your sleeve and hung on your chest.

When I awoke the pillow was still wet. I was still weeping.

I felt tired through and through. And at the same time I felt light, as though I had laid down a burden.

I lay smiling for a time, wondering if the mole had really disappeared. I had trouble bringing myself to touch it.

That is all there is to the story of my mole.

I can still feel it like a black bean between my fingers.

I have never thought much about that little mole beside your nose, and I have never spoken of it, and yet I suppose I have had it always on my mind.

What a fine fairy story it would make if your mole really were to swell up because you put mine in it.

And how happy I would be if I thought you in your turn had dreamed of my mole.

I have forgotten one thing.

"That's what I hate," you said, and so well did I understand that I even thought the remark a sign of your affection for me. I thought that all the meanest things in me came out when I fingered the mole.

I wonder, however, if a fact of which I have already spoken does not redeem me: it was perhaps because of the way my mother and sisters petted me that I first fell into the habit of fingering the mole.

"I suppose you used to scold me when I played with the mole," I said to my mother, "a long time ago."

"I did—it was not so long ago, though."

"Why did you scold me?"

"Why? It's a bad habit, that's all."

"But how did you feel when you saw me playing with the mole?"

"Well . . ." My mother cocked her head to one side. "It wasn't becoming."

"That's true. But how did it look? Were you sorry for me? Or did you think I was nasty and hateful?"

"I didn't really think about it much. It just seemed as though you could as well leave it alone, with that sleepy expression on your face."

"You found me annoying?"

"It did bother me a little."

"And you and the others used to poke at the mole to tease me?"

"I suppose we did."

If that is true, then wasn't I fingering the mole in that absent way to remember the love my mother and sisters had for me when I was young?

Wasn't I doing it to think of the people I loved?

This is what I must say to you.

Weren't you mistaken from beginning to end about my mole?

Could I have been thinking of anyone else when I was with you?

Over and over I wonder whether the gesture you so disliked might not have been a confession of a love that I could not put into words.

My habit of playing with the mole is a small thing, and I do not mean to make excuses for it; but might not all of the other things that turned me into a bad wife have begun in the same way? Might they not have been in the beginning expressions of my love for you, turned to unwifeliness only by your refusal to see what they were?

Even as I write I wonder if I do not sound like a bad wife trying to seem wronged. Still there are these things that I must say to you.

TRANSLATED BY EDWARD SEIDENSTICKER

Night Train

The pale light of daybreak—
The fingerprints are cold on the glass door,
And the barely whitening edges of the mountains
Are still as quicksilver.
As yet the passengers do not awaken;
Only the electric light pants wearily.
The sickeningly sweet odor of varnish,
Even the indistinct smoke of my cigar,
Strikes my throat harshly on the night train.
How much worse it must be for her, another man's wife.
Haven't we passed Yamashina yet?
She opens the valve of her air pillow
And watches as it gradually deflates.
Suddenly in sadness we draw to one another.
When I look out of the train window, now close to dawn,
In a mountain village at an unknown place
Whitely the columbines are blooming.

Cats

Two pitch-black cats
On a melancholy night roof,
From the tip of their taut tails
A threadlike crescent moon hovers hazily.
"Owaa. Good evening."
"Owaa. Good evening."
"Ogyaa. Ogyaa. Ogyaa."
"Owaa. The master of this house is ill."

Harmful Animals

>Particularly
>When something like a dog is barking
>When something like a goose is born a freak
>When something like a fox is luminous
>When something like a tortoise crystallizes
>When something like a wolf slides by
>All these things are harmful to the health of man.

The Corpse of a Cat

>The spongelike scenery
>Is gently swollen by moisture.
>No sign of man or beast in sight.
>A water wheel is weeping.
>From the blurred shadow of a willow
>I see the gentle form of a woman waiting.
>Wrapping her thin shawl around her,
>Dragging her lovely vaporous garments,
>She wanders calmly, like a spirit.
>Ah, Ura, lonely woman!
>"You're always late, aren't you?"
>We have no past, no future,
>And have faded away from the things of reality.
>Ura!
>Here in this weird landscape,
>Bury the corpse of the drowned cat!

The New Road of Koide

>The road that has newly been opened here
>Goes, I suppose, straight to the city.
>I stand at a crossway of the new road,
>Uncertain of the lonely horizon.
>Dark, melancholy day.

The sun is low over the roofs of the row of houses.
The unfelled trees in the woods stand sparsely.
How, how, to restore myself to what I was?
On this road I rebel against and will not travel,
The new trees have all been felled.

Hagiwara Sakutarō (1886-1942)

Composition 1063

Ours are simple fences in the Ainu style.
We plotted and replotted mulberry trees
In our inch of garden,
But even so, couldn't make a living.
In April
The water of the Nawashiro was black,
Tiny eddies of dark air
Fell like pellets from the sky
And birds
Flew by with raucous calls.
These fields full of horned stones
Where horsetails and wormwood have sprouted
Are cultivated by women
Dropping their litters
Patching together the ragged clothes of the older children,
Cooking and doing the village chores,
Shouldering the family discontents and desires,
With a handful of coarse food
And six hours sleep the year round.
And here
If you plant two bushels of buckwheat you get back four.
Are these people, I wonder,
So much unlike
The many revolutionaries tied up in prisons,
The artists starved by their luck,
Those heroes of our time?

Miyazawa Kenji (1896-1933)

Song

Don't sing
Don't sing of scarlet blossoms or the wings of dragonflies
Don't sing of murmuring breezes or the scent of a woman's
   hair.
All of the weak, delicate things
All the false, lying things
All the languid things, omit.
Reject every elegance
And sing what is wholly true,
Filling the stomach,
Flooding the breast at the moment of desperation,
Songs which rebound when beaten
Songs which scoop up courage from the pit of shame
These songs
Sing in a powerful rhythm with swelling throats!
These songs
Hammer into the hearts of all who pass you by!

Nakano Shigeharu (born 1902)

Spring Snow

It has snowed in a place where snow rarely falls,
Steadily, piling into drifts.
The snow covers all things
And all that it covers is beautiful.
Are people, I wonder, prepared for the ugliness of the thaw?

Early Spring

Midnight
A rain mixed with snow fell,
It trickled desolately on the bamboo thicket.
The dream dealt with another's heart.
When I awoke
The pillow was cold with tears.

—What has happened to my heart?
The sun shines in mildly from tall windows,
A humming rises from the steelworks.
I got out of bed
And poked with a stick the muck in the ditch;
The turbid water slowly began to move.
A little lizard had yielded himself to the current.
In the fields
I push open black earth.
The wheat sprouts greenly grow.
—You can trust the earth.

Kitagawa Fuyuhiko (born 1900)

Morning Song

On the ceiling: the color of vermilion
   Light leaking in through a crack in the door
Evokes a rustic military band—my hands
   Have nothing whatever to do.

I cannot hear the song of little birds.
   The sky today must be a faded blue.
Weary—too tired to remonstrate
   With anyone else's ideas.

In the scent of resin the morning is painful,
   Lost, the various, various dreams.
The standing woods are singing in the wind.

Flatly spread out the sky,
   Along the bank go vanishing
The beautiful, various dreams.

The Hour of Death

The autumn sky is a dull color
A light in the eyes of a black horse

The water dries up, the lily falls
The heart is hollow.

Without gods, without help
Close to the window a woman has died.
  The white sky was sightless
  The white wind was cold.

When she washed her hair by the window
Her arm was stemlike and soft
  The morning sun trickled down
  The sound of the water dripped.

In the streets there was noise:
The voices of children tangling.
But, tell me, what will happen to this soul?
Will it thin to nothingness?

Nakahara Chūya (1907-1937)

TRANSLATED BY DONALD KEENE

Isu yosete	Drawing up a chair
Kiku no kaori ni	In the scent of chrysanthemums
Mono wo kaku	I write my verses.

Mizuhara Shūōshi (born 1892)

The Imperial Tombs at Mukden

Ryō samuku	The great tombs are cold:
Jitsugetsu sora ni	In the sky the sun and moon
Terashiau	Stare at each other.

Kareno basha	In the withered fields
Muchi pan-pan to	A horse-carriage whip sharply
Sora wo utsu	Cracks against the sky.

An Ancient Statue of a Guardian King [1]

Kaze hikari	Wind and the sunlight—
Mukabaki no kin	Here, the gilt of a cuirass
Hagiotosu	Peels off and falls.

Natsu no kawa	The summer river—
Akaki tessa no	The end of a red iron chain
Hashi hitaru	Soaks in the water.

Yamaguchi Seishi (born 1901)

---

[1] At the Shin Yakushi-ji, a temple in Nara of the eighth century. The contrast is drawn between the sunshine outside and the silent darkness inside the building, where the once resplendent statue stands.

Guntai no	The tramping sound
Chikazuku oto ya	Of troops approaching
Shūfūri	In autumn wind.

Banryoku no	In the midst of
Uchi ya ako no ha	All things verdant, my baby
Haesomuru	Has begun to teethe.

Sora wa taisho no	The sky is the blue
Aosa tsuma yori	Of the world's beginning—from my wife
Ringo uku	I accept an apple.

Nakamura Kusatao (born 1901)

In the middle of the night there was a heavy air raid. Carrying my sick brother on my back I wandered in the flames with my wife in search of our children.

Hi no oku ni	In the depths of the flames
Botan kuzururu	I saw how a peony
Sama wo mitsu	Crumbles to pieces.

Kogarashi ya	Cold winter storm—
Shōdo no kinko	A safe-door in a burnt-out site
Fukinarasu	Creaking in the wind.

Fuyu kamome	The winter sea gulls—
Sei no ie nashi	In life without a house,
Shi no haka nashi	In death without a grave.

Katō Shūson (born 1905)

TRANSLATED BY DONALD KEENE

THE FIREFLY HUNT

[Sasameyuki, III, 4] by Tanizaki Junichirō (born 1886)

The publication of Tanizaki's novel Sasameyuki, *begun during the war, was discontinued by government order on the grounds that it was incompatible with wartime discipline, and not until 1946-1948, when the three volumes of the completed work finally appeared, could readers judge the magnitude and beauty of Tanizaki's masterpiece. The title of the work means, roughly, snow that is falling thinly as opposed to thickly falling flakes of snow, and refers to the fragile beauty of Yukiko, one of the four sisters around whom this novel of life in the Japan of 1936-1941 is centered.*

In the episode presented here, three of the sisters, together with the daughter of Sachiko, the second sister, go to visit a family named Sugano who live in the country.

•

It was a strange house, of course, but it was probably less the house than sheer exhaustion that kept Sachiko awake. She had risen early, she had been rocked and jolted by train and automobile through the heat of the day, and in the evening she had chased over the fields with the children, two or three miles it must have been. . . . She knew, though, that the firefly hunt would be pleasant to remember. . . . She had seen firefly hunts only on the puppet stage, Miyuki and Komazawa murmuring of love as they sailed down the River Uji; and indeed one should properly put on a long-sleeved kimono, a smart summer print, and run across the evening fields with the wind at one's sleeves, lightly taking up a firefly here and there from under one's fan. Sachiko was entranced with the picture. But a firefly hunt was, in fact, a good deal different. If you are going to play in the fields you had better change your clothes, they were told, and four muslin kimonos—prepared especially for them?—were laid out, each with a different pattern, as became their several ages. Not quite the way it looked in the pictures, laughed one of the sisters. It was almost dark, however, and it hardly mattered what they had on. They could still see each other's faces when they left the house, but by the time they reached the river it was only short of pitch dark. . . . A river it was called; actually it was no more than a ditch through the paddies, a little wider perhaps than most ditches, with plumes of grass bending over it from either bank and almost closing off the surface. A bridge was still dimly visible a hundred yards or so ahead. . . .

They turned off their flashlights and approached in silence; fireflies dislike noise and light. But even at the edge of the river there were no fireflies. Perhaps they aren't out tonight, someone whispered. No, there are plenty of them—come over here. Down into the grasses on the bank, and there, in that delicate moment before the last light goes, were fireflies, gliding out over the water in low arcs like the sweep of the grasses. . . . And on down the river, and on and on, were fireflies, lines of them wavering out from this bank and the other and back again . . . sketching their uncertain lines of light down close to the surface of the water, hidden from outside by the grasses. . . . In that last moment of light, with the darkness creeping up from the water and the moving plumes of grass still faintly outlined, there, far, far, far as the river stretched, an infinite number of little lines in two long lines on either side, quiet, unearthly. Sachiko could see it all even now, here inside with her eyes closed. . . . Surely it was the impressive moment of the evening, the moment that made the firefly hunt worth while. . . . A firefly hunt has indeed none of the radiance of a cherry blossom party. Dark, dreamy, rather . . . might one say? Perhaps something of the child's world, the world of the fairy story in it. . . . Something not to be painted but to be set to music, the mood of it taken up on a piano or a koto. . . . And while she lay with her eyes closed, the fireflies, out there along the river, all through the night, were flashing on and off, silent, numberless. Sachiko felt a wild, romantic surge, as though she were joining them there, soaring and dipping along the surface of the water, cutting her own uncertain line of light. . . .

It was rather a long little river, as she thought about it, that they followed after those fireflies. Now and then they crossed a bridge over or back . . . taking care not to fall in . . . watching for snakes, for snake eyes that glowed like fireflies. Sugano's six-year-old son, Sosuke, ran ahead in the darkness, thoroughly familiar with the land, and his father, who was guiding them, called uneasily after him, "Sosuke, Sosuke." No one worried any longer about frightening the fireflies, there were so many; indeed without this calling out to one another they were in danger of becoming separated, of being drawn apart in the darkness, each after his own fireflies. Once Sachiko and Yukiko were left alone on one bank, and from the other, now brought in clear and now blotted out by the wind, came voices calling, "Mother." "Where is Mother?" "Over here." "And Yukiko?" "She is over here too." "I've caught twenty-four already." "Don't fall in the river."

Sugano pulled up some grass along the path and tied it into something like a broom; to keep fireflies in, he said. There are places famous for fireflies, like Moriyama in Omi, or the outskirts of Gifu; but the fireflies there are protected, saved for important people. No one cares how many you take here, Sugano said; and Sugano took more than anyone. The two of them, father and son, went boldly down to the very edge of the water, and Sugano's bundle of grass became a jeweled broom. Sachiko and the rest began to wonder when he might be ready to think of going back. The wind is a little cold; don't you think perhaps. . . . But we are on the way back. We are going back by a different road. On they walked. It was farther than they had thought. And then they were at Sugano's back gate, everyone with a few captured fireflies, Sachiko and Yukiko with fireflies in their sleeves. . . .

The events of the evening passed through Sachiko's mind in no particular order. She opened her eyes—she might have been dreaming, she thought. Above her, in the light of the tiny bulb, she could see a framed kakemono that she had noticed earlier in the day: the words "Pavilion of Timelessness," written in large characters and signed by one Keido. Sachiko looked at the words without knowing who Keido might be. A flicker of light moved across the next room. A firefly, repelled by the mosquito incense, was hunting a way out. They had turned their fireflies loose in the garden earlier in the evening, and considerable numbers had flown into the house. But they had been careful to chase them out before closing the doors for the night—where might this one have been hiding? In a last burst of energy it soared five or six feet into the air; then, exhausted, it glided across the room and lighted on Sachiko's kimono, hanging on the clothes rack. Over the printed pattern and into the sleeve it moved, flickering on through the dark cloth. The incense in the badger-shaped brazier was beginning to hurt Sachiko's throat. She got up to put it out, and while she was up moved on to see to the firefly. Carefully she took it up in a piece of paper—the idea of touching it repelled her—and pushed it out through a slot in the shutter. Of the scores of fireflies that had flickered through the shrubbery and along the edge of the lake earlier in the evening, there were almost none left—had they gone back to the river?—and the garden was lacquer-black.

TRANSLATED BY EDWARD SEIDENSTICKER

THE MOTHER OF

CAPTAIN SHIGEMOTO

[Shōshō Shigemoto no Haha, Chapters IX and X, 1950]
by Tanizaki Junichirō

The Mother of Captain Shigemoto is a novel of ninth-century Japan, and much of its material is based on actual events, as recorded in Heian literature. It deals mainly with an old man married to an extremely beautiful young wife who is his joy and treasure. The Prime Minister, hearing of her beauty, by a ruse manages to steal her from the old man, leaving him to spend his days in fruitless attempts to forget her. Captain Shigemoto was the child of the old man and his young wife, and he appears as a small boy in the following episode.

•

Shigemoto had one terrible memory of his father. He could never forget it. His father was at the time in the habit of sitting for days and nights on end in quiet meditation, and Shigemoto, at length overcome with curiosity about when he ate and slept, stole away from the nurse one night to the altar room and, sliding the door open a crack, saw in the faint light his father still kneeling as he had been earlier in the day. Time passed and still he knelt motionless as a statue, and presently Shigemoto slid the door shut and went back to bed; but the next night curiosity came over him again, and again he went to look and saw his father as on the preceding night. And then, the third night it must have been, he was taken with the same curiosity and tiptoed to the altar room; but this time, as he looked through the narrow crack in the door, scarcely allowing himself to breathe, he noticed that the light on the tallow wick was flickering in spite of the stillness of the air, and at that moment his father's shoulders rose and his body moved. The motion was infinitely slow and deliberate. At first Shigemoto could not see what it meant, but presently his father, one hand pressed to the matting, his breathing heavy as though he were lifting an object of extraordinarily great weight, pushed his body from the floor and stood upright. Because of his age he could have gotten up but slowly in any case, and the long hours of unrelieved kneeling had so paralyzed his legs that he could pick himself up only with this special effort. In any case he was up, and he walked, almost staggered, from the room.

Shigemoto followed him, bewildered. His father's gaze was fixed dead ahead, he looked neither to the left nor to the right. He marched down the stairs, slipped his feet into a pair of sandals, stepped to the ground. The moon was a clear, crystalline white, and Shigemoto could remember a humming of insects that suggested the autumn; but he remembered too how when he slipped into a pair of grownup's sandals himself and went out into the garden, the soles of his feet were suddenly cold, as though he had stepped into water, and the bright moonlight, laying the landscape over white as with frost, made him feel that it could indeed have been winter. His father's shadow, swaying as he walked, was sharp against the ground. Shigemoto stayed far enough behind to avoid stepping on it. He would very probably have been seen had his father turned around, but his father seemed deep in meditation still, and when presently they had gone out the gate he walked firmly ahead as though he knew clearly where he was going.

An old man of eighty and a child of seven or eight could not have gone very far. Still to Shigemoto it seemed something of a walk. He followed his father at a distance, now seeing him and now cut off from him; but there were no other travelers on the road, and his father's figure reflected the moonlight so white in the distance that there was no chance of losing him. The road was lined at first with the earthen walls of fine mansions. Presently these gave way to poor fences of woven bamboo and to low, disconsolate roofs with shingles held down by stones, and these in turn became less regular, separated more and more by pools of water and by open spaces in which autumn grasses grew high. The insects in the clumps of grass were silent as the two approached, and began humming again as they moved away, noisier and noisier, now steady as a rain shower, the farther they walked from the city. Finally there were no houses at all, only a field of autumn grass stretching wide in every direction and a narrow country road twisting through it. There was but th one road, and yet as it wound now to the left and now to the right, lined with grasses taller than a man, Shigemoto's father sometimes disappeared from sight around a bend, and Shigemoto moved up to within ten or fifteen feet of him. The boy's sleeves and his skirt became soaked with dew as he separated the grasses that hung down over the road, and cold drops seeped down inside his collar.

His father crossed a bridge over a small river, and instead of following the road on ahead, turned downstream along the sand in the narrow river bottom. A hundred yards or so below, on a slightly raised stretch of level ground, there were three or four mounds of earth, each one soft and fresh, the tombstones above them a gleaming white, even the epitaphs clear in the moonlight. Some graves had small pines or cedars in place of tombstones; others had in place of the mound a railing with a heap of stones inside and on top of it a five-stone marker; and still others, the rudest of all, had neither stone nor mound, but only a straw mat to cover the body, and an offering of flowers. Several of the tombstones had fallen over in the recent storm, and a number of mounds had washed away, leaving parts of bodies exposed.

Shigemoto's father wandered among the mounds as though he were looking for something. Shigemoto followed, almost close enough now to step on his heels. If his father knew of it he gave no sign, not even once turning around. A dog, hungry for flesh, jumped suddenly from a clump of grass and scurried off somewhere, but Shigemoto's father did not glance up. The boy could tell even from behind that he was intent on his quest, that his whole spirit seemed poured into it. The old man stopped, and Shigemoto, stopping as suddenly, saw below him a sight that made his hair stand on end and his skin go cold.

The light of the moon, like a fall of snow, covered everything over with a phosphorescent light and obscured its form, and at first Shigemoto could not make out exactly what the strange object laid out there on the ground could be; but as he stared he saw that it was the bloated, rotting corpse of a young girl. He knew it was a young girl from the flesh of the limbs and from the color of parts of the skin. The long hair, however, had peeled off like a wig, scalp and all, the face was a lump that looked as though it had swollen up and been beaten flat, the entrails had begun to pour out, the body was crawling with maggots. One can perhaps imagine the horror of the scene, there in moonlight bright as day. Shigemoto stood as if tied to it, unable to turn his head, to move, much less to cry out. He looked at his father. His father had walked quietly up to the corpse, and now, bowing reverently before it, he knelt down on a straw mat beside it. Taking the same rigid, statue-like position he had had in the altar room, he lost himself again in meditation, sometimes looking down at the corpse, sometimes half-closing his eyes.

The moon came out yet brighter, as though polished to its last perfection. The solitude embracing them seemed to grow more intense. Except for a rustling in the autumn grasses as now and then a breeze passed, there was only the shrilling of the insects, ever louder. The sight of his father, kneeling there like a lone shadow, made Shigemoto feel as though he were being pulled into a world of eerie dreams; but, whether he wanted to return or not, the smell of putrefying flesh struck his nostrils with a force that brought him back to the real world.

It is not clear exactly where Shigemoto's father looked upon the dead woman. There were probably open charnels scattered over the Kyoto of the day. During epidemics of smallpox or measles, when the dead were many, a vacant space was chosen, any space would do, where bodies could be dumped and buried hurriedly under a token covering of earth or a straw mat, partly from fear of contagion, partly for want of better means of disposal. This no doubt was such a ground.

While his father knelt in meditation over the corpse, Shigemoto crouched behind the mound, trying to quiet his breath. The moon started down in the west, and as the cluster of grave markers behind which the boy was concealed sent a lengthening shadow off across the earth, his father at last arose and started back for the city. Shigemoto followed him along the road they had come. It was just as they crossed the little bridge and started off into the moor and the autumn grasses that Shigemoto was startled by his father's voice.

"My boy . . . my boy, what do you think I was doing there?" The old man stopped in the narrow road and turned back to wait for Shigemoto. "I knew you were following me. I had something to think about, and I let you do as you wanted."

Shigemoto said nothing. His father's voice grew softer, there was a gentleness in his manner. "I have no intention of scolding you, my boy. Tell me the truth. You were watching me from the start?"

"Yes." Shigemoto nodded. "I was worried about you," he added by way of apology.

"You thought I was crazy, didn't you?" His father's mouth twisted into a smile. Shigemoto would have guessed that he laughed a short, weak laugh, though it was too faint to hear. "You are not the only one. Everyone seems to think I am crazy. . . . But I'm not. There is a reason for what I did. I can tell you what it is if it will help you. . . . Will you listen to me?"

These are the things Shigemoto's father talked of as they walked side by side back to the city. There was no way for the boy to know even vaguely what they meant, and we have in his diary not his father's words but the adult observations Shigemoto later added. The question was that of the Buddhist "sense of foulness." I am ignorant myself of Buddhist teachings, and I have the gravest doubts whether I can get over a discussion of the problem without error. I am much indebted to a Tendai scholar whom I have frequently visited and who has lent me reference works. From the start I have seen that the problem is a complex one not to be mastered without effort. There would seem to be no need to become deeply involved here, however, and I shall touch on only those points that seem necessary to my story.

Though there may be others as good, I have found the best simple work on the subject to be that *Companion in Retirement* of which the author is either the priest Jichin or the priest Keisei, it has never been decided which. The *Companion* is a collection of anecdotes about the accomplishments of illustrious priests, and tales of conversion and salvation that were missed by earlier collections. In the first volume are stories like "How a Lowly Priest Perfected the Sense of Foulness in His Spare Time," "How a Lowly Individual Saw the Light After Viewing a Corpse Laid Out on a Moor," and "The Woman's Corpse in the River Bed at Karahashi," and in the second volume, "How the Lady in Waiting Displayed Her Foul Form." One can see well enough in stories like these what the sense of foulness is.

To take one example from the collection:

Long ago a saintly priest on Mt. Hiei near Kyoto had a lesser priest in his service. A priest the latter was called, but he was in fact little more than a temple servant who performed miscellaneous services for the sage. He was a young man of the greatest devotion and reliability, serving the sage well and carrying out his orders with never a mistake, and the sage had no little confidence in him. As time passed the young priest took to disappearing, no one knew where, when night fell, and returning again early the following morning. He must be visiting a woman at the foot of the mountain, the sage began to suspect. The latter's disappointment and annoyance, though he remained silent, were extreme. The youth would reappear in the morning looking somehow morose, crestfallen. He seemed to avoid the eyes of the other priests, to be always on the verge of tears; and the others, from the sage down, concluded that very likely the lady at the foot of the mountain was being difficult—undoubtedly that was it. One night the sage sent a man out to follow him. The young priest went down the west slope of the mountain to what are now the outskirts of Kyoto, and on to the Rendai Moor. The other followed after him, at a loss to explain what this might mean. The youth wandered over the moor, now here, now there, and presently, making his way up to an indescribably putrid corpse, lost himself in prayer beside it, opening his eyes, closing them, now and again giving himself up to the most unrestrained weeping. All through the night this continued, and when the dawn bells began to ring he finally dried his tears and went back up the mountain. The man following him was deeply moved. He too was in tears when he arrived back at the temple. What had happened? the sage asked. The fellow had reason to be gloomy, the other answered, and told everything he had seen. "And that is why he disappears every evening. Our crime has been a fearful one indeed for having doubted so saintly a person."

The sage was astonished. Thereafter he revered his subordinate as no ordinary individual. One morning when the youth had brought in the porridge for breakfast, the sage, making sure that no one else was present, turned to him. "They say you've mastered the sense of foulness. I wonder if it's true."

"It is not. That is for the great ones with learning, not for the likes of me. You should be able to tell from looking at me whether I would be capable of anything like that."

"No, no—everyone knows about it. As a matter of fact I've been doing honor to you myself for some time now. You must tell me everything."

"Perhaps I can say something, then. I don't pretend to have gone very far, but I begin to think I understand a little."

"You will surely be able to give us a sign of what you have done. Suppose you try concentrating on this porridge."

The young priest took the tray, put a cover on the porridge, and for a time closed his eyes in intense meditation. When he took off the lid the porridge had changed to a mass of white worms. The sage wept unashamedly. "You shall be my teacher," he said, and brought the palms of his hands together in supplication.

—That is the story of "How a Lowly Priest Perfected the Sense of Foulness in His Spare Time." It is, the author of the *Companion in Retirement* adds, a "most edifying one"; and the founder of the Tendai sect too has written that it is possible for even the unwise to gain insight into the nature of things by going to the edge of a grave and looking at a foul corpse. Our humble priest no doubt knew of the method. It is written in the *Method of Suspension and Contemplation*[1] that "mountains and rivers are foul, food and

[1] *Maka Shikan,* a major text of the Tendai sect of Buddhism.

clothing are foul, rice is like white worms, clothing is like the skin of a stinking thing." So wonderful was the understanding of the priest that quite spontaneously his works fell into harmony with the teachings of the holy texts. An Indian monk once said that a bowl is like a skull and rice like worms, and in China the priest Tao Hsüan taught that a bowl is like a man's bones and rice like his flesh. But a thing of surpassing promise it was for an ignorant priest, who can have known nothing of these pronouncements, to be able to demonstrate their truth. Even if one cannot follow him to the ultimate point he reached, one can still find the five desires growing weaker, the workings of the spirit changing, if one but recognizes the principle taught. "Those who have not seen the truth are stirred to the deepest covetousness by that which seems of good quality, and their resentment is not small at the rag that seems the opposite; the fine and the base may change, but that from which arises the cycle of birth and rebirth is eternal. . . . How pitiful, how profitless are worldly illusions. One can but think that only the trivia of a dream cause men to look with dread on resting in the eternal."

To come back to our story. It is clear from Shigemoto's diary that his father too was trying to train himself to the sense of foulness, that the enchanting figure of the beauty who had deserted him— the "lost crane" of the Po Chü-i poem, "whose voice has gone silent behind the green clouds, whose shadow is sunk in the brightness of the moon"—was always with him; and that in the excess of his grief he had summoned up his will to beat back the vision. He first explained the sense of foulness that night, then told how he wanted somehow to forget his bitterness at the woman who had deserted him, and his love for her, to wipe away the image still shining in his heart, to put an end to his suffering. Some might consider him insane, he said; but such was the discipline he had chosen.

"Then you've been out before?" Shigemoto asked. His father nodded with the greatest emphasis. For some months now, choosing moonlit nights, he had waited for the house to be quiet and gone out in search of enlightenment, not to one specific place but to any charnel on the edge of the moor, and had stolen back again at dawn.

"And has it helped you?" Shigemoto asked.

"No." His father stood quiet in the road. He heaved a deep sigh and looked off toward the moon over the distant hills. "It hasn't helped me forget. This enlightenment isn't so easy to come by as they say." He ignored Shigemoto after that even when the boy spoke to him, and captive of his thoughts, said scarcely a word the rest of the way back to the house.

That was the only night Shigemoto went out after his father. Since his father had stolen out unnoticed so many times before, undoubtedly he wandered out afterwards too. Late the next night, for instance, Shigemoto thought he heard his father's door open softly. His father did not ask him to come along, however, and Shigemoto did not try to follow.

Sometimes in later years Shigemoto wondered what could have made his father pour forth his heart thus for a still naive and uncomprehending child; but that was the only time in his life that he and his father talked together at such length. I use the expression "talk together" although in fact his father did most of the talking. At first the words were grave, they had a gloomy heaviness that weighed down the boy's heart, but presently it was as though the old man was appealing to his son, and at the end—Shigemoto could not be sure it was not his imagination—the voice seemed to contain a sob. Shigemoto could remember a childish fear that his father, so deranged that he quite forgot it was but a small child he was talking to, could not hope for enlightenment, that his labors would come to nothing. Shigemoto was sorry for his father, tormented day and night by that beloved image until he sought relief in the way of the Buddha. He could think of his father as a wretched and piteous figure. But, to speak plainly, Shigemoto could not repress a certain hostility, very near anger, at the father who made no attempt to preserve the beautiful figure of his mother, who sought rather to turn it into the loathsome image of a corpse left by the road, into a thing putrid and revolting.

He was only a little short, indeed, of calling out to his father, "I want to ask a favor. Please don't turn my mother's memory into something dirty." Several times during the talk he was on the point of bursting out with it, and each time he was only able to restrain himself with difficulty.

Some ten months later, toward the end of the following year, his father died. Was he able finally to gain release from the world of fleshly desire? Was he able to see her for love of whom he had so burned as no more than a worthless lump of putrefying flesh; was he able to die purified, ennobled, enlightened? Or was he, as young Shigemoto had foreseen, even at the last unredeemed by the Buddha; was that eighty-year-old breast, when it drew its final breath, aflame with passion, tortured again by the image of its love? Shigemoto had no way of knowing. To judge from the fact that his father's death was not one to arouse envy for its peace and repose, however, Shigemoto thought that those forebodings of his had not been without point.

Ordinary human sentiment would suggest that a husband unable to forget his runaway wife might do well to love all the more the only son she has borne him, that he might try to ease his pain even a little by transferring some of his affection to the boy. Shigemoto's father made no such attempt. If he could not have back the wife who had deserted him, he would not be distracted, he would not be led aside, by anyone else, not even by the child in whom his blood was joined to hers—so intense was the love of Shigemoto's father for his mother. Shigemoto had some few memories of times when his father had spoken softly to him, but without exception they were occasions when the two were talking of Shigemoto's mother, and on any other subject his father was only chilly to him. Shigemoto did not resent his father's coldness. As a matter of fact it made him happy to think that his father was so filled with love for his mother that he could give no attention to the child Shigemoto himself. His father grew colder and colder after that night, until it came to seem that the boy had quite disappeared from his mind. He was as one who gazes always at the blank space before his eyes. Shigemoto learned nothing from his father of his spiritual life during that last year, but he did notice that his father returned again to the wine he had given up, that even though he was shut up in the altar room as before the image of the Bodhisattva disappeared from the wall, and that in place of the sutras he presently took again to reciting the poetry of Po Chü-i.

TRANSLATED BY EDWARD SEIDENSTICKER

VILLON'S WIFE

[Villon no Tsuma, 1947] by Dazai Osamu (1909-1948)

Dazai Osamu, a member of a rich and influential family, was widely known during his lifetime, particularly to the younger generation, for his dissipation and excesses. His writings are autobiographical at least to the extent that we find in most of them the personage of a dissolute young man of good family, but Dazai was also gifted with a fertile imagination. His celebrity as a writer came after the war, with such stories as "Villon's Wife" and the novel The Setting Sun.

•

I was awakened by the sound of the front door being flung open, but I did not get out of bed. I knew it could only be my husband returning dead drunk in the middle of the night.

He switched on the light in the next room and, breathing very heavily, began to rummage through the drawers of the table and the bookcase, searching for something. After a few minutes there was a noise that sounded as if he had flopped down on the floor. Then I could hear only his panting. Wondering what he might be up to, I called to him from where I lay. "Have you had supper yet? There's some cold rice in the cupboard."

"Thank you," he answered in an unwontedly gentle tone. "How is the boy? Does he still have a fever?"

This was also unusual. The boy is four this year, but whether because of malnutrition, or his father's alcoholism, or sickness, he is actually smaller than most two-year-olds. He is not even sure on his feet, and as for talking, it's all he can do to say "yum-yum" or "ugh." Sometimes I wonder if he is not feeble-minded. Once, when I took him to the public bath and held him in my arms after undressing him, he looked so small and pitifully scrawny that my heart sank, and I burst into tears in front of everybody. The boy is always having upset stomachs or fevers, but my husband almost never spends any time at home, and I wonder what if anything he thinks about the child. If I mention to him that the boy has a fever, he says, "You ought to take him to a doctor." Then he throws on his coat and goes off somewhere. I would like to take the boy to the doctor, but I haven't the money. There is nothing I can do but lie beside him and stroke his head.

But that night, for whatever reason, my husband was strangely gentle, and for once asked me about the boy's fever. It didn't make me happy. I felt instead a kind of premonition of something terrible, and cold chills ran up and down my spine. I couldn't think of anything to say, so I lay there in silence. For a while there was no other sound but my husband's furious panting.

Then there came from the front entrance the thin voice of a woman, "Is anyone at home?" I shuddered all over as if icy water had been poured over me.

"Are you at home, Mr. Otani?" This time there was a somewhat sharp inflection to her voice. She slid the door open and called in a definitely angry voice, "Mr. Otani. Why don't you answer?"

My husband at last went to the door. "Well, what is it?" he asked in a frightened, stupid tone.

"You know perfectly well what it is," the woman said, lowering her voice. "What makes you steal other people's money when you've got a nice home like this? Stop your cruel joking and give it back. If you don't, I'm going straight to the police."

"I don't know what you're talking about. I won't stand for your insults. You've got no business coming here. Get out! If you don't get out, I'll be the one to call the police."

There came the voice of another man. "I must say, you've got your nerve, Mr. Otani. What do you mean we have no business coming here? You amaze me. This time it is serious. It's more than a joke when you steal other people's money. Heaven only knows all my wife and I have suffered on account of you. And on top of everything else you do something as low as you did tonight. Mr. Otani, I misjudged you."

"It's blackmail," my husband angrily exclaimed in a shaking voice. "It's extortion. Get out! If you've got any complaints I'll listen to them tomorrow."

"What a revolting thing to say. You really are a scoundrel. I have no alternative but to call the police."

In his words was a hatred so terrible that I went goose flesh all over.

"Go to hell," my husband shouted, but his voice had already weakened and sounded hollow.

I got up, threw a wrap over my nightgown, and went to the front hall. I bowed to the two visitors. A round-faced man of about fifty wearing a knee-length overcoat asked, "Is this your wife?", and, without a trace of a smile, faintly inclined his head in my direction as if he were nodding.

The woman was a thin, small person of about forty, neatly dressed. She loosened her shawl and, also unsmiling, returned my bow with the words, "Excuse us for breaking in this way in the middle of the night."

My husband suddenly slipped on his sandals and made for the door. The man grabbed his arm and the two of them struggled for a moment. "Let go or I'll stab you!" my husband shouted, and a jackknife flashed in his right hand. The knife was a pet possession of his, and I remembered that he usually kept it in his desk drawer. When he got home he must have been expecting trouble, and the knife was what he had been searching for.

The man shrank back and in the interval my husband, flapping the sleeves of his coat like a huge crow, bolted outside.

"Thief!" the man shouted and started to pursue him, but I ran to the front gate in my bare feet and clung to him.

"Please don't. It won't help for either of you to get hurt. I will take the responsibility for everything."

The woman said, "Yes, she's right. You can never tell what a lunatic will do."

"Swine! It's the police this time! I can't stand any more." The man stood there staring emptily at the darkness outside and muttering, as if to himself. But the force had gone out of his body.

"Please come in and tell me what has happened. I may be able to settle whatever the matter is. The place is a mess, but please come in."

The two visitors exchanged glances and nodded slightly to one another. The man said, with a changed expression, "I'm afraid that whatever you may say, our minds are already made up. But it might be a good idea to tell you, Mrs. Otani, all that has happened."

"Please do come in and tell me about it."

"I'm afraid we won't be able to stay long." So saying the man started to remove his overcoat.

"Please keep your coat on. It's very cold here, and there's no heating in the house."

"Well then, if you will forgive me."

"Please, both of you."

The man and the woman entered my husband's room. They seemed appalled by the desolation they saw. The mats looked as though they were rotting, the paper doors were in shreds, the walls were beginning to fall in, and the paper had peeled away from the storage closet, revealing the framework. In a corner were a desk and a bookcase—an empty bookcase.

I offered the two visitors some torn cushions from which the stuffing was leaking, and said, "Please sit on the cushions—the mats are so dirty." And I bowed to them again. "I must apologize for all the trouble my husband seems to have been causing you, and for the terrible exhibition he put on tonight, for whatever reason it was. He has such a peculiar disposition." I choked in the middle of my words and burst into tears.

"Excuse me for asking, Mrs. Otani, but how old are you?" the man asked. He was sitting cross-legged on the torn cushion, with his elbows on his knees, propping his chin on his fists. As he asked the question he leaned forward toward me.

"I am twenty-six."

"Is that all you are? I suppose that's only natural, considering your husband's about thirty, but it amazes me all the same."

The woman, showing her face from behind the man's back, said, "I couldn't help wondering, when I came in and saw what a fine wife he has, why Mr. Otani behaves the way he does."

"He's sick. That's what it is. He didn't used to be that way, but he keeps getting worse." He gave a great sigh, then continued, "Mrs. Otani, my wife and I run a little restaurant near the Nakano Station. We both originally came from the country, but I got fed up dealing with penny-pinching farmers, and came to Tokyo with my wife. After the usual hardships and breaks, we managed to save up a little and, along about 1936, opened a cheap little restaurant catering to customers with at most a yen or two to spend at a time on entertainment. By not going in for luxuries and working like slaves, we managed to lay in quite a stock of whisky and gin. When liquor got short and plenty of other drinking establishments went out of business, we were able to keep going.

"The war with America and England broke out, but even after the bombings got pretty severe, we didn't want to be evacuated to the country, not having any children to tie us down. We figured that we might as well stick to our business until the place got burnt down. Your husband first started coming to our place in the spring of 1944, as I recall. We were not yet losing the war, or if we were we didn't know how things actually stood, and we thought that if we could just hold out for another two or three years we could somehow get peace on terms of equality. When Mr. Otani first appeared in our shop, he was not alone. It's a little embarrassing to tell you about it, but I might as well come out with the whole story and not keep anything from you. Your husband sneaked in by the kitchen door along with an older woman. I forgot to say that about that time the front door of our place was shut, and only a few regular customers got in by the back.

"This older woman lived in the neighborhood, and when the bar where she worked was closed and she lost her job, she often came to our place with her men friends. That's why we weren't particularly surprised when your husband crept in with this woman, whose name was Akichan. I took them to the back room and brought out some gin. Mr. Otani drank his liquor very quietly that evening.

Akichan paid the bill and the two of them left together. It's odd, but I can't forget how strangely gentle and refined he seemed that night. I wonder if when the devil makes his first appearance in somebody's house he acts in such a lonely and melancholy way.

"From that night on Mr. Otani was a steady customer. Ten days later he came alone and all of a sudden produced a hundred-yen note. At that time a hundred yen was a lot of money, more than two or three thousand yen today. He pressed the money into my hand and wouldn't take no for an answer. 'Take care of it please,' he said, smiling timidly. That night he seemed to have drunk quite a bit before he came, and at my place he downed ten glasses of gin as fast as I could set them up. All this was almost entirely without a word. My wife and I tried to start a conversation, but he only smiled rather shamefacedly and nodded vaguely. Suddenly he asked the time and got up. 'What about the change?' I called after him. 'That's all right,' he said. 'I don't know what to do with it,' I insisted. He answered with a sardonic smile, 'Please save it until the next time. I'll be coming back.' He went out. Mrs. Otani, that was the one and only time that we ever got any money from him. Since then he has always put us off with one excuse or another, and for three years he has managed without paying a penny to drink up all our liquor almost singlehanded."

Before I knew what I was doing I burst out laughing. It all seemed so funny to me, although I can't explain why. I covered my mouth in confusion, but when I looked at the lady I saw that she was also laughing unaccountably, and then her husband could not help but laugh too.

"No, it's certainly no laughing matter, but I'm so fed up that I feel like laughing, too. Really, if he used all his ability in some other direction, he could become a cabinet minister or a Ph.D. or anything else he wanted. When Akichan was still friends with Mr. Otani she used to brag about him all the time. First of all, she said, he came from a terrific family. He was the younger son of Baron Otani. It is true that he had been disinherited because of his conduct, but when his father, the present baron, died, he and his elder brother were to divide the estate. He was brilliant, a genius in fact.

In spite of his youth he was the best poet in Japan. What's more, he was a great scholar, and a perfect demon at German and French. To hear Akichan talk, he was a kind of god, and the funny thing was that she didn't make it all up. Other people also said that he was the younger son of Baron Otani and a famous poet. Even my wife, who's getting along in years, was as enthusiastic about him as Akichan. She used to tell me what a difference it makes when people have been well brought up. And the way she pined for him to come was quite unbearable. They say the day of the nobility is over, but until the war ended I can tell you that nobody had his way with the women like that disinherited son of the aristocracy. It is unbelievable how they fell for him. I suppose it was what people would nowadays call 'slave mentality.'

"For my part, I'm a man, and at that a very cool sort of man, and I don't think that some little peer—if you will pardon the expression—some member of the country gentry who is only a younger son, is all that different from myself. I never for a moment got worked up about him in so sickening a way. But all the same, that gentleman was my weak spot. No matter how firmly I resolved not to give him any liquor the next time, when he suddenly appeared at some unexpected hour, looking like a hunted man, and I saw how relieved he was at last to have reached our place, my resolution weakened, and I ended up by giving him the liquor. Even when he got drunk, he never made any special nuisance of himself, and if only he had paid the bill he would have been a good customer. He never advertised himself and didn't take any silly pride in being a genius or anything of the sort. When Akichan or somebody else would sit beside him and sound off to us about his greatness, he would either change the subject completely or say, 'I want some money so I can pay the bill,' throwing a wet blanket over everything.

"The war finally ended. We started doing business openly in black-market liquor and put new curtains in front of the place. For all its seediness the shop looked rather lively, and we hired a girl to lend a little charm. Then who should show up again but that damned gentleman. He no longer brought women with him, but

always came in the company of two or three writers for newspapers
and magazines. He was drinking even more than before, and used
to get very wild-looking. He began to come out with really vulgar
jokes, which he had never done before, and sometimes for no good
reason he would hit one of the reporters he brought with him or
start a fist fight. What's more, he seduced the twenty-year-old girl
who was working in our place. We were shocked, but there was
nothing we could do about it at that stage, and we had no choice
but to let the matter drop. We advised the girl to resign herself to
bearing the child, and quietly sent her back to her parents. I begged
Mr. Otani not to come any more, but he answered in a threatening
tone, 'People who make money on the black market have no business
criticizing others. I know all about you.' The next night he showed
up as if nothing had happened.

"Maybe it was by way of punishment for the black-market business we had been doing that we had to put up with such a monster. But what he did tonight can't be passed over just because he's
a poet or a gentleman. It was plain robbery. He stole five thousand
yen from us. Nowadays all our money goes for stock, and we are
lucky if we have five hundred or one thousand yen in the place. The
reason why we had as much as five thousand tonight was that I had
made an end-of-the-year round of our regular customers and managed to collect that much. If I don't hand the money over to the
wholesalers immediately we won't be able to stay in business. That's
how much it means to us. Well, my wife was going over the
accounts in the back room and had put the money in the cupboard
drawer. He was drinking by himself out in front but seems to have
noticed what she did. Suddenly he got up, went straight to the back
room, and without a word pushed my wife aside and opened the
drawer. He grabbed the bills and stuffed them in his pocket.

"We rushed into the shop, still speechless with amazement, and
then out into the street. I shouted for him to stop, and the two of
us ran after him. For a minute I felt like screaming 'Thief!' and
getting the people in the street to join us, but after all, Mr. Otani is
an old acquaintance, and I couldn't be too harsh on him. I made up
my mind that I would not let him out of my sight. I would follow

him wherever he went, and when I saw that he had quieted down, I would calmly ask for the money. We are only small business people, and when we finally caught up with him here, we had no choice but to suppress our feelings and politely ask him to return the money. And then what happened? He took out a knife and threatened to stab me! What a way to behave!"

Again the whole thing seemed so funny to me, for reasons I can't explain, that I burst out laughing. The lady turned red, and smiled a little. I couldn't stop laughing. Even though I knew that it would have a bad effect on the proprietor, it all seemed so strangely funny that I laughed until the tears came. I suddenly wondered if the phrase "the great laugh at the end of the world," that occurs in one of my husband's poems, didn't mean something of the sort.

And yet it was not a matter that could be settled just by laughing about it. I thought for a minute and said, "Somehow or other I will make things good, if you will only wait one more day before you report to the police. I'll call on you tomorrow without fail." I carefully inquired where the restaurant was, and begged them to consent. They agreed to let things stand for the time being, and left. Then I sat by myself in the middle of the cold room trying to think of a plan. Nothing came to me. I stood up, took off my wrap, and crept in among the covers where my boy was sleeping. As I stroked his head I thought how wonderful it would be if the night never never ended.

My father used to keep a stall in Asakusa Park. My mother died when I was young, and my father and I lived by ourselves in a tenement. We ran the stall together. My husband used to come now and then, and before long I was meeting him at other places without my father's knowing it. When I became pregnant I persuaded him to treat me as his wife, although it wasn't officially registered, of course. Now the boy is growing up fatherless, while my husband goes off for three or four nights or even for a whole month at a time. I don't know where he goes or what he does. When he comes back he is always drunk; and he sits there, deathly pale, breathing heavily and staring at my face. Sometimes he cries and the tears stream down his face, or without warning he crawls into my bed and holds me tightly. "Oh, it can't go on. I'm afraid. I'm afraid. Help me!"

Sometimes he trembles all over, and even after he falls asleep he talks deliriously and moans. The next morning he is absent-minded, like a man with the soul taken out of him. Then he disappears and doesn't return for three or four nights. A couple of my husband's publisher friends have been looking after the boy and myself for some time, and they bring money once in a while, enough to keep us from starving.

I dozed off, then before I knew it opened my eyes to see the morning light pouring in through the cracks in the shutters. I got up, dressed, strapped the boy to my back and went outside. I felt as if I couldn't stand being in the silent house another minute.

I set out aimlessly and found myself walking in the direction of the station. I bought a bun at an outdoor stand and fed it to the boy. On a sudden impulse I bought a ticket for Kichijoji and got on the streetcar. While I stood hanging from a strap I happened to notice a poster with my husband's name on it. It was an advertisement for a magazine in which he had published a story called "François Villon." While I stared at the title "François Villon" and at my husband's name, painful tears sprang from my eyes, why I can't say, and the poster clouded over so I couldn't see it.

I got off at Kichijoji and for the first time in I don't know how many years I walked in the park. The cypresses around the pond had all been cut down, and the place looked like the site of a construction. It was strangely bare and cold, not at all as it used to be.

I took the boy off my back and the two of us sat on a broken bench next to the pond. I fed the boy a sweet potato I had brought from home. "It's a pretty pond, isn't it? There used to be many carp and goldfish, but now there aren't any left. It's too bad, isn't it?"

I don't know what he thought. He just laughed oddly with his mouth full of sweet potato. Even if he is my own child, he did give me the feeling almost of an idiot.

I couldn't settle anything by sitting there on the bench, so I put the boy on my back and returned slowly to the station. I bought a ticket for Nakano. Without thought or plan, I boarded the street-car as though I were being sucked into a horrible whirlpool. I got off at Nakano and followed the directions to the restaurant.

The front door would not open. I went around to the back and entered by the kitchen door. The owner was away, and his wife was cleaning the shop by herself. As soon as I saw her I began to pour out lies of which I did not imagine myself capable.

"It looks as if I'll be able to pay you back every bit of the money tomorrow, if not tonight. There's nothing for you to worry about."

"Oh, how wonderful. Thank you so much." She looked almost happy, but still there remained on her face a shadow of uneasiness, as if she were not yet satisfied.

"It's true. Someone will bring the money here without fail. Until he comes I'm to stay here as your hostage. Is that guarantee enough for you? Until the money comes I'll be glad to help around the shop."

I took the boy off my back and let him play by himself. He is accustomed to playing alone and doesn't get in the way at all. Perhaps because he's stupid, he's not afraid of strangers, and he smiled happily at the madam. While I was away getting the rationed goods for her, she gave him some empty American cans to play with, and when I got back he was in a corner of the room, banging the cans and rolling them on the floor.

About noon the boss returned from his marketing. As soon as I caught sight of him I burst out with the same lies I had told the madam. He looked amazed. "Is that a fact? All the same, Mrs. Otani, you can't be sure of money until you've got it in your hands." He spoke in a surprisingly calm, almost explanatory tone.

"But it's really true. Please have confidence in me and wait just this one day before you make it public. In the meantime I'll help in the restaurant."

"If the money is returned, that's all I ask," the boss said, almost to himself. "There are five or six days left to the end of the year, aren't there?"

"Yes, and so, you see, I mean—oh, some customers have come. Welcome!" I smiled at the three customers—they looked like workmen—who had entered the shop, and whispered to the madam, "Please lend me an apron."

One of the customers called out, "Say, you've hired a beauty. She's terrific."

"Don't lead her astray," the boss said, in a tone which wasn't altogether joking, "she cost a lot of money."

"A million-dollar thoroughbred?" another customer coarsely joked.

"They say that even in thoroughbreds the female costs only half-price," I answered in the same coarse way, while putting the sake on to warm.

"Don't be modest! From now on in Japan there's equality of the sexes, even for horses and dogs," the youngest customer roared. "Sweetheart, I've fallen in love. It's love at first sight. But is that your kid over there?"

"No," said the madam, carrying the boy from the back room in her arms. "We got this child from our relatives. At last we have an heir."

"What'll you leave him beside your money?" a customer teased.

The boss, with a dark expression, muttered, "A love affair and debts." Then, changing his tone, "What'll you have? How about a mixed grill?"

It was Christmas Eve. That must have been why there was such a steady stream of customers. I had scarcely eaten a thing since morning, but I was so upset that I refused even when the madam urged me to have a bite. I just went on flitting around the restaurant as lightly as a ballerina. Maybe it is only conceit, but the shop seemed exceptionally lively that night, and there were quite a few customers who wanted to know my name or tried to shake my hand.

But I didn't have the slightest idea how it would all end. I went on smiling and answering the customers' dirty jokes with even dirtier jokes in the same vein, slipping from customer to customer, pouring the drinks. Before long I got to thinking that I would just as soon my body melted and flowed away like ice cream.

It seems as if miracles sometimes do happen even in this world. A little after nine a man entered, wearing a Christmas tricornered paper hat and a black mask which covered the upper part of his face. He was followed by an attractive woman of slender build who looked thirty-four or thirty-five. The man sat on a chair in the corner with his back to me, but as soon as he came in I knew who it was. It was my thief of a husband.

He sat there without seeming to pay any attention to me. I also pretended not to recognize him, and went on joking with the other customers. The lady seated opposite my husband called me to their table. My husband stared at me from beneath his mask, as if he were surprised in spite of himself. I lightly patted his shoulder and asked, "Aren't you going to wish me a merry Christmas? What do you say? You look as if you've already put away a quart or two."

The lady ignored this. She said, "I have something to discuss with the proprietor. Would you mind calling him here for a moment?"

I went to the kitchen, where the boss was frying fish. "Otani has come back. Please go and see him, but don't tell the woman he's with anything about me. I don't want to embarrass him."

"If that's the way you want it, it's all right with me," he consented easily, and went out front. After a quick look around the restaurant, the boss walked straight to the table where my husband sat. The beautiful lady exchanged two or three words with him, and the three of them left the shop.

It was all over. Everything had been settled. Somehow I had believed all along that it would be, and I felt exhilarated. I seized the wrist of a young customer in a dark-blue suit, a boy not more than twenty, and I cried, "Drink up! Drink up! It's Christmas!"

In just thirty minutes—no, it was even sooner than that, so soon it startled me, the boss returned alone. "Mrs. Otani, I want to thank you. I've got the money back."

"I'm so glad. All of it?"

He answered with a funny smile, "All he took yesterday."

"And how much does his debt come to altogether? Roughly— the absolute minimum."

"Twenty thousand yen."

"Does that cover it?"

"It's a minimum."

"I'll make it good. Will you employ me starting tomorrow? I'll pay it back by working."

"What! You're joking!" And we laughed together.

Tonight I left the restaurant after ten and returned to the house with the boy. As I expected, my husband was not at home, but that didn't bother me. Tomorrow when I go to the restaurant I may see him again, for all I know. Why has such a good plan never occurred to me before? All the suffering I have gone through has been because of my own stupidity. I was always quite a success at entertaining the customers at my father's stall, and I'll certainly get to be pretty skillful at the restaurant. As a matter of fact, I received about five hundred yen in tips tonight.

From the following day on my life changed completely. I became lighthearted and gay. The first thing I did was to go to a beauty parlor and have a permanent. I bought cosmetics and mended my dresses. I felt as though the worries that had weighed so heavily on me had been completely wiped away.

In the morning I get up and eat breakfast with the boy. Then I put him on my back and leave for work. New Year's is the big season at the restaurant, and I've been so busy my eyes swim. My husband comes in for a drink once every few days. He lets me pay the bill and then disappears again. Quite often he looks in on the shop late at night and asks if it isn't time for me to be going home. Then we return pleasantly together.

"Why didn't I do this from the start? It's brought me such happiness."

"Women don't know anything about happiness or unhappiness."

"Perhaps not. What about men?"

"Men only have unhappiness. They are always fighting fear."

"I don't understand. I only know I wish this life could go on forever. The boss and the madam are such nice people."

"Don't be silly. They're grasping country bumpkins. They make me drink because they think they'll make money out of it in the end."

"That's their business. You can't blame them for it. But that's not the whole story is it? You had an affair with the madam, didn't you?"

"A long time ago. Does the old guy realize it?"

"I'm sure he does. I heard him say with a sigh that you had brought him a seduction and debts."

"I must seem a horrible character to you, but the fact is that I want to die so badly I can't stand it. Ever since I was born I have been thinking of nothing but dying. It would be better for everyone concerned if I were dead, that's certain. And yet I can't seem to die. There's something strange and frightening, like God, which won't let me die."

"That's because you have your work."

"My work doesn't mean a thing. I don't write either masterpieces or failures. If people say something is good, it becomes good. If they say it's bad, it becomes bad. But what frightens me is that somewhere in the world there is a God. There is, isn't there?"

"I haven't any idea."

Now that I have worked twenty days at the restaurant I realize that every last one of the customers is a criminal. I have come to think that my husband is very much on the mild side compared to them. And I see now that not only the customers but everyone you meet walking in the streets is hiding some crime. A beautifully dressed lady came to the door selling sake at three hundred yen the quart. That was cheap, considering what prices are nowadays, and the madam snapped it up. It turned out to be watered. I thought that in a world where even such an aristocratic-looking lady is forced to resort to such tricks, it is impossible for anyone alive to have a clear conscience.

God, if you exist, show yourself to me! Toward the end of the New Year season I was raped by a customer. It was raining that night, and it didn't seem likely that my husband would appear. I got ready to go, even though one customer was still left. I picked up the boy, who was sleeping in a corner of the back room, and put him on my back. "I'd like to borrow your umbrella again," I said to the madam.

"I've got an umbrella. I'll take you home," said the last customer, getting up as if he meant it. He was a short, thin man about twenty-five, who looked like a factory worker. It was the first time he had come to the restaurant since I started working there.

"It's very kind of you, but I am used to walking by myself."

"You live a long way off, I know. I come from the same neighborhood. I'll take you back. Bill, please." He had only had three glasses and didn't seem particularly drunk.

We boarded the streetcar together and got off at my stop. Then we walked in the falling rain side by side under the same umbrella through the pitch-black streets. The young man, who up to this point hadn't said a word, began to talk in a lively way. "I know all about you. You see, I'm a fan of Mr. Otani's and I write poetry myself. I was hoping to show him some of my work before long, but he intimidates me so."

We had reached my house. "Thank you very much," I said. "I'll see you again at the restaurant."

"Good-bye," the young man said, going off into the rain.

I was wakened in the middle of the night by the noise of the front gate being opened. I thought that it was my husband returning, drunk as usual, so I lay there without saying anything.

A man's voice called, "Mrs. Otani, excuse me for bothering you."

I got up, put on the light, and went to the front entrance. The young man was there, staggering so badly he could scarcely stand.

"Excuse me, Mrs. Otani. On the way back I stopped for another drink and, to tell the truth, I live at the other end of town, and when I got to the station the last streetcar had already left. Mrs. Otani, would you please let me spend the night here? I don't need any blankets or anything else. I'll be glad to sleep here in the front hall until the first streetcar leaves tomorrow morning. If it wasn't raining I'd sleep outdoors somewhere in the neighborhood, but it's hopeless with this rain. Please let me stay."

"My husband isn't at home, but if the front hall will do, please stay." I got the two torn cushions and gave them to him.

"Thanks very much. Oh, I've had too much to drink," he said with a groan. He lay down just as he was in the front hall, and by the time I got back to bed I could already hear his snores.

The next morning at dawn without ceremony he took me.

That day I went to the restaurant with my boy as usual, acting as if nothing had happened. My husband was sitting at a table reading a newspaper, a glass of liquor beside him. I thought how pretty the morning sunshine looked, sparkling on the glass.

"Isn't anybody here?" I asked. He looked up from his paper. "The boss hasn't come back yet from marketing. The madam was in the kitchen just a minute ago. Isn't she there now?"

"You didn't come last night, did you?"

"I did come. It's got so that I can't get to sleep without a look at my favorite waitress's face. I dropped in after ten but they said you had just left."

"And then?"

"I spent the night here. It was raining so hard."

"I may be sleeping here from now on."

"That's a good idea, I suppose."

"Yes, that's what I'll do. There's no sense in renting the house forever."

My husband didn't say anything but turned back to his paper. "Well, what do you know. They're writing bad things about me again. They call me a fake aristocrat with Epicurean leanings. That's not true. It would be more correct to refer to me as an Epicurean in terror of God. Look! It says here that I'm a monster. That's not true, is it? It's a little late, but I'll tell you now why I took the five thousand yen. It was so that I might give you and the boy the first happy New Year in a long time. That proves I'm not a monster, doesn't it?"

His words didn't make me especially glad. I said, "There's nothing wrong with being a monster, is there? As long as we can stay alive."

TRANSLATED BY DONALD KEENE

TOKYO

[Shitamachi, 1948] by Hayashi Fumiko (1904-1951)

Most of the characters in Hayashi Fumiko's writings belong to the Tokyo lower classes. She portrays them with realism and compassion, probably because as a young woman she experienced the hardships of their life. Her descriptions of postwar Tokyo are among the most somber and moving. Asakusa, where much of the action of "Tokyo" takes place, is an amusement district vaguely corresponding to Montmartre. It has a Buddhist temple dedicated to Kannon, the Goddess of Mercy. A description of the same scene sixty years earlier may be found in The River Sumida.

•

It was a bitter, windy afternoon. As Ryo hurried down the street with her rucksack, she kept to the side where the pale sun shone down over the roofs of the office buildings. Every now and then she looked about curiously—at a building, at a parked car—at one of those innumerable bomb sites scattered through downtown Tokyo.

Glancing over a boarding, Ryo saw a huge pile of rusty iron, and next to it a cabin with a glass door. A fire was burning within, and the warm sound of the crackling wood reached where she was standing. In front of the cabin stood a man in overalls with a red kerchief about his head. There was something pleasant about this tall fellow, and Ryo screwed up her courage to call out,

"Tea for sale! Would you like some tea, please?"

"Tea?" said the man.

"Yes," said Ryo with a nervous smile. "It's Shizuoka tea."

She stepped in through an opening in the boarding and, unfastening the straps of her rucksack, put it down by the cabin. Inside she could see a fire burning in an iron stove; from a bar above hung a brass kettle with a wisp of steam rising from the spout.

"Excuse me," said Ryo, "but would you mind if I came in and warmed myself by your stove a few minutes? It's freezing out, and I've been walking for miles."

"Of course you can come in," said the man. "Close the door and get warm."

He pointed towards the stool, which was his only article of furniture, and sat down on a packing case in the corner. Ryo hesitated a moment. Then she dragged her rucksack into the cabin and, crouching by the stove, held up her hands to the fire.

"You'll be more comfortable on that stool," said the man, glancing at her attractive face, flushed in the sudden warmth, and at her shabby attire.

"Surely this isn't what you usually do—hawk tea from door to door?"

"Oh yes, it's how I make my living," Ryo said. "I was told that this was a good neighborhood, but I've been walking around here since early morning and have only managed to sell one packet of tea. I'm about ready to go home now, but I thought I'd have my lunch somewhere on the way."

"Well, you're perfectly welcome to stay here and eat your lunch," said the man. "And don't worry about not having sold your tea," he added, smiling. "It's all a matter of luck, you know! You'll probably have a good day tomorrow."

The kettle came to a boil with a whistling sound. As he unhooked it from the bar, Ryo had a chance to look about her. She took in the boarded ceiling black with soot, the blackboard by the window, the shelf for family gods on which stood a potted sakaki tree. The man took a limp-looking packet from the table, and unwrapping it, disclosed a piece of cod. A few minutes later the smell of baking fish permeated the cabin.

"Come on," said the man. "Sit down and have your meal."

Ryo took her lunch box out of the rucksack and seated herself on the stool.

"Selling things is never much fun, is it?" remarked the man, turning the cod over on the grill. "Tell me, how much do you get for a hundred grams of that tea?"

"I should get thirty-five yen to make any sort of profit. The people who send me the stuff often mix in bad tea, so I'm lucky if I can get thirty yen."

In Ryo's lunch box were two small fish covered with some boiled barley and a few bean-paste pickles. She began eating.

"Where do you live?" the man asked her.

"In the Shitaya district. Actually I don't know one part of Tokyo from another! I've only been here a few weeks and a friend's putting me up until I find something better."

The cod was ready now. He cut it in two and gave Ryo half, adding potatoes and rice from a platter. Ryo smiled and bowed slightly in thanks, then took out a bag of tea from her rucksack and poured some into a paper handkerchief.

"Do put this into the kettle," she said, holding it out to him.

He shook his head and smiled, showing his white teeth.

"Good Lord no! It's far too expensive."

Quickly Ryo removed the lid and poured the tea in before he could stop her. Laughing, the man went to fetch a teacup and a mug from the shelf.

"What about your husband?" he asked, while ranging them on the packing case. "You're married, aren't you?"

"Oh yes, I am. My husband's still in Siberia. That's why I have to work like this."

Ryo's thoughts flew to her husband, from whom she had not heard for six years; by now he had come to seem so remote that it required an effort to remember his looks, or the once-familiar sound of his voice. She woke up each morning with a feeling of emptiness and desolation. At times it seemed to Ryo that her husband had frozen into a ghost in that subarctic Siberia—a ghost, or a thin white pillar, or just a breath of frosty air. Nowadays no one any longer mentioned the war and she was almost embarrassed to let people know that her husband was still a prisoner.

"It's funny," the man said. "The fact is, I was in Siberia myself! I spent three years chopping wood near the Amur River—I only managed to get sent home last year. Well, it's all in a matter of luck! It's tough on your husband. But it's just as tough on you."

"So you've really been repatriated from Siberia! You don't seem any the worse for it," Ryo said.

"Well, I don't know about that!" the man shrugged his shoulders. "Anyway, as you see, I'm still alive."

Ryo closed her lunch box, and as she did so, she studied him. There was a simplicity and directness about this man that made her want to talk openly in a way that she found difficult with more educated people.

"Got any kids?" he said.

"Yes, a boy of six. He should be at school, but I've had difficulty getting him registered here in Tokyo. These officials certainly know how to make life complicated for people!"

The man untied his kerchief, wiped the cup and the mug with it, and poured out the steaming tea.

"It's good stuff this!" he said, sipping noisily.

"Do you like it? It's not the best quality, you know: only two hundred and ten yen a kilo wholesale. But you're right—it's quite good."

The wind had grown stronger while they were talking; it whistled over the tin roof of the cabin. Ryo glanced out of the window, steeling herself for her long walk home.

"I'll have some of your tea—seven hundred and fifty grams," the man told her, extracting two crumbled hundred-yen notes from the pocket of his overalls.

"Don't be silly," said Ryo. "You can have it for nothing."

"Oh no, that won't do. Business is business!" He forced the money into her hand. "Well, if you're ever in this part of the world again, come in and have another chat."

"I should like to," said Ryo, glancing around the tiny cabin. "But you don't live here, do you?"

"Oh, but I do! I look after that iron out there and help load the trucks. I'm here most of the day."

He opened a door under the shelf, disclosing a sort of cubbyhole containing a bed neatly made up. Ryo noticed a colored postcard of a film actress tacked to the back of the door.

"My, you've fixed it up nicely," she said smiling. "You're really quite snug here, aren't you?"

She wondered how old he could be.

2

From that day on, Ryo came regularly to the Yotsugi district to sell tea; each time she visited the cabin on the bomb site. She learned that the man's name was Tsuruishi Yoshio. Almost invariably he had some small delicacy waiting for her to put in her lunch box—a pickled plum, a piece of beef, a sardine. Her business began to improve and she acquired a few regular customers in the neighborhood.

A week after their first meeting, she brought along her boy, Ryukichi. Tsuruishi chatted with the child for a while and then took him out for a walk. When they returned, Ryukichi was carrying a large caramel cake.

"He's got a good appetite, this youngster of yours," said Tsuruishi, patting the boy's close-cropped head.

Ryo wondered vaguely whether her new friend was married; in fact she found herself wondering about various aspects of his life. She was now twenty-nine, and she realized with a start that this was the first time she had been seriously interested in any man but her husband. Tsuruishi's easy, carefree temperament somehow appealed to her, though she took great care not to let him guess that.

A little later Tsuruishi suggested taking Ryo and Ryukichi to see Asakusa on his next free day. They met in front of the information booth in Ueno Station, Tsuruishi wearing an ancient gray suit that looked far too tight, Ryo clad in a blue dress of kimono material and a light-brown coat. In spite of her cheap clothes, she had about her something youthful and elegant as she stood there in the crowded station. Beside the tall, heavy Tsuruishi, she looked like a schoolgirl off on a holiday. In her shopping bag lay their lunch: bread, oranges, and seaweed stuffed with rice.

"Well, let's hope it doesn't rain," said Tsuruishi, putting his arm lightly round Ryo's waist as he steered her through the crowd.

They took the subway to Asakusa Station, then walked from the Matsuya Department Store to the Niten Shinto Gate, past hundreds of tiny stalls. The Asakusa district was quite different from what Ryo had imagined. She was amazed when Tsuruishi pointed to a small red-lacquered temple and told her that this was the home of the famous Asakusa Goddess of Mercy. In the distance she could hear the plaintive wail of a trumpet and a saxophone emerging from some loud-speaker; it mingled strangely with the sound of the wind whistling through the branches of the ancient sakaki trees.

They made their way through the old-clothes market, and came to a row of food-stalls squeezed tightly against each other beside the Asakusa Pond; here the air was redolent with the smell of burning oil. Tsuruishi went to one of the stalls and bought Ryukichi a stick of yellow candy-floss. The boy nibbled at it, as the three of them walked down a narrow street plastered with American-style billboards advertising restaurants, movies, revues. It was less than a month since Ryo had first noticed Tsuruishi by his cabin, yet she felt as much at ease with him as if she had known him all her life.

"Well, it's started raining after all," he said, holding out his hand. Ryo looked up, to see scattered drops of rain falling from the gray sky. So their precious excursion would be ruined, she thought.

"We'd better go in there," said Tsuruishi, pointing to one of the shops, outside which hung a garish lantern with characters announcing the "Merry Teahouse." They took seats at a table underneath a ceiling decorated with artificial cherry blossoms. The place had a strangely unhomelike atmosphere, but they were determined to make the best of it and ordered a pot of tea; Ryo distributed her stuffed seaweed, bread, and oranges. It was not long before the meal was finished and by then it had started raining in earnest.

"We'd better wait till it lets up a bit," suggested Tsuruishi. "Then I'll take you home."

Ryo wondered if he was referring to her place or his. She was staying in the cramped apartment of a friend from her home town and did not even have a room to call her own; rather than go there, she would have preferred returning to Tsuruishi's cabin, but that too was scarcely large enough to hold three people. Taking out her purse, she counted her money under the table. The seven hundred yen should be enough to get shelter for a few hours at an inn.

"D'you know what I'd really like?" she said. "I'd like us to go to a movie and then find some inn and have a dish of food before saying good-bye to each other. But I suppose that's all rather expensive!"

"Yes, I suppose it is," said Tsuruishi, laughing. "Come on! We'll do it all the same."

Taking his overcoat off the peg, he threw it over Ryukichi's head, and ran through the downpour to a movie theatre. Of course there were no seats! Standing watching the film, the little boy went sound asleep, leaning against Tsuruishi. The air in the theatre seemed to get thicker and hotter every moment; on the roof they could hear the rain beating down.

It was getting dark as they left the theatre and hurried through the rain, which pelted down with the swishing sound of banana leaves in a high wind. At last they found a small inn where the landlord led them to a carpeted room at the end of a drafty passage. Ryo took off her wet socks. The boy sat down in a corner and promptly went back to sleep.

"Here, he can use this as a pillow," said Tsuruishi, picking up an old cushion from a chair and putting it under Ryukichi's head.

From an overflowing gutter above the window the water poured in a steady stream onto the courtyard. It sounded like a waterfall in some faraway mountain village.

Tsuruishi took out a handkerchief and began wiping Ryo's wet hair. A feeling of happiness coursed through her as she looked up at him. It was as if the rain had begun to wash away all the loneliness which had been gathering within her year after year.

She went to see if they could get some food and in the corridor met a maid in Western clothes carrying a tea tray. After Ryo had ordered two bowls of spaghetti, she and Tsuruishi sat down to drink their tea, facing each other across an empty brazier. Later Tsuruishi came and sat on the floor beside Ryo. Leaning their backs against the wall, they gazed out at the darkening, rainy sky.

"How old are you, Ryo?" Tsuruishi asked her. "I should guess twenty-five."

Ryo laughed. "I'm afraid not, Tsuru, I'm already an old woman! I'm twenty-eight."

"Oh, so you're a year older than me."

"My goodness, you're young!" said Ryo. "I thought you must be at least thirty."

She looked straight at him, into his dark, gentle eyes with their bushy brows. He seemed to be blushing slightly. Then he bent forward and took off his wet socks.

The rain continued unabated. Presently the maid came with some cold spaghetti and soup. Ryo woke the boy and gave him a plate of soup; he was half asleep as he sipped it.

"Look, Ryo," Tsuruishi said, "we might as well all stay the night at this inn. You can't go home in this rain, can you?"

"No," said Ryo. "No, I suppose not."

Tsuruishi left the room and returned with a load of quilted bedrolls which he spread on the floor. At once the whole room seemed to be full of bedding. Ryo tucked up her son in one of the rolls, the boy sleeping soundly as she did so. Then she turned out the light, undressed, and lay down. She could hear Tsuruishi settling down at the other end of the room.

"I suppose the people in this inn think we're married," said Tsuruishi after a while.

"Yes, I suppose so. It's not very nice of us to fool them!"

She spoke in jest, but now that she lay undressed in her bedroll, she felt for the first time vaguely disturbed and guilty. Her husband for some reason seemed much closer than he had for years. But of course she was only here because of the rain, she reminded herself. . . . And gradually her thoughts began to wander pleasantly afield, and she dozed off.

When she awoke it was still dark. She could hear Tsuruishi whispering her name from his corner, and she sat up with a start.

"Ryo, Ryo, can I come and talk to you for a while?"

"No, Tsuru," she said, "I don't think you should."

On the roof the rain was still pattering down, but the force of the storm was over; only a trickle was dropping from the gutter into the yard. Under the sound of the rain she thought she could hear Tsuruishi sigh softly.

"Look Tsuru," she said after a pause. "I've never asked you before, but are you married?"

"No. Not now," Tsuruishi said.

"You used to be?"

"Yes. I used to be. When I got back from the army, I found that my wife was living with another man."

"Were you—angry?"

"Angry? Yes, I suppose I was. Still, there wasn't much I could do about it. She'd left me, and that was that."

They were silent again.

"What shall we talk about?" Ryo asked.

Tsuruishi laughed. "Well, there really doesn't seem to be anything special to talk about. That spaghetti wasn't very good, was it?"

"No, one certainly couldn't call it good. And they charged us a hundred yen each for it!"

"It would be nice if you and Ryukichi had your own room to live in, wouldn't it?" Tsuruishi remarked.

"Oh yes, it would be marvelous! You don't think we might find a room near you? I'd really like to live near you, Tsuru, you know."

"It's pretty hard to find rooms these days, especially downtown. But I'll keep a lookout and let you know. . . . You're such a wonderful person, Ryo!"

"Me?" said Ryo laughing. "Don't be silly!"

"Yes, yes, you're wonderful . . . really wonderful!"

Ryo lay back on the floor. Suddenly she wanted to throw her arms around Tsuruishi, to feel his body close to hers. She did not dare speak for fear that her voice might betray her; her breath came almost painfully; her whole body tingled. Outside the window an early morning truck clattered past.

"Where are your parents, Tsuru?" she asked after a while.

"In the country near Fukuoka."

"But you have a sister in Tokyo?"

"Yes. She's all alone, like you, with two kids to take care of.

She's got a sewing machine and makes Western-style clothes. Her husband was killed several years ago—in the war in China. War, always war!"

Outside the window Ryo could make out the first glimmer of dawn. So their night together was almost over, she thought unhappily. In a way she wished that Tsuruishi hadn't given up so easily, and yet she was convinced that it was best like this. If he had been a man she hardly knew, or for whom she felt nothing, she might have given herself to him with no afterthought. With Tsuruishi it would have been different—quite different.

"Ryo, I can't get to sleep." His voice reached her again. "I'm wide awake, you know. I suppose I'm not used to this sort of thing."

"What sort of thing?"

"Why—sleeping in the same room with a girl."

"Oh Tsuru, don't tell me that you don't have girl friends occasionally!"

"Only professional girl friends."

Ryo laughed. "Men have it easy! In some ways, at least. . . ."

She heard Tsuruishi moving about. Suddenly he was beside her, bending over her. Ryo did not move, not even when she felt his arms around her, his face against hers. In the dark her eyes were wide open, and before them bright lights seemed to be flashing. His hot lips were pressed to her cheek.

"Ryo . . . Ryo."

"It's wrong, you know," she murmured. "Wrong to my husband. . . ."

But almost at once she regretted the words. As Tsuruishi bent over her, she could make out the silhouette of his face against the lightening sky. Bowed forward like that, he seemed to be offering obeisance to some god. Ryo hesitated for a moment. Then she threw her warm arms about his neck.

3

Two days later Ryo set out happily with her boy to visit Tsuruishi. When she reached the bomb site, she was surprised not to see him before his cabin, his red kerchief tied about his head. Ryukichi ran ahead to find out if he were home and came back in a moment.

"There are strangers there, Mamma!"

Seized with panic, Ryo hurried over to the cabin and peered in. Two workmen were busy piling up Tsuruishi's effects in a corner.

"What is it, ma'am?" one of them said, turning his head.

"I'm looking for Tsuruishi."

"Oh, don't you know? Tsuruishi died yesterday."

"Died," she said. She wanted to say something more but no words would come.

She had noticed a small candle burning on the shelf for family gods, and now she was aware of its somber meaning.

"Yes," went on the man, "he was killed about eight o'clock last night. He went in a truck with one of the men to deliver some iron bars in Omiya, and on their way back the truck overturned on a narrow bridge. He and the driver were both killed. His sister went to Omiya today with one of the company officials to see about the cremation."

Ryo stared vacantly before her. Vacantly she watched the two men piling up Tsuruishi's belongings. Beside the candle on the shelf she caught sight of the two bags of tea he had bought from her that first day—could it be only two weeks ago? One of them was folded over halfway down; the other was still unopened.

"You were a friend of his, ma'am, I imagine? He was a fine fellow, Tsuru! Funny to think that he needn't have gone to Omiya at all. The driver wasn't feeling well and Tsuru said he'd go along to Omiya to help him unload. Crazy, isn't it—after getting through the war and Siberia and all the rest of it, to be killed like that!"

One of the men took down the postcard of the film actress and blew the dust off it. Ryo stood looking at Tsuruishi's belongings piled on the floor—the kettle, the frying pan, the rubber boots. When her eyes reached the blackboard, she noticed for the first time a message scratched awkwardly in red chalk: "Ryo—I waited for you till two o'clock. Back this evening."

Automatically she bowed to the two men and swung the rucksack on her back. She felt numb as she left the cabin, holding

Ryukichi by the hand, but as they passed the bomb site, the burning tears welled into her eyes.

"Did that man die, Mamma?"

"Yes, he died," Ryo said.

"Why did he die?"

"He fell into a river."

The tears were running down her cheeks now; they poured out uncontrollably as she hurried through the downtown streets. They came to an arched bridge over the Sumida River, crossed it, and walked along the bank in the direction of Hakuho.

"Don't worry if you get pregnant," Tsuruishi had told her that morning in Asakusa, "I'll look after you whatever happens, Ryo!" And later on, just before they parted, he had said, "I haven't got much money, but you must let me help you a bit. I can give you two thousand yen a month out of my salary." He had taken Ryukichi to a shop that specialized in foreign goods and bought him a baseball cap with his name written on it. Then the three of them had walked gaily along the streetcar lines, skirting the enormous puddles left by the rain. When they came to a milk bar, Tsuruishi had taken them in and ordered them each a big glass of milk. . . .

Now an icy wind seemed to have blown up from the dark river. A flock of waterfowl stood on the opposite bank, looking frozen and miserable. Barges moved slowly up and down the river.

"Mamma, I want a sketchbook. You said I could have a sketchbook."

"Later," answered Ryo. "I'll get you one later."

"But Mamma, we just passed a stall with hundreds of sketchbooks. I'm hungry, Mamma. Can't we have something to eat?"

"Later. A little later!"

They were passing a long row of barrack-like buildings. They must be private houses, she thought. The people who lived there probably all had rooms of their own. From one of the windows a bedroll had been hung out to air and inside a woman could be seen tidying the room.

"Tea for sale!" called out Ryo softly. "Best quality Shizuoka tea!"

There was no reply and Ryo repeated her call a little louder.

"I don't want any," said the woman. She pulled in the bedroll and shut the window with a bang.

Ryo went from house to house down the row calling her ware, but nobody wanted any tea. Ryukichi followed behind, muttering that he was hungry and tired. Ryo's rucksack dug painfully into her shoulders, and occasionally she had to stop to adjust the straps. Yet in a way she almost welcomed the physical pain.

4

The next day she went downtown by herself, leaving Ryukichi at home. When she came to the bomb site she noticed that a fire was burning inside the cabin. She ran to the door and walked in. By Tsuruishi's stove sat an old man in a short workman's overcoat, feeding the flames with firewood. The room was full of smoke and it was billowing out of the window.

"What do you want?" said the old man, looking round.

"I've come to sell some Shizuoka tea."

"Shizuoka tea? I've got plenty of good tea right here."

Ryo turned without a word and hurried off. She had thought of asking for the address of Tsuruishi's sister and of going to burn a stick of incense in his memory, but suddenly this seemed quite pointless. She walked back to the river, which reflected the late afternoon sun, and sat down by a pile of broken concrete. The body of a dead kitten was lying upside down a few yards away. As her thoughts went to Tsuruishi, she wondered vaguely whether it would have been better never to have met him. No, no, certainly not that! She could never regret knowing him, nor anything that had happened with him. Nor did she regret having come to Tokyo. When she had arrived, a month or so before, she had planned to return to the country if her business was unsuccessful, but now she knew that she would be staying on here in Tokyo—yes, probably right here in downtown Tokyo where Tsuruishi had lived.

She got up, swung the rucksack on her back, and walked away from the river. As she strolled along a side street, she noticed a hut which seemed to consist of old boards nailed haphazardly together.

Going to the door, she called out, "Tea for sale! Would anyone like some tea?" The door opened and in the entrance appeared a woman dressed far more poorly than Ryo herself.

"How much does it cost?" asked the woman. And, then, seeing the rucksack, she added, "Come in and rest a while, if you like. I'll see how much money we've got left. We may have enough for some tea."

Ryo went in and put down her rucksack. In the small room four sewing women were sitting on the floor around an oil stove, working on a mass of shirts and socks. They were women like herself, thought Ryo, as she watched their busy needles moving in and out of the material. A feeling of warmth came over her.

TRANSLATED BY IVAN MORRIS

[from Kamen no Kokuhaku, 1949] by Mishima Yukio (born 1925)

With the publication of the novel Confession of a Mask, *from which these extracts are taken, Mishima Yukio established himself as a writer of the first rank. The novel is apparently autobiographical, although Mishima has denied this. In the following sections the "I" of the novel is about fourteen years old.*

•

One morning just after a snowfall I went to school very early. The evening before, a friend had telephoned to say there was going to be a snowfight the next morning. Being by nature given to wakefulness the night before any greatly anticipated event, I had no sooner opened my eyes too early the next morning than I set out for school, heedless of the time.

The snow scarcely reached my shoetops. And later, as I looked down at the city from a window of the elevated train, the snow scene had not yet caught the rays of the rising sun and looked more gloomy than beautiful. The snow seemed like a dirty bandage hiding the open wounds of the city, hiding those irregular gashes of haphazard streets and tortuous alleys, courtyards and occasional plots of bare ground, which form the only beauty to be found in the panorama of our cities.

When the still almost empty train was nearing the station for my school, I saw the sun rise beyond the factory district. The scene suddenly became one of joy and light. Now the columns of ominously towering smokestacks and the somber rise and fall of the monotonous slate-colored roofs cowered behind the noisy laughter of the brightly shining snow mask. It is just such a snow-covered landscape which often becomes the setting for a tragic riot or revolution. And even the faces of the passers-by, suspiciously wan in the reflection of the snow, reminded me somehow of conspirators.

When I got off at the station in front of the school, the snow was already melting, and I could hear the water running off the roof of the express company building next door. I could not shake the illusion that it was the radiance which was splashing down. Bright and shining slivers of it were suicidally hurling themselves at the sham quagmire of the pavement, all smeared with the slush of passing shoes. As I walked under the eaves, one sliver hurled itself by mistake at the nape of my neck. . . .

Inside the school gates there was not yet a single footprint in the snow. The locker room was still closed fast, but the other rooms were open.

I opened a window of the second-year classroom, which was on the ground floor, and looked out at the snow in the grove behind the school. There in the path which came from the rear gate, up the slope of the grove, and led to the building I was in, I could see large footprints; they came up along the path and continued to a spot directly below the window from which I was looking. Then the footprints turned back and disappeared behind the science building, which could be seen on a diagonal to the left.

Someone had already come. It was plain that he had ascended the path from the rear gate, looked into the classroom through the window, and, seeing no one there, had walked on by himself to the rear of the science building. Only a few of the day students came to school by way of the rear gate. It was rumored that Omi, who was one of the few, came each morning from some woman's house. But he would never put in an appearance until the last moment before class formation. Nevertheless, I could not imagine who else might have made the footprints, and judging by their large size, I was convinced that they were his.

Leaning out the window and straining my eyes, I saw the color of fresh black soil in the shoe tracks, making them seem somehow determined and powerful. An indescribable force drew me toward those footprints. I felt that I wanted to throw myself headfirst out of the window to bury my face in them. But, as usual, my sluggish motor nerves protected me from my sudden whim. Instead of diving out the window, I put my satchel on a desk and then scrambled slowly up onto the window sill. The hooks and eyes on the front of my uniform jacket had scarcely pressed against the stone window sill before they were at daggers points with my frail ribs, producing a pain mixed with a sort of sorrowful sweetness. After I had jumped from the window onto the snow, the slight pain became a pleasant stimulus, filling me with a trembling emotion of adventure. I fitted my overshoes carefully into the footprints.

The prints had looked quite large, but now I found that they were almost the same size as mine. I had failed to take into account the fact that the person who had made them was probably wearing overshoes too, as was the vogue among us in those days. Now that the thought occurred to me, I decided that the footprints were not large enough to be Omi's. . . . And yet, despite my uneasy feeling that I would be disappointed in my immediate hope of finding Omi behind the science building, I was still somehow compelled to follow after the black footprints. Probably at this point I was no longer motivated solely by the hope of finding Omi, but instead, at the sight of the violated mystery, was seized with a mixed feeling of yearning and revenge toward the person who had come before me and left his footprints in the snow.

Breathing hard, I began following the tracks.

As though walking on steppingstones, I went moving my feet from footprint to footprint. The outlines of the prints revealed now glassy coal-black earth, now dead turf, now soiled packed snow, now paving stones. Suddenly I discovered that, without being aware of it, I had fallen into walking with long strides, exactly like Omi.

Following the tracks to the rear of the science building, I passed through the long shadow which the building threw over the snow, and then continued on to the high ground overlooking the wide athletic field. Because of the mantle of glittering snow which covered everything, the three-hundred-meter ellipse of the track could not be distinguished from the undulating field it enclosed. In a corner of the field two great keyaki trees stood close together, and their shadows, much elongated in the morning sun, fell across the snow, lending meaning to the scene, providing the happy imperfection with which Nature always accents grandeur. The great trees towered up with a plastic delicacy in the blue winter sky, in the reflection of the snow from below, in the lateral rays of the morning sun; and occasionally some snow slipped down like gold dust from the crotches formed against the tree trunks by the stark, leafless branches. The roof ridges of the boys' dormitories, standing in a row beyond the athletic field, and the copse beyond them, seemed to be motionless in sleep, and everything was so silent that even the soundless slipping of the snow seemed to echo loud and wide.

For a moment I could not see a thing in this expanse of glare.

The snow scene was in a way like a fresh castle-ruin—this legerdemain was being bathed in that same boundless light and splendor which exists solely in the ruins of an ancient castle. And there in one corner of the ruin, in the snow of the almost five-meter-wide track, enormous Roman letters had been drawn. Nearest to me was a large circle, an *O*. Next came an *M*, and beyond it a third letter was still in the process of being written, a tall and thick *I*.

It was Omi. The footprints I had followed led to the *O*, from the *O* to the *M*, and arrived finally to the figure of Omi himself, just then dragging his overshoes over the snow to finish his *I*, looking down from above his white muffler, both hands thrust in his overcoat pockets. His shadow stretched defiantly across the snow, running parallel with the shadows of the keyaki trees in the field.

My cheeks were on fire. I made a snowball in my gloved hands and threw it at him. It fell short.

Just then he finished writing the *I* and, probably by chance, looked in my direction.

"Hey!" I shouted.

Although I feared that Omi's only reaction would be one of displeasure, I was impelled by an indescribable passion, and no sooner had I shouted than I found myself running down the steep slope toward him. As I ran a most undreamed-of sound came reverberating toward me—a friendly shout from him, filled with his power:

"Hey! don't step on the letters!"

He certainly seemed to be a different person this morning. As a rule, even when he went home he never did his homework but left his school books in his locker and came to school in the mornings with both hands thrust in his overcoat pockets, barely in time to shed his coat dexterously and fall in at the tail end of the class formation. What a change today! Not only must he have been whiling away the time by himself since early morning, but now he welcomed me with his inimitable smile, both friendly and rough at the same time—welcomed me, whom he had always treated as a snotnosed child, beneath contempt. How I had been longing for that smile, the flash of those youthful white teeth!

But when I got close enough to see his smiling face distinctly, my heart lost its passion of the moment before, when I had shouted "Hey!" Now suddenly I became paralyzed with timidity. I was pulled up short by the flashing realization that at heart Omi was a lonely person. His smile was probably assumed in order to hide the weak spot in his armor which my understanding had chanced upon, but this fact did not hurt me so much as it hurt the image which I had been constructing of him.

The instant I had seen that enormous *OMI* drawn in the snow, I had understood, perhaps half unconsciously, all the nooks and corners of his loneliness—understood also the real motive, probably not clearly understood even by himself, which brought him to school this early in the morning. . . . If my idol had now mentally bent his knee to me, offering some such excuse as "I came early for the snow fight," I would certainly have lost from within me something even more important than the pride he would have lost. Feeling it was up to me to speak, I nervously tried to think of something to say.

"The snow fight's out for today, isn't it?" I finally said. "I thought it was going to snow more though."

"H'm." He assumed an expression of indifference. The strong outline of his jaw hardened again in his cheeks, and a sort of pitying disdain toward me revived. He was obviously making an effort to regard me as a child, and his eyes began to gleam insolently. In one part of his mind he must have been grateful to me for not making a single inquiry about his letters in the snow, and I was fascinated by the painful efforts he was making to overcome this feeling of gratitude.

"Humph! I hate wearing children's gloves," he said.

"But even grownups wear wool gloves like these."

"Poor thing, I bet you don't even know how leather gloves feel. Here—"

Abruptly he thrust his snow-drenched leather gloves against my cheeks. I dodged. A raw carnal feeling blazed up in me, branding my cheeks. I felt myself staring at him with crystal-clear eyes. . . .

On the switchboard of my memory two pairs of gloves crossed wires—those leather gloves of Omi's and a pair of white ceremonial gloves. I did not seem to be able to decide which memory might be real, which false. Perhaps the leather gloves were more in harmony with his coarse features. And yet again, precisely because of his coarse features, perhaps it was the white pair which became him more.

Coarse features—even though I use the words, actually such a description is nothing more than that of the impression created by the ordinary face of one lone young man mixed in among boys. Unrivaled though his build was, in height he was by no means the tallest among us. The pretentious uniform which our school required, resembling a naval officer's, could scarcely hang well on our still immature bodies, and Omi alone filled his with a sensation of solid weight and a sort of sexuality. Surely I was not the only one who looked with envious and loving eyes at the muscles of his shoulders and chest, that sort of muscle which can be spied out even beneath a blue serge uniform.

At my school it was the custom to wear white gloves on ceremonial days. Just to pull on a pair of white gloves, with mother-of-pearl buttons shining gloomily at the wrists and three meditative rows of stitching on the backs, was enough to evoke the symbols of

all ceremonial days—the somber assembly hall where the cere-
monies were held, the box of Shioze sweets received upon leaving,
the cloudless skies under which such days always seem to make
brilliant sounds in mid-course and then collapse.

It was on a national holiday in winter, undoubtedly Kigensetsu.
That morning again Omi had come to school unusually early.

The second-year students had already driven the freshmen away
from the swinging-log on the playground at the side of the school
buildings, taking cruel delight in doing so, and were now in full
possession. Although outwardly scornful of such childish playground
equipment as the swinging-log, the second-year students still had a
lingering affection for it in their hearts, and by forcibly driving
the freshmen away they were able to adopt the face-saving pretense
of indulging in the amusement half derisively, without any seriousness. The freshmen had formed a circle at a distance around the
log and were watching the rough play of the upperclassmen, who
in turn were quite conscious of having an audience. The log, suspended on chains, swung back and forth rhythmically, with a bat-
tering-ram motion, and the contest was to make each other fall off
the log.

Omi was standing with both feet planted firmly at the mid-point
of the log, eagerly looking around for opponents; it was a posture
which made him look exactly like a murderer who has been brought
to bay. No one in our class was a match for him. Already several
boys had jumped up onto the log, one after another, only to be cut
down by Omi's quick hands; their feet had trampled away the
frost on the earth around the log, which had been glittering in the
early morning sunlight. After each victory Omi would clasp his
hands together over his head like a triumphant boxer, smiling pro-
fusely. And the first-year students would cheer, already forgetting
he had been a ringleader in driving them away from the log.

My eyes followed his white-gloved hands. They were moving
fiercely, but with marvelous precision, like the paws of some young
beast, a wolf perhaps. From time to time they would cut through
the winter morning's air, like the feathers of an arrow, straight
to the chest of an opponent. And always the opponent would fall to

the frosty ground, landing now on his feet, now on his buttocks. On rare occasions, at the moment of knocking an opponent off the log, Omi himself would be on the verge of falling; as he fought to regain the equilibrium of his careening body, he would appear to be writhing in agony there atop the log, made slippery by the faintly gleaming frost. But always the strength in his supple hips would restore him once again to that assassin-like posture.

The log was moving left and right impersonally, swinging in unperturbed arcs. . . .

As I watched, I was suddenly overcome with uneasiness, with a racking, inexplicable uneasiness. It resembled a dizziness such as might have come from watching the swaying of the log, but it was not that. Probably it was more a mental vertigo, an uneasiness in which my inner equilibrium was on the point of being destroyed by the sight of his every perilous movement. And this instability was made even more precarious by the fact that within it two contrary forces were pulling at me, contending for supremacy. One was the instinct of self-preservation. The second force—which was bent, even more profoundly, more intensely, upon the complete disintegration of my inner balance—was a compulsion toward suicide, that subtle and secret impulse to which a person often unconsciously surrenders himself.

"What's the matter with you, you bunch of cowards! Isn't there anyone else?"

Omi's body was gently swinging to the right and left, his hips bending with the motions of the log. He placed his white-gloved hands on his hips. The gilded badge on his cap glittered in the morning sun. I had never seen him so handsome as at that moment.

"I'll do it!" I cried.

My heartbeats had steadily increased in violence, and using them as a measure, I had exactly estimated the moment when I would finally say these words. It had always been thus with moments in which I yield to desire. It seemed to me that my going and standing against Omi on that log was a predestined fact, rather than merely an impulsive action. In later years, such actions misled me into thinking I was "a man of strong will."

"Watch out! Watch out! You'll get licked," everyone shouted. Amid their cheers of derision I climbed up on one end of the log. While I was trying to get up, my feet began slipping, and again the air was full of noisy jeers.

Omi greeted me with a clowning face. He played the fool with all his might and pretended to be slipping. Again, he would tease me by fluttering his gloved fingers at me. To my eyes those fingers were the sharp points of some dangerous weapon about to run me through.

The palms of our white-gloved hands met many times in stinging slaps, and each time I reeled under the force of the blow. It was obvious that he was deliberately holding back his strength, as though wanting to make sport of me to his heart's content, postponing what would otherwise have been my quick defeat.

"Oh! I'm frightened—how strong you are! —I'm licked. I'm just about to fall—look at me!" He stuck out his tongue and pretended to fall.

It was unbearably painful for me to see his clownish face, to see him unwittingly destroy his own beauty. Even though I was now gradually being forced back along the log, I could not keep from lowering my eyes. And just at that instant I was caught by a swoop of his right hand. In a reflex action to keep from falling, I clutched at the air with my right hand and, by some chance, managed to fasten onto the fingertips of his right hand. I grasped a vivid sensation of his fingers fitting closely inside the white gloves.

For an instant he and I looked each other in the eye. It was truly only an instant. The clownish look had vanished, and instead, his face was suffused with a strangely candid expression. An immaculate, fierce something, neither hostility nor hatred, was vibrating there like a bowstring. Or perhaps this was only my imagination. Perhaps it was nothing but the stark, empty look of the instant in which, pulled by the fingertips, he felt himself losing his balance. However that may have been, I knew intuitively and certainly that Omi had seen the way I looked at him in that instant, had felt the pulsating force which flowed like lightning between our fingertips, and had guessed my secret—that I was in love with him, with no one in the world but him.

At almost the same moment the two of us fell tumbling off the log.

I was helped to my feet. It was Omi who helped me. He pulled me up roughly by the arm and, saying not a word, brushed the dirt off my uniform. His elbows and gloves were stained with a mixture of dirt and glittering frost.

He took my arm and began walking away with me. I looked up into his face as though reproving him for this show of intimacy. . . .

For all that, it was a supreme delight I felt as I walked leaning on his arm. Perhaps because of my frail constitution, I usually felt a premonition of evil mixed in with every joy; but on this occasion I felt nothing but the fierce, intense sensation of his arm—it seemed to be transmitted from his arm to mine and, once having gained entry, to spread out until it flooded my entire body. I felt that I should like to walk thus with him to the ends of the earth.

But we arrived at the place for class formation, where, too soon, he let go of my arm and took his place in line. Thereafter he did not look around in my direction. During the ceremony which followed, he sat four seats away from me. Time and time again I looked from the stains on my own white gloves to those on Omi's.

TRANSLATED BY MEREDITH WEATHERBY

SHORT BIBLIOGRAPHY

GENERAL WORKS

Aston, W. G. *A History of Japanese Literature*. London, 1889.

Bonneau, Georges. *Histoire de la littérature japonaise contemporaine*. Paris, 1940.

Keene, Donald. *Anthology of Japanese Literature*. New York, 1955.

————. *Japanese Literature*. New York, 1955.

Okazaki, Yoshie. *Japanese Literature in the Meiji Era*, tr. by V. H. Viglielmo. Tokyo, 1955.

Sansom, George. *The Western World and Japan*. New York, 1950.

PROSE

Akutagawa, Ryūnosuke. *Hell Screen*, tr. by W. H. H. Norman. Tokyo, 1948.

————. *Kappa*, tr. by S. Shiojiri. Osaka, 1947.

————. *Rashomon and Other Stories*, tr. by T. Kojima. New York, 1952.

Dazai, Osamu. *The Setting Sun*, tr. by Donald Keene. New York, 1956.

Elisséev, Serge, tr. *Neuf nouvelles japonaises*. Paris, 1924.

Futabatei, Shimei. *An Adopted Husband*, tr. by B. Mitsui and G. M. Sinclair. New York, 1919.

Hino, Ashihei. *Wheat and Soldiers*, tr. by Baroness Shidzué Ishimoto. New York, 1939.

Kobayashi, Takiji. *The Cannery Boat*. New York, 1933.

Mishima, Yukio. *The Sound of Waves*, tr. by Meredith Weatherby. New York, 1956.

Nagai, Kafū. *Le Jardin des pivoines*, tr. by Serge Elisséev. Paris, 1927.

Natsume, Sōseki. *Kokoro*, tr. by I. Kondo. Tokyo, 1941.

————. *La Porte*, tr. by R. Martinie. Paris, 1927.

Osaragi, Jirō. *Homecoming*, tr. by B. Horwitz. New York, 1954.

Ozaki, Kōyō. *The Gold Demon*, tr. by A. and M. Lloyd. Tokyo, 1905.

Tanizaki, Junichirō. *Ashikari and the Story of Shunkin*, tr. by R. Humpherson and H. Okita. Tokyo, 1936.

————. *Some Prefer Nettles*, tr. by E. G. Seidensticker. New York, 1955.

POETRY

Bonneau, Georges. *Anthologie de la poésie japonaise.* Paris, 1935.

———. *Lyrisme du temps présent.* Paris, 1935.

Hughes, Glenn and Iwasaki, Y. T. *Fifteen Poets of Modern Japan.* Seattle, 1928.

———. *Three Women Poets of Modern Japan.* Seattle, 1936.

Ishikawa, Takuboku. *A Handful of Sand,* tr. by S. Sakanishi. Boston, 1934.

Matsuo, Kuni and Steinilber-Oberlin. *Anthologie des poètes japonais contemporains.* Paris, 1939.

Yosano, Akiko. *Tangled Hair,* tr. by S. Sakanishi. Boston, 1935.

DRAMA

Bowers, Faubion. *Japanese Theatre.* New York, 1952.

Iwasaki, Y. T. and Hughes, Glenn. *New Plays from Japan.* London, 1930.

———. *Three Modern Japanese Plays.* Cincinnati, 1923.

Kikuchi, Kan. *Tōjūrō's Love and Four Other Plays,* tr. by Glenn W. Shaw. Tokyo, 1925.

Kurata, Hyakuzō. *The Priest and His Disciples,* tr. by Glenn W. Shaw. Tokyo, 1922.

Tanizaki, Junichirō. *Puisque je l'aime,* tr. by C. Jacob. Paris, 1925.

Yamamoto, Yūzō. *Three Plays,* tr. by Glenn W. Shaw. Tokyo, 1935.

NOTE: A much more extensive bibliography may be found in Borton, Hugh, *et al., A Selected List of Books and Articles on Japan in English, French and German.* Cambridge (Mass.), 1954.